The Process of Investigation: Concepts and Strategies for Investigators in the Private Sector

Third Edition

The Process of Investigation: Concepts and Strategies for Investigators in the Private Sector

Third Edition

CHARLES A. SENNEWALD, CSC, CPP
JOHN K. TSUKAYAMA, CPP, CFE, PCI

With contributions by David E. Zulawski, CFI, CFE;
and Douglas E. Wicklander, CFI, CFE

ELSEVIER

Amsterdam • Boston • Heidelberg • London
New York • Oxford • Paris • San Diego
San Francisco • Singapore • Sydney • Tokyo
Butterworth-Heinemann is an imprint of Elsevier

Acquisitions Editor: Pamela Chester, Mark Listewnik, Jennifer Soucy
Editorial Assistant: Kelly Weaver
Marketing Manager: Christian Nolin
Project Manager: Sarah M. Hajduk
Cover Designer: Shelagh Armstrong Artist, Inc.
Cover Printer: Phoenix Color
Printer: The Maple-Vail Book Manufacturing Group

Butterworth–Heinemann is an imprint of Elsevier
30 Corporate Drive, Suite 400, Burlington, MA 01803, USA
Linacre House, Jordan Hill, Oxford OX2 8DP, UK

 Recognizing the importance of preserving what has been written, Elsevier prints its books on acid-free paper whenever possible.

Library of Congress Cataloging-in-Publication Data
Sennewald, Charles A., 1931–
   The process of investigation : concepts and strategies for investigators in the private sector / Charles A. Sennewald, John K. Tsukayama ; with contributions by David E. Zulawski and Douglas E. Wicklander. — 3rd ed.
      p.   cm.
   Includes index.
   ISBN 0-7506-7950-6 (hardcover : alk. paper)   1. Criminal investigation.   2. Detectives.
I. Tsukayama, John K.   II. Title.
   HV8073.S39 2006
   363.25—dc22   2006009668

British Library Cataloguing-in-Publication Data
A catalogue record for this book is available from the British Library.

ISBN 13: 978-0-7506-7950-3
ISBN 10: 0-7506-7950-6

For information on all Butterworth–Heinemann publications visit our Web site at www.books.elsevier.com

Printed in the United States of America
06   07   08   09   10   10   9   8   7   6   5   4   3   2   1

DEDICATION

To

My mother Katherine
Honey Rose
The Holy Spirit

Denise
Spike

Table of Contents

PREFACE   ix

ACKNOWLEDGMENTS   xi

I.   **FUNDAMENTALS OF SECURITY INVESTIGATION**   1

    Chapter 1.   The Investigative Process   3

    Chapter 2.   A Comparison of Public and Private Sectors   9

    Chapter 3.   Qualities of the Investigator   17

    Chapter 4.   Managing the Investigative Function   29

II.   **METHODS OF SECURITY INVESTIGATION**   39

    Chapter 5.   Undercover Investigations   41

    Chapter 6.   Surveillance   53

    Chapter 7.   Background Investigations   67

    Chapter 8.   Discovering Covert Crimes   79

III.   **BUILDING A CASE**   93

    Chapter 9.   Interviews and Interrogations   95

    Chapter 10.   An Overview of the Interview and Interrogation Process   113
                   By David E. Zulawski, CFI, CFE; and Douglas E. Wicklander, CFI, CFE

Chapter 11.	Evidence	139
Chapter 12.	Written Statements, Admissions, and Confessions	153
Chapter 13.	The Use of Informants	167
Chapter 14.	Report Writing and Note Taking	181

IV. APPLYING INVESTIGATIVE STRATEGIES   195

Chapter 15.	Problems Arise: The *What* of Investigation	197
Chapter 16.	Crime and Solution: The *How* of Investigation	201
Chapter 17.	Identifying Suspects: The *Who* of Investigation	213
Chapter 18.	Finding Information: The *Where* of Investigation	225
Chapter 19.	The Time Factor: The *When* of Investigation	239
Chapter 20.	Establishing Motive: The *Why* of Investigation	251

V. TECHNOLOGICAL AND SPECIALIZED INVESTIGATIVE TECHNIQUES   263

Chapter 21.	Imagery	265
Chapter 22.	Computers in Private Sector Investigations	279
Chapter 23.	Targeted Violence Investigations	299

SOURCES   317

INDEX   321

Preface

We noted when this book was first published in 1981 that for too long the art and science of professional investigation had been deemed the exclusive realm of the public sector. Textbooks on investigation traditionally had been written by and for those in public law enforcement and, invariably, these books included such topics as homicide and rape. Although interesting, these subjects have little, if any, practical application for investigators in the private sector. In the two decades since, the private sector fully came of age and in some areas was at the forefront of the development of new techniques and professional practices.

This book was written to serve the needs of this recognized professional class of investigative practitioners. We have tried to cover in detail those investigative skills that will always be so essential in private security investigation: surveillance techniques, interviewing and interrogation, evidence, confessions and written statements, among others. An effective book on investigation must go beyond mere detail, however; the investigators in the real world and the book must deal with the day-in and day-out challenges that confront them. Throughout the book, we have included cases and examples based on our own experiences, as well as those of keen investigators of centuries and millennia past. In this third edition we've folded in the unique talent of two other nationally known experts whose experience clearly enhance the value of this material. In dealing with such a wide variety of situations, we share the approaches and strategies that have helped each of us in the hope that they can be of some assistance to others.

Acknowledgments

Two of the experts involved in the development and training of computer forensic techniques kindly have allowed their wisdom to be shared through this book. They are Michael R. Anderson of New Technologies, Inc. and Mr. Carlton Fitzpatrick, of the Financial Fraud Institute, Federal Law Enforcement Training Center (FLETC), U.S. Department of the Treasury. We are indebted to them for their willingness to bolster our admittedly scanty knowledge in this arcane area. We're also grateful for the contribution of Doug Wicklander and Dave Zulawski for sharing their expertise in our effort to provide investigative strategies for students and professionals alike.

I. FUNDAMENTALS OF SECURITY INVESTIGATION

Chapter 1

The Investigative Process

An investigation is the examination, study, searching, tracking, and gathering of factual information that answers questions or solves problems. It is more of an art than a science. Although the person engaged in investigation is a gatherer of facts, he or she must develop hypotheses and draw conclusions based on available information. The investigative process, that is to say, is a comprehensive activity involving information collection, the application of logic, and the exercise of sound reasoning.

The end result of an investigation is the factual explanation of what transpired, if the incident or issue is history, or what is occurring, if the issue is of the present.

The investigative process is not limited to the criminal justice and security fields. It is an activity found, to one extent or another, in virtually all areas of human endeavor. Academicians are investigators, supervisors faced with disciplinary problems are investigators, antique appraisers are investigators, medical doctors are investigators — just to name a few. Sherlock Holmes with the deerstalker hat and magnifying glass may be the art's most familiar image, but investigation does not belong exclusively to the arena of crime or the realm of cops and robbers.

Just as the art of investigation belongs to no one province, so no one has all the answers as to precisely how any investigation can lead to the desired solution. Too many facets are involved in the process of information collection, application of logic, and sound reasoning. Some such facets include intuition, luck, mistakes, and the often touted "gut feeling." No single textbook of formulas is possible; no one book (or author) can stand alone as the ultimate authority. Our purpose, then, is an overview of investigative concepts, strategies, suggestions, guidelines, hints, and examples that can be useful to any investigator.

TWO CATEGORIES OF INVESTIGATION

There are two categories of investigation: constructive and reconstructive. Constructive investigations are covert in nature, performed in secrecy. This type of inquiry occurs while the suspected activity is taking place or anticipated. An example might be an investigation into a complaint that a member of middle management solicits sexual favors from female subordinates and reaps favors accordingly. The purpose of the constructive investigation is to determine if objectionable activity is taking place.

Reconstructive investigations are necessary when an event has taken place and the investigator must recreate what happened after the fact. This type of investigation is usually overt in nature, carried out in the open.

THE INVESTIGATIVE PROCESS

As it pertains to the security industry, the investigative process is organizationally oriented as opposed to being community oriented. Its objective in this setting is to seek answers to the basic questions — the what, who, where, when, how, and why — regarding a condition, incident, or action deemed organizationally unacceptable, or to meet organizational objectives. Internal dishonesty, for example, is an organizationally unacceptable activity. The background investigation of a prospective new employee would meet one organizational objective.

Most of the investigative process takes place in the collection of information. This gathering or collection is based on communication and observation. The answers to the six basic investigative questions will be developed through communication — that is, the written or spoken word — or by observation — that is, physical evidence that can be observed (whether by human eye or microscope), touched, or in any way quantitatively measured.

Communication

Communication includes information received from informants, information developed through the interview process, and information obtained in interrogations.

Consider a simple example. A homeowner, hearing the glass of his front window breaking, runs to the room and commences an immediate inspection to determine the cause. He observes a baseball lying among the pieces of broken glass. Sticking his head out of the broken window, ball in hand, he shouts to a silent group of youngsters in the street. "Okay, you guys, which one of you did it?" As he asks the question, simultaneously he observes that a boy named Harry is holding a baseball bat. Based on the facts thus far gathered, he forms a hypothesis that Harry struck the ball with the bat, causing the ball to enter the homeowner's living room through the window.

Up to this point the homeowner, in a natural investigative role as a victim, has had only the benefit of his own powers of observation in forming his hypothesis. But now a couple of the boys in unison say, "Harry did it." The investigative process has advanced through communication from informants. "Did you do it, Harry?" asks the homeowner. "Yes, sir," answers Harry, dropping his head. The question and its answer are two other basic elements of communication — interrogation and admission.

Ideally, as in this example, the investigator's work is simplified if given some direction by an informant, if witnesses are available and willing to cooperate, or if a suspect is known and can be interrogated. Such simplification is not to suggest that all is easy in the communications aspects of investigation. Quite the contrary! Developing informants, or developing a climate in which employees or nonemployees voluntarily will confide in you is not easy. It takes talent. The ability to extract painlessly all the information a witness may have requires training and experience. Only a skillful interviewer can get the specialist to explain the workflow of the finance unit so it is and understandable.

Finally, the ability to interrogate, and in that interrogation to obtain voluntary confessions, requires a high level of skill. The point to be drawn is that communicatio, necessarily easy to manage well, is often extremely helpful to the investigative process. ...ately, it is not always available. In such circumstances the investigator must rely totally on observation, at least during the initial phases of his inquiry, as he seeks to know the what, who, where, when, how, and why of a situation.

Observation

Scientific technology, in such areas as DNA analysis, forensic computer data examination, finger-printing, infrared photography, motion picture photography, videotape, and document analysis, to name but a few, plays a vital role in the observatory aspects of modern investigation. In our judgment, perhaps too much emphasis has come to be placed on technology and too little on man's powers of observation.

This is not to suggest that, because computers and the Internet are so sophisticated, we should return to only paper files and printed books. It is to emphasize that the common denominator of both information technology and paper records is the aggregation and recall of useful information. Total reliance on computers leaves us vulnerable to total information loss should a computer virus attack, prolonged power outage, or critical hard-drive crash occur. In an investigation we want to gather, organize, analyze, and present factual information, and we should be able to conduct online research, dig through mountains of paper, hold video conferences, prepare multimedia presentations, or use any other means available to us.

A remarkably wider range of important information is available to us through our own powers of observation than through the use of a laboratory. To see, to touch, to smell, and to hear are all forms of observation. Did you ever touch the hood of an automobile to determine if it had been driven recently as evidenced by its warmth? Did you ever mark the label on a bottle of liquor to determine later if someone was taking unauthorized sips? Such uses of the power of observation are as natural and commonplace as eating and breathing. Consider the example of a shopper who returns to a new car, parked in the shopping center's lot, only to find a scratch, dent, or ding in the car door. It is pre-dictable (natural and commonplace) that this unskilled observer will promptly inspect the adjacent automobile to determine if any part of that car reveals, at a height corresponding to the damage to the new car, any evidence of paint fragments that would prove culpability — coloration of victimized vehicle on suspect vehicle, or vice versa.

If, in fact, the power of observation is natural and commonplace in seeking investigative answers and solving problems, why is it that those who are professionally charged with conducting investiga-tions fail to understand, fully appreciate, and maximize such powers? The answer, perhaps, can be found in modern technology, which mitigates against our need to fine-tune our own faculties. Just a few decades ago people had to rely on their own resources. We do not. We hardly tap our capabilities because we do not have to. In our advanced and sophisticated society, there is relatively little need to be observant. Take the weather as an example. Today we have 24-hour access to specialized cable sta-tions that broadcast televised reports on tomorrow's weather based on the use of real-time satellite imagery. Through the Internet we can view for ourselves the weather from government satellite pictures that are literally "up to the minute." Meteorologists predict; we accept. Yet, even now, there are men and women who can predict the weather with remarkable accuracy by observing nature in the raw — by observing cloud formation, density, coloration, direction, temperature fluctuation, and so on. Divers and fishermen will tell you that on a calm day when all the seagulls sit in the water, bad weather is coming fast — and their predictions are at least as accurate as official forecasts. In terms of observatory skills, people are only as resourceful as their needs. Consider life and death. "Natural births" are currently the norm. To observe, if not assist, in delivery is quite a revelation to most people today. In the not too distant past, most births were "natural." As for death, what can the urban man or woman know of the natural phenomenon when we live in a society where one's loved one usually dies in a medical facility and is wheeled away while the grieving survivors are ushered out, and the "remains" are not seen again until presented for viewing? In the recent past, the body, with all the changes that naturally occur, was observed by the survivors. They saw, felt, and if there was undue delay, smelled the effects of death. They may not have used the words now employed, but they knew postmortem lividity and rigor mortis, and a great deal more.

Early "professional" investigators, not yet dependent upon what is commonly considered modern investigative technology, made superior use of keen observation, common sense, and healthy skepticism in their investigations. The forerunners of the famed Scotland Yard Criminal Investigation Department (CID) Inspectors were a group of detectives in London who worked for British magistrates at a small station on Bow Street. They were famous for their willingness to set out within a quarter of an hour for any point in the kingdom where their dogged assistance in solving crimes was needed. These detectives became known as the Bow Street Runners, and operated from 1749 to 1839.

When the Runners were called out of London to assist in inquiries, they would be paid by the persons seeking that assistance. Often they were paid by victims of crimes who chose not to rely solely on the village policemen to identify and catch culprits. Thus, they were operating as private sector investigators, with powers no greater than those of a modern corporate investigator. An example of close observation and commonsense analysis being used to solve a crime is an investigation conducted by Bow Street Runner Henry Goddard, as follows:

A Southampton woman named Mrs. Maxwell was awakened at about 1:00 A.M. on January 10, 1835, by the sounds of gunfire and a fight somewhere in her house. Rushing to the hall, she and other residents of the home found that her butler had interrupted a burglary by two men, traded pistol shots with them, and finally chased them off. They also found her valuables bundled up and apparently discarded by the burglars during their flight. Maxwell sent to London for the services of a Runner to investigate this frightening robbery. Goddard was sent to investigate. During his investigation he spoke with Mrs. Maxwell and interviewed the butler, Joseph Randall. Randall related that he had gone to bed at approximately 11:00 P.M. after making sure that all doors and windows on the ground floor were locked. He was awakened by a strange noise but lay still. He then saw a small "bull's eye" lantern being held at arm's length. Such a lantern, like a modern flashlight, projects light only forward, through a small round window. Randall saw the shadow of the man holding the lamp, and also saw another man standing behind.

Randall was afraid and pretended to sleep, even as the men approached his bed and shined the light on his face. They were apparently convinced that he was asleep and quietly exited. Randall reached under the pillow with his right hand for the pistol he kept on his left. As he did so a shot was fired from outside. Randall told Goddard, "The bullet whizzed by my ear and passed through the pillow and the backboard of the bedstead against the wall behind and dropped on the floor, and had it not been for my turning round to reach my pistol they would have left me a corpse, for as I lay the bullet must have entered my chin and lodged in the gullet."[1]

Randall returned fire, cried out to awaken the household, and ran into the hallway where he struggled with the men, and eventually drove them off. Goddard's own words best describe his investigation:

> Having paid the greatest attention to the above statement, I requested him to conduct me to the door where the thieves made their entry. After I had examined it I found that some considerable force had been used, no doubt by a Jemmy [pry-bar]; but I also found the impression on the outside did not appear to my mind to correspond with the inside. This observation I kept to myself. I then proceeded to the plate closet [in which valuable silver items were secured] and saw similar impressions, which also did not tally, and I felt satisfied it was not the work of a Cracks-man [burglar]. I then asked him to show me his pistols and also the mould and bullets if he had any. He went to the cupboard and produced the pistols, the mould, and about a dozen bullets, saying, "That is the mould I cast the bullets in."
> "Have you got the bullet that was fired at you?" I asked.
> He put his hand in his pocket and, pulling out a bullet, said, "Yes, here it is, I found it on the floor at the back of the bedstead."
> I examined it and found some part of it to be a little flattened. On comparing it with the other bullets I had got in my possession it appeared to correspond with them as if it had been cast in the same mould. I made no remark. I left, and soon after my return to the hotel I occupied myself for some little time in looking at the discharged bullet; and on comparing it closely with the others I discovered a very small round pimple on all the bullets, including the one alleged to have been discharged. In looking into the mould there was a very little hole hardly so large as the head of a small pin, and this I found accounted for the pimples.[2]

Goddard was suspicious of several things he had observed:

1. The pry marks on the outside of the door to the house did not match those found on the interior doorframe.
2. The pry marks on the plate closet similarly did not properly match.
3. The unique characteristic of the "pimple" on the bullet purportedly fired by the burglars matched those found on the bullets made by Randall for his own pistols.

Goddard was also suspicious of one other aspect of what Randall told him. Randall claimed to have seen the shadow of the man holding the bull's eye lamp at arm's length, in front of the lamp. A man holding a bull's eye, or a modern flashlight, in this way cannot cast a shadow unless he is actually pointing it back at himself.

Goddard confronted Randall, who confessed to having contrived the whole story in the hopes that Mrs. Maxwell would reward him for bravely defending her home. Randall said that he had used a crowbar a week before the staged robbery on the interior doorframe. On the night in question he went outside and used the tool to make the exterior marks, but because it was so dark he did not line up the marks perfectly.

Careful observation and interpretation of what is observed are as crucial to the twenty-first century investigator as it was to Goddard of the nineteenth century. We will be discussing modern technology and its uses in this text; however it must be understood that in criminal investigation even the most sophisticated technology is useless unless it is combined with common sense, professional skepticism, and an investigator's persistent attempt to arrive at the truth.

THE CREATIVE PROCESS IN INVESTIGATION

The foregoing experience may appear to involve a considerable amount of creative imagination. That does not make it inappropriate — just the opposite. Be it reconstructive or constructive, the development of information by communication or by observation, the entire investigative process is as creative in nature as it is scientific.

Investigation is an imaginative process. Despite all the modern technological assistance available to the investigator, and regardless of what marvelous things machines and computers can do, for the successful investigator there is no substitute for the God-given gifts of imagination and creativity.

Chapter 2

A Comparison of Public and Private Sectors

The fundamental difference between the investigative process in the public and in the private sectors is the objective. The primary objective of investigations in the public sector is to serve the interests of society. If those interests are best served by removing or otherwise punishing those who commit offenses against the public good, then the reconstructive method of investigation is used. When the purpose of the public sector investigation is to inhibit and suppress criminal activity — prostitution and gambling are two examples — then constructive, covert techniques are employed.

The primary objective of the investigative process in the private sector is to serve the interests of the organization, not society as a whole. If those interests are best served by removing or otherwise punishing those who criminally attack the organization, or whose performance in any way defeats or impedes organizational goals, the reconstructive strategy is used where the conduct is a matter of history. Where that conduct or activity is ongoing, constructive, covert techniques must be applied.

It is interesting to note that what serves the best interests of society may not necessarily serve the best interests of the organization, and vice versa. For example, society's interests are protected when an embezzler is prosecuted and sentenced to prison. There are occasions, however, when the embezzler, having banked all his thefts, would be happy to return the stolen funds in order to avoid prosecution. Such an agreement would be unacceptable in the public sector. A seasoned private sector investigator, on the other hand, is not concerned primarily with prosecution and sentencing. Recovery of the loss might be a more important achievement, better serving the interests of the private organization. More often than not, investigations in the private sector that deal with criminal behavior result in serving the public sector's objective as well as the organization's, despite the fact that there is a fundamental difference in the perception of the crime. Wherein lies that perceptual difference? It comes from differing views of the victim. The public investigator sees society (the "people") as the victim, whereas the corporate investigator views his organization as the victim. More specifically, forgery detectives in a law enforcement agency consider forgers to be a general menace to the community. Investigators of a banking institution or credit-granting company regard the forger whose target is their organization as a very real, immediate threat to the financial stability of the organization. From the viewpoint of the private investigator, the forger must be stopped not because he is breaking the law, but because he is damaging or victimizing the organization.

Different perceptions and different objectives have a direct impact upon the strategies and the character of the investigative process in the two sectors, leading to other differences. Public investigators usually are armed, for example, private investigators unarmed. Other interesting differences that invite comparison require more examination.

SOURCE OF AUTHORITY AND FUNDING

The public investigation represents the sovereignty of government, whose authority is vested in constitutional, statutory law and even case law. Its efforts are financed by public funds, replenished through taxation.

The private investigator represents management or his client, with some authority derived from statutory and case laws. The same authority is afforded to any citizen, such as the power to make arrests under certain conditions, although that power and authority are unknown to most private citizens. In addition, the private security investigator has delegated authority from senior company management.

SOURCES OF INFORMATION

In the public sector, there are relatively few limitations to such information as criminal records, government records, and files at municipal, county, state, and federal levels. On the other hand, there are accelerating limitations on private access to public records.

JOB SECURITY

Most investigators in the public sector are in a civil service system with clearly defined job security, and labor unions represent many as well. The private investigator has reasonable job security (as opposed to the unreasonableness of some civil service and labor contracts), provided by the organization's human resource policies. Normally, corporate or company investigators are not part of a labor bargaining entity.

SCOPE OF WORK

Public investigators tend to specialize in specific areas of concentration, depending on the agency, department, or assignment. They are burglary detectives, forgery detectives, homicide detectives, state or federal narcotics investigators, immigration investigators, and so on.

Private security investigators tend to be "generalists," although some specialize in such areas as forgery or fraud when employed by finance and credit companies. They are generalists not only in the sense of working across the broad spectrum of business and commercial interests, ranging from quiet investigations into indiscretions related to executive romantic involvement with subordinates to tracking down counterfeiting of corporate negotiable instruments, such as coupons, event tickets, and company checks, but also in the attendant need for wide-ranging information, intelligence, and skills.

IMAGE

Public investigators can command immediate respect and attention based on the color of authority, generally supported by impressive credentials, such as badges. Although inherited, such authority must continue to be earned to maintain that favorable image.

Although many in private security have attempted to copy their public cousins' credentials, an ever-growing number recognize that respect and attention rightfully are based on demonstrated intelligence, effective interpersonal skills, and a genuine concern and respect for others.

CIVIL LIABILITY

Public investigators engaged in day-in and day-out activities are relatively free from civil actions because of governmental immunity. Civil action filings, if they occur at all, usually follow only extremely aggravated incidents. In this respect governmental agencies are not as tempting a target as, for example, a utility company.

In the private sector, investigators are relatively vulnerable to civil actions as a result of exposure in their daily work, irrespective of culpability. An investigator who interrogates an employee on documented evidence of dishonesty can easily expose the company to an unfair labor practice suit, slander or libel suit, extortion (e.g., promising a suspected employee he or she will not be referred to the police in exchange for an admission of culpability), or to charges of false imprisonment or malicious prosecution. Large companies are inviting targets — the bigger, the better.

TRAINING AND EDUCATION

Once on the job, the public investigator attends publicly funded schools, classes, or academies, usually of high quality, from basic in-service training to advanced and specialized courses, depending on the area of specialization. At the end of the 1950s, only thirteen institutions of higher learning offered a bachelor's degree in Police Science and Administration, or a similarly designated program. Today, more than 450 U.S. universities and colleges offer undergraduate and graduate degree programs in police science, criminal justice, and law enforcement administration. Just a few short years ago, investigators in the private sector invariably came from the governmental agencies. The public sector was the training ground. College curriculums rarely included courses in security. This situation has been changing rapidly. More investigators are coming up within the organization, and proportionately fewer retired or former public sector investigators are entering private industry. This change is attributable primarily to the growing numbers of young college graduates with associate, bachelor, and even graduate degrees in criminal justice or administration of justice as well as degrees in security administration, men and women who see definite career opportunities in large, successful firms.

Academia is beginning to recognize security as a separate discipline. Now there are perhaps a few dozen institutions of higher learning worldwide that offer programs leading to undergraduate as well as graduate degrees in security management. We can expect to see their degree-holders increasingly influencing the private sector in this new century. In addition, there simply are more security jobs available than in the past.

Security and Loss Prevention has become a recognized part of organizational existence, with more emphasis on proprietary protection and less reliance on the public sector for protective support.

Thus, there are more security administration classes in the schools, more very professional training programs such as the American Society for Industrial Security's Assets Protection course, Wicklander and Zulawski's interviewing and interrogation seminars and a host of other professional programs, from telecommunication security to computer fraud. Most of these programs and seminars are funded privately and conducted by competent practitioners. As the various industry hubs of technological innovation in Washington, California, Massachusetts, and elsewhere have propelled the general society into the information age, so it is with at least one sector of the protective professions. Information security professionals are often persons whose training and experience have been obtained strictly in the private sector. Many come to the profession not from law enforcement, but from information sciences, and are used frequently as consultants to government investigators, attorneys, and accountants. Their own specialized professional societies, such as the Information Systems Security Association (ISSA) and the Information System Audit and Control Association (ISACA), and certifications are becoming established.

TECHNICAL RESOURCES

In carrying out an investigation, officials in the public sector are able to call upon an extensive arsenal of such technical resources as questioned document examiners, crime laboratory facilities, forensic computer analysts, computer reconstruction artists, and fingerprint classification specialists, to name just a few. Within the private sector, the investigator has limited access, if any at all, to such publicly supported resources. He or she must seek out and assume the cost for any such services available through a comparatively small number of private sources. The practical effect of this difference is that the private investigator simply cannot call upon the same resources as freely, but rather, must draw on his or her own resources, must be more resourceful.

PROFESSIONALISM

Such agencies as the Federal Bureau of Investigation have attained a high level of respected professionalism, both in fact and in profile, by virtue of their reputation, known standards, and visibility through the media (both in fictional entertainment and factual news reporting). To a lesser extent, this is true of other law enforcement agencies at the state and local level. Perhaps the epitome of investigative professionalism is the homicide detective in a modern metropolitan police force. In general, the premise that criminal investigators in the public sector are indeed professional, in every sense of the word, goes relatively unchallenged; however, unseen by the general public's eye are the unsolved crimes, some of international note. But in most cases, respect for their work is rightfully deserved.

The same is not as universally true in the private sector. Investigators in this area are too often thought of in terms of "private eyes" and commercially available detectives who handle skip-tracing cases or develop evidence for divorce hearings. The general public — and, for that matter, many investigators in the public sector — have little awareness of or appreciation for the corporate investigator. When one thinks of the FBI, investigations leap instantly to mind. When one thinks of United Airlines, traveling is the first thought association, not investigations. Some people are even surprised to learn that commercial firms have investigators on the payroll. Very professional and highly skilled investigators thus go virtually unnoticed outside the upper echelons of the organization. But times are changing.

These investigators now have available to them specialized training programs offered by the private sector. This is not second-best training either, as is evidenced by the fact that most federal and other government investigative agencies pay substantial fees to have their most talented personnel attend the same private programs. Professional specialty societies have formed, which offer certifications subject to education, experience, and examination requirements as rigorous as those applied to certified public accountants and other professions. The Certified Protection Professional (CPP) and Professional Certified Investigator (PCI) designations earned through the American Society for Industrial Security, the Certified Fraud Examiner (CFE) designation awarded by the Association of Certified Fraud Examiners, and the Certified Security Consultant (CSC) awarded by the International Association of Professional Security Consultants are four of the gold standards by which modern practitioners in security and investigations are measured and known. Regrettably, the range or spectrum of talent, from superior to marginal or poor, remains broader in the private sector than is generally the case in the public sector. There are still a large number of unprofessional, unsophisticated, and unskilled "investigators" in the security industry. And whereas the general public may never hear of the genuine achievements of the professionally trained and qualified private investigator, they will certainly be made aware of the illegal, immoral, or sloppy work of the unprofessional practitioner.

Twenty-five years ago, when the first edition of this text appeared, it read "*(on) balance, then, the mantle of professionalism is much more generally worn in the public sector, without question. But time and trends are shifting that balance. It would be interesting to reconsider this question in the year 2000.*" Today, as a result of two and a half decades of growing and elevated professional standards in the private sector coupled with the reduction of public resources, private sector investigative professionals have taken their place as innovators and are respected as full colleagues by many law enforcement leaders, attorneys, and an increasingly informed public. And today, interestingly, in sharp contrast to twenty-five years ago, more criticism of public sector investigations has surfaced, such as the handling of the Waco, Texas, siege, the O.J. Simpson homicide crime scene investigation, the Colorado Springs JonBenet Ramsey murder investigation, and the still unsolved disappearance of an American high school graduate on the island of Aruba in the Caribbean, a world-class resort island and government with an allegedly sophisticated police agency.

CAREER PATHS

In the public sector investigative agency — the FBI, for example — the entry-level position would certainly include pure investigatory responsibilities. In a generalized agency, such as a police department, the position of investigator is a promotional and relatively low position in the organizational structure, at the rank of or equivalent to sergeant. From detective or investigator, one can move up to supervisorial investigator (lieutenant), then to a management-level position (captain or chief of detectives). This means that one can advance vertically while remaining in an investigative career.

In the private sector, there is a more pronounced trend toward moving talent up into the investigative position as a part of the individual's development and growth. The goal is usually administrative as opposed to investigative, although some individuals may choose to make a career of investigative work. Consequently, high-ranking positions in the security industry are usually filled by men and women with investigative experience. By contrast, high-ranking positions in a police department, as an example, are often filled by men and women who have never worked exclusively as an investigator.

ASSISTANCE

Few investigations, public or private, develop in a vacuum. The very nature of the investigative process involves calling on others for information or assistance.

In the public sector, irrespective of departmental and jurisdictional rivalries (which do exist), the exchange and flow of information are rarely, if ever, denied the investigator. It is an unwritten rule that one investigator will share information and assist another if such assistance is sought.

With regard to the assistance provided by informants, it has often been said that the success of any detective in large measure rests upon his or her sources of information. Tips are provided by those seeking favor or "tolerance" — prostitutes and drug addicts, for example — by spurned or jealous lovers seeking revenge, and by a whole host of other sources, anonymous and otherwise, acting from an endless variety of motives, all desirous of seeing a culprit caught. To a lesser extent, monetary rewards also generate information. There is little in the way of rivalries or jealousy in the private sector to hinder cooperation. An investigator for one utility company can call on a similar firm and, as a rule, count on and receive prompt assistance. This form of cooperation knows no political boundaries. Using such publications as the ASIS membership directory, which alphabetizes members by personal as well as organizational name, one investigator can call another across the country. If he is unknown at the receiving end, that party can verify the identity and affiliation of the caller by use of the same directory. Once identity is established, information is exchanged.

The use of informants in the private sector is another matter. It is unusual for employees to inform on their fellow workers; few people wish to "become involved." More often than not, a customer shopping in a store who witnesses a theft will not report that theft; the typical reaction is to look the other way. Nor does the private investigator have the same "leverage" that a police officer can use to encourage informants to talk. A powerful tool for the public sector, tips are not a significant factor in most successfully concluded private investigations.

Exceptions are noteworthy and in some areas are increasing, usually within the format of a structured and well-publicized "silent witness" incentive award program. If such programs guarantee anonymity for the informant, they stand a good chance of surviving. And if they survive, information of remarkable value will come in. Courts have established strong incentives for companies to establish such anonymous programs, especially for discreet reporting of sexual harassment, and it is to be expected that an increasing number of corporations will offer them to their employees.

PERSONAL ACHIEVEMENT

Without question, all investigators experience a real sense of achievement when a criminal is taken into custody at the successful resolution of a case, especially if the investigation has been lengthy and difficult. Bearing in mind, however, that the real objective of criminal investigations in the public sector is the successful prosecution of the offender, it must be recognized that there is a high (and rising) level of frustration for investigators in this area. The work of the investigator can bring little lasting satisfaction when, as happens all too frequently in the present climate, trial court decisions are reversed in the appellate courts. And if appellate reversals based on liberal interpretations of the law do not bring frustration, wrist-slapping sentences handed down by the court will do it. The reward of satisfaction for the professional investigator must be found in the investigative process itself — the means, not the end. To bring a case to a conclusion, identifying the suspect and causing his incarceration — even if only temporarily — brings a sense of personal achievement (and helps to preserve sanity), even if the final result fails to accomplish the ultimate objective.

Because the stated objective of the investigator in the private sector lies in the protection and general welfare of the organization, such down-the-line possibilities as unsuccessful prosecution, light sentencing, appellate reversals, or even failure to indict, although certainly disappointing to some degree, do not bring anything like the level of frustration commonly experienced in the public sector. Why? The mere exposure and eradication of a gang counterfeiting corporate negotiable instruments, for example, and the destruction or seizure of their means of continuing production, genuinely satisfy organizational goals. The investigators can take satisfaction from the knowledge that they have put an end to a source of loss or threat. Similarly, to identify and subsequently to cause the termination of an employee who ingeniously falsified his time records or travel expenses — organizational activities considered more a violation of trust and of the employer-employee relationship than criminal acts — can and do bring real job satisfaction. For these reasons there is probably a healthier climate of self-worth and job satisfaction today in the private than the public sector of investigation.

OVERLAPPING MISSIONS

There have evolved a number of reasons why the private sector has begun to rely more heavily upon private investigative professionals. Private organizational objectives are oriented principally toward profit. Many of the crimes perpetrated against those same corporations involve attacks upon the assets and profitability of the organizations.

Frequently however, companies do look at public prosecution of employee criminals as a desirable deterrent to future similar episodes. Such prosecutions also give heart to the honest employees in the company who detest dishonesty in the work force.

Unfortunately, with the emphasis in public law enforcement upon illegal drug suppression and violent crime reduction, property crimes perpetrated against faceless corporate victims receive second-level priority. This, combined with understaffed police agencies, have forced companies, in effect, to find their own solutions.

This is not to say that the average city police detective is not sympathetic to the plight of a corporate victim, but rather he or she simply will not be afforded the time needed to undertake a lengthy investigation. We increasingly have found that prosecution of criminals who steal from companies is much more likely to occur if the case has been worked fully to a point where the district attorney's office can begin to bring charges with little, if any, labor on the part of the police department. As more cases investigated by the private sector are successfully prosecuted, both prosecutors and police detectives have begun to trust and respect the quality of the cases they will receive. An indication that trust and respect are growing is the fact that in a few instances we have been called upon by government

ate and direct the efforts of combined private-public criminal investigative task
ilability and expertise make this a logical choice.

In dwelling at some length in this chapter on the differences that can be observed between public and private investigators, it is not our purpose to widen the gap between them, but rather to identify those differences for better understanding of common interests and goals. With increased understanding, how much easier it is to communicate and to work together!

Chapter 3
Qualities of the Investigator

To the uninitiated, the aspirant, and the distant observer, there is an aura of romanticism surrounding the investigator and his work. That illusion is quickly dispelled in the light of reality. The real world of investigative work is hard, demanding, and rarely glamorous. Occasionally a case may come along that is exciting, or one in which the answers come easily, but as a rule investigation is a tedious, exhausting, frustrating, time-consuming, and sometimes dirty (in the literal sense) process. Invariably the novice investigator is somewhat dismayed by the difference between his or her preconceptions of the nature of the work and the reality.

Crimes are not solved by ingenious and clever supersleuths, but by hard-working men and women who universally share one common denominator: perseverance. In the words of Samuel Johnson, "Great works are performed, not by strength, but perseverance." This investigative virtue is defined as "holding to a course of action, belief, or purpose without giving way; steadfastness . . . continuing strength or patience in dealing with something arduous. It particularly implies withstanding difficulty or resistance" in striving for a goal.[3] Perseverance is the one overriding human trait or characteristic among the many deemed necessary, or at least highly desirable, for investigative work. What are the others? One authority, Donald Schultz, lists fifteen "desirable attributes of an investigator."[4] Charles O'Hara boils it down to three: character, judgment, and the ability to deal with people.[5] And the familiar "green book," *Municipal Police Administration*, has its own list, including "the ability to be deceptive."[6] Collating, modifying, deleting, and adding to the suggestions in these sources, we have identified twenty-one qualities or characteristics that are necessary in the effective investigator. The qualities or characteristics are:

1. Observant
2. Resourceful
3. Patient
4. People-oriented
5. Understanding of human behavior
6. Knowledgeable about legal implications of the work

7. A skilled communicator
8. Receptive
9. Possessed of a sense of well-being
10. Dedicated to the work
11. A self-starter
12. Skeptical
13. Intuitive
14. Energetic
15. A good actor
16. Capable of sound judgment
17. Logical
18. Intelligent
19. Creatively imaginative
20. Of good character
21. Professional

Invariably a successful investigator will possess, in varying degrees, each of these traits, either as innate or learned qualities. (Following the discussion and amplification of each trait, a self-scoring survey is provided for personal insight at the end of this chapter.)

POWERS OF OBSERVATION

Skill in observation does not come naturally. It must be learned, and it must be practiced. It requires *seeing* as opposed to merely looking; and, after seeing, the ability to draw intelligent conclusions.

An underlying characteristic of a good observer is curiosity. If you are curious about a person, the power of observation can reveal a great deal. In personal appearance and grooming, for instance, are fingernails manicured or dirty? Are the nails chewed? Is the hair of conventional cut, long and shaggy, or carefully styled? Has the hair been colored? Is clothing color coordinated? In current fashion? Are the shoes shined? Heels run down? Is the person dapper or sloppy in appearance? If in casual dress, are there any stains such as paint or grease that could indicate what the person does around the home or at work? Are there any personal items of jewelry or accessories that might tell you something? If a man, is he wearing a college ring? Fraternal or service ring? A Timex or Rolex watch? Religious medals? If he is wearing a metal belt buckle with the Coors logo, is he a martini drinker?

Apply the same close observations to an automobile. Fingerprints on the interior of windows suggest children. The same is true if there is popcorn on the rear seat or floor. What kind of decals or stickers are visible? Would a bumper sticker reading "I'd rather be skiing" tell you anything? What kind of debris is present on the front floor mats? Are there cigarette butts in the ashtray? If so, what brand? Is there lipstick on the butts? Are there a great many butts? Obviously, there is much to see, and much can be learned by observing. This is not to say that intelligent, concise, or totally accurate conclusions can always be drawn from any given observation. But valid conclusions can often be made. Think of

Did the
fail or su
what was

the wife who waits up for her husband and observes lipstick on his collar. He can speak eloqu
the power of observation!

RESOURCEFULNESS

The resourceful person is one who, when one path or strategy is blocked or comes to a dead end, finds another. He thinks in terms of alternatives: If this does not work, something else will. If the information is not available at one source, he will turn to another. The person who lacks resourcefulness has a tendency to give up when the initial plan or strategy fails. *Canned Hacks*

In one investigation concerning activities that were occurring in a cocktail lounge, it was vital that I get into that bar during the evening hours, unnoticed. But on the preceding evening the bartender had become suspicious of my presence and purpose and had begun pointing me out to the patrons as an investigator. He would surely do the same if I went in again on this critical evening. If he could be lured away from the location just for thirty minutes, I could go in and secure the last needed evidence. The question was how to get him out? Across the street from the bar was a pay phone. I entered the booth. I knew the bartender's name and also his home address. Dialing the bar, I asked for the bartender by name. He came to the phone, the noise of the bar audible in the background. I identified myself as a fire captain and asked if he lived in the apartment building at 7373 Hightower Parkway. "Yes," he answered. "Why do you ask?"

I told him the apartment building had caught fire and many items of furniture and personal property had been carried out by tenants and firemen. "Can you come right down and identify your effects?"

"Who's calling?" he asked in disbelief.

"Captain Glenn, Engine Company 461," I replied.

"You say my apartment building caught fire?" he asked incredulously, obviously alarmed.

"In this confusion I can't say specifically whose apartments are damaged. I'm telling you the building has been fire and water damaged, and there are a lot of personal effects that need to be identified and secured. Are you coming or not?" "I'll be right there, Captain. Give me fifteen minutes."

From the phone booth I watched him leave the bar, get into his car and drive off. I entered the bar and accomplished my mission before he returned.

I saw him in court later. We looked at each other. Nothing was said because nothing needed to be said. He knew.

PATIENCE

The quality of patience is not only a virtue in investigative work, it is essential, particularly in surveillance assignments. It is not uncommon in surveillance assignments for investigators to have to sit in a parked automobile day after day, week after week. The average man would give up, but patience pays off for the investigator.

We did hear of one impatient investigator, but he did not last long.

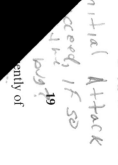

...EOPLE

...e people-oriented. He must be comfortable around and with people. Our ...rmation are observation and people. People communicate, and there is a ...en the amount of rapport between two people and the amount of com- ...ual who likes and enjoys others acts like a human magnet; he attracts ...ncomfortable around others subconsciously avoid or shun them, and that is ...or who enjoys people is usually very adaptable in adjusting to a wide spectrum of different types of people. He is comfortable with the dock worker as well as an executive, with a person on welfare or resident of a main street flophouse as well as a political or government official.

There is also something to be said for kindness and respect for others: It pays off when the investigator is seeking assistance and information. This applies not only in developing informants but also in the day-in and day-out gathering of what appears to be inconsequential information.

UNDERSTANDING HUMAN BEHAVIOR

In addition to the human understanding involved in being people-oriented by nature, there is another aspect of understanding human behavior that is important for the investigator. It belongs in the area of practical psychology. The investigator has to have a fine sense for what makes most people "tick." There are times when it is appropriate to cry, even for men; there are also times when it is not appropriate. That is true of laughter, sarcasm, anger, resentment, and the whole range of emotions and responses. Sensitivity to the reactions and emotions of others can throw light on the investigator's task. Dealing effectively with human responses can make the difference between success and failure. With the person who is experiencing shame, the empathetic investigator can keep communication alive. The investigator who fails to appreciate or understand that person's feelings may act or react in a way that closes communication.

UNDERSTANDING THE LEGAL IMPLICATIONS

The investigator in the public sector today is very sensitive to the legal implications of his actions. This is not always equally true in the private sector. This may be due, in part, to the very clear distinction between public and private law enforcement that has existed in the past, particularly in the private security man's immunity from such restrictions as the Miranda requirements. That situation is rapidly changing. The private security investigator may or may not be caught up in the same legal problems as the public law enforcement officer, but the lines of difference are no longer so clearly drawn. And many other legal ramifications affect the work of the private investigator, particularly as it pertains to making arrests and the discharge of employees. The trend is to focus on how and what the investigator did, rather than what the accused did.

The investigator must therefore be sensitive to the gray areas of the law, as well as clearly defined legal limitations on his actions.

EFFECTIVE COMMUNICATION SKILLS

Because report writing is such an integral part of the investigative process, the investigator must have writing skills. In addition, he must have the ability to articulate his case effectively, be it an oral presentation of the status or findings of a case to management or testifying in an administrative or judicial hearing. Cases are lost and won by the manner in which witnesses project, especially verbally. Good delivery, in terms of enunciation, clarity, conviction, and choice of words, adds credibility to the facts of the case. Conversely, mumbled, hesitant, or hard-to-understand oral presentations, and presentations filled with slang or other poor choices of words, tend to discredit an otherwise good case.

RECEPTIVITY

The quality of receptiveness means being open-minded. That includes an interest and willingness to listen to other opinions, and even to ask for them. Further, it includes the willingness not only to listen but to consider weighing the merits of other ideas, suggestions, and opinions, and when appropriate, accepting them. The unreceptive person who rejects external sources, who has strong tendencies to pursue an investigation in his or her own way, tends to work in a trench, becoming blind to alternatives. The effective investigator must remain open for fresh input.

By way of illustration, in 1978 we were approached by someone who asked if we would be interested in meeting with a graphologist to discuss the possibility of utilizing graphology in background investigations. Graphology, the study of handwriting for the purpose of analyzing the writer's character, struck me as something akin to fortune telling. The caller asked me to keep an open mind and at least give the graphologist — a young woman — the opportunity to prove her ability to identify indicators of dishonesty in the handwriting of our employees. With some skepticism we agreed.

We gathered sample handwriting of four of our most trusted employees and the handwriting of four former employees who had been discharged for dishonesty. There was absolutely no way the graphologist could know anything about the eight individuals. The "test" analysis was overseen by my very able assistant, an attorney by education and a former FBI agent. To his dismay, the young woman not only identified the former employees as having "traits of dishonesty," but she was also able to identify other interesting personality characteristics of several employees in the sample with startling accuracy. We called on the graphologist again to assess the promotability of three key security executives in the organization, and her analysis of the three was so accurate it was uncanny. We asked another security executive to identify the three subjects by reading her analysis only; he was able to identify each of them correctly.

By being receptive to a new idea, graphology, we broadened our own horizon.

SENSE OF WELL-BEING

An investigator must feel good about himself, his skill, his ability to perform the task at hand, no matter how complex or difficult. This feeling is more than self-confidence, because it includes experiencing the rewards of a job well done.

The sense of well-being also includes personal and professional security. The investigator is not always looking over his shoulder, wondering how long he will remain in the investigation unit; he is comfortable in the knowledge that his performance level is high. Another expression of this quality is self-esteem.

One who lacks this sense of well-being will spend more time and energy on himself than his assignment, and his work will suffer in consequence.

DEDICATION TO THE WORK

How many wives and how many husbands have said, "You're more dedicated to your job than to me!" Outstanding investigators are unequivocally dedicated to their work. Invariably, families suffer, personal affairs are neglected, yard work goes undone, personal business goes unattended — all because the demands of the job take priority.

A dedicated investigator does not wear a watch to know when to go home. He wears a watch to record in his notebook the time of an event, interview, receipt of information, or action. This dedication is not unique to investigators, of course. It can be found in doctors, educators, scientists, and military officers, to name but a few, invariably in successful ones. There is something awesome and wonderful about so loving one's work, as long as the dedication is not an escape from some problem. Of the many who may have suffered because of that single-mindedness, most have survived and are richer and stronger for their trial. And for those dedicated individuals who caused the suffering, the time comes when they make it up, many times over, for they too are richer and stronger because they have fought the best battle.

SELF-INITIATIVE

The demands of the investigative process require an individual with initiative, a "self-starter." Working within the guidelines established by the organization, he or she accepts assignments and pursues them in a uniquely unstructured fashion. Rarely is there only one way or one specific time to resolve the issue at hand. The investigator must be able to act on his own. The work should never require official or managerial prodding or supervision. Most supervision is advisory in nature. The man or woman who counts on a superior to say "start" and "stop" should not be in the investigative business.

HEALTHY SKEPTICISM

A healthy skepticism in investigation means taking everything in with "a grain of salt," not fully accepting anything with blind faith, yet not necessarily rejecting anything because of the source. Everything is listened to, everything is looked at, nothing is sacred, nothing is a fact until it is proven or measures up to known and acceptable standards. Healthy skepticism keeps investigators sharp and accurate. If someone says it was raining on a given night, and that information is vital to the case, the healthy skeptic will confirm that information with official records of the weather service.

This quality has to be private, not open. Only a fool would openly display the attitude, "I'm from Missouri, you'll have to show me." Such a posture can be self-defeating, because many people resent skepticism, particularly when it is directed toward what they say or believe.

INTUITION

The notion of a "woman's intuition" would seem to preclude men having the same instincts, which is far from the case. To be intuitive is no more or less than the familiar "gut feeling." It is the sense of knowing something without the use of a rational process or evidence provided by the five physical senses. Intuition is commonly manifested in the area of attempted deception. An experienced investigator may have no concrete proof that someone is lying, but nonetheless experiences a strong intuition that the person lied. It is a hunch, a feeling that cannot be explained but is an indicator for action or direction. Many cases have been resolved because an investigator paid attention to this intuition or followed a hunch.

ENERGY AND STAMINA

Investigators are not desk-bound executives. They are workers, always on the move — looking, probing, digging, asking, comparing. Their work requires a person with a high energy level. Its demands impact on the mental as well as the physical reservoirs of strength and stamina. Despite the fatigue and frustrations, despite the setbacks and reversals, despite the failures that inevitably occur, the investigator must have the reserves of energy that enable him to keep going.

ACTING SKILLS

In Shakespeare's *Hamlet*, Hamlet instructs the troupe of players, "Let the words fit the action and the action fit the words." The advice suits investigators as well as actors.

The investigator must be able to assume a wide variety of roles, and he must be able to change roles quickly and fittingly. Whatever the role — fire captain, old wartime buddy, the "bad guy" in the interrogation strategy, or friend — each calls for versatility. Call it deception if you will. The ability to act or be deceptive is a prime requisite in the effective investigator. In one case, evidence suggested that the firm's computerized list of customers had somehow fallen into the hands of an insurance agent. The agent appeared to be soliciting business through mailings to our customers. It was determined that the insurance agent had contracted with an independent mailing service for a quantity of mailings. Further investigation revealed that the principal of the mailing service, call him Mr. Brown, was a part-time operator, his regular employment being that of supervisor with a major mailing service — the very service subscribed to by my employer. The circumstances appeared to indicate that Mr. Brown was building his own mailing lists by making extra runs of the lists of his employer's clients. It was necessary, however, to confirm this suspicion.

Brown ran his part-time business out of his garage. I contacted him at his residence by phone and said that a friend had referred me to him. I told him I was in town for a very short time, that I was from another part of the state, that I was the director of a Christian fund-raising foundation, and that we were interested in expanding our appeal to a select part of the Los Angeles market on a test basis only. If the test reflected a favorable response, I told him, we would then be interested in discussing a contract. In the meantime, all I wanted was to purchase a list of 1,000 residents in a specific geographical area with a given income range. The geographical and income requirements matched those of my company's customers.

In response to Mr. Brown's questions, I gave him a fictitious name for myself and the foundation. When he asked for my telephone number I told him that I was almost impossible to reach because I traveled a great deal. We agreed on a price for the mailing list, with payment in cash, and set a meeting time in the lobby of a large downtown hotel the following week. At the appointed time and place, after a brief discussion of my foundation, I examined the multipage list of names and addresses Mr. Brown provided and paid him for the list in currency. We parted on my promise to get back to him within thirty days.

Careful comparison of the purchased list against our customer list proved negative. During additional phone conversations I asked for more lists, but Brown was unable to deliver new names. Another appointment was set up in the hotel lobby. This time I was accompanied by an investigative associate. Our intention was to disclose our identity and determine how Brown had obtained a few of our customers' names and addresses — the few we knew about. Mr. Brown was astonished upon learning my true identity. During our quiet interrogation in the corner of the hotel's coffee shop, he admitted taking home overruns and set-up runs of the address labels that were considered waste or trash. This was subsequently confirmed. The handling of "waste" at the primary mailing service's facility also was corrected. Our investigation established beyond doubt that our computerized customer list had not been stolen or sold.

The particular strategy of deception or "cover story" used in this case was considered the best way to ensure that we arrived at the truth. And it worked.

GOOD JUDGMENT

Good judgment simply means the ability to make the right decision most of the time. When someone claims to exercise good judgment, he is really saying that his batting average is over .500, that he makes more good decisions than bad ones.

There are two elements involved in sound judgment. The first is the willingness to make decisions. Many people, including those in management roles, find decision-making difficult as well as unpleasant. The effective investigator is not reluctant to make decisions. The second factor is that most decisions, based on experience, intuition, and accumulated wisdom, must prove to be right. Note the qualification, *most* decisions, not all.

Bad judgment is somewhat easier both to identify and to define. Bad judgment occurs when the decision runs counter to the available data. Overloading an airplane and attempting to take off on a short runway are poor judgments. So is the attempt single-handedly to arrest a felon known to be armed and dangerous in a dark alley.

Another indication of poor judgment is making the same wrong decision more than once. The investigator does not live who has never made a mistake. The good ones do not repeat it.

THE EXERCISE OF LOGIC

A logical person is one capable of consistency in reasoning. In investigative work, logic is necessary in drawing reasonable conclusions based upon earlier events. A logical mind is able to see relationships between events past, present, and future.

For example, it is discovered that over the past six months quantities of titanium have been smuggled from the plant. Considering the availability of the material and existing controls, it is logical that the titanium was removed by an employee. Because titanium has little value or appeal for personal use, it is logical that the thief has a buyer, someone with a commercial need or a commercial source for titanium. The next logical investigative step might be to identify and contact the major legitimate suppliers of titanium in the area to (1) identify industries and firms that regularly purchase titanium; (2) determine if any regular customers have reduced their purchases of the metal while maintaining or even increasing their level of production; and (3) depending on the professionalism of the titanium supplier, advising them that stolen metal is in circulation and requesting that they pass along any information that comes to their attention. These are logical steps, in a sequential pattern that is reasonable.

INTELLIGENCE

Without question, an effective investigator must have higher-than-average intelligence. Most of the qualities already discussed — resourcefulness, understanding of people, communication skills, receptivity, initiative, skepticism, sound judgment, and a logical turn of mind — imply an agility of mind beyond the normal. Simply stated, a good investigator cannot be average; he must be smart.

One aspect of intelligence essential to the investigator is mental recall, or memory. The ability to remember small details, even those seemingly unrelated to the present case, can help make logical connections that aid in resolving the case at hand. Such details might include names, events, faces, an automobile, a phrase, a criminal's M.O. *(modus operandi)*. The investigator must have strong powers of memory.

CREATIVE IMAGINATION

The creative imagination is capable of transcending the reality of the present or apparent. Puzzles offer a useful demonstration. In Figure 3.1 there is a picture of a cake. How can you cut the cake with a knife, using only three straight strokes, so that you end up with eight pieces of cake, each of equal size?

Figure 3.1 Creative puzzle.

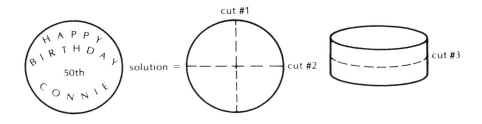

As another example, how can you change the number 9 (in Roman numerals) into the number 6 with the addition of only one line?

Solution: IX + S = SIX

Such exercises are illustrations of the ability to see things in a different way, demonstrating a creative imagination.

In a practical way, *Municipal Police Administration* puts its finger on the essence of this ability: "Uncovering the facts of a crime by means other than direct interview and examination of physical evidence in the strict sense requires an active and practical imagination and the ability to substitute the mental processes of the culprit for one's own."[7] In other words, you must be able to think like a thief. What would you do next if you were the criminal? How would you dispose of the evidence if you were faced with his problem? Where would you go if you were in his shoes?

For this writer, it is difficult to conceive of conducting an investigation without that creative imagination as part of the overall strategy.

GOOD CHARACTER

For many years I worked for and with a "grand lady," a woman of strong principles, Koral Vaughn, senior vice president of the Broadway Department Stores, now deceased. She used to say that personnel employees and security employees must be "like Caesar's wife, above reproach." It is hard to add to that.

SENSE OF PROFESSIONALISM

An investigator, in particular a criminal investigator (and the bulk of investigative work in the private sector is criminal), is always "on stage." On or off the job, what we do, how we do it, what we say, and how we say it reflect on the image of our profession. Like other professionals, the investigator must maintain high standards of conduct.

One good rule to follow will be familiar to most investigators: What you do on the job, hear on the job, see on the job, and say on the job, should *stay* on the job. But discretion is only one aspect of investigative professionalism. Because of the investigator's high visibility, such qualities as courtesy, a sense of fair play, gentleness, good grooming, pleasantness, and humility will evoke respect and admiration for the investigator individually and, collectively, for the investigative professional.

A SELF-QUIZ

Figure 3.2 provides a self-quiz for the present or potential investigator. Bearing in mind such qualities as good character and a sense of professionalism, grade yourself as fairly and objectively as possible. Whatever your score, there will always be room for improvement. Make it a goal to move those Xs one box to the left.

	STRONG	ABOVE AVERAGE	AVERAGE	BELOW AVERAGE	WEAK
MARK APPROPRIATE BOX WITH AN "X"	**5**	**4**	**3**	**2**	**1**
1. Are you really observant, seeing instead of looking?					
2. Are you resourceful, able to find other ways to go?					
3. How patient are you?					
4. Are you comfortable with and do you really like people?					
5. Do you have a feeling for how people tick?					
6. Do you know the legal "down-side risks" of the job?					
7. Do you write and speak well?					
8. Do you invite and accept other people's input?					
9. Are you comfortable and confident as an investigator?					
10. Do you consider yourself dedicated to your work?					
11. Are you a person of initiative?					
12. Are you a healthy skeptic?					
13. Do you get "gut feelings" and act upon them?					
14. Are you considered energetic on the job?					
15. How good an actor are you?					
16. Do you have a reputation for using good judgment?					
17. Are you strong in logical reasoning?					
18. Rate your own I.Q. range with 110 as the average.					
19. Are you a creative person?					
20. How would you rate yourself as a person of principles?					
21. How do you rate your sense of professionalism?					

Each box has a numeric value as shown in the top line.
Add up the columns and enter the total score here.
Maximum score attainable is 105. The average score is 63.
An investigator should score above 75.

Figure 3.2 Investigator's personal quiz.

Twelve Rules For Success

Remember:

The value of time
The success of perseverance
The pleasure of working
The dignity of simplicity
The worth of character
The power of kindness
The influence of example
The obligation of duty
The wisdom of economy
The virtue of patience
The improvement of talent
The joy of originating
                                        -Marshall Field

Figure 3.3 All investigators should be mindful of the direct applicability of these virtues to their profession.

TRUE SUCCESS

Marshall Field's maxims, listed in Figure 3.3, are an example of the kind of simple personal code that true professional investigators adopt to guide them as they practice their art. To be a competent technician should not be all one strives for. Good character and professionalism create success, and pave the way for daily personal satisfaction. How we obtain our success ultimately earns us far more than the sum of our individual successes, especially in terms of that gift that only we can bestow: self-respect.

Chapter 4

Managing the Investigative Function

There is a school of thought that supports the concept that a good manager need not possess the technical skills of those being managed. Where that approach may be valid in some or even many areas of management, the concept proves invalid when it comes to managing or, more precisely, supervising investigators. The reason is that the very nature of the work demands far more freedom of movement, more alternatives, and more creativity on the part of the investigator than other security functions. To manage the highly motivated and creative individuals who perform in this more "free-wheeling" kind of work requires that the supervisor be someone who has already been down that road, one who understands, through experience, what is going on.

The manager of an investigation unit performs five different roles, each of which requires investigative experience. Such a manager functions as

1. An investigative counselor
2. An investigative trainer
3. An investigative controller
4. An investigative motivator
5. An investigative evaluator

THE MANAGER AS INVESTIGATIVE COUNSELOR

Because the investigative process is not a precise science, the investigator on assignment — including the experienced investigator — needs the active counsel of a knowledgeable person about where he has been in the case, where he is now, and where he should go next.

This counseling activity is an informal and open exchange of ideas. It is exploratory, creative, and thought provoking. It involves bouncing ideas off one another and "off the wall." It means bringing together the sum total of yesterday's experiences that should throw light on the direction of today's investigation.

This counseling role should not be misconstrued as one in which the manager sits as the oracle of wisdom. He functions, rather, as a participant in the discussion, one who can make significant contributions by virtue of his investigative skills and experience.

The key to effective counseling is the process itself. It should be a process that creates a climate in which one person stimulates another with ideas or strategies that could materially contribute to the successful conclusion of a given case. The following exchange exemplifies this kind of dialogue.

Investigator: "The guy has simply dropped out of sight. He's not been seen or heard of for over a year."

Supervisor: "What about the last known residence? No request for forwarding mail, or information about a moving or storage van?"

"No, he was in a cheap hotel, lived out of a suitcase."

"Check for address changes at the Department of Motor Vehicles?"

"Yep. Nothing."

"Did you check the usual databases?"

"I checked the commercial databases we subscribe to plus the simple web-based people-finder sorts of services. I got old telephone numbers, addresses, and neighbor's names and telephone numbers. Running those down gave us nothing."

"Could he be locked up somewhere?"

"Checked that too. I know for a fact he's not incarcerated in a federal institution or in any of the neighboring states."

"How about a monastery, like that Trappist place in Utah?"

"I didn't check that but I really doubt it. He was too much of a party guy — drugs and booze. Say, that gives me an idea. He really liked his meth. He could be in an outpatient or even maybe a residential rehab program. If he did bottom out on drugs, he's probably living on the street or in a shelter if he's lucky. Never thought of that before. . . ."

In this exchange the manager is not giving advice in the strict sense of the term. He is stimulating the investigator with questions that, in this example, led the investigator to discover a logical step he had not taken.

In some circumstances the counseling process may be advisory in nature. This is simply another dimension of the process. The investigator who has doubts about the wisdom of interviewing a given witness, for example, can have the benefit of his manager's feelings. The essence of the process is dialogue, involving the exchange of ideas and agreement on strategy.

THE MANAGER AS TRAINER

You cannot teach a student the art of calligraphy, how to fly an airplane, or how to wrestle until you, the teacher, have first mastered those skills. The same is true in teaching investigative skills. Teaching and developing such skills are vital responsibilities of the manager. This is particularly true in the training of newly assigned investigators, or novices.

In his role as trainer, the manager has a number of options and combinations of options. Ideally, a combination of all available options would be used, including the manager's direct involvement, on-the-job training with an experienced investigator, classroom instruction, and participation in college programs and seminars.

Direct Involvement

The manager may personally conduct an investigation from beginning to end, with the trainee working alongside. As the case unfolds, step by step, the manager explains the whys and wherefores and answers questions. The student thus learns the logic or rationale of the investigative process, and, with the manager as teacher, he or she learns the business the right way from the start — the manager's way. For all practical purposes the manager's way is the right way, when one considers the fact that the manager is the evaluator of the investigator's performance.

On-the-Job Training with Others

A second training option is to assign the novice to work with an experienced investigator for so-called on-the-job training. Although this is the most popular method of training, it does have its drawbacks. The most conspicuous problem is that the trainee tends to pick up the more experienced partner's bad as well as good habits. An otherwise excellent investigator who tends to be sloppy with his note-taking because of an unusual capability of mental recall will pass along to the novice the notion that note-taking is not important. If the novice does not have the same recall ability, this flaw in the learning process can have serious consequences later.

Although the manager may choose to delegate the training to a seasoned subordinate, the manager must still assume the final responsibility for training and follow-up to ensure that bad habits or gaps in the learning process are corrected.

Another form of training is the formalized or structured classroom experience. Here there is a wide variation of possibilities, from instruction given by the manager to instruction by a number of seasoned investigators, each teaching in areas where they have particular expertise, to utilizing an outside training consultant. This form of training has genuine value as part of the learning process.

The quality and creativity of classroom training are limited only by the manager's imagination. Take, for example, a program we designed for instruction in the art of interrogation. We held a one-day interrogation workshop for all investigators of my organization. In preparation for the seminar, all participants were required to submit an actual interrogation situation in which they had experienced difficulty. On the day of the training session, selected situations were read aloud to two randomly selected investigators, one of whom was charged with playing the role of the interrogator while the other acted as the interrogatee. The "interrogation" was acted out before the assembled group of investigators, while being filmed on videotape with sound. Following the dramatized enactment of the interrogation situation, the confrontation was subjected to a critique by the entire group. This proved to be a meaningful learning experience for all involved.

As an extension of this classroom experience, we later developed a self-study interrogation workbook that covered the basics of interrogation, the dos and don'ts, and then exposed the student to one of the previously videotaped situations. The video-workbook program contained three situations. After reading the first situation, the student was instructed to close the book and turn on the television set. The situation he had just read about was dramatized on the screen. At the conclusion of the first filmed sequence a message on the screen directed the student to turn the set off and return to the workbook, where a series of questions about the interrogation just witnessed had to be answered. After the student had viewed all three situations and answered the questions about each, he could then compare the answers with those printed in the back of the book.

This variation on the classroom approach to learning had three clear advantages: (1) The novice investigator engaged in a learning experience alone, without tying up the time of the manager or another investigator. (2) The learning experience was nonthreatening. The student's answers were unknown to anyone else, and thus his own private and confidential assessment of doubtful or incorrect answers (as measured against those in the back of the workbook) could serve as a useful guideline. (3) The learning process was experiential. The student could privately live the role of the interrogator on the television screen.

A variation on the classroom training method we used would be to show videotape of actual interrogations recorded while they occurred. Some organizations use this as a means of protecting against false claims of abuse or misrepresentation by its investigators. The investigators in the workshop can as a group provide suggestions on how the interrogation could be improved upon.

This does, however, require a proper collegial atmosphere among the staff so that input is always framed as suggestions, not critiques. When done correctly, this is a powerful way to bring fresh insights to even the most experienced interrogator. Another benefit to using actual interrogation tapes is that it exposes trainees to a range of real suspects' reactions and ploys, which is something otherwise limited by the acting ability of the role players.

Outside Classes

Another way the manager can discharge his responsibility as trainer is to arrange or require attendance at local college classes in relevant subjects or seminar sessions on investigative skills. Although the availability of such programs will vary in different areas, this type of formal training is rapidly increasing and is of unquestioned value.

Professional groups sponsor concentrated seminars within their specialties, the calendar for which may frequently be found at the Internet site of the society or association. As an added benefit, many associations will post alerts for similar training available from private companies or other associations within common areas of interest. Such training, often designed for advanced practitioners who have limitations on the amount of time they can stay away from their usual duties, can be expected to be densely packed with practical information and techniques. This is especially true if the training is organized and sponsored at the national or international organization level. Sometimes, local chapter training is of lesser quality with respect to training materials and presentation style of the trainers.

THE MANAGER AS CONTROLLER

In the manager's role as controller there are four areas of concern: organization and span of control, records, expenses, and equipment.

Organization and Span of Control

Span of control as a management concept refers to the number of subordinates reporting directly to a superior. In an earlier book we took the position that a good span of control in a security organization is six persons.[8] But in the case of investigators, this effective span of control can be extended because of the nature of the worker and the nature of the work. As Schultz observes, "Highly qualified and motivated investigation personnel obviously require less supervision, thus making it possible to extend the normal limits of a span of control."[9]

In the organization diagrammed in Figure 4.1, for example, only one manager or supervisor is needed for the investigation unit. However, as Schultz concludes correctly, "Under no circumstances should a supervisor in investigation be required to have more than 10 subordinates reporting to him."[10] Thus, if a security organization has more than ten investigators, organizational design as it pertains to investigations comes into play. Here another principle of organization is applicable, the logical division of work, according to which investigators are divided by either their purpose, process or method, clientele, time, or geography.[11] In the organization shown in Figure 4.2, three supervisors working under the manager should be capable of exercising effective control over as many as thirty investigators.

Records

The primary or master record in the investigative unit is the investigative assignment ledger, which should be a computerized record to which staff will make update entries. Staff computer user rights should not allow individual investigators to delete or modify existing entries. Although there are special-purpose case management programs available with quite extensive capabilities, even simple word processing and spreadsheet programs can be quite adequate. Every investigation conducted by the organization is posted in this control ledger by date received or date the case was opened, case file number, name of suspect or arrestee, if any, the name of the investigator to whom the case is assigned, status report dates, remarks, and final disposition. The simplified illustration of ledger data in Figure 4.3 is presented in strict chronological case assignment order, much as it is initially created, and represents how a manual method of compilation would appear.

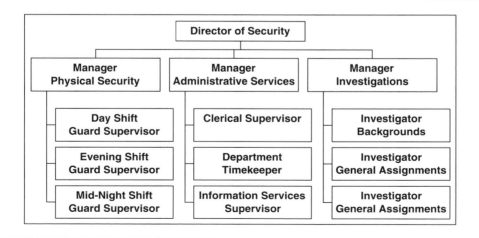

Figure 4.1. Organization with less than ten investigators.

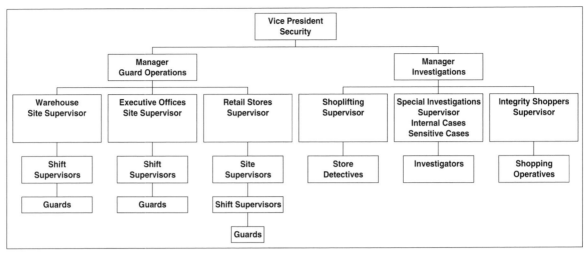

Figure 4.2.   Organization with more than 10 investigators.

DATE	FILE #	SUSPECT/ARRESTEE	INVESTIGATOR	1st REPORT	REPORT	REPORT	REMARKS
01/04/0	B-2-05		Childs	01/05/05	01/11/05	03/07/05	
01/06/05	SP-1-05	Learant, Oscar	Moss	01/06/05			Arrested juvenile. Turned over to PD.
01/09/05	BI-1-05	Turner, Helen	Childs	02/02/05			Update OK.
01/09/05	S-1-05		Hernandez	01/11/05	02/09/05		Lewd calls to Accounting Div.
01/10/05	E-2-05	Farmer, Charles	Childs	01/11/05			Employee terminated.
01/11/05	B-3-05	Jackson, Wiles & White, Samuel	Hernandez	01/12/05	01/13/05	03/01/05	Detective Hogan reports arrests. Recovery being held as evidence.
01/16/05	M-1-05		Childs	01/17/05	02/11/05		Fence cutting.
01/16/05	E-3-05	Reed, Malissa	Hernandez	01/19/05			
01/17/05	E-4-05	Borowiler, Harry	Moss	01/18/05	02/21/05	03/06/05	Employee resigned.

Figure 4.3.   Investigative assignment ledger.

Figure 4.4 shows the same information, computerized, and sorted by the individual investigator. It tells the manager, who examines it on March 7th, the following information:

Investigator Childs: On January 4 he was assigned a company burglary investigation (file designation B), the second of the year (file #2=B-2-05). He filed his first report the following day, a supplemental report six days later, and another report on March 7. The matter is pending.

On January 9, Childs was assigned the first background investigation of the year (BI-1-05), which he completed and filed on February 2. On January 16 he was assigned the first malicious mischief case for the year (M-1-05). A day later he filed his first report on this case, with a second report following almost a month later. The problem of someone cutting the exterior fence line is still pending.

INVESTIGATOR	DATE	FILE #	SUSPECT/ARRESTEE	1st REPORT	REPORT	REPORT	REMARKS
Childs	01/04/05	B-2-05		01/05/05	01/11/05	03/07/05	
Childs	01/09/05	BI-1-05	Turner, Helen	02/02/05			Update OK.
Childs	01/10/05	E-2-05	Farmer, Charles	01/11/05			Employee terminated.
Childs	01/16/05	M-1-05		01/17/05	02/11/05		Fence cutting.
Hernandez	01/09/05	S-1-05		01/11/05	02/09/05		Lewd calls to Accounting Div.
Hernandez	01/11/05	B-3-05	Jackson, Wiles & White, Samuel	01/12/05	01/13/05	03/01/05	Detective Hogan reports arrests. Recovery being held as evidence.
Hernandez	01/16/05	E-3-05	Reed, Malissa	01/19/05			
Moss	01/06/05	SP-1-05	Learant, Oscar	01/06/05			Arrested juvenile. Turned over to PD.
Moss	01/17/05	E-4-05	Borowiler, Harry	01/18/05	02/21/05	03/06/05	Employee resigned.

Figure 4.4. Computerized investigative assignment ledger. Sorted by Investigator.

Investigator Moss: On January 6, she was assigned a special investigation, the first of that classification for the year (SP-1-05). The same day she identified juvenile Learant as the suspect and referred that juvenile to the police, who took over the case. There was nothing more for her to do and the matter was closed (cleared). On January 17, Moss was assigned an employee case, the fourth of the year (E-4-05). This case was cleared from the books some weeks later, on March 6, when the suspect resigned.

Investigator Hernandez: On January 9, he was assigned the first sex crime of the year (S-1-05), a lewd phone call problem that is continuing but has not been resolved. Hernandez has kept abreast of the case, filing monthly supplemental reports. On January 11, he was assigned the third burglary case (B-3-05). He filed his initial investigative report the next day. On the following day the ledger reflects a report from a local police detective advising that the patrol division had picked up two suspects. The case is awaiting trial. On January 16, Hernandez was assigned the third employee investigation of the year (E-3-05). He submitted his first report three days later, but since then no activity in connection with that case has been recorded.

Bear in mind that this sample reflects only the assignments over a two-week period, and the three investigators naturally would have other cases assigned prior to the initial date of the sample.

Obviously, then, the investigation assignment ledger provides the manager with a wealth of information.

- It is a single source that reflects the total caseload of the organization.
- It is a single source that reflects the quantitative status of a given classification of case.

By the 16th of January, for example, four employee cases had been formalized. By August the then current page of the ledger might tell the manager at a glance that the 64th employee investigation for the year was just assigned.

- It serves as a reminder to follow up on cases still pending.
- It serves as a guide as to which investigator might or might not be assigned to the next case.
- It is the source for the compilation of monthly activity or production statistics, by unit as well as by individual investigator.

The ledger computer file (which should be backed up on a daily basis, as well as printed regularly and kept in paper form by the manager) is a strong supervisory tool. Consider, for example, Hernandez' case # E-3-05. Examining the ledger on March 7, the manager notes that Hernandez submitted one report on this case on January 19. There are no remarks to indicate any activity or status, and the case is still open. Thus, the sheet signals a possible problem. It should alert the manager to go to the investigation files and pull # E-3-05. Let us say, for the sake of illustration, that the one report dated 1/19/05, as indicated in the ledger, concludes with this statement: "Investigation will continue when the subject employee returns from his medical leave of absence." More than six weeks have passed. Is the suspected employee still on medical leave? Or has the employee returned but Hernandez has failed to keep up with the case? Whether the employee has returned to work or not, the investigator should have checked within a thirty-day period and, if the employee was still on leave, a brief supplemental report to that effect should have been written. The manager can point out this lapse to Hernandez.

The other key record is the monthly activity report for each investigator. Such a report is simply a summation of each investigator's work, covering the number of cases assigned, the number closed, number pending, number of arrests or apprehensions, value of recoveries, and any other data deemed significant to the organization. Such data are computed in terms of the month in question (for example, February, 2005), this month last year (February, 2004), this year to date (January–February, 2005), and last year to date (January–February, 2004).

Expenses

Ideally, the investigative unit of the security department should have its own salary and sundry expense budgets, originally prepared and subsequently monitored by the manager.

In *Effective Security Management*, 3e, summarizing the chapter on planning and budgeting, this area of the manager's responsibility is expressed in a nutshell:

> Planning and budgeting go hand-in-hand; a budget is a plan stated in financial terms. Budgeting requires a realistic estimate of programs and their costs, and an allocation of resources to achieve planned objectives.
>
> Because budgets are prepared well in advance, effective budget management requires thinking ahead, anticipating needs based on relatively predictable conditions. The budget then becomes a tool. . . .[12]

Each month the manager should analyze the expenditures of his section. Let us say that he originally planned for 40 hours of overtime for his staff but during the last month actually incurred 80 hours of overtime, a 100% increase over the plan. The manager must review the work record to determine who worked the excess overtime and why. The extra overtime may or may not have been necessary. Periodic review and evaluation of these and other expenses are simply other important ways of controlling the operation of the investigative unit.

Equipment

Equipment used by investigators, such as two-way radios, video camcorders, binoculars, audio recorders, weapons, surveillance trucks, digital cameras, and so on, requires strict controls. All forms of such equipment should be secured in a locked equipment room with the key controlled by the manager. When an investigator has need of equipment, say a camera, it should be assigned to the investigator on an equipment control sheet that reflects the following: date checked out, description of equipment (by equipment number or serial number), case file number, investigator's name, person checking the equipment out, condition of equipment going out, signature of investigator taking possession, date equipment is returned, condition of equipment returned, and signature of person receiving the returned equipment. Unless such controls are in place and faithfully administered, equipment will invariably end up missing or mysteriously damaged.

With respect to the condition of equipment and record of damage, this control is not designed to make investigators pay for damages. It is designed, rather, to prevent a situation in which equipment is urgently needed but is discovered to be broken or otherwise inoperable. With proper control, if any piece of equipment is damaged on one case, that damage will be caught and promptly repaired, so the equipment will be ready for use the next time.

As an alternative, if the investigative unit is especially small and there is enough equipment to do so, permanent issues of frequently used equipment can be made. This can facilitate the rapid response to incidents by investigators who always have "their own" equipment available to them. This is especially desirable if investigators frequently have to work upon short notice after normal office hours. An additional benefit to this arrangement is the increased familiarity that comes from using the same piece of gear every time. A rapidly developing mobile surveillance is not the time to try to remember how to turn on an unfamiliar camcorder, especially if it is a nighttime situation. It has also been our experience that people tend to take better care of equipment they "own" and no one else uses. After all, they can blame no one else if repair issues are not addressed, and they will directly suffer the consequences of neglect if failures occur in the field later.

THE MANAGER AS MOTIVATOR

Because most individuals in investigative work are or should be highly motivated, managerial expertise in this area will best be demonstrated by what he should not be: a demotivator.

What can cause a motivated employee to lose dedication and enthusiasm? In large part such demotivation is the result of managerial styles or practices that restrict the investigator's decision-making opportunities, emphasize criticism rather than praise, take credit when that credit rightfully belongs to the investigator, restrict the investigator's freedom of movement, or in a host of other ways express the negative characteristics so frequently found in the work environment.

Investigators who are empowered to evaluate situations and then to act will advance investigations smoothly and regularly. Those who are continually checked on by their bosses will develop the habit of constantly stopping for reassurance and guidance. Instead, they should be competently trained, given the means to do the job, and encouraged to execute workable plans of their own development, free to exploit opportunities that present themselves.

Really effective and motivated investigators may indeed be prima donnas, but of all employees they require a light touch on the reins. The best managerial approach to them is expressed in an article entitled "Give Your People the Opportunity to Fail," in *Security Management* magazine. It reads, in part, ". . . we find the decision-making process is the result and reflection of one's judgment and/or creativity. Management either respects and values the judgment and/or creativity of each employee, or they don't. How can an employee's true capabilities be known if the individual is over-supervised, overruled, unduly limited, reversed and corrected?"[13] This of course assumes that they have advanced in their training and professional development to have reached journeyman status. Trainees do need more assistance and quality checking, but even in those instances, the proper training progression should result in ever-lessening monitoring.

Even those who might take issue with this thinking in general would be hard pressed to refute its logic as applied to the work climate of those engaged in investigative work. The manager responsible for investigators must have outstanding people-management skills as well as a strong background in investigative fieldwork. Unskilled managers can and do drive valuable investigative talent to look for work with other companies or in the public sector. In addition, unless some level of appropriate risk-taking is encouraged among investigators, managers will find themselves virtually planning each investigation themselves. It is in both the organization's and manager's best interest to avoid this by properly managing and motivating their professional investigators.

THE MANAGER AS EVALUATOR

There are two common managerial errors found in performance evaluations as applied to the investigative function. The first is the attitude or belief that evaluations should be an annual event, usually preparatory to salary reviews. The second is the error of rating the person rather than that person's performance.

The effective manager recognizes that the evaluation of each investigator's performance is an ongoing process, based on case after case, and one that should be reviewed at least monthly. That review will begin with the monthly individual statistical summary. If the investigator's work is rated marginal, questionable, or below accepted standards for the month of March, the matter should be discussed at that time, not months later. To put this in another way, the investigator should never be surprised by his standing in the eyes of the manager. Everyone needs and wants to know how he is doing, and it is encouraging and stimulating to know that your work is under constant review as you progress through the year. Even the knowledge of failing to meet acceptable standards, when this evaluation is handled in an objective way, provides encouragement to the employee in terms of knowing exactly what is expected of him and what he must do to reach accepted standards of performance. On the other side of the coin, rare is the employee who is not motivated to even better performance when praised for his or her work.

Objectivity in evaluation is essential. The manager cannot afford to rate investigators as personalities. Each must be rated on the basis of what he does or fails to do — on performance. It is all too easy to fall into the trap of rewarding likable and popular personalities with high marks, or to rate less attractive people with lower marks. Even the wisest manager can sometimes be blinded by the halo effect of an outstanding but isolated incident or swayed in his judgment by the fact that an individual is highly popular. Avoid these traps. Evaluate everyone, like it or not, based on the record.

II. METHODS OF SECURITY INVESTIGATION

Chapter 5

Undercover Investigations

Undercover investigations are essentially intelligence or "spy" operations within any given area or unit of a corporation. As such, the investigation is definitely covert in its nature and operation. Effectively, no one should know an investigation is in progress other than those directly responsible.

The obvious advantage of an undercover operation is that it gives management an accurate picture of what is occurring in detail, on a day-to-day basis, in a designated area of the organization. As a rule, management does not really know what is going on in line units. It relies on supervision to keep superior officers apprised. Obviously, poor or dishonest supervisors will not report on themselves or their subordinates.

Another invaluable aspect of this covert activity is that the undercover investigator is in position not only to observe dishonesty but also to participate in it, along with all the other employees who have chosen to become involved. This provides security and management with intimate details of employee theft and other illegal activities. As an example, the shipping and receiving supervisor might be compromised by a female subordinate as a result of a one-time sexual encounter. The female employee and two other receiving clerks are stealing from the firm by signing off receipts that reflect more goods than actually received. The differences are being divided among the three and various truck drivers delivering the goods. The compromised supervisor knows what is happening but conveniently disappears from the dock when trucks come in. An undercover agent assigned to work in that area as a forklift operator (assuming he is an effective agent) soon would become involved in the thefts. He would also readily discover why the supervisor never seems to be in the area when the illegal activity occurs.

Undercover investigations may be conducted on a random basis or they may be undertaken with specific targets, for example, when there is information or suspicion of dishonesty in a given area, such as the shipping and receiving department in the preceding illustration. Random assignments are simply tests of work areas. If dishonesty or any other form of unacceptable conduct exists in that area, it will be discovered. Unacceptable behavior might include the use of alcohol or drugs on the job, cheating on the time clock, gross carelessness that causes damage to materials, equipment, or goods, or any number of other actions that commonly constitute problems in the work environment.

The objectives of constructive or undercover investigations in the private sector are:

1. To discover internal dishonesty.
2. To identify all parties involved in the dishonest activity.
3. To identify the organizational, operational, or physical failure that contributed to or permitted the dishonesty to occur.
4. To purge the organization of all guilty employees (or outsiders who contract for or otherwise service the organization).
5. To correct those deficiencies identified in #3.

Additional benefits from this particular protection strategy include discovery and subsequent correction of conditions that are counterproductive to the best interests of the organization, such as poor supervisory practices, unsafe conditions, wasteful practices, sanitation problems, legal compliance failures, industrial espionage, and internal sabotage.

It should be clear that undercover investigations in the private sector focus on internal operations involving employee conduct and performance. It follows that the strategy used to detect and apprehend shoplifters (customers, not employees) who commit theft in a retail organization is not the same as an undercover investigation. Rather, it is a plainclothes, constructive, observatory program (as opposed to participatory) that has little, if anything, to do with employee dishonesty.

TECHNIQUES AND METHODS

Arranging for Undercover Agents

Outside agencies typically will be used to obtain, train, and place undercover agents. Later we will discuss the reasons why in-house investigators should not be used on these assignments. There are many things that must be considered during the selection of an agency and the design of the assignment:

1. Agency Qualifications. Does the agency specialize in workplace misconduct investigations or is this just another of numerous sidelines it dabbles in? Has the agency controlled undercover operations in the past or will they be "learning on the job"?
2. Agent Characteristics. The company and the agency should be completely clear on the desirable characteristics and traits for the prospective agents. Special qualifications and experience should be understood. For example, an undercover delivery driver should possess the requisite type of driver's license for the equipment to be operated. The agency should profile the targeted workforce so that a compatible individual can be recruited.
3. Recruiting/Qualifying Process. The company should clearly understand all the methods being employed by the agency for the recruitment of the agent. The agency should shoulder the responsibility of conducting a thorough background investigation of the would-be agent and present the company with the results for its consideration. The company should expect to pay a fee for the recruiting expenses and services associated with finding the right person for the job. These charges should be explicitly understood in advance.

4. Hourly and Report Fees. Agencies typically will charge the company a per-hour fee for the agent's time from which some premium pay is given to the agent in addition to the normal wages paid to the agent as an employee. In addition there often will be some number of hours charged for the services of the professional investigator controlling the agent's activities. Some agencies also offer the agents an incentive bonus per report filed on time, to be paid at the end of the assignment. The company should agree to all fees and expenses to be incurred in advance to prevent later misunderstandings. A budget for each type of fee and expense should be set and continuously monitored by the company security executive in charge of the project.

5. Agent Control Guidelines. The agent's investigative services should be controlled solely by the outside agency. She must not acknowledge to anyone within the company the true nature of the work she is providing. If the company security personnel attempt to exercise routine direction of the agent, lines of communication and control will be blurred and they will rapidly become ineffective as accountability is muddled. At best it leads to a confused agent, at worst miscommunications arise, which can lead to the agent or the entire project being compromised. This all being said, the company, agency, and agent must establish a method of emergency contact by the company security executive if it is learned that the agent's cover identity has been badly compromised and may be in danger.

6. Insurance and Risk Management. It is a good idea for the agreement between the company and the outside agency to include some form of indemnity for the company for the unauthorized and negligent actions of the agency or the agent. Having the agency provide a certificate of additional insurance to the company in which the company is named as an insured party on the agency's insurance policy should be mandatory. This is a good thing to have done, especially if something unfortunate should happen during the operation that results in later lawsuits.

Undercover operations are an area where it is prudent to have the engagement contract and the overall project reviewed by an experienced employment law attorney who intimately knows the company, its culture, and risk tolerance.

The Fair Credit Reporting Act (FCRA) had been interpreted by the Federal Trade Commission staff as creating a number of complex and problematic burdens on employers using third-party investigators to examine employee misconduct. Due to the objections of employers, investigators, and attorneys, Congress amended FCRA with the Fair and Accurate Credit Transactions Act of 2003 (FACTA).

FACTA clarified the requirements imposed upon employers when using outside investigators to examine employee conduct, whether or not undercover investigation is employed. If employers wish to take adverse action against employees as a result of such outside investigation, the following apply:

1. The subject matter of the investigation should be employment related.
2. The investigation should be pursuant to preexisting written policies of the employer.
3. The investigation can also be looking into compliance with federal, state, or local laws and regulations.

4. The employee must be given a summary of the investigation, but that summary can exclude the names of persons who gave information in the investigation.
5. The employee does not have to be given a complete copy of the investigation report upon which the adverse action is based.
6. The report may be given only to the:
   a. Employer or the employer's agent
   b. Government agencies
   c. Or, as otherwise required by law

It should be understood that these provisions do not apply if the employer does not use an outside investigator to conduct the work. Therefore, an internal investigation, using only company employee investigators and undercover operatives, would not fall under the requirements of the Fair Credit Reporting Act.

Having the outside law firm actually engaging the investigative agency may also provide certain legal protections over the information generated by the undercover agent as legally privileged. It is clear that getting legal advice is now strongly advisable before undercover investigations are initiated.

Penetrating for Job Placement

A very important aspect of the undercover operation is the need for the investigator, agent, or operative to assume a false identity in the work force. For all intents and purposes, the agent is an impostor, posing as a janitor, assembler, stockman, clerk, accountant, waitress, EDP operator, warehouseman, or anything else — not excluding a possible role as a security employee within the security department. The fact that the false or assumed identity would not stand up to any searching scrutiny (as in a security background investigation) presents no problem, since the agent is security's operative. To fake a work history to meet a job's requirements is not difficult, and coworkers usually accept others at face value.

Undercover Investigation Engagement Agreement

This Agreement, made between **UC Inc.** (The Contractor) and **Dynamic Frozen Foods, Inc.** (The Client), shall constitute the terms and conditions under which the Contractor shall provide certain services to the Client.

Terms

1. The Contractor shall provide specialized services to investigate the matter of inventory losses recently incurred at the Client's Central Warehouse.
2. The Contractor shall recruit, train, and provide for approval, one to five suitable undercover agents (the Operatives) for placement in the Central Warehouse of the Client as a Janitor.

3. The Client shall interview the prospective Operatives until it has selected one for placement.
4. The Client shall pay to the Operative all pay, benefits, and allowances customarily afforded employees of the Client who occupy similar positions.
5. The Client shall exercise customary management prerogatives over the work done by the Operative that is customary to the position of Janitor within the Client's company.
6. The Contractor shall exercise exclusive control over, management of, communication with, and training of, the Operative in all investigative work done by the Operative.
7. The Client shall not make any direct contact with the Operative with respect to the investigative work performed by the Operative for the Contractor.
8. The Operative shall resign employment from the Client upon termination of assignment without claim against the Client.
9. The Contractor shall provide to the Client a daily report of observations reported by the Operative.
10. The Client shall not undertake any action that will reveal the true identity, nature of assignment, or dual employment status of the Operative at any time to any person except as may be required by law, except with the written authorization of the Contractor, on a case by case basis. The Client will not make any attempts to debrief, interview, direct, or question the Operative relative to the investigative services provided by the Operative on behalf of the Contractor.
11. The Contractor shall ensure that the Operative does not engage in any conduct that cannot be legally allowed by the Client. In those instances when the Operative is to be allowed by the Contractor to violate established work rules or policies of the Client, the Contractor will first receive verbal or written authority from the Client.
12. The primary point of contact for the Client shall be Mr. Charles B. Wilson, Investigator, and in the case of Mr. Wilson's unavailability, the alternate point of contact for the Client shall be Ms. Bernadette Bishop, Vice President, Security.
13. The Client will pay an hourly fee for each hour the Operative is present on Client premises or, if off premises, when actively engaged in the investigation. The fee will be $xx per hour.
14. In addition, the Client will pay an hourly fee of $xx per hour for control of the Operative to the Contractor. An estimated four hours per week will be charged.
15. The Client will pay for all reasonable expenses incurred by the Contractor and all applicable taxes that are occasioned by the services provided to the Client.

The Above Terms And Conditions Are Accepted
DYNAMIC FROZEN FOODS, INC.
By,

Bernadette Bishop   *June 15, 2005*

Its,   **Date**

Vice President, Security

There are two effective ways to penetrate the work force clandestinely. One is to have the assigned agent simply present himself to the unsuspecting personnel department representative as an applicant. In this approach the agent should be armed with a predesigned and memorized background and work history appropriate to the position sought. The other way is to work in close harmony with the human resources executive of the target unit or facility. This latter method requires written policy that specifically defines the relationship and responsibility of the personnel executive including, and this is most important, the admonishment that the executive is bound to absolute confidentiality regarding the presence or placement of an undercover agent, even if queried by the unit manager under whom the agent will be working.

This written policy should preferably be included in the personnel manual. It should state, in essence, that the placement of undercover agents in the work force as necessary is an acceptable protection strategy that has the full support of senior management. This is important because invariably you will find personnel people who believe that undercover operations are "dirty" or unethical, that undercover agents go about trying to entrap perfectly good employees, and report unfairly on management and personnel. Often there even will be those in human resources who, despite written policy, remain steadfastly opposed to the strategy of undercover investigation and will do whatever they can to undermine the program. This can potentially endanger the physical safety of the agent and should be dealt with swiftly and effectively. One solution to that kind of problem is to place an undercover agent in the human resources department itself, without the knowledge of the staff or their manager.

Important elements of the written policy would include the following:

- Human resources management should endeavor to place applicants sent by security unless, in their judgment, the applicant is totally unsuited for the position or placement and would be a conspicuous deviation from normal standards that would arouse suspicion.
- Only the human resources manager should know that an undercover agent is on assignment; absolutely no one else, including secretaries, should be privy to that knowledge.
- Personnel records should not be coded or in any way otherwise reflect the fact that an employee is an undercover agent.
- Once the undercover agent is in the workforce, he should not be laid off or otherwise terminated without consultation with the security department.
- The true identity of the undercover agent should not be revealed, even if such a request should come from the human resources manager's own supervisor.

The legal requirement for establishing the right to work in the United States currently imposed upon employers forces companies to view certain identity documents of each person hired. If a false identity is to be employed by the agent, we suggest that the company human resources executive fulfill these requirements by secretly inspecting the documents and completing the immigration and naturalization service form and keeping the form under close personal control. The agent should employ a ruse to avoid the normal form completion procedures of the company for as long as possible.

Many companies are surprisingly lax in this area. If this is not the situation in the case at hand, consideration should be given to creating a position to be filled by a temp agency specially contracted for this purpose. This often can be done without arousing too much attention, especially as companies are routinely outsourcing and downsizing operations. This allows the agent to be placed without ever becoming an employee and subjecting the company to those document requirements.

Of course, it is also possible that the agent will agree to use her true name and present bona fide documents. This greatly simplifies the placement process and, as long as false home address and telephone information is put into the personnel file, the protection of the agent can be somewhat assured.

Reporting

An undercover agent must submit a handwritten report for each shift worked. Typewritten reports are not satisfactory; and handwriting provides some protection against forged, altered, or fictitiously prepared reports. Each report should be signed and dated. Although the practice has questionable judicial or administrative value, the affixing of the agent's signature should follow some form of personal statement to the effect that he affirms or swears that the contents of the report are true and factual. Although it can never be known for sure, such a statement may have some influence on the agent's concern for the truth. (The veracity of undercover agents is discussed later in this chapter.) The thrust of the report should be the equivalent of a "shotgun" rather than a "rifle" attack; that is, the agent should comment on a wide variety of incidents, observations, and conversations during the last shift worked, instead of zeroing in on a specific highlight of the day or a particularly interesting facet of the job. The agent is not the one to determine what is or is not important, because he is not in a position to weigh the value of everything he hears or sees.

A full overview, uncensored, of what occurred in that agent's life on the job can be carefully evaluated by the investigator or security administrator. That is good raw intelligence.

The written report goes to the undercover agent's primary employer, the outside agency supplying the service. That report is transcribed into a typed report, in which the identity of the agent goes over to a coded numerical designation. For example, in 718-4423:

718 = Location, for example, St. Louis
4423 = Agent Conrad Bastilla, the 4423rd agent hired by the agency

The handwritten reports are maintained by the agency. The typed reports are forwarded to the security management of the company using the service. Obviously, if such reports ever fell into the wrong hands in the company, the identity of the undercover agent would be somewhat protected by the coded designation. The actual context of the reported activity would still likely compromise the agent's identity, especially if other participants read the report. Therefore, security management must ensure that the reports are received through secure channels such as being sent to the security manager's home, a special-purpose post office box, or secure e-mail address.

If possible and practical, it is desirable to have each agent also make a telephonic report on a phone answering/recording device maintained in the supervising investigator's office. That recorded call is a summary of the written report, which may take as much as five days to move through the typing and mailing process. The phone message will not only be fresh and current, but it could also provide the signal for closer supervision, including daily personal contact with the agent. When a case starts developing and the end is in sight, undercover agents must have specific instructions and directions.

Sometimes they need encouragement. One's heartbeat tends to increase, or another's courage tends to sag, as the drama approaches its climax.

Concluding the Case

The duration of a typical undercover investigation usually is measured in terms of weeks, and the undercover agent's effectiveness at a given location normally ends with the successful conclusion of the case. The reason is that the agent's involvement with dishonest employees necessitates his or her "termination" along with everyone else implicated in dishonesty. This strategy protects the agent's real identity and mission, since he is treated or processed no differently than the others involved.

This procedure suggests administrative rather than judicial action for detection of employee dishonesty. Why not follow the normal criminal justice system, beginning with the police arriving at the scene and taking into custody all participants? The answer is not simple. Following are some of its component parts:

- Once the police are aware of the investigation, the corporate investigator becomes "an agent of the police" and loses, in large measure, control over the investigation.
- The loss of control would handicap efforts to surface other incidental information that could be just as valuable to the organization as the original criminal theft investigation.
- The identity of the undercover agent, in every case, would be disclosed in court.
- The disclosure of an undercover agent in court automatically invites charges of entrapment.

Operative Report
Operative No. 01-86
Date: July 14, 2005
Place: Dynamic Frozen Foods, Inc. — Central Warehouse

1550 hrs.   I arrived at work, Mary Smith and Paul Jones were in a car located in a remote part of the parking lot. I think it was Mary's car. She's somebody who works on the day shift that I heard Paul was trying to date. When I went into the warehouse I saw Earl Marshall sitting in the break room reading a magazine and eating ice cream. Earl said that there were a couple of boxes of ice cream bars in the freezer that the day boss said we could eat because the box had broken. I took and ate one.

1600 hrs.   Paul and Earl punched in to work, put on their freezer coats and gloves and went into the freezer rooms to start work. I punched in and went to the janitorial closet and got my cart. I started cleaning the offices.

1730 hrs.   The night boss arrived at the warehouse. I don't know where he was, on other days he is here when I arrive. He called Paul and Earl out of the warehouse using the loudspeaker and they met in his office for about fifteen minutes.

1847 hrs.	I was startled by a blond haired woman who walked into one of the offices while I was vacuuming. She tapped me on the shoulder and made me jump. She was looking for the boss and I pointed to his office. She went into his office and he closed the door for about twenty-five minutes when they came out they left in his car. I overheard her say something about taking a cab to the warehouse. As the boss left he told me to tell the guys that he would be gone for the rest of the night.
1900 hrs.	Earl and Paul came out of the freezer rooms and took a break. I told them the boss was gone for the night. They laughed and said something about "now we can go crabbing." They quickly disappeared back into the warehouse.
2225 hrs.	I saw Earl and Paul leaving through a fire escape from freezer room no. 2 with case-sized boxes. They went to their cars and put one box into each of their trunks. They looked around and went back through the same door. I thought those doors were supposed to be alarmed, but I heard recently that the alarms were broken.
2230 hrs.	My shift done, I punched out, leaving Earl and Paul at work. They normally get off shift around mid-night, I think.

With the established liberalism in the courts, convictions are difficult to obtain. Even when won, they remain uncertain because of the possibility of appellate reversals, some of which are based on questionable logic. All this means that the degree of civil liability exposure is growing almost by the calendar month. The investigative efforts of the security department should be to protect the company, not to increase its exposure to civil liability. Administrative resolution of internal misconduct cases, including theft, normally by means of termination of employment, is an acceptable and safe alternative to criminal prosecution. As a matter of fact, many people are far more concerned about losing their jobs than they are over facing a confrontation with the police and court systems. The police and courts do not scare people as much as they used to. During the last decade, many people brushed their teeth in the morning knowing full well that they would be in jail by nightfall. Demonstrators for civil rights, antiabortion protesters, and current extremist animal-rights groups are good examples. But threaten a protesting assistant professor with discharge from the faculty and you will have numerous experiences with arrestees who beg to call their employers so they will not lose their jobs. There is a great deal more trauma and pain to employment discharges than is generally credited.

The undercover agent, therefore, is "terminated" along with those he identified as being undesirable employees, and no one is the wiser. That agent then awaits the next assignment, at another location.

Security department investigators would normally never go undercover in their own company. Undercover agents should be provided by an outside service agency that hires, trains, assigns, and supervises such agents as an ongoing part of the agency's professional services. The rationale for not using career security people in undercover criminal investigations is that, at some point into the investigation or at least at its conclusion, the undercover agent will be viewed by any number of employees as a partner or coconspirator in the criminal activity. Why? Because the undercover investigation is constructive, covert, and participatory. The agent's task is to be accepted by the employees who are engaged in dishonesty. The acceptance often includes such intimate relationships as wining, dining, and, yes, even romance (although the latter rarely occurs as part of the investigative plan). The resulting close association, which is a key to the success of the investigation, is treated as such at the moment of truth, the day the case is resolved. That resolution frequently includes "capture" of the undercover agent along with all the others involved in criminal conduct. A regular company investigator could hardly resume his normal role of investigator after playing the part of a bad employee. Besides compromising his effectiveness, that revelation would immediately invite a charge of entrapment.

PROBLEM AREAS

The Issue of Entrapment

Undercover investigations and entrapment are two processes closely intertwined in the minds of most people, so linked that separation is quite difficult, if not impossible, for some to perceive. But entrapment is easy to understand when one reflects on the process of planting seeds in a garden. Entrapment is the process where one person plants the seed of an idea to do wrong in another person's mind.

Following are two vignettes of employees in situations where theft occurs. In one case there is entrapment; in the other there is none. Which one entails entrapment?

Vignette #1: The Warehouse Dock. Two warehouse dock employees, Charlie and Roy, are working on a Saturday with their supervisor, Mr. Morgan. Charlie is an undercover agent. The facility normally is closed on Saturdays. This is an overtime assignment for the three; all the other employees are off duty.

At lunchtime Morgan decides that he would like fried chicken and french fries. He asks the others if they would like the same and volunteers to go get their lunches from a nearby fast food franchise. Charlie and Roy agree. Rather than walk through the building and leave by the authorized door, Morgan decides to take a shortcut to the parking lot. He jumps off the dock, unlocks the gate that is part of the security enclosure around the receiving area, and leaves that gate open for his return.

Charlie watches Morgan's car disappear down the street. He then approaches Roy and says, "Morgan won't be back for another twenty minutes. Why don't you pull your van over here and we'll both get ourselves a laptop computer. No one will ever know the difference." Roy thinks the idea is a good one, and the theft of two computers occurs.

Vignette #2: Kitchen Cleanup Time. Two kitchen helpers in a large hospital, Bill (the undercover agent) and Harris, are the last employees to leave late each night. Final chores include the garbage run (final trash and garbage trip down the service elevator to the dumpsters in the basement) and the mop-down. As he is dry-mopping the tile floor, Bill notices that the "walk-in box," or refrigerated room, was inadvertently left unlocked. He comments on that discovery to Harris. Dropping his mop, Harris hurries over to the door in question and tests it. The door opens. Harris then tells Bill, "Quick! Go get me a couple of plastic trash bags from the supply closet." Bill asks why, but Harris doesn't answer. He gestures with his hand toward the supply closet. Bill complies with the request.

Harris then motions Bill to follow him inside the box. He tells Bill to hold the large green plastic bag open. Harris then proceeds to place in the bag a carton of steaks, a ham, and several pounds of butter. Now humming mischievously, Harris waves Bill out of the room and locks the door to the box.

He takes the sack from Bill and pulls it across the floor to the cart already loaded with four garbage cans. Harris seals the bag containing the stolen food items, places that bag in a second one, and seals it. He then makes room in the nearly full garbage can for his bundle and covers it with garbage.

The bundle is deposited, along with the refuse, in a dumpster in the basement. Harris drives his car down to the trash area after work and picks up the stolen goods. Bill claims half the loot as his, but Harris gives him only the ham, promising more later. The ham is turned over to the hospital's security management as evidence.

Note the clear distinction between these two situations. In the first case, Roy was the victim of entrapment. Charlie, the undercover agent, planted the seed of the crime in Roy's mind by suggesting the idea. Roy's "garden," or mind, was devoid of the idea of stealing. In the second example, however, there was no entrapment even if the door was intentionally left unlocked. Leaving the door unlocked, and the agent's discovery of that condition, simply created an opportunity. Harris could ignore it, correct it, or take advantage of it. No seed of theft was planted. Had Bill, upon discovery of the open door, said, "Look! Some fool went off and left this thing unlocked. We could take off with half the stuff inside and no one would be the wiser," that would constitute entrapment. In either case, the key question in determining entrapment is this: Whose idea was it to commit theft? Who planted the seed?

Deception or "Double-Cross"

Another hazardous aspect of undercover investigations that must be understood and dealt with accordingly is the ever-present possibility of the undercover agent fabricating information. In some instances such fabrication may be the result of an agent's anxiety to please an overzealous investigator or supervisor who is pressing hard for derogatory information. In one actual case, an undercover agent reported the daily thefts of a coworker, actually going so far as to plant stolen goods under the front seat of the accused worker's auto and reporting the observed theft to security. When the truth was eventually, and painfully, brought out, the reason for this maliciousness on the part of the agent proved to be a personal one. The agent passionately disliked the coworker. He envied the other man's popularity, good looks, and "all-American boy" image, and he used this undercover position to "bring him down a notch or two."

How does one deal with this possibility of deception? First, recognize the possibility itself. Second, verify, directly or indirectly, all information submitted. If the agent reports that a group of employees attended a party at one's home on the weekend, it should be possible to verify that information. Even if it would be difficult or impossible to verify what happened and what was said at that party, at least a part of the agent's report would be confirmed. Third, look for inconsistencies that might occur between the written and verbal reports. A good time to reconcile information is just before interrogations commence. The agent's verbal summary, with some details, should not conflict with earlier reports if the agent is reliable. And last, be sensitive to the natural and normal reactions of the suspected employee during the interrogation. On occasion, detecting natural reactions of disbelief and innocence during an interrogation, this writer has suspended the questioning of the accused and commenced an interrogation of the accuser, securing admissions of deceptive and fabricated reports, some designed specifically to hide the agent's own acts of theft. The agent should be told that reports will be verified and, without specificity, that other collection methods are being simultaneously applied. Hidden CCTV cameras, manned surveillance, trash recoveries, can all be used to test the veracity of the agent's reports. If they tend to confirm the reports, management can more confidently rely on the work product from the agent. If otherwise, the company can attempt corrective action or simply end the project without alerting the agent that anything was amiss.

THE ABSENCE OF PROFESSIONALISM

There are some undercover agents who are truly professional. They have devoted years to this unique and fascinating kind of work, and their effectiveness is something to behold. But these are out-numbered by men and women who lack professional bearing or stature, let alone formal training and experience. Many individuals take such assignments either out of curiosity or to supplement their income while going to school. Using agents of this type in undercover work may be acceptable, but they need to be closely supervised, from the security side of their activity. Perhaps the application of the term "undercover investigator" to such agents is a misnomer. They are really intelligence agents used in an investigation supervised by investigators. To consider them as investigators in the strictest sense of the term might confer on them a degree of responsibility and decision-making that could prove counterproductive, if not simply unproductive. This use of undercover agents, in fact, comes down to security deploying nonsecurity people to assist in a security operation. As noted earlier, the people engaged in this very specialized work normally are provided by a contract service organization that deals specifically in providing undercover agents for any given need. Those agencies recruit through blind ads (using a post office box only as an address) and actively recruit college students. If, at any time during the course of the agent's assignment, his services are no longer wanted or needed, he can be terminated and instructed to report back to the primary employer. There is no employment com-mitment or guarantees between the company using the undercover agent and the agent, because the agent actually works for someone else.

This distinction is important with reference to the company's need to be consistent in its termi-nation practices. To better understand this, consider, as an example, an undercover agent who decided that he liked the position he was filling as an undercover agent, and disliked the service company that was paying him to function as an agent. Suppose that he stopped sending in his daily reports and even went so far as to tell everyone he worked with that he was an agent. When called up and terminated, he could not claim discrimination or inconsistent termination practices, because his assignment was secondary to his primary employment.

CONCLUSION

Regardless of the absence of widespread professionalism among undercover agents, and the potential risk of fraud or charges of entrapment, undercover investigations are a viable and, indeed, often essen-tial part of the overall strategy of protecting the company's assets. Failure to employ undercover inves-tigations is like a man denying himself eyeglasses when his vision is impaired or needs correction. It can leave the company blind to what is occurring within the organization, with particular reference to employee misconduct. There is no adequate substitute for this effective, internalized self-inspection and feedback process.

Chapter 6

Surveillance

Surveillance, an integral part of the investigative process, is the visual monitoring of a location or individual to determine what activities or conduct is occurring. This visual monitoring is accompanied by a *log*, a diary-type record of what is occurring within the surveillance picture. The log provides a documented chronology of what was observed.

The surveillance may be stationary, moving, or a combination of both. It may also be covert or overt, with an objective of detecting the commission of a crime or serious policy violation, gathering intelligence, preventing a crime, or all three. And surveillances may be conducted by the human eye or by means of electronic and mechanical hardware.

COVERT VERSUS OVERT SURVEILLANCE

There is a useful rule of thumb in determining the difference between covert and overt surveillance. Covert surveillances are normally detection oriented, whereas overt surveillances are usually prevention oriented.

As with all such rules, there are exceptions. For example, a covert surveillance of a fashion jewelry department operation with a primary objective of prevention could be an intelligence-gathering mission, developing every available detail surrounding that operation with an eye toward taking appropriate corrective action to reduce losses. Such intelligence could include (1) traffic patterns (customer counts by the hour, or fractions thereof), (2) number of customer theft incidents (customer-to-thief ratio), (3) type of merchandise stolen, (4) exact locations of thefts, (5) time of thefts, (6) what employees were doing when thefts occurred, (7) how thefts were effected, (8) employee staffing (break schedules, number on duty, etc.), and (9) employee dishonesty (discounting to friends, failure to record sales, putting jewelry on during store hours and then wearing it home).

By the same token, an overt surveillance of a precious jewelry department by means of the conspicuous placement of a CCTV camera could fail its primary objective of discouraging a robbery, but at the same time provide a tape of the robbery that could lead to the identification and subsequent apprehension of the robbers.

The distinction, then, between the objectives of covert and overt surveillances is not hard-and-fast. It does, however, offer a functional differentiation in most situations.

Surveillance by Human Eye

Whenever practical and possible, surveillances should be conducted by the human eye, without the use of any device or hardware, save binoculars. There is no substitute for the total comprehension afforded the observer — in terms of clarity, detail, color, and dimension (depth of field) — when he personally views the scene of an unfolding event.

This is not to suggest that the same scene should not also be recorded on film or videotape if possible, but the human eye provides the most reliable view. It may be sophisticated and less uncomfortable to monitor employees handling cash at a cash register with a history of shortages by means of CCTV with a pinhole lens, but any investigator experienced in such surveillances will testify that the human eye is more discerning, with less room for doubt and error. The flat surface of the television monitor fails to give the viewer the depth of field our minds are accustomed to and expect.

In addition, there is the interpretative value of the human mind where the observer directly witnesses an act or event. Most surveillance films cannot stand on their own. They require some interpretation.

Visual Surveillance Devices

Despite their limitations, surveillance cameras, in particular video cameras with time-lapse recorders, are invaluable in a number of situations, not the least those kinds of cases where it is impossible to conceal an investigator to conduct the surveillance. Another advantage of cameras is that they allow a multilocation coverage with one operator monitoring all locations, either simultaneously or in any sequencing pattern of switching from one location to another. CCTV cameras also do not become fatigued, distracted, or hungry.

In the security context, the camera has materially contributed to the investigative process. Many dishonest employees have been caught on a time-lapse video recorder while exiting the facility with stolen goods through covertly monitored doors, rummaging through office desks and files, or carrying out a whole host of other security-related violations, such as kicking vending machines to force out candy, drinks, or extra change. Such cameras have also captured on film outside culprits who victimize the company, such as bad check passers and holdup artists.

The camera's eye is effective in providing general information — who is entering a given door, who is receiving goods through a dock door, who is within a security-controlled work area, and such. For very specific or detailed information, the camera has shortcomings. In one investigation of thefts from a payment processing unit in which employees opened customers' envelopes containing statement heads and payments (not always in the form of bank checks), the camera was unable to detect the actual theft. It did, however, indicate to the investigator which employee was stealing by showing her suspicious behavior and furtive movements, which eventually led to her capture. The camera's deficiency in revealing specific details, in this particular case, included such puzzles as this: Did the subject put a customer's white envelope into the pocket of her work smock, or was that a white handkerchief or a note?

Even given these limitations, the use of CCTV cameras
ducting surveillance. Cameras as small as a tube of lipstick or
in numerous situations. Their cost is very minimal and their t
investigator. This will be addressed more fully later.

The Surveillance Log

The recording of what a surveillant observes can be by vc
it is taped, the notes must be transcribed at a later date. /
that they are immediately available, cost little in time, effor
are thereafter easily transmitted via e-mail to authorized
recorded logs. Another advantage is that the simple papei
in the field than do tape recorders, batteries, and tapes. There is nothing fancy of on-
log. Its purpose is no more than to record, briefly, what is observed and when, as exemplified in
Figure 6.1. There should be a separate log for each calendar day, even though one day's report could
have several pages. Each day, or each shift, should have a heading similar to that in the example,
showing the date, case under investigation (name and file number), and the identity of the investigator or investigators. If two or more surveillants are watching the same scene, only one should maintain the log. If two or more are surveying separate areas while on the same case, separate logs should
be maintained. These logs will then become a permanent part of the official case file.

THE STATIONARY SURVEILLANCE

Stationary surveillance positions may be fixed or permanent, short term, or very temporary.

Fixed Surveillance

Fixed or permanent surveillance positions are designed or constructed into a building or any other
structure, allowing for the visual monitoring of a given location within that building according to need.
Examples would include fixed positions over the back office of a cash counting room, where large sums
of currency are counted and prepared for deposit; permanent installations over gaming tables such as
in gambling casinos; and positions affording surveillance opportunities into sensitive work areas, such
as receiving or delivery docks, or where the general public has immediate access to valuable company
assets, such as a precious jewelry display in a retail store. The fixed positions themselves may be disguised or so unobtrusive that only the very alert or trained eye would detect them, or they may be conspicuously obvious. Examples of unobtrusive surveillance positions would include a full mirror where
one would normally expect to see one, such as a single full-length mirror in a men's clothing store, or
louvered vents that look like heating and cooling register openings in the upper portion of walls. An
example of a conspicuous position of surveillance would be a ceiling-mounted, closed-circuit TV
camera that pans back and forth in full view of employees or customers, with or without a light suggesting that it is functional. Another conspicuous surveillance position is the protruding two-way
mirror configurations commonly seen elevated on market and drugstore walls with a view down aisles
that have the greatest history of shoplifting losses.

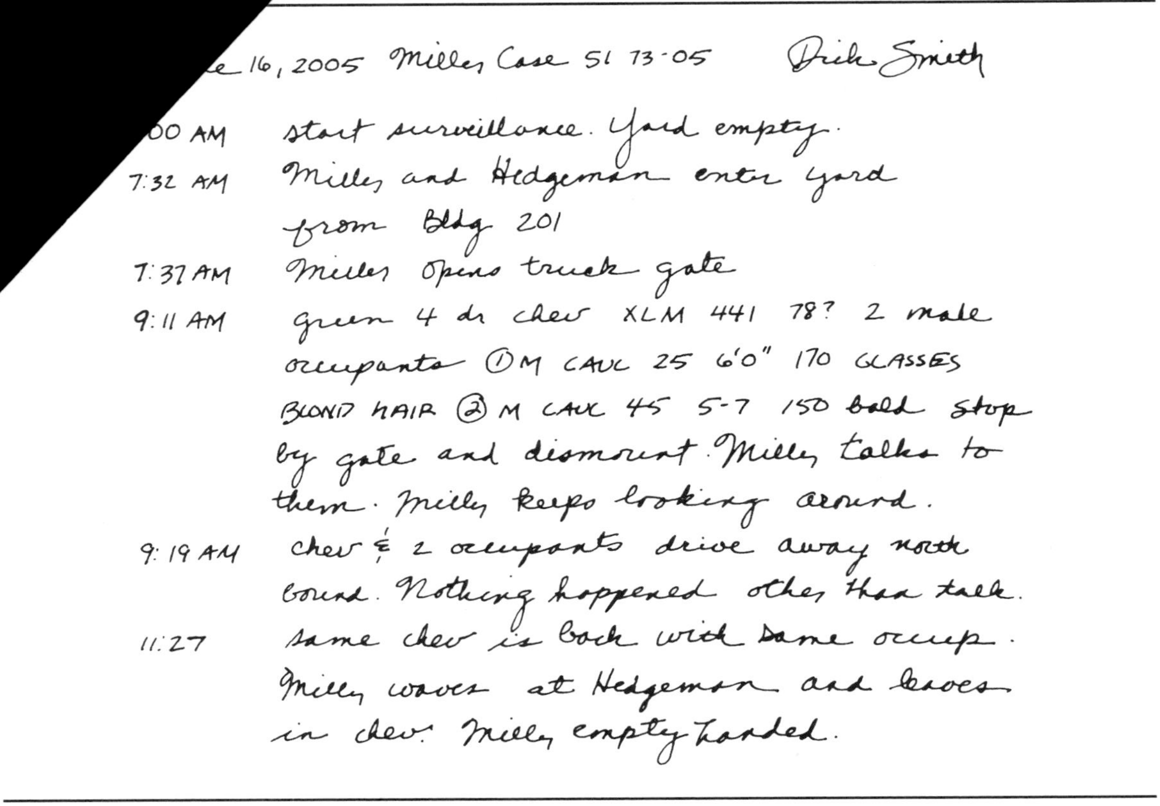

e 16, 2005   Miller Case 51 73-05   Dick Smith

00 AM	start surveillance. Yard empty.
7:32 AM	Miller and Hedgeman enter yard from Bldg 201
7:37 AM	Miller opens truck gate
9:11 AM	green 4 dr chev XLM 441 78? 2 male occupants ① M cauc 25 6'0" 170 glasses blond hair ② M cauc 45 5-7 150 bald stop by gate and dismount. Miller talks to them. Miller keeps looking around.
9:19 AM	chev & 2 occupants drive away north bound. Nothing happened other than talk.
11:27	same chev is back with same occup. Miller waves at Hedgeman and leaves in chev. Miller empty handed.

Figure 6.1.   Sample surveillance log.

Short-Term Surveillance

Short-term surveillance is for specific problem-solving situations. Positions selected might include rented houses, apartments, or rooms affording a view of a targeted portion of company property, such as stockpiled assets, box cars on company railroad spurs, loading docks, a door or window through which there might be illicit traffic of people and/or goods, or a section of perimeter fencing where unauthorized penetration is suspected.

One case involving this type of surveillance developed after the discovery that a set of double doors on the front of a department store were being found unlocked several days a week. There was no question that the doors were locked each night at closing time. A test of the swing of the doors with the burglary alarm turned on revealed that they would open one foot before the alarm actuated. This created the possibility that someone could remain in hiding while the store was being closed and, later, could unlock the door, open it less than twelve inches, and pass out through the narrow opening large quantities of merchandise without setting off the alarm. The same culprit could then return to his hiding place and emerge only after the store was again open to the public. This possibility ha[d] be resolved.

Two investigators rented a hotel room that directly overlooked the front doors in question. For several nights they took turns observing the closing procedure through binoculars, ensuring that the doors were indeed locked, and monitoring the doors until they were opened again in the morning. After close to one hundred consecutive hours of work, it was discovered that the door had a faulty tumbler in the lock mechanism. The vibration of passing buses during the early morning hours would infrequently cause the bolt to fall. The problem was solved, though not with the solution anticipated.

It is not uncommon to place under surveillance locations other than the immediate company property. Examples might include the residence of an employee suspected of dishonesty to observe him unload company equipment or property from his auto after work; the gathering place of suspects, such as a local bar; or any other location where stolen company property might be stored, divided up, or otherwise disposed of.

When property other than a hotel or motel is rented for surveillance purposes, it should be done surreptitiously, using some pretext, and ideally under an assumed name. Investigators, like criminals, can obtain good false identification; and as far as references are concerned, other members of the investigative staff or even personal friends can vouch for the "roomer." As a rule, however, establishments in the areas where surveillance is needed are not especially discriminating about who is moving in.

The point is that the owner or landlord should be given no reason to be interested in or curious about the rental. To take a landlord or apartment manager into your confidence borders on pure folly. Being privy to a secret operation creates an overwhelming irresistible itch that must be satisfied — a satisfaction that comes from telling someone else. In this way the contagion spreads. The rented facilities must obviously remain covert in nature, and if handled as such usually prove very productive. Certainly there is some risk of a leak, but the short duration of the surveillance, and the professional status of the management concerned, will tend to minimize the risk.

For short-term surveillances, vehicles, particularly campers or vans modified to accommodate surveillance personnel, can be very effective. The van innocently parked on the street or in a parking lot rarely arouses suspicion. If the vehicle must be parked dangerously close to the surveillance objective, ruses can be employed. For example, the vehicle can be boldly driven to the desired spot, where two investigators dismount, each on his own side, slam the doors shut, and, in animated conversation, leave the scene. Secreted in the rear of the closed van is the surveillance team. If there is no legal or reasonable way to park where it is necessary, or if overnight parking would be either illegal (hence no reasonable person would do it) or suspicious, an effective ruse is for the vehicle to "break down" at the desired location. As long as the van is not needed for moving surveillance, visual proof of the breakdown can be offered by having the driver (and passenger, if manpower is available) jack up one corner of the vehicle, remove the wheel, place blocks under the axle to prevent the vehicle from slipping off the jack, and then depart with the surveillance team hidden inside. It is amazing how acceptable a disabled vehicle is, even to those who should be wary.

An example of an ultra-sophisticated surveillance platform is shown in Figure 6.2. This vehicle is custom equipped for a single purpose: covert surveillance. The cost of outfitting such a vehicle generally restricts this kind of platform to law enforcement agencies. Sometimes camouflaging the true purpose of a van can run to much more colorful approaches. A Dodge van was used as a modified surveillance vehicle in one case where warehouse employees were peddling stolen television sets, radios,

Figure 6.2.   A sophisticated professional surveillance vehicle. Photos courtesy of The Mattman Company, Escondido, California.

and stereo component parts to a "fence" in a neighboring community. The fence was, in fact, a storefront rented by a combined public and corporate investigative team. The store was wired for sound recordings. The van parked in the rear alley next to the store's back door, where all the nefarious activity took place, was painted and disguised as a fresh fish delivery truck. On each side of the van was mounted a ship's steering wheel, a decorative addition to the seafood theme. The hub of each wheel accommodated the lens of a camera, manned by a team of two investigators secreted inside the van.

Very Temporary Surveillance

Very temporary surveillances can last anywhere from one half-hour to two weeks (at the outside), depending on the circumstances. They may be conducted, for example, from adjacent building rooftops or office windows, with the owner's knowledge and permission, often on the basis of reciprocity should the need arise. In one case an undercover agent phoned from a pay phone and reported that an employee was going to stash a stereo set in the trash area outside a certain door at lunchtime. Later in the afternoon he would leave work early, drive his car to the trash area, put the stereo in the trunk, and drive off. The only place from which we could survey the trash area was a neighboring company's rooftop. Within a half-hour we had identified the management person responsible for that building, presented our case, and obtained permission to place an investigator on the roof. The roof was flat with an 18-inch parapet. A head showing over that parapet would have been disastrous as far as our case was concerned. However, because the roof was flat, there were four-inch by eight-inch water drains through the barrier, creating little windows through which a man in a prone position could observe the area under surveillance. Equipped with binoculars and a walkie-talkie, the investigator observed the secretion and later recovery of the stolen merchandise. Following his directions over the radio system, investigators were able to block the culprit's car with their vehicles, and he was captured.

Hardware Used in Stationary Surveillances

Hardware that can assist in stationary surveillance work includes cell phones, two-way radios, 35-mm cameras with telephoto lenses, digital still cameras, VHS-C or 8-mm video camcorders, binoculars, tripod-mounted telescopes, and "jerry rigs," or improvised devices limited only by the imagination. Improvisation can be an important part of the investigator's art, as two examples may suggest. One is a trigger device activated by a string attached to the sliding door of a boxcar. When the boxcar is entered at night, the string is pulled, turning on a small, unobtrusive light. The thieves are unable to see that light, which signals that a crime is in progress. Another device was improvised by students of a college who were experiencing frequent forcible entries into the soft drink dispensing machine sitting outside their dormitory. They wired the coin box so that, if it were removed, all the dorm lights would go on along with a loud bell. They all slept peacefully during the "surveillance." When the machine was attacked again, the surprised thief found himself surrounded by a large number of very incensed young men.

THE MOVING SURVEILLANCE

Moving surveillances are by far the most difficult to achieve and the most vulnerable to discovery. The objective of a moving surveillance is usually that of determining an unknown location — where the subject lives, works, plays, conducts affairs, disposes of stolen goods, meets others, and so on. Once the location is known, the *where* of the investigative quest, then other strategies, including stationary surveillance, can surface details connected with that location.

Moving surveillances can be accomplished on foot (especially in crowded urban areas), or by means of bicycle, moped, motorcycle, automobile, public transportation, or, though it sounds like the implausibility of television drama, by plane or helicopter. Any means that is available and practical can be used, as long as it enables the investigators to follow the subject to a location the knowledge of which is germane to the investigation.

The risk in the moving surveillance, as in any covert surveillance, is discovery by the person or persons being followed. Such discovery — called *burning* — can have disastrous consequences for the investigation. It may cause the subject to destroy or otherwise dispose of evidence, to discontinue criminal activities before the case can be developed fully, or to suspend those activities temporarily only to resume them with a whole new set of strategies. It will induce a heightened awareness in the subject resulting in appropriate defensive maneuvers. And it may result in public or organizational exposure of the security department's surveillance activity, which would have embarrassing consequences. (The notorious Watergate affair was neither more nor less than the discovery of a surveillance, although that case involved illegal means to effect the surveillance, a strategy not propounded here.)

The trick, then, is to avoid discovery. Following are some suggestions to minimize that risk.

Foot Surveillance

- Keep several people between yourself and the subject being watched.
- Never watch the back of your subject's head. Many individuals can sense being watched or stared at.
- Watch the subject from the waist down, especially the legs and feet.
- If the subject stops to window gaze, visit with someone or buy a paper, and if your stopping would be obvious, keep walking past him. If possible, enter a building or store ahead of the subject and, from its recesses, watch for him to resume his movements and to pass by.

Public Conveyance Surveillance

- Never sit directly behind the subject.
- Sit several seats ahead of the subject, on the same side of the vehicle, as long as there is no way for him to exit behind you unobserved.
- Watch the subject from the waist down, especially the legs and feet.
- Absolutely avoid eye contact with the subject.
- If in a bus that stops, or will stop within the short distance of one block, remain in the bus to the next stop after the subject alights if he appears nervous, or if you can see through a rear or side window the direction the subject takes after leaving the bus.

Auto Surveillance

- Whenever possible, have two or more vehicles involved in the surveillance, with voice (radio or cell phone) contact capability.

- Use female investigators as drivers as well as riders.
- Female investigators riding in the car should sit close to a male driver.
- Follow as far back as distance, traffic, road design, and conditions will al back, the better.
- Do not follow in the same lane in which a subject is driving. That lane tends to be more "blind." Other lanes permit turns and expressway exiting in a less *reactive* manner.
- With multiple vehicle surveillances, a decoy vehicle can follow the target relatively closely. When the subject makes a change in direction, turning left or right, the decoy should continue straight ahead. The intent of this maneuver is to cause the subject, if he is at all suspicious of a tail, to enjoy a false sense of confidence that he is not being followed.
- In multiple vehicle surveillances, have the autos "leap-frog" each other at appropriate time intervals, the trailing vehicle moving up to the forward position and the lead vehicle dropping back to the end of the line.
- Be aware of the importance of "body language" while in a moving surveillance. Tense concentration is discernible. An arm draped over the seat backrest, or resting in the door's window frame, gives the appearance of a relaxed and unconcerned driver or occupant.

Hardware Used in Moving Surveillances

All the hardware listed for stationary surveillances is used also in moving surveillances, with the exception of time-lapse VTR (videotape recording in slow motion) and telescopes, which are impractical where there is too much motion.

MOVING AND STATIONARY SURVEILLANCE

When the decision is made to place an individual or group under combined moving and stationary surveillance, such a determination obviously indicates the need for a very intensive and comprehensive investigation during which every move of the subjects must be recorded. This in turn suggests 24-hours-a-day surveillance, the jargon for which is "Put 'em to bed and get 'em up."

Those recommendations made for moving and stationary surveillance separately apply as well when the two methods are used concurrently. Different demands upon the same individuals to carry out each assignment are unreasonable, particularly in view of the pressure and tension involved in moving surveillance. Moreover, the higher risk of losing a subject during moving surveillance must be taken into account. If a separate team is handling the fixed location — say, at the subject's residence — they will be in place to observe the subject's arrival home. Comparison of notes between the moving and fixed surveillance teams, with attention to the time interval, would indicate if the subject proceeded directly home from the point where he was lost or if he stopped somewhere in between.

The importance of such an unaccounted for stop is illustrated by a case in which a bartender had been observed by security consuming, on an ongoing basis, large quantities of vodka while on duty. He was subsequently discharged for consuming alcoholic beverages while on duty and for the theft of such beverages. The subject denied the allegation, claiming that he was only drinking water. He claimed that, as a staunch supporter of Alcoholics Anonymous and a former alcoholic, he would be the last person to drink again. He convinced some civic-minded leaders in the community to bring pressure on the company that terminated him.

In the absence of any physical or other tangible evidence to support the company's position, it was incumbent upon the company to prove the subject to be other than what he claimed — in other words, to prove that he was not an abstainer from alcohol. He was placed under moving surveillance in the hope that he could be observed spending time in a bar.

During the first day of surveillance, the subject went to a private residence where he spent the entire day. When he left that location, his direction appeared to be toward home. He was lost at a large, multisignal, controlled intersection. The moving surveillance team arrived at his residence some ten minutes ahead of the subject, who pulled directly into his garage (which had an automatically controlled door) and entered the house.

The next day was a carbon copy of the first. The primary difficulty in surveillance was the controlled intersection, about two miles from the subject's residence. The interval between the time the subject was lost at that intersection and the time of his arrival home indicated that he was stopping en route, but not long enough to have a drink. Inspection of the logical route from the key intersection to his home revealed the presence of a liquor store. On the following day an investigator was in that store's parking lot on stationary surveillance when the subject pulled in. On that occasion, and for several consecutive days, the subject was observed purchasing a quart of vodka. The company's administrative action, discharge, was upheld, as a result of evidence obtained through combined moving and stationary surveillance.

Checkpointing

A practical strategy in following a subject to his final destination when the subject is "tail-wise" or otherwise difficult to follow the entire distance is *checkpointing*.

Checkpointing involves piecing together sections of the subject's route, one day at a time, until the entire route is identified. Most people tend to be creatures of habit, and that is reflected in the routes they will take to familiar places. The route each of us takes from home to work each day, for example, is relatively predictable.

Checkpointing can be a strategy of choice, because it is less dangerous than trying to stay with a subject along his entire route, or it may be a necessity if, for example, the subject makes an abrupt turn that is not negotiable by the surveillance vehicle. The accompanying map (see Figure 6.3) shows the southerly route of a subject and the three checkpoints required to develop the entire route. On the first day of the surveillance, the subject's unexpected left turn onto Cimarron Avenue (west of the traffic circle) led to the designation of checkpoint A the following morning. The surveillance vehicle was in place, facing south on Cimarron, when the subject drove by, and he was picked up at that point. Similar procedures at checkpoints B and C enabled investigators to chart his entire route. Each checkpoint is simply a calculated anticipation or prediction, based on prior observations, of the route the subject will take.

Presurveillance Planning

Surveillance rarely occurs as a surprise to the investigators. As such, they normally are in control of where and when the surveillance is to commence. Therefore, there is no excuse if every effort is not made to create a thorough presurveillance plan. Investigators armed with appropriate information,

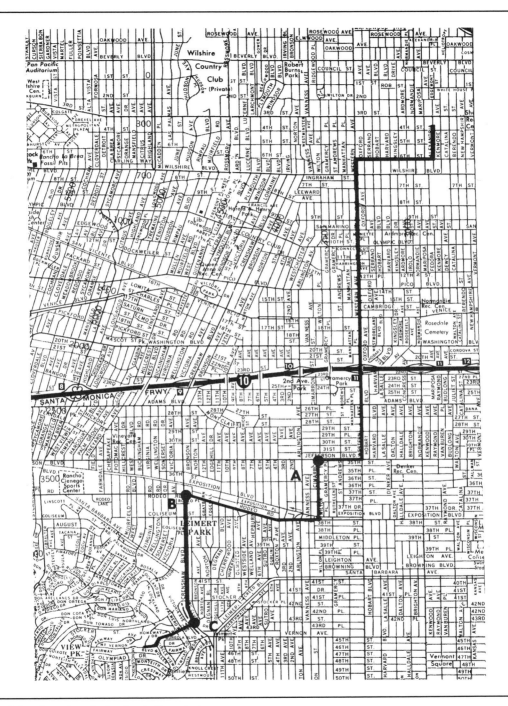

Figure 6.3. Sample of checkpointing strategy.

equipment, and a game plan can often do much more than those who merely "show up and hope for the best." There are several factors to include in such planning.

1. Location Descriptions. Are the address and description of any location the subject is likely to visit known? Have surreptitious reconnaissance images been recorded of those locations (either by camcorder, digital still, or 35-mm film camera)? Have those pictures been shared with all investigators on the team?

2. People. What is known about the key associates of the subject, including coworkers, household members, and coconspirators? Are pictures or descriptions of those people and any vehicles they possess available? What about the same for the primary subject? Are their home addresses, telephone numbers, and places of employment known?

3. Scheme. What is known about the scheme being practiced by the subject(s)? Is it a simple matter of putting cash in a pocket or does the theft require a flatbed truck and a forklift? Are company secrets being spirited off property on documents, or should the surveillants be alert for computer diskettes? Are particular banks, pawnshops, or commercial establishments believed to be key to the execution of the scheme?

4. Safety. Is there anything in the background of the persons placed under surveillance that indicates a high risk of physical danger to the surveillance team? Does the subject have a history of violence or associate with those who do? Does the subject carry or own weapons? Does the subject customarily drive at extremely high speeds? Has the subject ever previously known that he has been under surveillance?

5. Law Enforcement. Consideration should be given whether local police should be advised of the team's presence in the surveillance area. In quiet residential neighborhoods, people parked in cars at night for long periods can arouse the suspicion of anyone, including the neighborhood watch members. Advance contact with the local police, at the lieutenant or sergeant level, can go far in avoiding the spectacle that accompanies a felony stop by three cars of uniformed police officers with guns drawn. This is not only embarrassing and likely to alert the subject to something unusual occurring, but can be dangerous if the responding police mistakenly feel threatened in some way. A courteous "heads up" notification to the police need not disclose confidential details, but is appreciated by the police and ultimately is in the surveillance team's own best interest.

Surveillance is one area where the need to give the field personnel as much information as possible cannot be emphasized enough. When contact is lost due to traffic or other factors, smart investigators in possession of good intelligence information can react quickly. Speed of reaction is crucial. Consider this. When contact is lost with a subject driving at 30 miles per hour, in one minute she is a half-mile away from where last seen. In five minutes she will be two miles further away. Unless the surveillance team can instantly search in intelligently chosen directions, the ever-widening circle of error will halt the operation.

CONCLUSION

All the hardware useful in moving or stationary surveillance, naturally, is applicable to combined surveillances. A successful surveillance may also depend on additional practical considerations including allowance for biological needs. There are occasions when investigators cannot abandon a moving or stationary surveillance assignment to satisfy natural urges. Experienced investigators will carry food, water, napkins, and an empty container that can accommodate any need. Other useful items might include a small portable radio (with ear plug), a cushion for comfort, and even a blanket. These few necessities, packed in a briefcase or small tote bag, can take some of the pain and weariness out of a long surveillance. In brief, plan ahead!

The fruits of such planning and attention to detail can be substantial. Surveillance is clearly a vital investigative strategy that can significantly contribute to detection, prevention, and organizational intelligence.

Chapter 7

Background Investigations

No investigative function serves the best interests of the corporate organization more than the employee screening process — the background investigation. Cases demanding investigative expertise come and go, day in and day out. Even truly exciting and significant cases involving large monetary risks or losses come and go, though with less frequency. But despite the importance or magnitude of any given case, the humble background investigation remains preeminent in its overall importance.

Screening applicants through the pre-hire investigation, and new employees by means of post-hire investigations, is loss prevention in the purest sense. Loss prevention *begins* internally, with the employee; only following that does it deal with the nonemployee. A companywide antishoplifting program, as an example, can be neutralized or otherwise made unproductive before it begins, if the very employees whose involvement in the program is essential are thieves themselves.

And theft is only one concern in determining who is employed by the corporation or seeking employment. As a case in point, a post-hire investigation by a major retailer disclosed that one of its new employees selling shoes in the children's shoe department had a criminal history of child molestation. It requires little imagination to speculate over the possible harm that might have resulted from this situation — and the potential for civil litigation. There has been an increasing tendency for the courts to extend the area of corporate responsibility for the safety and security of guests or customers. If a motel chain can be held civilly liable for not providing adequate security for its guests, as was found in a hallmark case in which a guest was raped on company property by a nonemployee,[14] how much more liable would a retailer be for employing a known pedophile and placing him in a children's department or in an amusement arcade? In a similar vein, what is the responsibility of a hospital hiring a laundry employee who has a history of setting fires, a convicted arsonist, or pyromaniac? Or a financial institution hiring an embezzler or forger? Or a major oil company hiring an alcoholic to captain one of its super-tankers?

Do such offenders voluntarily come forward, either in the employment interview or on the application for employment, and admit that they have a propensity to molest children, set fires, commit fraud, or drink too much? Hardly. Their natural impulse is to hide what they know would disqualify them for employment. Because they must work, they will take great care to conceal such derogatory information in order to protect their own best interests.

It follows that an equal if not greater degree of care must be taken by the employer to ensure that only the best candidates are selected and subsequently retained on the payroll. So-called probationary periods are designed, in large measure, to ensure that the employer has the opportunity to examine, observe, and study new employees prior to the commitment or contract of protected employment.

The marriage contract offers a useful analogy. The application for employment is equivalent to a proposal of marriage. The probationary period is analogous to the engagement period. Successful completion of the probationary period (acceptance of the new employee as a regular employee) leads to the wedding. Once the two parties are married, separation is difficult and often painful indeed. The background investigation must complete its careful examination of the prospective bride or groom before the wedding date.

WORKPLACE VIOLENCE

In recent times the issue of workplace violence has become increasingly significant to employers. Although gauging the likelihood that an individual will become violent in the workplace may be difficult for even experienced forensic psychiatrists, the company has in the pre-hire and post-hire background investigations the best opportunity to reduce its exposure to this risk. If a separation is called for, it is far better to do so early in the employment relationship than after years of stored-up frustration over real or imagined slights "suffered" by the worker. These sometimes fuel the violence-prone employee to lash out at coworkers, supervisors, and innocent bystanders.

To carry the marriage analogy further, we know that spouse abusers stalk, assault, and murder their ex-spouses months and years after the break-up of the marriage. A company and its employees are no less vulnerable after a long-term relationship with an increasingly abusive employee. The thorough background investigation will, it is hoped, prevent the violence from coming to the workplace by avoiding the relationship altogether.

Pre-Hire Investigations

Ideally, all background investigations should be conducted prior to the job offer. As a practical reality, however, there are a number of conditions that mitigate against the ideal. A prompt or timely job offer many times captures highly desirable candidates (those who appear on the surface, at least, to be highly desirable). The applicant could be lost to another company because of the inherent delay involved in background checks. In larger companies, the sheer volume of applicants for employment dictates that only the most critical positions be given a full examination prior to the job offer. Other positions, those considered less critical in terms of risk, can receive a quick initial surface check and later, after the new employee has started work, can be subjected to a closer examination. A cashier or security employee, for example, would be a high-risk position, while a dishwasher or gardener would normally be a low-risk situation.

THE APPLICATION PACKAGE

When does the background investigation process begin? In well-run organizations it starts months and years before the applicant ever arrives at the human resources office to seek employment. Key to the success of a thorough background investigation, and the subsequent employment relationship, is the initial set of papers that the applicant fills out in seeking the job. Ideally, a team of human resources managers, security executives, and legal advisers should collaborate to design the total package of documents that awaits the prospective applicant.

The papers include much more than merely the preprinted application form, although much care must be given to the form itself. Here are some of the documents that organizations should consider including in their application packets.

1. The Application. The form should require disclosure of all jobs held in the prior seven-year period. In some cases, employers will seek a history of all jobs ever held. The name, address, and telephone number of the employer should be required along with the name and telephone number of the person who directly supervised the applicant. The application should contain a separate space where the applicant is required to certify that the information provided covers all employment held during the required period. This can go a long way later to overcoming the claim that the applicant "forgot" to list the one job from which he was fired for theft. Also, the application should call for at least three personal references who are not relatives or former employers, along with their day and evening contact information.

2. Fair Credit Reporting Act Waiver. The legal department should draw up a form upon which the applicant provides authorization for the company to obtain credit reporting agency reports, both before and during employment. This can be an important document during subsequent employment should the employee ever become the subject of an extensive investigation in which the company retains outside investigative or research assistance.

3. Education Waiver. The applicant should fill out a form authorizing the release of information contained in all educational records kept at schools, colleges, or trade schools. The form should include the applicant's social security number, date of birth, and all names under which the applicant was enrolled. The date of birth should be used only as an individual identifier, not as a means of illegally discriminating due to age. Some institutions desire this information in order to be sure which "John Jones" they are being asked about.

4. Blanket Information Authorization. The applicant should sign a form in which she specifically authorizes former employers, supervisors, coworkers, acquaintances, landlords, doctors, and others to provide all information sought by the employer. Again, this form should list the precise identifiers of the applicant. The authorization also should include a waiver of liability for providing information in good faith. Some jurisdictions provide statutory protections for this kind of information release. If so, the specific statute should be cited on the form. It is amazing how much information can be obtained from otherwise hesitant former employers once an offer is made to fax the authorization form to them.

5. Unemployment Verification Form. A form should be made that requires the employee to list each period of unemployment during the prior seven years. A reason for the unemployment should be listed along with information of how the individual met basic living expenses during those times. The name and telephone number of someone who can verify that information should be required.

6. Background Investigation Acknowledgment. The applicant should be given a notice to sign that informs him that a condition to employment or continued employment is the

satisfactory completion of a background investigation. It should advise the applicant that failure to accurately provide information necessary to the investigation will be grounds for separation. This will cover both the proven intentionally false application and the uncertainty that accompanies a claim that untrue information was provided as a "mistake." The form also should notify the employee that her assistance in the investigation is required so that if employment and education documents are later needed, or additional references are required, the employee understands that they must be provided. Finally, the employee must be advised that even if there is no proven falsity or derogatory information developed, if for some reason the provided information cannot be reasonably verified (due, for instance, to the burning down of the school records building), the company may consider the background investigation impossible to complete and this alone may be grounds for separation. It is important that a consistent application of this practice is applied to all similarly situated applicants in order to reduce unwarranted claims of illegal discrimination.

The Master Indice File

The heart of an effective pre-hire investigative procedure would be the creation, maintenance of, and referral to a master alpha indice (index) file. This is a negative base reference source, containing the names of dishonest or otherwise undesirable individuals, known to the company specifically and to the industry generally. For example, the security department of a major hospital should maintain an index card or computer file on every person arrested for crimes committed on or against the hospital, its employees, patients, and guests. The names of every employee of the hospital terminated for cause also should be included. Such a file would be considered the bare base, or minimum.

Ideally, in this context, all the hospital security departments in a given metropolitan area would pool their information so that the name of a nurse caught stealing at one hospital would end up in the master indice file of the other hospital security departments. Better yet, that nurse's name would be added to the master file in one central location servicing all hospitals in that area. All departments participating in the program would have access to that file by telephone, mail, or computer.

Such central data repositories are not uncommon in the retail and horseracing industries, to cite two quite different examples. In the former, store or mutual store protective associations serve as the central repository of all known and reported retail-related offenders, such as shoplifters, dishonest employees, credit card forgers, and bad check passers. In the thoroughbred horseracing industry, files containing the names of known touts, cheats, pick-pockets, "past-posters," con artists, and hustlers that follow the horses are maintained. Any individual so identified is *persona non grata* at the track.

Although such files appear to be engaged in a blacklisting operation, they are, in fact, legal and in compliance with the Federal Fair Credit Reporting Act. If an individual is denied employment or terminated for falsifying either an employment application or a bonding application, based on information contained in that centralized file, the reason for the rejection is made known to the person in question. Armed with that information, the individual denied employment might challenge and/or examine any records used to justify the decision.

The bottom line in any such situation is this: Is the information in the central file accurate, and does that information refute an applicant's or new employee's claim? To take a specific example, if an applicant writes the word "no" in answer to the question, "Have you ever been discharged from any previous employment?," and that answer is untruthful because he indeed has been discharged, the existence of the file itself is not at fault. It is the untruthfulness of the applicant that is at fault. The file did not deny the applicant a job; the applicant denied himself the job.

It should be pointed out, conversely, that many an applicant who has been straightforward with prospective employers regarding derogatory information in his background has been hired despite that information. Enlightened employers respect truthfulness, and sometimes will base a hiring decision, in some measure, on the fact that the candidate had the courage to honestly discuss problems of the past.

The central repository, or master indice file, does not contain all the details surrounding the negative information. It will include only the basic data: full name of the subject, date of birth, identification (Social Security number, driver's license, etc.), nature of the incident, location and date of the incident, and file reference number.

Operationally, the program works in this manner. A background investigator for company A discovers an applicant's name in the centrally maintained master file. Armed with that basic data, the investigator then phones or visits company B, the company that had direct involvement with the applicant in question and has on file the complete information on the incident of concern. Company B's investigator confirms the derogatory information, which is contrary to the applicant's statements.

If the investigation is in a pre-hire mode, the investigator advises the personnel representative of his own company that there is documented evidence that the applicant has not been truthful, and recommends that a job offer should not be made. If the investigation is post-hire, the investigator, along with a personnel representative, interviews the new employee, focusing on the discrepancy at issue. Invariably, the employee admits falsification on his application and is then terminated. Prior to the conclusion of that interview, the investigator advises the employee that the information was discovered through a search of the central files. The employee is provided with the location, hours, and other applicable conditions under which, if the employee so chooses, the relevant files may be examined. That prerogative, or option, rarely is exercised.

Past Employment Verification

A primary component of the entire screening process is the verification of past employment. Key questions that must be answered are the following:

1. Was the applicant in fact employed by the company claimed?
2. If so, was the applicant employed for the period of time claimed?
3. Was the applicant employed in the capacity claimed? For example, if the applicant claims supervisory responsibilities, was he indeed a supervisor?
4. Did the applicant leave the company for the reason stated?
5. Is the applicant eligible for rehire? If not, why?
6. Were the applicant's earnings as claimed? (This applies, as a rule, only to middle or upper management positions.)
7. Was the applicant involved in any instances of violence, threats, drug or alcohol use on the job, or sex harassment allegations?

In pre-hire investigations, these questions usually can be answered by a telephone conversation with a responsible official of the past employer, such as a personnel representative, the owner, or someone in the security department. The latter, if such a department exists, is preferable. When any derogatory information to these very basic questions is received, the investigator must ask complete follow-up questions so that a clear picture of the alleged events can be obtained. Getting the names and contact information of witnesses to those events may also prove critical later.

If the applicant is unknown to the industry — that is, not in the negative indice file — previous employment has been verified, and the applicant has been recommended as eligible for rehire, the chances are that the applicant is not a high risk. In such cases this quick background check could suffice, bearing in mind, however, that more extensive checking must be done in the post-hire period.

This is not to suggest that other pre-hire work is unnecessary. The amount of effort in background screening that constitutes minimal standards is *directly* related to a given company's (or security department's) assessment of organizational needs, the sensitivity of the position in terms of risk, and the security resources available for background investigation. Take security resources, as an example. If five investigators normally are assigned to the screening unit and the company becomes embroiled in a labor dispute, it is quite conceivable that the demands and priorities for investigators could deplete the screening unit, reducing it to one or two people available. That obviously would impact on both the quantity and quality of background investigations.

Other areas that can usefully be explored in the pre-hire (or post-hire) investigation include, but are not limited to, the following:

1. Does the applicant have a criminal record?
2. Does the applicant have the skill or education claimed?[15]
3. Is the applicant financially responsible?
4. Does the applicant have a general reputation for honesty and good moral behavior?
5. Does the applicant have a political or social bias that would mitigate against successful job performance? (Consider, for example, a member of the American Nazi Party who would be obliged, by virtue of the job, to work cooperatively and closely with blacks and Jews. Or a staunch activist opposed to nuclear energy whose job would include development of public relations materials, on a contractual basis, for a utility company operating a nuclear power facility.)

Answers to these questions are not in themselves the determiners of employment, but they do constitute arenas for dialogue. A conviction for a misdemeanor (a petty or minor crime) would not necessarily be grounds for employment rejection (pre-hire) or discharge (post-hire) unless the applicant lied on the application or bonding form. The expanded dialogue or discussion would include such questions as (1) What was the original criminal charge? (2) Was the offense one involving moral turpitude? (3) Does the crime have any relation to, or in any way impact on, the position being sought by the applicant? The ultimate hiring decision would be based on the merits and circumstances of the individual case.

The Neighborhood Check

Neighbors and landlords often know a great deal more about a person than might be suspected. They are familiar with an individual's comings and goings, his sensitivity to others, his predilection for noisy parties, his drinking and drug habits, his morality, his concern for his children (as demonstrated by involvement with scouting or other organized activities, family outings, how the children are supervised, how they are dressed, etc.), his standards of home maintenance, care for the yard or for the automobile, and so on. If the applicant was or is a renter, the landlord can tell the investigator if rent payments are made punctually or not, and if payment is made by cash, money order, or bank check. (If by bank check, the landlord can probably advise as to which bank and the branch.) Can such information as the method of paying rent be significant? What if the applicant pays by cashier's check or money order? Could this indicate that he has no bank checking account because of trouble with the bank? Has the bank closed the account for insufficient funds or some other abuse? These are questions that the investigator may wish to explore.

A former landlord generally will be eager to speak revealingly about a former renter who left the property in poor condition or when all accounts were not settled amicably. (It is interesting to note that most people who are compelled, for whatever reason, to speak in a negative or derogatory way about someone will almost invariably temper such comments by attempting to say something favorable as well — perhaps as a salve to the conscience.)

On the other hand, the investigator often will encounter those who have derogatory information or strong suspicions about the applicant in question but are reluctant to speak unfavorably about someone looking for work. Sympathetic persons in such a situation face a real dilemma. Here is a responsible representative from a reputable company looking for "advice," asking for "my opinion." (My reputation could be on the line. I don't want to lie but at the same time I don't want to hurt Harry's chances for a job, and I certainly don't want Harry to discover that I said something that hurt him. Still, he does have a drinking problem. . . .)

How does the investigator overcome this kind of problem? By giving the interviewee a way to tell you what you need to know. The way is to provide an *option*. The investigator should avoid boxing the person in by requiring, for example, a "yes" or "no" answer to the question, "Would you recommend Harry for a position with our firm?" Instead, the question should provide an option. The investigator might say, "We're considering Harry for one of two positions. One is highly sensitive, with a great deal of responsibility. The other is a more average type of assignment with less responsibility. Which of the two would you recommend Harry for?" This gives the interviewee a palatable way of saying that Harry is not a good candidate. Under these circumstances, an endorsement for the so-called average job is, in reality, no endorsement at all.

The neighborhood check, knocking on doors and asking people how well they knew or know the applicant and what their assessment of his qualifications is, can be a gold mine of information — and also of surprises. A casual question may evoke the response that "The police were just here last week looking for him." Or the unsolicited revelation that "They are very generous people. Did you know they just adopted another little Asian girl, on top of being foster parents for the county's unwanted new babies?" The point is that there is often much to be learned in these neighborhood checks that can be very revealing, pro or con, and that otherwise would remain unknown.

POST-HIRE SCREENING

Once the applicant is an employee, the post-hire screening activities must be finalized as quickly as possible within the firm's probationary period. Irrespective of how thorough the pre-hire investigation

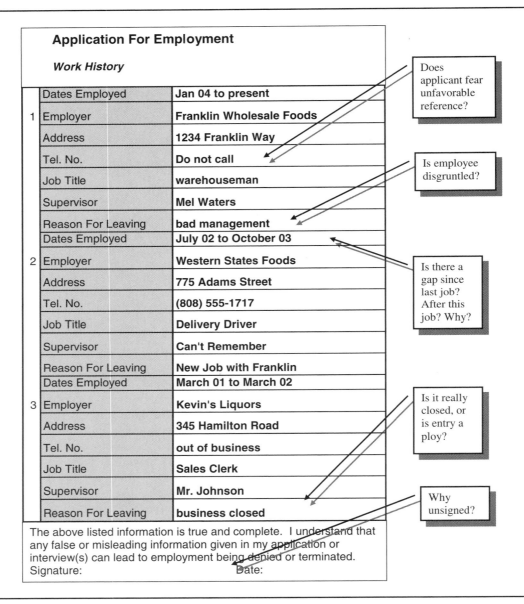

Figure 7.1. Excerpt from application for employment. Red flags may be present in this example.

has been, two important remaining steps are required. The first is the careful inspection of the bond or bonding form for content. The second, and most productive, is comparison of the bond form to the application form.

What is a bond? A bond, fidelity form, or bonding form is a document provided by an insurance carrier that indemnifies employers against loss caused by employee criminal conduct, or, if the company is self-insured, it is the document completed by the employee after being hired, said document calling for information prohibited on the application for employment (such as date of birth). Note that it is legal to request such information after the employee has been hired, since there is no longer any question of discrimination in hiring. The source of the bonding form is unimportant; the important consideration is that it should exist and be used.

One important feature of this form, which is almost a carbon copy of the application form (except for the additional information just noted), is that it becomes the security department's employment record for every employee of the company. The value of this from a security point of view is self-evident. An employee's original application for employment rightfully belongs to and remains in the personnel files. The bond, however, in great measure duplicates the information in personnel files. Consequently, should the need for an investigation arise, the security department is not dependent upon the personnel department for information. This also avoids the possibility of compromising an early-stage investigation by reducing the number of persons who know that security has an interest in a particular employee. This is best for the security of the investigation and also the privacy and reputations of employees against whom no negative information is later developed or who are completely cleared of wrongdoing.

Examination of the Bond

The bonding form, which is permanently in the control of the security department after its satisfactory completion, can be examined carefully for the following indicators of possible deception:

1. Questions not answered or left blank.
    Example question: "Have you ever been convicted for an offense other than a minor traffic violation?"
    Comment: The employee who has been so convicted is often afraid to lie and will attempt to avoid falsifying the document by not answering the question.
2. Unexplained gaps in the employment history.
    Example: 10/94 to 6/95   Ace Trucking Co.
        6/95 to 3/96   Koskovich Tire & Brakes
        6/96 to 6/99   Dennis & Son, Inc.
    Comment: The period from March 1996 to June 1996 is unaccounted for. Was he ill? Was he in jail for theft from the tire and brake shop? It must be determined what the employee was doing for that period of time.
3. Erasure or strike-outs and scratch-outs.
    Comment: To be unsure of or to change one's mind in answering a question such as the reason for leaving a job is a danger signal, an indicator of possible deception (not a fact, it should be emphasized, but an indicator worth exploring).

4. Answers that presumably cannot be checked.
   Example: Giving as a "reason for leaving" the answer: "went out of business."
   Comment: This answer is a convenient and common technique of hiding employment with a firm, still actually in business, from which one was discharged, or for covering time spent in incarceration. It can also be used to fill a period of "unexplainable unemployment" (such as incarceration) with an unverifiable job history.
5. Failure to affix the required signature at the conclusion of questions (bottom of the form).
   Comment: Failure to sign the form could be indicative of a reluctance, conscious or otherwise, to perjure oneself.

There is a logic to an honest person's work history. The investigator must therefore be sensitive to the *illogical*, as demonstrated in the following case history.

Discovery of a significant amount of liquor unaccounted for from the gourmet department of a major department store prompted the reexamination of all employees assigned to that department. One female employee's bond reflected previous employment as a sales clerk for a liquor store located on Hollywood Blvd. in Hollywood. Her stated reason for leaving that job was, "Went out of business." The answer seemed illogical. If there was, in fact, such a store in that location it should have been a thriving business. Investigation determined through business and licensing records that there had been such a store. The owner was traced. He confirmed that he had gone out of business and added, "My employees stole me blind." Had our employee worked for him? "Yes," he replied, "and though I couldn't prove it, there's no doubt in my mind that she was one of the thieves." The employee was then placed under surveillance. Within a week she and two outside confederates were detected using the old "scam" in which the customer purchased an item and the employee filled the bag with unpaid-for merchandise. In this specific case, close to $100 worth of liquor was being carried out with each $6.00 purchase.

Comparing the Bond to the Application

There is an underlying strategy involved in comparing the bonding form to the application for employment. In the normal sequence of events, an applicant presents himself to the personnel department and completes an application for employment, which is a relatively comprehensive personal and work history. A few days later the applicant, after a minimal background check, is offered employment commencing the following Monday. When the new employee appears at the appointed time to begin work, a period of perhaps five to fourteen days will have passed after the original application was completed. On his first day on the new job, the employee is given the bonding form, which is, as previously suggested, closely equivalent to the application for employment document. The test is, if the applicant lied on the original application form, can that person remember, with precision, the original falsehoods and duplicate them after a lapse in time? Experience tells us no. They will try, but the variances will stand out noticeably when the two documents are compared side by side.

Comparison, then, is necessary. If there is no comparison, the screening process is deficient. This comparison is so vitally important that consideration should be given to having the two documents as nearly identical in format as possible. If the bonding form is provided by an insurance carrier, the company could redesign the application for employment form to match the format of the bond. If the company is self-insured (either having no insurance against internal theft, or a policy with a deductible so high that it precludes practical application), the bonding form can easily be printed so that, when it is placed side-by-side with the application, the corresponding data are visually comparable. This should also be true on the reverse sides of the two forms. I've suggested the bond be on a colored paper so there's a contrast between the two similar documents, which makes for easier examination and processing. Bonds received by security from personnel that reflect unanswered questions or have not been signed should be returned to personnel for further processing. Erasures or strike-outs call for no action other than deeper investigation.

Variances, discrepancies, or contradictions should be handled by security, not personnel. This is done in an interview conducted by the background investigator, witnessed by a personnel representative. The thrust of that low-keyed confrontation is, simply, "Please explain." In most cases the employee will admit falsification. In some cases satisfactory explanations will be offered, removing the reason for concern. In a relatively small number of cases an employee will, out of fear or desperation, cling to the falsehood, insisting that it is true. In these instances logic usually will give the investigator direction. For example, if the employee insists that he or she worked for a company the investigator knows never existed, then the employee should be asked to bring in a W2 form (IRS earnings and tax withholding statement). If an employee swears that criminal records discovered by the investigator reflect the arrest of his twin brother, then the employee should be asked to bring in his birth certificate. An honest employee can support his claims; sooner or later the dishonest person will run out of explanations.

Employment Verification and Reference Letters

In pre-hire screening, as we have seen, verification of past employment usually is by telephone. In the post-hire period a rather common practice in the private sector in verifying past employment is to send out a form letter asking for employment verification and eligibility for re-hire, requesting that the form be completed and returned. This is an acceptable strategy, particularly for low-risk positions, but only if the following procedures are followed.

1. A control must be maintained, showing every letter sent out and reflecting when it has been returned.
2. Verification letters not returned in a reasonable time must be followed up by security, either by telephone or in person. An ex-employer or company receiving the verification letter, and with something derogatory to say, often will be reluctant to reduce that information to writing for fear of accusations of defamation of character or some other repercussion. The alternative is to say nothing. This failure to respond, if properly controlled by the point of origin of the request, personnel, signals the need to make further inquiry.
3. Variances in dates of employment as reflected by returned letters should be reported to security. (There is usually little if any reluctance on the part of former employers to reflect discrepancies.)
4. "Not eligible for re-hire" responses must be pursued further, either by personnel, or if personnel is unable to obtain a satisfactory explanation, by security.

All too often this area of employment verification becomes routine and its true value is lost, primarily because these controls and follow-up procedures are not fully understood and consistently practiced.

Other Suitability Measures

Depending on the sensitivity of the position sought by the applicant, and the policies of the company, some of the following techniques also are used in employment situations.

1. Paper and Pencil Tests. A number of companies offer tests in which the applicant responds to a set of questions intended to measure past activities of an undesirable nature as well as predictability of future misconduct. Violent tendencies, drug use, and honesty are factors often measured.
2. Polygraph. Although federal and state legislation in the past two decades have definitely limited the use of this technique in preemployment situations, there are a small number of industries (drug manufacturing, nuclear power industry, banking, etc.) where the use of the polygraph is still allowed.
3. Litigation History. A check of the court records in the places the applicant has worked and resided can bring out important information regarding lawsuits brought by and against the applicant, as well as convictions and divorces. Even if there was never a conviction for assault, a civil judgment awarded against the applicant by a bodily injury plaintiff should be reviewed carefully to see if violence by the applicant was the cause. Likewise, a sexual harassment suit against the applicant or other discrimination claims should be reviewed closely for information of legitimate importance to the employer. Bankruptcies and divorce files can also provide extensive information about the individual that may be of bona fide use for certain positions.

Ongoing Investigations

Background investigations of prospective or new employees will consume the bulk of the screening effort, but such investigations should not be limited only to such employees. As the case history of a liquor department theft described earlier in this chapter indicated, a background check of a suspected employee or group of employees can be productive in specific investigations. In addition, an ongoing program of updating background information on key personnel — people in the computer, finance, personnel, and security areas, for instance — should be part of the screening unit's responsibility. Only such a comprehensive and continually updated program can ensure that only the best possible people come into the company, remain in it, and rise in its ranks.

Drug Testing

Drug testing as a pre-employment situation is more an HR than security function, especially as it is routine rather than exceptional when done, and does not require investigative expertise and judgement. It is also closely regulated by most states, and touches on ADA (Americans with Disabilities Act) issues, again normally best addressed by HR. If a failure in routine testing occurs, again the response tends to be an automatic nonselect by HR.

Chapter 8

Discovering Covert Crimes

Criminal conduct, in most cases, is all too apparent. The corporate victim, like the individual who is attacked, is usually aware of the crime and its consequences.

The list of overt crimes is endless. Rather typical examples might include the hijacking of a company tractor and trailer, the burglary of a warehouse, an extortion attempt involving threats against the life of an executive or members of his family, a fire purposefully set in the workplace, the rape of an employee departing late in the parking facility, the robbery of a cashier, assault against an employee, the overnight disappearance of a laptop computer from an accountant's desk, malicious destruction of the firm's landscaping accomplished by vandals driving a vehicle through the flower beds, checks drawn on accounts with insufficient funds or on closed accounts, threatening or obscene e-mail or phone calls, and so on, ad infinitum.

Even when accomplished in stealth, such crimes are quickly known. They call for a reconstructive investigation as a response to a historical event.

There are also a great many criminal acts, most of a larcenous nature, and other forms of unacceptable behavior that are so subtle and surreptitious in nature that the crime or offense often goes undetected, and its consequences are not immediately apparent. Some, in fact, are never known with any degree of certainty.

Such covert crimes have a number of characteristics that set them apart from overt crimes against the organization. Those characteristics are:

- They usually are committed by persons considered trustworthy.
- The acts tend to be ongoing in nature as opposed to a single, spectacular incident.
- Some of the acts tend to be shrouded in uncertainty (i.e., was it intentional or was it an error?).

This last characteristic is one of the chief problems with covert crimes. For example, consider the case of a retailer who buys 100 bottles of perfume. After an inventory he determines that he has ten bottles left in stock. Sales records, however, show that he sold eighty-five bottles. Five cannot be accounted for. Were they stolen? Did a crime occur? What happened to the missing bottles? There are a number of possible explanations for this single commonplace situation.

1. The shipment was short in the first place.
2. Salespeople opened some bottles as samples for customers to smell.
3. Someone broke bottles in an accident but was afraid to report the loss.
4. The bottles were shoplifted by customers.
5. They were stolen by employees.
6. They were overlooked in a multiple item transaction and inadvertently not recorded as sold.
7. They were given away by salespersons paid on a commission basis who were trying to please known customers in the hope of later sales.
8. They were intentionally given by salespersons to friends or relatives.

When this range of possibilities is extended over the activity of the entire organization, it becomes clear that the problem of exposing and properly identifying covert crimes is enormously complex. Obviously, a number of investigative strategies must be practiced in order to surface covert activity. Because of the range and diversity of businesses and industries in the private sector, it is impossible for any list of strategies to be all-inclusive or even notably comprehensive. The strategies discussed in the rest of this chapter, however, should serve as a sound basic list. They may also serve as a stimulant to the more enterprising investigator, prompting her own adaptations and creative variations. These fundamental strategies included the following:

1. Deployment of undercover agents in the work force.
2. Taking physical inventories.
3. Refund letter circulation program.
4. Daily audit of sales registers.
5. Checking continuity of register transaction numbers.
6. Integrity shopping/testing.
7. Bank check reconciliation program.
8. Cash counts.
9. Exit interviewing.
10. Checking for "ghost" employees.
11. Vendor verification.
12. Intelligence surveillance.
13. Physical inspections.
14. Use of suggestion box or award programs.
15. Financial analysis.
16. Odometer checks.
17. Shoplifting surveillance.

DEPLOYMENT OF UNDERCOVER AGENTS

Undercover investigation by covert agents planted in the work force has been discussed at length in a previous chapter. Suffice it to repeat here that numerous incidents of internal dishonesty that would otherwise never be known or identified are surfaced by this strategy. In the words of Saul Astor, "Without question, the major means of eliminating internal crime has always been and always will be internal intelligence — especially through undercover investigation."[16]

Physical Inventories

There are essentially three types of inventories. The first is the annual or semiannual inventory that should be a normal operating practice in any business that has a stock of supplies, materials, equipment, or goods on hand. Simplistically stated, this kind of inventory is a comparison of the "book" inventory (what the records indicate should be on hand) with the physical or actual inventory (results of a count of what is really there). Ideally the totals should match: a recorded total of 100 units should be equaled by a count of 100 units. More often than not, however, the actual count reflects fewer units on hand, thus creating a shortage. The enlightened and realistic approach to this shortage is to assume that at least part of the shortage reflects dishonesty, indicating that covert crime exists. Not to take this annual inventory is to operate blind.

The second type of physical inventory is the daily accounting of specific materials or goods, such as narcotics in a health service or hospital environment. Any variation, shortage, or overage should arouse suspicion. The third kind of inventory is clandestine. Specific items are secretly counted and, after a designated period of time, again are subjected to a secret verifying count. A truck, for example, is loaded with boxes for shipment the following morning. During the night the truck is entered and the boxes are counted again, at which time the vehicle is secured by seal, lock, or both. When the truck arrives at its destination, the receiving end of the shipment, the boxes are unloaded under observation and again recounted. A shortage in the count under these circumstances would expose dishonesty, with the driver the prime suspect. Obviously this type of inventory is capable of many variations.

Refund Letter Circularization Program

In those business operations where customers are given refunds, a document must be generated by an employee that reflects the amount, date, reason for the refund, and the full name and address of the person receiving the refund. A letter circularization program is an ongoing strategy designed to verify refunds. A letter is sent to the party receiving the refund by First Class U.S. mail, return postage guaranteed. In essence, the letter asks if the transaction was handled efficiently and courteously. The exact amount of the refund is noted in the letter, and a prestamped return envelope is enclosed.

Ordinarily, one of five things will happen in response to the refund letter:

1. The letter will be answered, stating that the transaction was satisfactory (or even that the employee was discourteous in some instances). No dishonesty is in evidence.
2. There will be no response, which probably means that the refund was legitimate, the customer simply not bothering to reply.
3. The customer will reply they know of no such refund, there must be an error. Clearly this suggests the possibility of a fraudulent transaction.
4. The customer will reply to the effect that the actual refund was for a smaller amount than shown. This suggests the strong possibility that someone inside the company is manipulating the documents by raising the figure of the sale *after* the legitimate transaction — changing a $25.00 refund to $35.00, for example, and pocketing the $10.00 difference.

5. The postmaster will return your original envelope marked "no such address," "undeliverable," "no such party at address," and so on. This also strongly suggests that the refund transaction was fraudulent. Many cases of internal dishonesty have been exposed by this routine strategy of refund verification.

Daily Audit of Cash Registers

Among other things, a cash register or sales terminal is an adding machine that totals the day's receipts — all receipts, both cash and charge. Unless registers and terminals are audited daily, thefts may go undetected.

The proper audit process requires that the cash be counted by someone other than the person who made the sales. Another person, working independently, receives the register/terminal totals (in the form of an inner "detail" or "journal" tape) and copies of the charge transactions. This second independent auditor adds the charges and compares this to the total sales. The sum of the charges and the independently counted cash receipts should be equal to the register tape total.

Example: The tape reflects sales of $436.11 for the day. The count of charge receipts amounts to $207.09. For the register to balance, confirmation is needed of a total of $229.02 in cash received and counted. The person counting cash receipts must not know what is expected. If he knew that $229.02 was required to balance but actually counted $239.02 in cash, the difference of $10.00 would be unaccounted for and readily subject to theft. If cash receipts of only $209.02 were counted and reported, the holder of the register tape and charge receipts would record a shortage of $20.00, which would have to be investigated.

Checking Register Transaction Numbers

Most cash registers are designed to imprint transaction numbers chronologically, usually in terms of up to four digits. In other words, the register/journal tape reflects the number of the transaction each time the register is activated, 1 to 9,999 in sequence.

In some registers it is physically possible to reset the transaction wheel, and in some firms this is done each morning. This practice is dangerous. It creates the possibility for a dishonest employee to "steal" a given number of sales without detection, since there is no continuity in the transaction numbers from day to day. A much better practice is to have the numbers run continuously. Thus, if the last sale of the day on Monday is transaction number 3483, the first time the register is used on Tuesday it will record number 3484. The strategy is to physically or electronically deny access to the transaction wheel or counter mechanism and to verify the continuity of transaction numbers on a daily basis. Missing numbers immediately will suggest manipulation and dishonesty.

Integrity Testing

The most common and hard-to-detect method of theft from the cash register is for the dishonest employee simply to accept money from customers and fail to record it. One way to detect this type of theft is integrity testing, commonly known as "shopping." Investigators hired for this purpose pose as regular customers making normal purchases. At the same time they are able to observe sales recording practices.

As Roger Griffin, a nationally known authority in this field, observes:

> The fact that the cash accepted by the employee goes into the register at the time of the purchase is of no importance. It is extremely rare when the employee fails to record and then places the cash directly into his pocket. When a person begins to manipulate his cash by not recording sales, he can make the register come out over or short, as he chooses.
>
> The employee keeps track of the unrecorded funds and at some propitious moment takes out the total accumulated for the day. An employee sometimes takes out an even amount (ten, fifteen, or twenty dollars) while he is verifying his change fund at the beginning of the day and then makes up the shortage by failing to record an equivalent amount of money.[17]

Where the money is not taken out beforehand but accumulated throughout the day in amounts not recorded, the person on the cash register must keep a running account of the total unrecorded. This "accounting" can take the obvious form of actually writing down the amount each time in a little notebook. Since this might create suspicion, another technique is to use loose coins at the side of the register. For example, if the employee places $12.00 from a sale in the register without recording it, he places a dime and two pennies to the side. Later, if a $5.00 transaction is not recorded, a nickel is set aside. Those 17 cents in coins would not appear suspicious to an observer, but they represent to the dishonest employee $17.00 in the drawer that he can safely remove when the time is right. In describing the shopping test, Griffin goes on to say:

> It is vital to understand that the typical test performed by the shopping investigator involves payment for an article in a manner which gives the employee a *choice* of whether to ring or not to ring the payment on the register.
>
> A simple test is to pay for an item with exact change and casually walk away not waiting for a receipt. Regular customers consistently make this type of purchase. At this point the employee stands at the register with the money *in his hand*. He has a perfectly free choice of whether he records the money or places it unrecorded into the cash drawer."[18]

It should be added that the money does not always go into the register drawer. The method of theft depends on the kind of setting or circumstances. If the employee works alone or unobserved, for example, in a small gift shop in a resort area, and there are no customers in the store after a transaction has gone unrecorded, the money may go directly into pocket, shoe, handbag, bra, or wherever it can be concealed.

Virtually everyone has been an unwitting instrument in this very prevalent type of theft. It is especially frequent when a purchase is an afterthought. After paying for his initial purchase, the customer suddenly decides, "Oh, I think I'll have a pack of cigarettes after all." He then leaves the exact change on the counter and departs. The cash register clerk is free to record the extra transaction or not.

The display screen on the cash register was designed from the beginning to show the customer how much he was being charged. If the display shows "NO SALE" or an underring (the clerk records a sale of $15.88 when the actual amount was $25.88), something is clearly amiss. This may account for the number of displays that have been turned away from the customers or covered up with advertisements, cartoons clipped from magazines, and other convenient camouflage. The same risk exists in those casino/gaming operations wherein the computerized keno terminal "reads" a player's ticket and only the casino employee can read the screen displaying the winning amount.

Bank Check Reconciliation

The bank check reconciliation process for a business is very much the same as that used by the individual balancing his private checking account. It involves comparing cancelled checks issued against the original record. The objective is to ensure against or to catch checks that have been stolen or counterfeited, or on which the amount has been increased fraudulently. Although this procedure should take place several times a year, it is routinely neglected. It is important that the personnel conducting the bank check reconciliation do so properly. They must actually handle the cancelled checks along with the bank statement and check register. A number of years ago we investigated a case for a government client in which a county treasurer issued checks of five and six figures to a business in which he had an interest and then made false entries in the computerized journal, indicating that another legitimate county vendor had received the payments. The reconciliation clerk missed the fraud because she was examining only the bank statement and the check register. Had she also looked at the actual checks she would have clearly seen the discrepancy in payee names. Hundreds of thousands of dollars were diverted this way, which was bad enough, but the much larger theft of currency (nearly one million dollars) would have been discovered much sooner.

Cash Counts

There are three types of cash counts, all of which are necessary parts of an effective accountability procedure. The first and most commonly used count is one in which the responsible party is obliged to count regularly and record the amounts of funds under his control. The second is the surprise count, usually an internal audit type of activity. The last, and the one that interests us most here, is the secret count.

A common practice in business is to do what is called bulk or "bundle" counting; the money is counted on the basis of the face value of bundled or banded packs. Knowing that one way to steal from funds is to slip one or two bills from a banded pack and place that bundle (which is now short) to the rear of the vault, the investigator carrying out a secret count will count each bill in a pack, ignoring what the band indicates is in that bundle. The regular employees are not aware of this count. Banded packs that are found short present strong evidence that someone is either stealing outright, knowing that regular counts are only bundle counts, or is using company money with the intention of replacing it.

Exit Interviews

The right kind of exit interview may surface dishonesty or other conditions unknown to management. What is referred to here is not the customary final interview usually conducted by a personnel employee, but rather a multiple-page form that asks a number of questions about supervision, working conditions, treatment on the job, what needs correcting, and so forth. Such an interview has the potential of identifying such problems as favoritism, time-clock violations, spurious accident claims, general loafing and shirking in a given unit, safety hazards, even dishonesty.

The trick is to get the departing employee to be frank. Most employees know a great deal but feel intimidated about telling what they know. Many simply will not answer truthfully such questions as "Why are you leaving?" The usual response is "a better opportunity" somewhere else. To encourage openness in responding to the interview, the interviewer must have a solid reputation for being trustworthy or the interview must be conducted anonymously. One effective method is to send the interview form home with the departing employee, along with a stamped, preaddressed envelope, and request that the form be returned by mail. If the work environment has been in any way threatening, however, the procedure may be ineffective. An alternative approach is to send the interview form to the former employee a week or two after he leaves, asking in a brief cover letter, that the individual be completely frank. Assurances should be given that anything said will be held in the strictest confidence, or the individual can be invited to complete and return the form without identifying himself.

Checking for "Ghost" Employees

A "ghost" employee is simply a nonexistent employee for whom payroll checks are issued and cashed. A number of ghosts can haunt a business. One might be a fictitious name and identity, even including social security number, created by a supervisor at a work location somewhat removed from the main facility.

Another might be the product of the imagination of an enterprising personnel employee who has set up a file on the ghost, including name and hours of pay in the document that activates the issuance of payroll checks regularly. A third form of ghost might be an actual person who died or was terminated but for whom the necessary paperwork was not generated to stop the automatic issuance of checks. The former employee, or friend, or relative of the deceased who receives the checks either has a place where they can be cashed or simply opens a bank account under that name where the checks can be deposited. There are two ways to check for this type of fraud. One is to have an independent person, such as an internal auditor accompanied by someone from security, intercept the checks at the point of generation. The auditor then distributes the checks to each employee in person, perhaps even requiring signatures of the recipients. This should be done at least once annually. Another method, also used on an annual basis, is to mail all W-2 forms to employees. Fictitious addresses will cause those envelopes to be returned. With reference to such mailings, it is important that employees should never be permitted to use a post office box as a home address on company records. The use of a post office box in itself could be indicative of a problem. Other means of detecting ghost employees consists of conducting simple analysis of employee records. Ensuring that there is actually a personnel file on each employee listed on the payroll is very simple, but a rather clear way of discerning which "employees" are bogus.

Even if an embezzler has gone to the trouble of fabricating a false employee jacket, the fictitious files will be apparent once they actually are handled and reviewed. They will lack the miscellaneous documents found in any long-term employee file. Missing will be the leave slips indicating a need to stay home with a sick child, attend a funeral, or serve jury duty. Annual updates for tax forms, and other periodic insurance forms will not appear. Employee evaluations, commendations, or reprimands will also be lacking. Even evidence of raises, promotions, and annual vacations will be nonexistent. We investigated one case where the ghost employee was an actual person who had come in and been hired, but was paid by a supervisor who never had her come to work. But for an accidental discovery, the "employee" would have sailed along for many years, right into retirement. Her file was as thin as a brand-new hire, even though she had been on the books for over a dozen years.

Another analytical method is to search the payroll register for employees with the same address. This sometimes is used to allow for several paychecks to be mailed to the same individual. Look also at cancelled paychecks on a periodic basis. If you determine that checks are being deposited to a common account, or are being endorsed and signed over to another employee, further investigation is warranted. Obviously, in the case of electronic direct deposits to employee accounts, the searching for common account numbers also is indicated, and probably easier to achieve through computerized data sorting.

Verification of Vendor or Resource

More common than ghost employees are ghost vendors, suppliers, or other resources. Again, internal dishonesty is indicated. The most common culprits are receiving agents, purchasing agents or buyers, and accounts payable personnel.

A typical theft by the receiver involves initiating a receiving document to verify receipt of a shipment and forwarding it to the person in the company who pays the bills. The receiving record is matched to a fictitious invoice mailed to the company by the dishonest receiving agent. The invoice may be very formal and legitimate in appearance, or it can be the common form available in a stationery store. It is simply a demand for payment for merchandise delivered to the company. The fake receiving document confirms receipt of the merchandise, making the bill due and payable.

The dishonest purchasing agent or buyer may claim that he received merchandise, perhaps claiming that material was delivered through the front door rather than through the receiving department, or he may act in collusion with a receiver to create a false receipt. Even more free to steal is an agent who obtains blank receiving documents, which he can simply complete and forward to accounts payable. The purchasing agent then invoices the company. The receiving document confirms the invoice and payment is made.

A dishonest accounts payable employee can, like the buyer or purchasing agent, generate his own illicit receiving documents, or he can use voided or illegible copies of legitimate receiving records to create a supporting document for the invoice.

The possible variations of this type of internal theft are almost limitless, depending on the company and its policies, procedures, and controls. In each case goods or services are paid for that were never received. Payment goes to unscrupulous companies who over-invoice, knowing that receiving records will have been altered, or to nonexistent firms that are simply "mail drops" for the dishonest employee.

The strategy to prevent this kind of theft is to confirm that all companies that invoice the parent company actually exist. As with employee addresses, post office box numbers can be a warning signal. Every legitimate business has an office, plant, building, warehouse, or other facility. The investigator should go to the address of every firm in question and confirm that it exists. If the address turns out to be a private residence, ownership or tenancy should be confirmed. The residence might be that of a relative or close friend of an employee. Again, analytical techniques can be an important method of ferreting out the fictitious vendor. Reviewing the invoice numbers from a particular vendor can be quite revealing. Sometimes the dishonest employee goes to great lengths to create very impressive-looking computer-generated invoices. They rarely, however, take care to ensure that those invoices carry all the logical progressions that mark the legitimate item. They sometimes will submit the identical invoice from period to period, bothering to alter only the date and purchase order number. The exact quantity of goods can be repeated every time; frequently even the same invoice number is used. This is especially true if they merely are deleting limited information from a saved computer document file and printing the new invoice. The investigator must ask himself the obvious questions. Is it logical that our operation actually would purchase fifty truck tires a month? Can we even store that many? Have we ever used fifty truck tires in even a single year of normal operations?

In other cases the thief will phony up a fresh invoice, but will either fail to ensure that the new invoice number is higher than those from earlier invoices, or will have the new invoice number represent an illogical interval. For instance, if the vendor is supposedly a supplier of common auto parts, is it logical to have two invoices generated weeks or months apart being in immediate sequence? Legitimate invoice numbers should represent an interval of hundreds or thousands of invoice numbers.

Investigators must be familiar enough with normal business transactions to recognize those which are too regular, too large, or just plain too strange to be legitimate.

Intelligence Surveillance

As discussed at length in Chapter 6, intelligence surveillance is the covert monitoring of a location or workplace for the purpose of determining exactly what is transpiring there.

Surveillance can be by the human eye or the eye of a camera. The human eye is more discriminating if there is a great deal of traffic and activity. The eye of the camera is most satisfactory in isolated situations — for example, when focused on a remote door, which is not to be used except in emergencies. The camera used in connection with a time-lapse video recorder can tell the investigator in minutes what happened over many hours.

Physical Inspections

Physical inspections constitute a potential gold mine of interesting discoveries for the security investigator. The careful examination of a window (recall our earlier discussion of the power of observation in the investigative process) can reveal dust disturbances indicating passage of someone or something through an opening not intended to be used. A door wedged open that was supposed to be locked, a carefully concealed tear in a perimeter fence, a light bulb loosened so that an area will be dark that should be brightly illuminated — these and countless other telltale signs can alert the investigator to a potential problem.

In one case, physical inspection of a night depository disclosed that the perimeter alarm system had been defeated. A typical depository is like a closet built against the interior side of a building's outside wall. It has two locked doors, each having the key-way on the outer side of the door. One key will open the outer door from the exterior of the building, providing access to the depository, but the inner door is blank. The same works in reverse when the inner door is opened with its key from inside the building.

Normally the exterior door is not alarmed; the inner door must be alarmed. The function of the depository is for the pickup of goods, documents, and such, during hours when the building is closed. A courier service usually makes the pickup and delivery, and the courier is provided with the exterior door key. In the case in question, the inner door was equipped with alarm contacts of the plunger design. When the inner door was closed and locked, the plungers were forced deep into their receptacle. The continuous alarm circuit was then intact. With this arrangement, opening the door while the alarm system was turned on would permit the spring-loaded plunger to come out, triggering the alarm. Physical inspection revealed that someone, obviously an employee working inside the building, had taken a toothpick and jammed the plunger down in its housing, so the door could be opened without the plunger coming out.

This discovery indicated more than a prank. It meant that someone had copies of the keys to the two depository doors. It was not difficult to work out how conspirators might use those keys. One party could remain inside the building after closing, gather up all the goods desired, and place them in the depository. He could then lock the door and remain in hiding until the building opened in the morning, emerging from his hiding place and sauntering out unnoticed (or appearing for work as an employee). Meanwhile, an outside accomplice could come by in the middle of the night, open the outer door, remove the stolen contents, and relock the door, leaving no evidence that a theft had occurred. If it was too dangerous to remain all night inside the building, another possibility would be to enter the depository during the night, rap on the exterior door to signal waiting associates, pass quantities of stolen goods through to the outside and, when the theft was completed, simply close the inner door. Since the inner door could not be locked from the depository side, the thieves in this case would have to hope that no one would notice or regard as important the fact that the inner door was unlocked. The thieves, of course, would lock the exterior door from the outside before departing.

Inspections of any alarmed facility should include "swinging" (i.e., opening every door and window on the system, one at a time, while the alarm system is turned on, in order to verify that a signal actually is being received on the enunciator panel or central station board). Failure to receive a signal could indicate an opening that has been bypassed and is being used for criminal purposes while the facility is closed. Since the presumption would be that no theft had occurred because there was no alarm, modest or judicious thieves would go completely undetected.

Experience will alert the investigator to signs of criminal or improper activity that might otherwise go unnoticed. My years of service as a metropolitan vice investigator have made me aware of common indicators of sexual activity in public or company restrooms. Whereas dirty words or obscene pictures scrawled on the walls generally can be ignored as the work of juvenile minds, very small messages written clearly in the grout line between tiles, usually soliciting sexual activity, are suggestive of a more serious problem; so are holes bored in the walls between partitioned toilets. Obviously, all such holes must be covered and the walls of restrooms painted or washed as frequently as necessary. More to the point of our present discussion, however, is the fact that physical inspections must be alert to any evidence of activity out of the ordinary.

Suggestion Box and Award Systems

Suggestion box and award programs are discussed at length in Chapter 12. Such programs can be a valuable source of information for the security investigator. Employees generally know a great deal about what is going on within the company, including illicit activity. Since most employees may be reluctant to approach anyone openly with such information, even when they strongly disapprove of what they observe, the key is to provide a vehicle for employees to communicate with management (and security) by some legitimate means. A variety of such programs have proved effective in exposing dishonesty by providing a structured vertical communication system. Such programs should provide assurances of confidentiality or, if necessary, anonymity for the informant.

Financial Analysis

The use of straightforward financial analytical techniques should not be avoided by an investigator. One needs no formal accounting training or experience to apply them, merely a sound understanding of the business of the company. At the macro level, analysis of the financial statements of the company or operating unit is easily done if several consecutive periods (years, quarters, months, weeks, etc.) are compared. This comparison of different periods is known as a *horizontal analysis* and calls for the investigator to look at changes in certain factors from period to period. For instance, if for three years the company purchased approximately $300,000 in long-distance telephone services and in the fourth year that number jumps to $500,000, the investigator should look for explanations. Is it the victim of a telecommunications fraud, or has the company opened a major telemarketing center?

Another method of analysis is to look at ratios within single financial statements and testing their reasonableness; this is known as a *vertical analysis*. An example would be noting that in one quarter the company purchased $8,000 in ground beef and sold $10,000 worth of hamburgers. If it is not obvious to the investigator that 80% represents an alarmingly high food cost, she should check with managers of her own company or other similar companies to determine what an acceptable cost ratio would be. Similar ratios can be applied to almost any sections of a financial report that bear some logical basis to one another, such as room nights sold in a hotel compared to total numbers of sheets and towels laundered.

In the area of cashiering, simple financial analysis again pays big dividends. Analyzing easily assembled data can reveal important information. Suppose, for example, a convenience store is suffering unexplained inventory shortages and it is suspected that one of the cashiers is not ringing all sales and pocketing the resulting cash. Information regarding the hours worked, total number of transactions rung, and the total dollar sales of each employee, when logically analyzed, can help to zero in on a suspect. Learning which employee has the lowest number of sales per hour worked, or the smallest sales per shift is significant, especially if the poor performance follows the employee regardless of which shifts he works. Comparing the various employees' trends for only a few days or weeks worth of data can virtually answer the *who* of an investigation before the investigator even leaves his office.

Cash register systems also can provide a wealth of information, routinely ignored by companies. Many of the production measures noted earlier can be pulled electronically from these systems. Also, some specialized measurements can be taken. Some systems will measure the time during which the cash register drawer is open. If the average length of time for most employees is thirty seconds, and one employee posts an average of five minutes, it is quite likely that the employee is leaving the drawer open in order to conduct transactions without the necessity of ringing sales.

Odometer Checks

If employees are compensated for the miles they drive their car on company business, the form used to request reimbursement should require not just the number of miles driven, but the full odometer reading before the business trip and the full reading at the conclusion of the trip. Periodic comparison of actual readings on the vehicles parked in the company lot with the mileage statements is an effective method of detecting fraud. Many a weekend trip to the mountains, desert, or lake has been charged to the employer as a business trip. For that reason the best time to record odometer readings is Monday morning.

SHOPLIFTING SURVEILLANCE

As shoplifting is a covert crime, the action of the sneak thief, so is its detection a covert strategy. It is a very difficult strategy to learn and practice. Good shoplifting investigators, more commonly referred to as either detectives or operatives, are hard to find. Many candidates are trained but few develop into outstanding achievers. Those who do are aware of their skills and are frequently difficult to supervise. They are typically people of exceptional courage, having been in many scrapes while making arrests. Most have seen more criminal acts performed than a police officer with the same years of work experience. They love their work, and will turn down promotional opportunities if the promotion will take them "off the floor." They are deserving of great respect and admiration.

In shoplifting surveillance, knowledge of techniques used by the shoplifter is as important as the detective's own stratagems. Some shoplifting strategies are as follows.

1. Put merchandise on and wear it out as though it belongs to the wearer. In some cases women will come into a store wearing only underwear under a buttoned up coat. They will then put on a dress, belt, and sweater after removing the price tags and wear the merchandise out of the store.
2. Put merchandise on beneath one's outer garments and wear the stolen items out concealed. A lot of swimwear and intimate apparel are stolen this way.
3. Place soft, folded items such as sweaters under the coat and armpit.
4. Push items off a counter so they fall into a waiting shopping bag.
5. Place articles in the bag of a previous purchase.
6. Carry into the store empty bags of the same or other stores and fill these bags with items while the shoplifter is shielded behind piles or racks of merchandise or in the privacy of a fitting room.
7. Hand merchandise to children who accompany you and let the children carry it out.
8. Wear special "boosting" coats that have hooks sewn on the inside to accommodate soft goods that are quickly placed there.
9. Wear special "boosting" coats that have a modified lining that makes the whole coat a huge pocket.
10. Carry booster boxes into the store. Such boxes appear to be ready to mail, wrapped, and string-tied, or they may be disguised as fancy gift boxes. They are empty and have a false or trapdoor, or the bottom or side may be fitted with a spring-type hinge. Push the goods in and the false side gives way; withdraw the hand and the side snaps back to its original position.
11. Wear special "booster" bloomers, similar to old-fashioned ladies' underwear that comes down just above the knee. The legs of the garment are tied, or strong elastic is used so that

stolen merchandise will not slip out. Stolen goods are pushed down the front of the bloomers, or an accomplice can push goods down the back.

12. Hide stolen items in the crotch area. Even items as bulky as a fur coat or several men's suits folded up can be hidden in this way between the thighs of a woman wearing a long, full skirt or dress, who simply walks out of the store after concealing the items. Even typewriters have been removed in this fashion.

13. Switch price tags. A garment's $50.00 price tag and barcode is replaced by a $25.00 tag and barcode from another item, and the more expensive article is then purchased at the lower price. Similar switching is often done with boxed items. For example, four cubes of margarine are removed from the package and replaced with four cubes of pure butter, which is then purchased at the price of the margarine.

14. Pick up merchandise and immediately take it to a clerk, demanding your money back.

15. Run into the store, grab items, and run out to a waiting car, catching everyone by surprise (if you are noticed at all).

The foregoing list is by no means exhaustive, but it should offer some insight into the endless variety of ways that retail merchandise can be stolen. To combat this highly prevalent form of loss, investigators must be as alert and imaginative as their adversaries.

Some detection strategies are as follows.

1. Dress in keeping with the store's clientele so as to blend into the crowd.

2. Watch for the customer who is more interested in what is going on around him than in the merchandise. A bona fide customer is interested in price, size, color, value, and such. The shoplifter is interested in who might be watching. (This is known as *eyeballing*.)

3. Once a person considered a likely shoplifter appears on the scene, stay with him until absolutely satisfied that your original assessment was wrong.

4. During that continuous surveillance of a suspect, the detective should see the customer approach and select the item to be stolen.

5. After the shoplifted item has been selected, the detective must then observe its concealment or he must know exactly where it is.

6. The investigator must ensure that the stolen article is not disposed of before an arrest can be made. This means the culprit must be kept under a continuous and uninterrupted surveillance. This is the most difficult part of the detective's job. People are easily frightened and will imagine they have been detected stealing even when they have not been. They will then dispose of stolen articles with as much stealth as was used in taking them.

7. The detective must be certain that the article supposedly stolen was not purchased.

8. Covert pursuit and surveillance must continue without interruption until the subject carries the stolen article or articles out of the store, where he is then intercepted and arrested. (Apprehension outside the store is not necessarily a legal requirement. It does, however, strengthen the charge that the shoplifter intended to take permanent possession of the stolen items without paying for them. Obviously, if a shoplifter is stopped while still inside the store, it is easier to claim that he had no intention of not paying for the goods, insisting rather that

he wished to shop for other items or to compare the original selection with other goods to ensure there was a color match, etc.)

9. Experienced shoplifting detectives will attempt to avoid a confrontation when a thief is stopped. This usually is accomplished by talking the person back into the store in a low-key, nonthreatening manner. The severity of the real consequences — arrest and prosecution — should become apparent only after the shoplifter is safely inside an office of the store, where resistance or combativeness would prove fruitless.

Two final observations should be made about shoplifting surveillance. The first is that most shoplifters are not hardened criminals or professional thieves. There are professional shoplifters, but they constitute a small percentage of all those who steal from retailers. The second point of note concerns the application of electronic article surveillance (EAS), special tags attached to goods that can be removed or deactivated only by sales personnel at the time of purchase. Otherwise the tags will cause activation of a sensing monitor at the store's exits when anyone attempts to leave with them. More and more manufacturers are placing tags on or in their goods at the time of packaging. Everything from CDs to videotapes to books are guarded by these tags. Even though they can sometimes be defeated, article surveillance of this type has done more to discourage or prevent the crime of shoplifting in all types of retail establishments than any other single strategy.

III. BUILDING A CASE

Chapter 9

Interviews and Interrogations

Once a crime, act or incident has occurred, the reconstructive process has but two sources to draw on: (1) the physically observable (i.e., physical evidence) and (2) the written or spoken word of those who witnessed or in one way or another participated in the act or incident. *Example*: a forklift shears off a sprinkler head in a warehouse operation with resultant water damage to valuable goods. Under the "physically observable," we would have such evidence as:

- The parts of the sheared sprinkler head
- The pipe from which the head had been sheared
- The point of impact on that part of the forklift that struck the head
- The condition of the forklift operator (if the investigator is on the scene shortly after the accident)
- The "hard copy" of the central station receiving the water flow signal, and the time the flow stopped
- The wet and damaged goods

Now that is a great deal of physical evidence, yet we probably could not determine if the incident was an accident, an act of negligence, or intentionally done (e.g., for spite). To complete the picture, we really need the written or spoken word of those who witnessed or in one way or another participated in the incident. What the supervisor saw and heard, what the receiving clerk saw and heard, and what the forklift driver himself has to say should provide the investigator with sufficient information to resolve the matter. The obtaining of the "word" is achieved through effective interviewing and/or interrogation. This chapter will address the spoken word. Chapter 12 will deal with the spoken word reduced to writing.

Interviewing and interrogating are two distinctly different processes, although they both have essentially the same objective. They both seek insight into and information about a specific question or issue. Interviewing and interrogating are question and answer exchanges between one who seeks information (in our context, the investigator) and the individual who is believed to possess the information being sought. The key difference between the interview and the interrogation is in the person being questioned. The interview is the questioning of a witness or any party not (at that point in time) suspected of involvement in the crime or act, and the interrogation is the questioning of a person who *is* suspected of involvement. An obvious consequence of the difference is that the interrogation at some point becomes accusatory and as such strikes the uninformed as being bad, or negative, with connotations of "grilling" or administering the old "third degree." For that reason, such professionals as James Gilbert, in his fine work, *Criminal Investigation*, recommend that all police questionings be referred to as interviews.[19] Be that as it may, the investigator must understand the two processes and approach each accordingly.

INTERVIEWING

Purpose of the Interview

Let's go back to the forklift operator who sheared off the sprinkler head. We have ample physical evidence of the consequences of the act. Our purpose in interviewing witnesses in this matter is to determine specific circumstances surrounding the "accident" to better understand *why* and *how* the incident occurred. Such information may, but more probably may not, be available from any source other than a witness. For example, we want to talk to the supervisor who was on the scene to determine the following:

1. Has the operator of the forklift been properly trained?
2. Has the operator had similar "accidents"?
3. Has the operator ever been warned about how he operates equipment?
4. Did the operator exhibit "normal" behavior prior to and after the "accident" or did he appear to be hazy, loud, or otherwise uncoordinated in movement or speech?
5. Is the operator considered a good employee or have there been problems or disagreements?
6. Is the operator content with his assignment?
7. When was the forklift last serviced? When were the brakes last serviced?
8. Was there sufficient illumination for the operator to see? (The supervisor could say he has personally complained that the lighting is insufficient in that area but management has not acted to correct the condition.)
9. Has that particular head ever been struck before?
10. Did the operator act concerned and chagrined or did he think it was funny?
11. Was the pallet on the forklift overloaded, blinding the operator's view?
12. Was there a particular rush to load or unload at that time?

The answers to such questions will fill out an otherwise incomplete picture of the incident. You can develop your own scenario of what really happened by answering each of the questions a number of different ways.

The Interviewer

The effective interviewer is the professional investigator of good grooming and poise. Articulate but soft-spoken, gentle but firm, he clearly demonstrates, by word and action, total objectivity (except where expressed empathy might encourage additional information and/or cooperation). A good interviewer engages in "active listening." He stays with the speaker by nodding his head in agreement, raising eyebrows at a particular point of interest, emitting low, audible "uh-huh's" as the interviewee talks. Set the climate in which the interviewee does the talking. Most people enjoy an audience and like to have their say, so be a good listener!

The effective interviewer also realizes that one, perhaps the biggest, impediment to getting all the relevant information the witness possesses is actually the interviewer himself. Interviewing is a lot like an archaeological dig; broad tools like shovels are used to expose rough forms hidden in the earth. When the outlines of the hidden artifacts are discovered, they are further unearthed not by pry-bars, but with gentle strokes of brushes. By boring in to the interview like a drill, the interviewer prematurely narrows the opening through which information can be observed. Much of importance can lie inches to the right or left of the hastily drilled channel.

Interview Dynamics

Any good interview for detailed verbal information will progress through a number of phases. The interviewer, being the presumed professional in the situation, has the best opportunity to guide the interview through the process. "Guide" is used advisedly because an investigator who seeks to control the interview will limit the amount of information actually received.

The importance of establishing rapport cannot be overstated. Rapport allows the witness to view the investigator as a human being open to receiving the information the witness desires to impart. Even in the case of the erstwhile reluctant witness, establishing good rapport during a patient process of interviewing can allow the witness to set aside some or all of his reluctance and opens the flow of information.

Rapport is established best by earnestly displaying the characteristics just suggested. In addition, taking a few moments at the start of the interview to discuss inconsequential matters allows the witness to begin a dialogue about nonthreatening issues while getting used to the stranger with whom they are forced to speak (you, the investigator). It takes little time to establish rapport and need not be elaborate. Simply by being polite, kind, and professional, the investigator reduces the tension for the witness and inspires confidence in the interviewer.

Rapport is actually a two-way transaction as it also allows the interviewer to obtain a fuller view of the witness. In fact, treating a person as if they were a cut-out "witness" caricature will be detected and resented. It also gets in the way of trying to understand the witness' perspective. This could easily lead the investigator to neglect asking a question that could be extremely useful in getting to the *whole* truth.

The interviewer should transition to the topic of the interview with a general statement of the situation and invite the person to tell everything she knows of the relevant events. Before asking any direct questions, the interviewer should get the witness to give a narrative of what happened. An example of this opening technique would be to say, "Mrs. Smith, we understand that you called our office to lodge a complaint this morning. Now this is very important to us, and perhaps you could tell us what happened today."

Once the witness has given the initial rendition, they should then be asked some open questions to encourage more information without the answers being suggested by the interviewer. For example, the simple question, "what else do you recall?" is surprisingly effective in having witnesses produce more information than they first mentioned. If during the narrative the witness seems to have stopped, expecting a direct question, the interviewer should avoid doing so and elicit more information by simply asking, "and then what happened?" Another open question could be, "what else did you see or hear?" The additional information gained from just a few moments of open questions can open whole areas of inquiry for the rest of the interview, or indeed the whole investigation.

Only after the investigator believes that open questioning has been exhausted of its full value should the interview progress to the specific questions. Even then, the first direct questions should be those suggested by what the witness said. Investigators often will come to interviews with questions suggested by information previously received. Those should be saved for last for three reasons. First, many of them may be answered during the information volunteered naturally by the witness. Second, the witness by that time should have been fully comfortable with answering all the investigator's questions and will be "softened up" to answer questions that earlier might have been uncomfortable for her to answer. Finally, the order of questioning (concentrating first on what the witness has to say) implies to the witness that the investigator thinks what she has to offer is important, not something to be dispensed with. It is just another means of maintaining good rapport.

At the close of the interview, after all the direct questions have been asked, the interviewer should close with two additional questions: "Is there anything else you would like to add or think would be important for us to know?" and "If we need to, may we call on you again?" The first question is a last attempt at wringing out the final detail left unsaid and also prevents the witness from later claiming that she had important information and would have related it "if only they had asked me for it." The second allows for the very real likelihood that the investigator will think of other questions to ask after leaving the interview. Any honest investigator will admit that "I should've asked . . . ." By closing the interview in this manner, the interviewer has left the door open for later obtaining more information.

An investigator who maintains excellent rapport during all interviews may be surprised at how often she gets further information volunteered by a previously interviewed witness. This is the reason why the witness should always be given the investigator's business card before the interview is concluded.

Interviewing the Victim

Victims are difficult to interview because they are reacting emotionally to their plight. The intensity of the emotion tends to be a delayed reaction, peaking after the reality of the incident sets in, then tending to dissipate with the passage of time. And the emotional reaction should be predictable. A female employee who received an obscene phone call will be frightened; an employee whose new automobile was broken into and damaged while in the company parking lot will be angry (with the culprit *and* the company); the employee who cashed her paycheck, only to have the cash stolen from her purse before the end of the day, will be frantic or depressed.

If as an interviewer you find yourself with the victim at the peaking of emotion, then do not push for information. Instead, get him a cup of coffee or let him light up a cigarette or whatever, biding for time. If time runs out because the shift is over and the victim must catch a bus or carpools with others, put the interview off until the next day. Forcing the interview is no more or less than "victimizing" the victim again. It builds resentment against the investigator or firm. On the other hand, to show concern for and sensitivity to a victim, *after getting the basic facts*, and advising him that the interview can wait until he feels better the following day, develops good will. (It is necessary to emphasize "after getting the basic facts" because the victim of certain crimes must immediately share basic information.)

The interview's ultimate objective is to gather *all* the facts, every fact possible; details are important. Take, for example, interviewing a witness/victim who is the recipient of an indecent phone call from an unknown suspect pretending to be doing a lingerie survey for a well-known local department store. The receiver of the call, when asked to describe what happened, will tell a "story." The "story" (not meant as a fabrication, but rather the retelling or recalling of the incident) will invariably leave out pertinent details. Following would be a typical retelling of the incident:

> This morning, I got a call from a man from your company who said his name was Mr. Barkins and he said he was doing a survey for the lingerie department. He asked if I would answer questions to the survey and I would then receive a certificate worth $25 to buy merchandise in your store. I said fine. He then asked my lingerie color preference, then my bra size, slip size, and panty size. I felt uncomfortable but answered. He then asked if I wore the brief panties or regular cut. I said brief. He then asked if I shaved to wear the briefs. I didn't think that was right so I just said no. Then he asked me if I didn't shave, did hair show. I was so shocked I couldn't think of an appropriate answer and then he asked me a filthy question, to which I slammed down the phone. That's what happened, from beginning to end.

After using open questions to elicit some additional facts, the interviewer must then develop unstated details. For example:

1. Does your telephone system have Caller ID or a last caller dial-back capability?
2. What time exactly did the caller call? Fix the time by association with her schedule or routine. What was she doing when the phone rang? Watching a favorite TV program? Still having coffee? Husband just left for work? and so forth.
3. Did he use the store's name first, or at first identify himself by name, claiming he was with the store?
4. Did he say he was *Mr.* Barkins or did he use a first name also?
5. Was the phone connection clear? Was it a cell phone call?
6. How old a man did he sound like?
7. Did you hear any sounds in the background, such as a radio or TV, phones ringing, sounds of traffic, voices, or no sounds whatsoever?
8. Did he sound like an educated man, in terms of his choice of words, diction, delivery, or sentence structure? (Qualify the answer by asking her to compare to husband, family, or friends.)
9. Any accent distinguishable?
10. Any other characteristic in his manner of speaking, for example, fast, slow, lisping, stutter, preceding questions with "ah," and so on?
11. Did he make any reference as to how or why he called you, for example, did he say the local credit bureau provided your name as a good customer in the community?
12. Is your telephone listed in the directory?
13. Have you made any lingerie or other intimate apparel purchases anywhere lately?

14. If your phone number is listed, how is it listed, under your own name or your husband's?
15. Did he ever refer to you by your first name, if it's not listed?
16. Are you well known in the community, by virtue of your personal, social, political activities, or is your husband so known?
17. Is it generally known in your neighborhood that you are alone during the morning?
18. Did the caller sound like anyone, even vaguely, you have met or known?
19. Would you be able to recognize the caller's voice if you heard it again?

Obviously the answers to these questions, and more, give the investigator details. And in that detail can be the key to the identity of the caller, if not in this incident, then in another. It is important that you ask only one question at a time, and, if the answer is appropriate and intelligent, determine if that answer deserves another question.

Sometimes, however, investigators deny themselves every detail by having, as an example, the wrong person conducting the interview. Consider the female employee who received an obscene phone call. If a male investigator were conducting that interview, some of the language during that conversation, language that could tie in with a past or future case, might not surface. A female investigator would probably obtain the entire conversation, word for word. Ideally, then, a female investigator would do the follow-up interviewing on sex-related offenses involving female victims. That is also true where children are witnesses. As a rule, small children will confide in a female more readily than in a male, and older people feel more at ease with investigators closer to their own age.

Interviewing Employees

Regrettably, many employees across the entire spectrum of business and industry tend to view the company's security department and investigators in the private sector with some degree of guarded alarm or suspicion. Certainly, in some industries in which there is a relatively high incidence of employee dishonesty, fear of security is understandable. In others it may be attributable to simply identifying security as an extension of management. But whatever the case, the interviewer should be tuned in to the rank-and-file's perception of security, and more particularly, the security department's investigation unit.

There are a number of ways to substantially reduce, if not eliminate, this negative perception, but that is not for this chapter, or even this text. The point is that, if this attitude is present in a company, it poses an obstruction to good communication between security and employees, making interviewing more difficult.

There are two ways to overcome built-in resistance (assuming, of course, that the interviewer meets the personal and professional standards set forth earlier in this chapter). The first is to conduct the interview whenever possible right in the employee's work area, as opposed to conducting it in an administrative office, which in itself is intimidating to some employees. This is accomplished by having the lead person or line supervisor accompany and then introduce the investigator to the employee to be interviewed, saying something to the effect of, "Mr. DeWindt of our security department needs your assistance on a company problem, so take whatever time he needs. You two can talk right here or maybe you'd be more comfortable over in the lounge. OK?" Standing around, or sitting, in the work area openly so all the other employees can see tends to allay the worker's concerns about his own well-being. It is then easier for him to share parts of his interview with coworkers when they ask him what it was all about — and they will! (Needless to say, this kind of interview should cover a matter other than internal dishonesty in that area.) Additionally, this kind of informal meeting tends to add dignity or importance to the employee. After all, security came to him. He wasn't summoned to their office. Last, that very work area and the activity the employee engages in could very well be germane to the investigation. It would therefore make sense to inspect the area with the employee witness.

The second kind of interview, particularly if the matter is internal dishonesty, can be handled in an administrative office where a supervisorial or personnel representative introduces security and remains quietly as a witness. Here again, the employee is introduced in a positive, nonthreatening way, such as, "Ms. McDonald of our security department is interviewing a number of employees about a delicate matter and she needs all the assistance she can get. I know you'll help if you can. I've been sitting here so why don't you sit right over there?"

Interviewing Nonemployees

The difference between interviewing nonemployees and employees is twofold. First, most nonemployees feel no obligation to cooperate, and second, most nonemployees do not have the same sense of dread or fear of corporate security, with the exception of subcontractors and service organizations that rely heavily on the company as their primary sources of income. Usually, these exceptions are eager to please and their cooperation can be counted on.

In interviewing the nonemployee, be it a client, customer, passerby, or what have you, the most universally productive approach to gain their cooperation is to suggest that somehow it is good for them — good as a client because service can be improved, good as a customer because prices can be kept down, good as a recipient because the neighborhood will be improved (or changed for the better), good as a citizen to carry out civic responsibility, good as an insurer because abuses can cause insurance rates to climb. And this approach need not be direct. It can be suggestive in nature. The good investigator will get cooperation.

Disciplinary and Investigative Interviews

There are two noticeable exceptions to the difference between the interview and interrogation, and for lack of better terms, we will refer to them as disciplinary and investigative. In each case, the employee is confronted with derogatory information indicating him but not accusing. An example of a *disciplinary interview* would be one in which the employee failed to perform as required, and that failure caused or contributed to a serious problem, but it is not possible to prove that the employee did so with intent. The failure might have involved leaving a dock door unlocked that resulted in a successful burglary. That employee could be under strong suspicion of being involved in that crime but it is unprovable. The interview would explore why and/or how he failed to secure that door, but without more substantial information, and without that employee all of a sudden blurting out an admission of involvement, the only recourse is disciplinary action, based on the admitted procedural failure. Depending upon the company and its rules, such an employee could be terminated following the interview.

In a disciplinary interview discussing an employee's failure to record a cash sale, a case in which there is substantial evidence that the employee did sell a service, goods, beverage, or whatever, but failed to record (i.e., ring it up on the cash register or terminal), the employee is asked to *explain* what happened to the transaction, the money specifically. We strongly suspect the employee pocketed that money but cannot *prove* it. The employee invariably "can't remember" or insists he put the money in the register, even if he failed to record it properly. Irrespective of what the employee admits, the employee is discharged for failure to follow an important rule: All cash transactions must be recorded at the time of sale. Discharge for this procedural failure is not uncommon in the retail industry.

An *investigative interview* is a vehicle to reiterate accusations of dishonesty by coworkers. The investigator acts discreetly as a somewhat disinterested third party. As an example, the investigation has identified internal dishonesty and now the culprits are in "custody." During the interrogation, one or more of those involved implicates someone either unknown to the investigation or someone suspected of involvement but against whom there is insufficient evidence for action. The company has two choices: (1) open an investigation into the activities of the accused (although the accused may not participate in dishonesty again because his confederates have been caught); or (2) confront the accused in an interview. That interview (preferably with a personnel representative present as a witness that the investigator did not *accuse* the employee) would be handled by the key investigator as follows: "Mr. James, I suspect you are aware of the fact that Mr. White is in trouble. He's told us everything. He told us you've been involved. We'd like to hear what you have to say." If Mr. James drops his head and admits dishonesty, the interview turns immediately into an interrogation. If, on the other hand, Mr. James denies involvement and claims his associates are lying, then, in the absence of any proof, Mr. James is apologized to for the inconvenience caused by his accusers and told that the company does not take the unverified word of one employee against another. He is then sent back to work. The employee may be wary, but he usually heaves a sigh of relief. Depending on the circumstances, a covert investigation may continue.

Checking Perceptions

As an aid to judgmental determinations, such as age, weight, distance, and height, ask the interviewee *your* age, weight, height, hair color, and so on. This check of his perceptions will help him as well as you in putting down relatively accurate information, which is so important to the investigation. Inquire also after any vision or hearing problems the interviewee may have. If she customarily wears corrective lenses and a hearing aid, did she use them at the time of the incident?

INTERROGATION

The interrogation is the oral examination of one believed to be responsible for the omission or commission of an act considered a public offense. One definition is an accusatory confrontation between a person standing accused and his accuser, the objective of which is to induce the accused to admit culpability. It is a psychological contest between an interrogator whose purpose is to get the accused to volunteer self-incriminating statements, and the accused who seeks to protect himself from the consequences of his conduct by assuming a posture of innocence or ignorance.

The first step in admitting culpability is an admission of wrongdoing. Upon that first admission, the skillful interrogator will build more admissions until all is disclosed. An example of building on the initial admission of merchandise theft by a warehouse employee, for instance, would probably unfold as follows:

Employee:	"OK. You've got me anyhow. I put the carton of CD players in my trunk just before I locked up for the night."
Interrogator:	"What prompted you to do that?"
Employee:	"I just needed the money."
Interrogator:	"How much did you get for the carton?"
Employee:	"$200.00 cash."
Interrogator:	"Who gave the $200?"
Employee:	"A guy named Willie. Don't ask me his last name 'cause I don't know."
Interrogator:	"Did you know Willie was willing to buy before you took the carton or did you take the carton and then look for a buyer?"
Employee:	"Willie and me already had talked about it. In fact, it was his idea for me to get the players because he said they're easy to sell."
Interrogator:	"When did you turn the carton over to him?"
Employee:	"That same evening, over behind Lucciani's delicatessen. I gave him the box and he gave me the money."
Interrogator:	"What did he do with the carton, once he had it?"
Employee:	"Well, he took, all the CD players out and put them on his shelf. He has shelves in his van, kind of like a store."
Interrogator:	"A van, like a store?"
Employee:	"Yeah, He's got a step-in van, you know, kind of like a converted parcel delivery truck."
Interrogator:	"Does he actually use it to sell from?"
Employee:	"Oh sure. In fact, later that evening, several customers in Lucciani's came out the back door and two of them bought a player. He's got all kinds of things, like Levi's, sweaters. One time, he had lugs of tomatoes. Never has the same stuff twice. Lots of people know Willie."
Interrogator:	"What does he look like?"
Employee:	(describes Willie)
Interrogator:	"What does the van look like?"
Employee:	(describes the van)
Interrogator:	"Would you be willing to work with us, and deliver more merchandise to Willie?"
Employee:	"Are you kidding? He'd kill me even if he knew I was just telling you about him. No way, man. No way!"
Interrogator:	"He won't find out from us you're talking to us."
Employee:	"God, I hope not. I'm sure your guys or the police will get him but keep me out of it. Fact is, I'm surprised he gets away with what he does. Everyone knows Willie."
Interrogator:	"How did you ever make this arrangement anyhow, the arrangement to deliver a carton of players to him?"
Employee:	"He asked me where I worked. Then one thing led to another and you know the rest."
Interrogator:	"How did you come to meet him?"
Employee:	"I bought a leather jacket from him, from his van."
Interrogator:	"When was that?"

Employee:	"Just after last Christmas."
Interrogator:	"Where was the van then?"
Employee:	"Sitting behind Mullin's gas station. He's there a lot."
Interrogator:	"If I saw his van there tomorrow afternoon, could I buy something?"
Employee:	"Not in the afternoon. He only works at night. Besides, he'd be suspicious of you 'cause he doesn't know you."
Interrogator:	"How does one get to know Willie?"

It is amazing how much information can be obtained through skillful interrogation. In this example, the interrogator obviously is interested in obtaining a full disclosure about Willie, a local "fence" or outlet for stolen goods. A great deal more information is yet to be developed concerning this case — for example, the number of previous thefts (involving Willie or not), how he defeated the company safeguards that permitted the removal of the carton from the premises, and so on.

The securing of this first admission is enhanced by the accused's sense of guilt — the knowledge that he or she *did* commit the wrongful act. Added to that naturally uncomfortable feeling is one's apprehension and uncertainty over just how much the interrogator knows. These factors result in an inner stress, a necessary element in any successful interrogation. Maintenance of stress will bring about an admission because of people's desire to be relieved from stress.

Invariably, an unsuccessful interrogation can be attributed to a shifting of stress from the accused to the accuser! The shifting occurs when the accused perceives that the interrogator is not knowledgeable of the facts surrounding the incident, or seems unsure of the accused's degree of guilt or involvement. Such perception gives the subject confidence. With confidence comes strength and hope. The perceptive interrogator, recognizing the growing confidence and strength of the accused, tends to lose heart. His composure is thus undermined and the stress is shifted from the accused to the interrogator. It is almost like a game that could be called, "Stress, Stress, Who Has the Stress?" If you have the stress, you can't win!

PREPARING FOR THE INTERROGATION

Essentially, the same standards set forth for the interviewer hold true for the interrogator except that the purposeful, soft-spoken approach should be replaced by a more aggressive articulation of questions. It is important to examine oneself in a mirror, if at all possible, immediately prior to commencing an interrogation to ensure that there is nothing distracting in appearance. Male interrogators should not wear lapel pins or any fancy tie tack and certainly not a little handcuffs tie tack. Female interrogators should not wear any jewelry other than one or two finger rings, a watch and a bracelet; no broach, necklace, or earrings unless the necklace is out of sight and the earrings are very small and do not dangle. You do not need a subject leaning forward, pretending to be honestly curious about a lapel pin or brooch, and saying, "Oh, do you belong to the Knights of Columbus?" Or, "What a lovely pin! What kind of stone is that?"

The interrogator should be as knowledgeable as possible about the subject's personal and work history — where he was born, schools attended, occupation of parents or spouse, and such. If the interrogator knows the accused's brother is in law enforcement, a line of questioning using that fact — such as, "Your brother Fred is a Connecticut state trooper. What would he say if he knew you were in this mess?"—could come as quite a shock to an unsuspecting subject. The statement suggests that the interrogator knows *everything*.

Another preparatory activity, time permitting, is scenario development, in which the interrogator anticipates possible responses and how each should be dealt with. Responses can be verbal or physical. An example of a verbal response might be, "I quit, resign my job at this very moment. That means I am no longer an employee. Either pay me off my salary due and release me, or arrest me!" If the interrogator has not thought that possibility through, he could be caught totally off guard and, as a consequence, be unable to effectively interrogate.

An example of a physical response could be the subject fainting or going into an epileptic seizure, or uncontrolled weeping. The effective interrogator is prepared for the unexpected.

If a file on the subject does not exist, prepare one, even if it is only a dummy file. Fill the file with numerous forms and written reports, anything to give the impression and appearance of a very comprehensive package. Have the subject's name boldly printed on the jacket or folder tab. During the interrogation such a file can be quietly referred to. Such a file has the following advantages:

1.   It gives the impression that a great deal of information has been gathered on the subject.
2.   It can be picked up and examined as though comparing the subject's answer against known facts.
3.   It might be used as a prop for the interrogator who wishes time to reorganize thoughts, or just to buy time.

Prepare yourself in terms of slowing down (be calm), feeling good about yourself and your preparation. Move forward with confidence and anticipate success (self-fulfilling prophecy, the Pygmalion Effect).

Needless to say, the single most crucial preparation step for an effective interrogation is for the investigator to know the case information cold. Being aware of every fact known to date allows the investigator to realize when the suspect has said something significant and worthy of later follow-up. It also lets the interrogator recognize when she is being lied to before being led fully "down the primrose path." Finally, this level of preparation prevents the interrogator from saying anything that will display ignorance of a key matter, something likely to pierce the intended display of being the all-knowing investigative professional. Instead, the subject will begin to think of the investigator as artless or plain dumb. Neither perception will be helpful to the interrogator.

The Setting of the Interrogation

Contrary to what many of us learned while in college, a bare-walled room, almost sterile, is really not necessary for conducting a successful interrogation (see Figure 9.1). Any regular business office will do, except the subject's own office, as long as it can be secured from interruptions such as a ringing phone or someone inadvertently walking in. If the room has a window to the outside, close the blinds to prevent the subject from fixing a gaze on some point in the distance or otherwise concentrating on what is happening out there (see Figure 9.2).

Place two straight-back chairs opposite one another, four to six feet apart, just outside one another's personal space. If possible, site one chair with its back to the door. The subject will sit in that

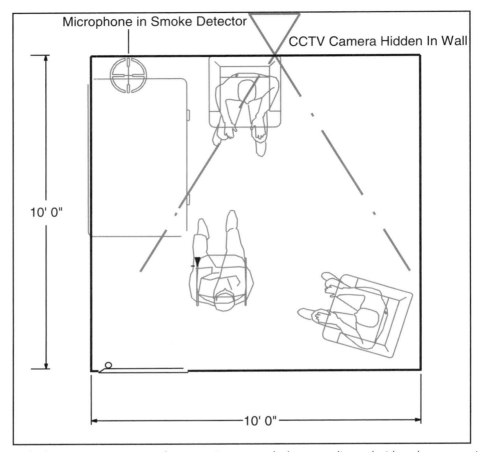

Figure 9.1.   Ideal interview situation. The room is not overly large, audio and video documentation is possible, the subject faces away from the door. If used, an observer sites to the side and rear of the subject. Prepared using *The CrimeZone*.

one, you the other. This prevents the subject from looking directly at the door and being constantly reminded that the literal and figurative "way out" of the interrogation is to simply get up and leave through it. The second important reason for this arrangement is that the person will have difficulty in later claiming that the investigator was physically blocking the exit from the room and coerced a confession (see Figure 9.3). For the same reason, having no lock on the door to the regular interrogation room is advisable. (This of course applies only in situations where no arrest has been made or is being contemplated.) First, sit in the subject's chair, and look beyond where you will be. What might prove to be a distraction? A picture? A calendar? Anything that might catch the subject's fancy or attention should be removed. Now, just slightly to the right of the subject's chair, place a third chair. That will be where the partner or witness will sit, just barely discernible in the subject's peripheral vision.

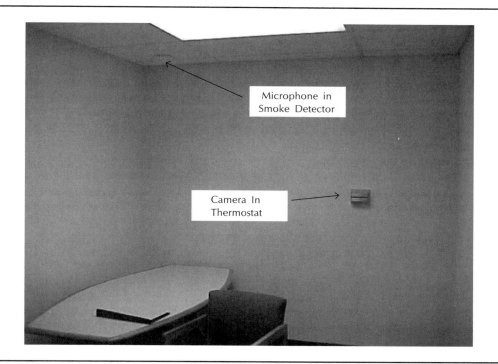

Figure 9.2. Typical interview room, wall devoid of distractions, nothing on table except relevant file, equipped for unobtrusive audio and video recording.

Notice how the interrogator does not sit behind a desk. A desk only builds a barrier between the two principals, something the interrogator does not want. As the investigator sees that the suspect is about to give in, pulling the investigator's chair more closely to the suspect will penetrate the personal space of the suspect. This must be done naturally, just as if you were moving closer to hear a friend who was talking softly. This "intimacy" will facilitate the production of first admission. A desk would interfere with this natural movement bridging the personal space. After the admissions start coming in, the desk can be used, but not until then.

Rid the room of any ashtrays, wastebaskets, or any other receptacle that might be used to put ashes into.

Place the subject's "file" prominently on top of the desk or any other logical place where the subject can see it. Be sure you have the physical evidence in the room so it can be displayed when appropriate.

Be certain the room is not too cold or warm, too bright or dark. It should be normal and comfortable. The author lost a case in court based on the fact that the interrogation was conducted under spooky and intimidating circumstances, conditions which, when described in court, were true enough

Figure 9.3.   Interview in progress. Note that the subject's path to exit is unobstructed, there are no barriers to communication or observation between the parties, and no lock on the doorknob.

but to which we were simply not sensitive at the time of the interrogation. That interrogation took place in a tool-and-storage room adjacent to the public toilets in a country park at night. To heat the interior of that room we were using an antique, fuel-oil-burning, cylindrical-type stove that stood on three short legs. For ventilation, and presumably for appearance, there was a row of little "windows" at the height of the flame inside the heater. We purposefully kept the lights out because we were expecting another arrest, so we interrogated in the room illuminated only by the orange flickering light thrown by the heater, dancing on the otherwise dark walls. We investigators were similarly illuminated. Although the subject was caught "red-handed," and admitted his guilt, the interrogation proved his salvation and our loss.

Beginning the Interrogation

Introduce yourself and your partner (or witness) as agents of the company in a direct and pleasant manner. Seat the subject and immediately take the opposing chair. Commence the interrogation along the following lines, depending on how it fits with a particular case, but always include the questions in this suggested opening:

"Mary — may I call you Mary? Good. Mary, we have a very important subject to discuss this morning, very important to you and very important to us. In fact, it probably will be the most important discussion you've ever been engaged in. But before we get into the question at hand, I do want to ask you a couple of questions, okay? Are you in any way sick or are you thirsty?"

Mary, with a curious expression, answers, "No."

"Do you take any kind of medicine?"

"No."

"Do you have to use the ladies' room?"

"No."

"Good."

The interrogator continues, "One more final point before we get started here, Mary, and that is my rule on lying. You have my solemn promise that at no time during our discussion will I lie to you. This is too important a matter for you to worry about me being deceptive. And by the same token, I'm asking you not to lie to me, no matter how much the truth hurts. Don't lie. This whole problem is too important to jeopardize it with lies. Do you understand that?"

Now the interrogator asks a series of relatively unimportant questions about the job and perhaps a few innocent questions about activities away from the job, all of which are designed to evoke "yes" answers. That is to establish a pattern of saying "yes"; it becomes easy to say "yes." When you get around to asking her a critical question, she may be in the mood to tell the truth.

Now if Mary gets a dry throat or says she has to use the toilet, the interrogator says, with raised eyebrow, "Why, Mary, just a very short time ago I asked you specifically if you were thirsty and you said you weren't. Why is your throat now dry? I can tell you with absolute certainty that the dry throat is a sure sign of guilt." The point is that asking those four questions at the outset of the interrogation precludes the possibility of an interruption that otherwise you would be unwise to refuse. Such interruptions obviously are designed by the accused to relieve stress.

Of course, you must not restrict the subject's freedom to leave unless you have the legal grounds to make an arrest and to do so is within corporate policy. If the subject indicates a desire to use the toilet or to leave, you should be persuasive, not coercive, in your attempts to avoid the interruption.

If the subject starts looking around for an ashtray while trying to extract a cigarette, tell the subject there is no ashtray in the room and that, during the discussion, you would appreciate it if he would not smoke. Don't tell him he cannot. *Ask* him not to or point out that the workplace is a non-smoking area per company policy or legal restriction. Why this stipulation? Because smoking soothes stress. A smoker denied a cigarette becomes distressed, adding to the very condition the interrogator wants. And there is nothing immoral or illegal in prohibiting smoking in certain areas at certain times.

If the subject starts to use profanity, admonish him immediately. Profanity is used as a substitute for other words. The individual who has difficulty in expressing himself tends to resort to the use of profanity, and such use makes him feel good about himself, intellectually or socially. Take away the "cuss words" and his vocabulary is dramatically reduced, or so it seems to him. That is also *stressful*. That is exactly what the interrogator wants. The admonishment would go something like this: "Please don't use profanity during our discussion here. This is too important an occasion to mar with profanity. I don't use it. I expect you not to use it." The admonishment should be made in a reasonable, not confrontational, tone so as not to create resentment in the subject and destroy all rapport. Of course, if the subject becomes verbally abusive toward you, rapport has already been largely lost and you can expect to call upon all your reserves of patience and professionalism to get it back and succeed in getting the confession.

Constantly observe the subject for indications of stress and for reactions to questions. If the subject starts picking at a fingernail, ask him to stop and concentrate on your questions and his answers. The eyes do two things: (1) your constant eye contact penetrates the guilty man's consciousness and creates stress; and (2) your eyes tell you when to ask the same question again; when to suddenly stand up and look down on the subject, then walk around the room and return to your chair; when to remain silent.

Other physical indications of stress include dry mouth, a bobbing Adam's apple, a paling complexion, beads of perspiration on the forehead, the onset of a tic (e.g., uncontrollable shaking, usually of the hands), inability or unwillingness to look the interrogator in the eye, and uncontrolled elimination of body waste.

To stand up and look down on a subject tends to subjugate the one seated. It is a way to reemphasize, if necessary, who is in control. Unquestionably, there are some theatrics involved here. Let us say the subject contradicts himself and realizes it. Upon hearing the contradiction, that could be an excellent time for the investigator to rise and, looking down, say, "Do you realize what you just said?" Or to rise and walk around the room while saying, "Well now, *that's* interesting! First you said the supervisor was in his office and *now* you say he was on the dock. Why would you change your story?" The stress is magnified because, in the mind of the subject, he is in more trouble than before and is "locked" into the chair, whereas the righteous person (the interrogator) is "free" to get up and walk around, as well as to look down on him (the unrighteous).

Could you imagine a blind man or woman conducting an interrogation? Highly unlikely!

Do's and Don'ts of Interrogation

Following is a list of other *Do's* and *Don'ts* that can be helpful to the security interrogator:

1. Do use silence as a weapon. Ask a direct question and then wait for the response. The silence may seem like a long time, but it is thundering in the mind and ears of the accused, to whom it seems like an eternity.
2. Do keep questions short.
3. Do ask only one question at a time.
4. Do question the answers.
5. Do guard yourself against giving away information.
6. Don't make promises of any kind.
7. Don't lose your patience or persistence—any anxiety you feel is much amplified in the subject.
8. Don't threaten an accused with discharge, police involvement, or violence.
9. Don't show surprise at any answers.
10. Don't use profanity. Some still believe the only way to communicate with tough employees or outsiders is to speak "their" language. Don't lower yourself to them; rather, raise them up to you.

11. Don't be a big shot. Arrogance and pomposity close communication lines, which defeats the interrogator's purpose.
12. Don't lie. It may be unwise to tell all. What you do tell must be truthful.
13. Don't ever lose your temper. If you lose your temper you "got the stress" and lose the interrogation. The subject will do and say things, both intentionally and by chance, that can make you angry. Resist this urge and remain the clinical professional.

Learning

Interrogation is something that is best learned through a combination of methods. Having successfully developed a number of competent investigators into accomplished interrogators we know that attending formal training seminars offered by a number of well regarded companies, observing actual interrogations, conducting role playing simulations, and being coached by more experienced interrogators are all part of a comprehensive approach to learning this fascinating and critical art. This process can take months, and more often years, to progress through to a level of competence and confidence. The process is never fully complete because each new interrogation session provides its own set of learning experiences for even the accomplished interrogator who is willing to honestly examine his performance.

In addition, many of the techniques and methods taught from a purely law enforcement or private detective agency context will differ from that which is advisable for a corporation's security investigator to employ. One example is the issue of deception. It is widely taught at respected interrogation seminars that deception employed against the subject is, within proper bounds, entirely permissible and to be encouraged. This is fine to admit later on the stand as a sworn police officer or private detective, whose positions in the eyes of the jury are simply as objective fact-finders in the fight against crime. The same conduct employed by the security department investigator can be looked upon as the oppression of a relatively powerless worker by a monolithic and greedy corporation. This perception can result in a loss of a prosecution in the criminal courts. If this happens, one can almost certainly expect a more disastrous airing before a civil jury in a suit against the company. The corporate investigator must always keep in mind his organizational mandate is to protect assets, not create unreasonable risk.

There are probably as many acceptable ways to conduct an interrogation as there are interrogators and subjects. This chapter is not intended to be an exhaustive treatise on the topic; indeed, many entire books have been written already. Instead, some basic information is presented as a starting point for each investigator's personal exploration of the field.

CONCLUSION

Remember, the person being interrogated is, after all, a human being who is psychologically and emotionally suffering at your hands. Most people want to confess. The interrogator can relieve that suffering by his genuine concern for the accused and the final resolution of the matter at hand. As a result, the accused senses that concern and wants to share with the interrogator. If that seems odd, it is closely parallel to the equally odd but well-documented phenomenon of kidnap victims becoming attached to their captors. The professional private sector investigator, functioning as an interrogator, is sensitive to human behavior and emotional needs, and by his behavior and attitude wins the confidence and respect of the man or woman in trouble. Once the subject respects and has confidence in that professional, the confession follows.

This will be, for many subjects, the first time they have admitted their misdeeds to anyone, including close friends and even spouses. The skillful interrogator should be honored by this fact and not treat the person with scorn or disdain. This is such a significant and cathartic event for many people who confess, that, if the interrogator has acted with empathy and professionalism, it is not at all uncommon for the person to leave actually thanking the investigator for helping him and earnestly shaking his hand. Not at all the popular image of interrogation.

Chapter 10

An Overview of the Interview and Interrogation Process

By David E. Zulawski, CFI, CFE; and Douglas E. Wicklander, CFI, CFE

Editor's Note

Proficiency in interviews and interrogations is so crucial to the success of investigators that we have elected to provide more in-depth information for those who desire an advanced understanding of the subject. We especially are pleased to have this contribution from two acknowledged masters of the art, and trust that it will be of immeasurable value to students and practitioners as they undertake these central tasks.

The most productive component of any investigation is the investigator's effective use of interviewing and interrogation. The process of interview and interrogation resolves more cases than any other forensic or laboratory examination of recovered evidence.

Unfortunately, many new investigators pay little attention to developing their skills and instead rely on techniques seen on television or in the movies. However, once an investigator understands the process of interview and interrogation it becomes readily apparent that it is an incredibly productive avenue of case resolution.

The difficulty in learning to effectively use interview and interrogation is that almost any technique or attempt to gain information may work at sometime. Simply sitting silently across from a suspect* might obtain a confession, but it is not a very effective or consistently reliable way of getting

---

* In this chapter the term *subject* will refer to someone who is a victim, witness, or suspect, and the interviewer is attempting to obtain or confirm information, but not a confession from the individual. The term *suspect* will be used when the investigation has focused on an individual who is believed to be responsible for the incident and the interrogator is attempting to obtain an admission or confession from that person.

one. As a result, the new investigator may be rewarded with a successful outcome even though the technique employed will not work well when applied against hundreds or thousands of other encounters. For example, one interviewer who was having difficulty obtaining information from suspects was asked to recount her approach to the interview. She related she would have the suspect placed alone in a room for a short period of time before she entered. She said when she arrived she would make strong eye contact with the suspect and slam the door. When asked why, she said it was a replication of her first interview when she had obtained a confession. In the previous example, the techniques employed were counterproductive, but the interrogator had been rewarded with a confession, which reinforced her continued use of the approach. Skilled interrogators know that the best techniques are the ones that work the most often with the most people.

DEMEANOR

Generally people who like others and are comfortable communicating tend to make the best interviewers and interrogators. They have a natural curiosity about people and their comfortable approach puts others at ease and open the lines of communication.

Even though television and the movies tend to portray the investigator as abrasive, demanding, and aggressive, this is almost always contrary to the personality of a good interviewer/interrogator. Instead, a good interviewer/interrogator will adjust his demeanor and personality to the individual with whom he is speaking, establishing a comfortable dialogue.

When attempting to obtain information either through an interview or interrogation the investigator must not appear to value either the information or confession excessively. When it appears to the subject that the information he possesses is of great importance, its value increases and the resistance to sharing the information may increase as well. During any negotiation the buyer is always at a disadvantage once the seller discovers the importance of the purchase to the buyer. Once discovered, the price always increases since it is now apparent that the buyer is unwilling to walk away. It is the same with information or a confession. The information possessed by the subject may actually be critical to the resolution of the investigation, but the investigator must use methods of rapport and persuasion to encourage the individual's cooperation without appearing to desperately need the information.

RAPPORT

Almost every interview and interrogation textbook addresses the necessity of establishing rapport between the investigator and the individual from whom he is seeking information. However, establishing rapport is often easier said than done.

Most people know someone who has the unique ability to walk into an establishment and within a short time talk with strangers like they are old friends. Others just never seem to grasp this skill. This ability to establish rapport is often as simple as finding something in common between yourself and another. It could be a community, interest, person, or even a question that leads to rapport.

Once rapport has been established an interesting phenomena called *mirroring* can be observed. Mirroring means the participants in the conversation unconsciously begin to posture themselves and pace their speech in similar fashions. People may stand the same way, moving to follow one another's posture change to maintain the comfort of rapport. This mirroring of behavior is the result of rapport.

Watch any conversation and the observer quickly will see by the group's body positioning whether they are in a state of rapport or conflict.

Depending on the individual, establishing rapport can be accomplished quickly or may take some time to achieve. People are much more likely to establish rapport when they do not feel threatened or uncertain about another's intentions. If the investigator is perceived as attempting to be unnaturally friendly, this likely will foster suspicion and resistance in the subject. Their uncertainty and distrust of the overly friendly investigator will result in less information being obtained.

INTERVIEW AND INTERROGATION

It is important that the investigator understand the distinction between the process of interview and interrogation. The dynamics of the two are exactly opposite and the investigator must clearly establish in his mind what he is attempting before talking with a subject.

An interview is a nonaccusatory fact gathering or behavioral provoking conversation to determine facts, sequence of events, alibis, or to confirm information with a victim, witness, or suspect. The interviewer allows the subject to do the majority of the talking by asking open-ended questions to encourage a narrative response. In the latter stages of the interview the investigator may use closed-ended questions to clearly establish or confirm details. Because of the dynamics of interviewing the investigator should not expect a confession, but only for the subject to confirm or deny information.

An interrogation is conducted when a suspect is believed to be guilty. It is a search for the truth to obtain admissions or confession, which independently confirm the investigative findings. The admissions or confession should support the details of the investigation and establish the individual's participation in the act. In an interrogation the interrogator seeks information that establishes the suspect's culpability and mental state, which will provide sufficient details to prosecute, discipline, or discharge the individual.

Behavior

Interviewing and interrogation is essentially a conversation between two people desiring information. Each is reacting to the other's questions and moods. An important aspect of interview and interrogation is the careful observation of the subject's behavior and then reacting to it. Observing the individual's behavior as he is questioned often provides the interviewer/interrogator clues to concealed information, plus it can assist in determining the person's candidness.

Carefully listening to the individual's word choice, speed of delivery, tonal qualities, and pauses may provide the astute interviewer with clues where to develop information. In addition, observing the physical behavior, attitudes, and behavioral changes during the course of questioning may also assist the interviewer in knowing where to develop additional information.

For behavioral clues to be relevant in detecting deception they must be on time and consistent. There is no single behavior either verbal or physical that always indicates an individual is being truthful or attempting to deceive. Instead, the interviewer must observe behavior and its timeliness and consistency to determine its usefulness for detecting deception.

For example, a subject may scratch his ear during the interview, which could indicate either his ear itched or he was under stress because of a question being asked. It will be the consistency of a response to either the question asked, topic introduced, or even a word used, which will indicate that the behavior is relevant. When the interviewer returns to the word, topic, or question does another behavioral response occur? This may or may not be the same physical behavior, but rather a consistent response to the stimulus of the topic, word, or question. It might occur that the first indication of stress was the scratching of the ear, next a folding of the arms, and finally the crossing of the legs. Although each of the behaviors is different, what is common is the consistency of some type of behavior occurring after the interviewer returns to a particular area of questioning. The preceding examples of behavior all consisted of movements after the stress, but just as relevant is the subject's lack of movement.

Behavior offers the interviewer/interrogator direction, and although it is observable its true meaning can be inferred only from the context of the conversation, never absolutely known. The interviewer/interrogator views the behavior of a subject in two ways: comparing the subject to the population as a whole and to the subject's normal everyday actions. First, the subject's behavior is compared to what most people's action would be in a given context. Does the subject's behavior conform to the population's norm or are the actions or attitudes different? If they appear different this may be a clue to deception or it may just be the individual's behavioral norm. The second thing that must be done is for the interviewer/interrogator to establish how the individual responds truthfully under the given set of circumstances of the current conversation.

Establish a Behavioral Norm

In either an interview or interrogation it is essential for the interviewer/interrogator to establish a behavioral norm for the individual being spoken with. The interviewer is attempting to identify the normal pattern of behavior for the individual when he is responding truthfully to questions in a given situation.

Being interviewed, even when truthful, may put the individual under some level of stress. Recognizing this, the interviewer asks biographical or nonissue related questions to which the individual is likely to respond truthfully. The interviewer calibrates the individual's speech pattern and physical behavior during this portion of the conversation and uses it as a tool of comparison when the conversation moves into those areas under investigation.

To establish the individual's behavioral norm the interviewer might ask questions where the answer is known or easily checkable. Those questions could be similar to the following:

- What is your current address?
- How old are you?
- How long have you been at your current job?
- What is your supervisor's name?

The interviewer may use questions like these to observe behavior associated with truthful information that readily is used by the subject every day, such as the individual's age or address. The interviewer also asks questions that require the individual to retrieve information from his long-term stored memory or to create responses. After carefully observing the individual's responses the interviewer now has a pattern of behavior to use as comparison when the subject retrieves short- and long-term information or creates an answer to a question.

As the interviewer moves from the behavioral norm questions into the issue under investigation he looks for changes in the subject's verbal and physical responses, which may indicate the individual is being deceptive or withholding information.

Movement and gestures may indicate stress or simply could be a method the subject uses to help explain the story. It is also common for someone attempting to deceive to lock themselves down, limiting any movements or gestures. The interviewer/interrogator concealing what is known from the investigation is in a unique position to evaluate the candidness of the subject and his associated behavior. The subject, if he chooses to, will attempt to lie and conceal derogatory information in a number of ways.

Types of Lies

During an interview or interrogation the subject may engage in a variety of different attempts at deception. There are five basic types of lies that the individual may use when attempting to deceive his interviewer.

The simple denial is the first type of lie, which would seem to be the easiest to carry off by the subject. "I didn't do it." Though its brevity and simplicity on the surface would seem to indicate that it would be chosen often, many guilty individuals avoid denying the incident directly. It seems that a direct denial of involvement creates a significant discomfort internally; psychologists call this cognitive dissonance. To avoid this, many deceptive individuals will go to great lengths to avoid having to say, "No, I didn't do it."

Instead, they will respond to a question that was not asked or talk off the subject, giving an indirect response to a question that simply could have been responded to with a denial. It is important for the interviewer to evaluate each response to a question in light of what was asked instead of simply accepting what on the surface may seem like a good answer.

For example, an interviewer may ask:

Interviewer: "Bob, let me ask you, did you steal that missing deposit?"
Subject: "You know, I didn't even know that that deposit was missing. I had been over in Trailorville at the shop most of the morning working on a tractor we were having problems starting."

Notice, in the previous exchange, the subject never denied stealing the missing deposit, but instead offered a piece of information that was not requested by the interviewer.

The second type of lie, the lie of omission, is the most commonly used by deceptive individuals. It is the simplest lie to tell because the subject merely relates the truth while leaving out information that would prove embarrassing or incriminating. The subject relates a sequence of true events, which, because true, can be told repeatedly in a consistent manner. It is only those details that would incriminate him that need to be left out. If the interviewer offers information that seemingly contradicted the subject's story he can defend himself by telling the interviewer that he "just forgot" to mention those details. A lie of omission can succeed only if the interviewer does not ask the detailed questions to force the subject to commit to a story or to be forced to fabricate one to cover his deception.

The third type of lie is the lie of fabrication. This type of lie is the most difficult for an individual to carry off since it requires inventiveness and good memory to remain consistent. A fabricated lie creates the most stress for the subject, which will result in leakage of deceptive behavior that the interviewer may be able to observe. An interviewer whenever possible should ask questions that will result in the deceptive subject manufacturing a story or details. These manufactured details and events will not hold up to inspection during the investigation since they do not exist outside the subject's mind. If the investigation can disprove the subject's sequence of events or details it may prove as damning as a confession of wrongdoing. Plus, an interrogator who can use the suspect's own lies to challenge him has a significant advantage should there ever be an interrogation.

Unfortunately for the subject, a lie of fabrication requires third parties, documents, or some other piece of nonexistent evidence to support it. Even stories agreed upon in advanced with coconspirators often will contain glaring contradictions and inconsistencies. If an interviewer suspects that the story has been concocted he should carefully ask about the details, which is where the contradictions most often will be found. When most stories or alibis are constructed there will be a discussion about what makes the most sense among the group. The problem then lies in the memories of the participants as they try to recall which variation was finally agreed upon. It is no wonder why there will be variations in the fabricated memories.

The fourth type of lie the interviewer may be faced with is minimization. In using the lie of minimization a subject offers a small admission in hopes that the interviewer will be satisfied and discontinue any further questioning. A subject under the influence may concede that "he had a beer or two," but continued to deny he was intoxicated. A cashier might minimize the admission of theft by acknowledging he took "some change for a soda" instead of admitting to taking a larger amount of money from the safe. In each of the preceding examples the individual's strategy was the same — offer a small, less incriminating admission in hopes that the interviewer or interrogator would be satisfied and discontinue the conversation. Generally, when this type of lie is used it is a strong indication that additional information is being withheld.

The final type of lie is the lie of exaggeration. This type of lie often is found on employment applications where the applicant exaggerates his qualifications and salary at previous positions. An interviewer might also find this type of lie with a witness who exaggerates the violence of an encounter or some other aspect of a conversation. This type of lie essentially uses the truth as its foundation, while exaggerating some aspects of the story.

Investigators also find that lies of exaggeration are used by informants who want to increase the value of their information or the interviewer's perception of the informant's importance. Informants often take some peripheral access to a previous case and through exaggeration, inflate the importance of their role in bringing it to a resolution. Remaining skeptical of the information provided by informants allows the interviewer an opportunity to carefully question each claim, looking for contradictions and places where points may be confirmed through investigation.

Remember that lies told by an individual during an interview can be as powerful as a confession. Subsequent investigation can establish the person's deception and destroy their credibility at trial or in a disciplinary hearing. The interviewer/interrogator must constantly be aware of the possibility the subject is withholding information or intentionally attempting to deceive. Changes in the subject's verbal and physical behavior along with the evaluation of the information offered will assist the interviewer in determining its veracity.

Preparation and Room Setting

Prior to any interview or interrogation there must be preparation for the encounter, both in terms of reviewing the investigative information and arranging the room setting. Most organizations have a policy or procedure for proceeding with investigative interviews or interrogations, which should be strictly followed. Often these policies will lay out the prior notifications required, criteria to interview, and selection of witnesses.

The interviewer should evaluate the subject to identify potential information and the probable level of cooperation that might be expected from the individual. Generally, a cooperative witness is handled easily by an interviewer and usually provides any information requested. However, this is not necessarily the case from all witnesses or suspects in an incident. Depending on the witness' anticipated level of cooperation, the interviewer may select a more or less formal location to conduct the conversation. In instances where the witness's cooperation may be suspect, a more formal interview may be appropriate.

The interviewer should also assess the elements of the crime or policy violation that may be important in proving the case. Questioning and information evaluation becomes easier when the interviewer has a clear idea of what must be proved. This also identifies what is relevant evidence that should be secured. Knowing what must be proved to obtain a conviction or termination assists the interviewer in developing questions to explore these areas more fully.

The interviewer also should be aware of any special areas of concern from the decision makers that also might indicate areas of inquiry. For example, it is not unusual for some decision makers to be concerned about whether or not the individual knew what he was doing was wrong. Once they have expressed this concern the interviewer can now address this area during his questioning and elicit responses that satisfy the decision makers' needs. There may also be less obvious legal aspects that may not be apparent to the interviewer, but may become important in subsequent litigation. Clearly identifying needs and concerns of investigative partners at the onset of the interviews will make each conversation more productive.

Another area of preparation is considering what the end result of the investigation will be. Is the organization interested in prosecution, termination, civil litigation, or some other decision? Knowing the end point of the investigation will allow the interviewer to allocate resources and investigative dollars in the most appropriate fashion. Since there are differing levels of proof in civil and criminal hearings, having an end point in mind helps direct the process.

One question that should always be asked is, "If this person has ever been previously interviewed, interrogated, or disciplined, how did he react?" People tend to fall into patterns of behavior, which either have been successful for them in the past encounters or have become a habit. Being able to anticipate the subject's attitude toward the interviewer/interrogator increases the likelihood of success by selecting appropriate strategies. By recognizing the possible pitfalls the interviewer can choreograph the conversation in ways most likely to assure its success. If the individual tends to react in a rude and aggressive fashion, the interviewer should attempt to find an approach that would avoid this particular response. This could include the selection of the interviewer, location of the interview, and perhaps even the selection of an appropriate witness.

The interviewer/interrogator should also consider whether or not a witness should be present during the conversation. Many organizations require a company witness be present during the encounter. The interviewer should preselect an appropriate witness, instructing him on his duties during the interview or interrogation. In general, the witness is told to sit quietly and observe without joining in the conversation unless instructed to do so by the interviewer. In some cases it may be appropriate for the witness to take notes of the encounter, especially noting times of specific admissions and the confession.

When a telephone interview or interrogation is going to be conducted, the witness may become critical in arranging the room, bringing the employee to the phone, and obtaining a statement. The witness, in this type of case, becomes the eyes and ears of the interviewer/interrogator onsite, handling all those things the investigator would normally do himself.

The interviewer/interrogator should also test any audio/visual recording devices that might be used to document the conversation. There may be background noise that will obscure the conversation, so a test of the system always should be conducted using the anticipated positioning of all parties. The audio/visual recording of an interview or interrogation should be performed only when authorized by an organization's policy and in accordance with state and federal eavesdropping laws.

The interviewer/interrogator also should consider the appropriateness of making an appointment with the subject. Interviewers will often find people much more cooperative when they have set aside time for the conversation; however, interrogators often find that when suspects have time to prepare for the encounter they become more resistant to a confession and difficult to handle. In the case of employee interviews, many of these problems can be overcome by planning with management for the associate's daily schedule, taking into account breaks, lunch, and dismissal times. To conduct a productive interview or interrogation there must be adequate time; sometimes this is just a phone call to management away.

Room Setting

The selection of a setting for the interview or interrogation is often a matter of convenience for the subject. In certain situations the interviewer may be talking with the victim, witness, or suspect at their residence or place of business. In these types of interviews it is difficult for the interviewer/interrogator to control the setting or distractions that may be present. On occasion, these distractions and inappropriate settings can be minimized by prearranging the interview with the individual, but the potential problems must be weighed against this course of action.

Regardless of the location chosen for the interview/interrogation, the overriding concern in preparing the environment should be establishing privacy for the conversation. The individual is being asked to admit to something that he may never have divulged to another. It is always more difficult to tell something confidential to a group than it is to a single interviewer.

Removing distractions also assists in establishing privacy for the conversation. The interviewer/interrogator should attempt to avoid interruptions in the conversation by turning off phones and when possible putting a Do Not Disturb sign on the door. Each of these actions may prevent a break in the encounter, which could disrupt the flow of information and break rapport.

Distractions in an interview/interrogation can vary widely. It could be loud noises from machinery or ringing phones, or as simple as people walking in and out of the room. When the location for the interview has been prearranged and under the control of the interviewer/interrogator, many of these types of distractions easily are avoided. This is more difficult to do when the interviewer/interrogator has no control over the setting because he is visiting the individual's home or place of business.

When selecting an interview room, generally it should be small and uncluttered. The interviewer should prearrange the seating for the subject, himself, and possibly a witness. Often a small table or desk is useful should a statement need to be taken. A room that comfortably holds three or four people is usually fine for the job. In most cases the room will be occupied by the interviewer/interrogator, the subject, and possibly a witness. However, there may be occasions where another party may be asked into the room to witness the subject's verbal or written statement, and having the extra space can be convenient.

Most interviewers will position the subject with his back to the door and the witness slightly behind and off to one side. The placement of the witness in this fashion avoids the distraction of having an additional person in the room and maximizes the feeling of privacy. By positioning the subject with his back to the door, the interviewer minimizes the accusation that the subject was being held against his will. Were the interviewer or witness to position themselves between the subject and the door this allegation would appear much more plausible.

The interviewer should position the subject across from himself without the barrier of a table or desk between them. By positioning the subject in this position the interviewer can observe the subject's demeanor and body language without having a desk interfere with his line of sight. In addition, positioning the interviewer directly across from the subject without a barrier allows the interviewer an opportunity to move closer should the need arise.

If the interview is going to be recorded, the subject's chair should be placed in such a fashion that he can be clearly observed and heard by the camera and microphone. In professional interview rooms often this is done with concealed equipment that does not influence the subject's statements or cooperation. Before using any audiovisual recording, the interviewer should investigate applicable state and federal laws regarding eavesdropping and adhere to company policy on recording interviews.

Interviewer Appearance and Demeanor

Another step prior to the interview or interrogation is to determine the appearance and demeanor of the interviewer/interrogator. The appearance of the interviewer/interrogator should always be clean and professional. The decision to dress up or down for the encounter should be based on the status of the subject and the clothing he normally wears. If an interviewer was going to talk to a senior-level executive it would be proper to dress up to the more formal level chosen by that individual; interviewing an hourly associate might lead to a much more casual form of dress.

Contrary to the detectives shown on television, an interviewer/interrogator is much more likely to gain the cooperation of an individual using a calm persuasive demeanor than an aggressive one. Even when dealing with hardened criminals the softer approach will be much more effective than attempting a hard, aggressive tack.

After considering the elements of the crime or policy violation, personality of the individual, arrangement of the room, and briefing of the witness, the interviewer is ready to begin his conversation with the subject.

CONDUCTING THE INTERVIEW

Understanding and Establishing the Case Facts

Before the interview, the interviewer reviews the available case facts and evaluates the implications of the information uncovered. If there are procedures or events that are not clear from the file it may be useful to conduct background interviews with people who can help the interviewer understand the information. Knowing in advance the process used by the witness to do his job will help the interviewer ask more specific questions, potentially identifying areas where the individual is being deceptive or omitting relevant information.

The interviewer should also evaluate what is known to determine other possible plausible explanations for the subject's actions. For example, a surveillance video observes a member of management removing merchandise from the company and placing it into his vehicle. This certainly could be a possible theft or there could be other less sinister reasons why the manager was putting merchandise in his car. The merchandise could be being transferred, returned to a vendor, or used in conjunction with a presentation, any of which would not be a theft. Before the interview it would be important for the interviewer to determine under what circumstances merchandise might legitimately be removed by employees, and who must authorize any removals. If there were legitimate circumstances why an employee might remove merchandise for transfer, the interviewer should know before the interview what authorizations are required and what paperwork is necessary for that to happen. This information would allow the interviewer to investigate whether or not this was a legitimate action, policy violation, or a theft.

In cases where there is specialized knowledge required the interviewer should conduct sufficient preliminary interviews with subject matter experts so he is familiar with the terminology used, ordinary operating procedures, and documents produced to conclude the task. In certain cases it may be useful to select a person with this knowledge as a witness or at least have him available for consultation during the interview.

Purpose of the Interview

The interviewer should be clear about what information the subject is likely to possess and any potential evidence that may be recovered during the conversation. Clearly identifying what the interview is trying to establish and what is going to be important to the resolution of the case often will point the interviewer to the areas of inquiry.

For example, if the interviewer was going to question the owner of a junkyard about used parts being substituted for new ones at a dealership, the interviewer has a number of areas of inquiry.

- What inventory system does he used to keep track of junked autos and the parts on his lot?
- When a used part is purchased what documents are created and how is payment made? Are signatures required?
- How are the parts removed from the vehicle?
- How are orders for a used part placed?
- How many regular customers for used parts exist in the area? Does a list exist?

- Do any of these regular customers retail used parts?
- Are there any unique serial numbers on the used parts that would link them back to vehicles in his junkyard?

These are but a few of the logical questions that might help provide additional areas of inquiry and identify potential evidence that might resolve the case. In addition, the owner's responses to these questions might identify other interviews that should be conducted to fully investigate the circumstances surrounding the case.

Types of Questions

In an interview, the subject is asked a variety of questions to produce information useful to the investigation. During an interview the subject should do the majority of the talking with the interviewer asking questions only where necessary to direct the individual's story or expand on details. Silence is an interviewer's best friend since most people will continue to talk, to fill the void in the conversation. As the subject continues to talk he often will expand on relevant information or offer new information not yet addressed.

Interviewers will use a variety of questions to develop information during the interview.

Open-Ended Questions. The interviewer uses open-ended questions to encourage a narrative response from the subject. These questions allow the subject to respond, selecting what he believes is important. An open-ended question such as, "Tell me what happened yesterday?" offers the subject an opportunity to tell his story regarding the events without direction from the interviewer. The subject offers his version of events, selecting and omitting details based on what he believes was important. The open-ended question offers the interviewer a framework for his questioning by first allowing the subject an opportunity to highlight what he believes are relevant points.

Expansion Questions. The interviewer, now having the framework of the story, can begin to expand it using the subject's own words. By using the subject's own words, the interviewer does not influence the story by either adding or directing the individual's responses. The subject, during his telling of the story, said, "After we had finished dinner we had a couple of beers and then later on we went to the movies." The expansion question might be, "Now, you said, after we finished dinner we had a couple of beers — what happened during that time?" The interviewer, recognizing that the subject had left something out between drinking beer and going to the movies, seeks to expand the individual's story into that missing time frame. Note that the question uses the subject's own words, adding nothing to contaminate the story, but encouraging the subject to expand on the details himself.

Closed-Ended Questions. Once the interviewer has had an opportunity to create a framework for the story, and expanded it, there may be specific details that must be determined. Closed-ended questions are designed to elicit the specific details. For example, the interviewer might specifically ask for the number of beers consumed. "Exactly how many beers did you drink before leaving for the movies?" Or, "What movie did you see?"

When using these questions, they should be presented in a neutral manner, not offering information, but rather encouraging the witness to provide specific information. It would be much better to say, "What color was the shirt?" than to ask, "Was the shirt blue?" By asking for confirmation of the color blue the interviewer inadvertently may taint an individual's recall or encourage him to provide faulty information not actually recalled. The description of the shirt as blue may require additional questions to understand exactly what color blue the witness saw.

Closed-ended questions are best saved until the end of the interview since they interrupt the flow of the story or sequence of events being recalled by the subject. Once the subject has committed to the overall story the interviewer now asks the specific questions to which he has an interest with less risk of tainting what the subject is saying. This is where the interviewer should make sure that he clearly understands what the subject means by a specific word. "You said he hurried. What did you mean by that?" The witness can now define what he means to make sure there is clarity in the communication.

Leading Questions. In most instances an interviewer should avoid using leading questions with a victim or witness. Many individuals can be extremely suggestible when responding to leading questions. They respond not with an actual memory, but rather with a response encouraged by the interviewer's question. Consider the difference between the words accident and crash. Using the term *crash* implies greater speed and a more violent impact, which could alter the witness's impression of the vehicle's speed and resulting damage. An interviewer should be aware that the younger the victim or witness the more suggestible he may be to altering his story because of the interviewer's leading questions. The easiest way to avoid contaminating the witness's statement is to use his words exactly when expanding the observation.

An interviewer should also attempt to keep his questions simple and to the educational level of the subject. Nothing creates more difficulty than using a compound question, such as, "Did he run through the yard and then jump over the fence?" The potential problem with a compound question is one part of it is accurate but the second part might not be. The witness simply could agree, accepting the inaccuracy, thus tainting the interviewer's impression of the event.

The Final Question. An extremely effective last question in the interview is, "Is there anything else that we should talk about?" This question can also be asked assumptively, "What else is there that we should talk about?"

It is amazing how often people will offer additional information or even make admissions of guilt when faced with this final question in the interview. Attorneys taking depositions often will ask this question to prod additional information from the witness being deposed. Many times attorneys will preface their most significant area of inquiry with the statement, "I am almost done here." This tactic often causes the witness to drop his guard, becoming more susceptible to giving up critical information to the most important areas of inquiry.

SELLING THE INTERVIEW

In some situations the interviewer must convince the subject to cooperate in the interview, which requires that the interviewer provide a reason. In essence, the subject is asking, "What's in it for me? Why should I cooperate?" Many people will provide information simply because they have done nothing wrong and see no harm in cooperation. However, in our litigious society many people are afraid of being drawn into a lawsuit or criminal proceeding that is not of their making. With the uncooperative witness the interviewer must work to encourage cooperation.

With a difficult subject the interviewer faces the hurdle of overcoming the individual's reluctance to cooperate. Most of the time the person has some concern that must be addressed by the interviewer before he can open a dialog with the individual. These concerns could be loss of wages, having to testify, giving up valuable time, retaliation, or even potentially involving themselves in a crime. Essentially, the interviewer must offer some benefit to the subject to encourage his cooperation. In most instances, the benefit provided by the interviewer will be some form of an intangible. These intangibles might include encouraging them to do the right thing, protecting the individual's self image, and on occasion, allowing the person to relieve their guilt.

A little honey goes a long way and an interviewer who is personable and takes the time to develop rapport with the subject is already a long way ahead of the game. People often will go out of their way to help someone that they like or have positive feelings toward. The interviewer who takes the time to express interest in the person and establish rapport will gain significant amounts of information when a more aggressive approach would have provided nothing.

STATEMENT ANALYSIS — THE UNTAINTED STORY

Whenever possible the interviewer should attempt to obtain an untainted story from the subject. As a story or sequence of events is told over and over, additional information is incorporated as a result of questions asked. The resulting story can have significant differences in content and emphasis from its first telling. The first telling of a story or sequence of events is the untainted version. In the untainted story the witness is telling the interviewer what he believes is important and omitting those areas he believes are not. This might be done in an attempt to deceive or it might be done simply as a means of telling the story in an expedient manner.

If a subject was asked to tell an interviewer what happened yesterday he would most likely respond with the significant details of the day. It would be unlikely for that person to tell every single event incorporating every detail that had occurred. To do so would be to tell a story that was unending.

> I woke up at 6:33 A.M. after my clock radio on the nightstand, which is set to WXJL, went off. I listened to one minute of the weather before I rolled onto my right side and pushing up I placed my left foot on the floor before slowly placing my right foot next to it. I felt a small twinge in my lower back that I attributed to the gardening I had done the previous day. I used my right hand . . .

It would be much more likely for someone to tell the story utilizing the highlights of the day:

> I woke up at 6:30 when my alarm went off. Then I went down and had breakfast before I showered and shaved. I got to work about quarter to nine and had a marketing meeting until about 10:30.

In this example the subject is selecting what he considers to be important points relating to what he did yesterday. Notice however, there are significant gaps of information in this telling. How long was breakfast? How did he get to work? How long did it take to get to work? Did the marketing meeting start immediately upon arrival or at some point later?

The untainted story does provide some indication for the interviewer whether or not the subject is being truthful. When evaluating the subject's story the interviewer compares the level of detail that preceded the incident, the incident itself, and the teller's relating of what followed the incident. In the untainted story these three components are likely to be comparable in the length and detail. However, when the untainted story's components are not equal it often indicates an attempt at deception. If the subject was attempting to deceive the interviewer using a lie of omission, thus deleting the incriminating components from his story, the resulting description of the incident likely will be shorter and contain less detail. This will contrast to the portions of the story that preceded or followed the event, which will have greater detail and length. However, once the subject has been questioned repeatedly about the incident it will naturally distort the parts by adding additional detail to the event itself in response to the questions. This does not indicate deception; it is simply a natural progression of a story with the witness incorporating details that were inquired about previously. Because a question was asked, the information requested must be important. Therefore, in the next telling the witness simply includes it so he does not have to answer the same question over again.

A careful examination of the subject's untainted story can assist the interviewer in evaluating its truthfulness and identify areas where omitted information may be sought. Some interviewers will have a subject write the untainted story about the incident in a statement form and conduct an extensive evaluation of the story and language used by the subject. This statement analysis can be effective in eliminating individuals from the incident as well as focusing on the guilty.

FACT GATHERING

Fact gathering interviews are generally one of the most easily accomplished since they primarily revolve around confirming facts and establishing information. These types of interviews seek to answer the questions who, what, where, when, how, and why. The interviewer often has an understanding of what information is available from the witness along with the types of documents or evidence available, so the focus of the interview is very directed.

These types of interviews often are conducted by making an appointment since the cooperation of the individual will be dependent on their ability to make time for the conversation. Since the interviewer merely is confirming or following up a previous inquiry, this interview is usually relatively focused on a particular piece of information. The location selected for this type of interview is often where the witness's access to the document or information is easily achieved.

LIFESTYLE INTERVIEWS

In certain investigations a lifestyle inquiry might be made into the background of a particular individual. Rather than identifying or confirming specific facts, this interview is designed to develop information about how an individual lives. These types of interviews tend to be much more broadly based and may address likes and dislikes, expenditures, travel, personality, and general demeanor.

The lifestyle interview may be conducted with neighbors, family members, friends, acquaintances, and coworkers. The purpose of the interview is to develop an understanding of how the subject lives his life, makes decisions, and spends his money. This type of information may be useful in the interrogation of the subject should he be proved to be involved. Lifestyle information also might be relevant when doing background investigations for preemployment selection.

COGNITIVE INTERVIEWING

Another type of interview is called the cognitive interview. The cognitive interview is designed to assist a cooperative victim or witness in recalling details about a particular incident. Researchers evaluating interviewing techniques determined that although many of the techniques and tactics used during the interview were effective, they were being used in an improper order. Through their research the cognitive interview was developed to take advantage of how memories are made, stored, and retrieved in the human mind.

When storing a memory, the victim or witness must first make the observation, store the memory, and then at some later point be able to retrieve it. There are a number of obvious difficulties in retrieving a memory. First, was the individual prepared to make the actual observation or was it, as in many instances, an unexpected event. Second, where was the memory stored by the individual? It could have been associated with a visual observation, a smell, a sound, taste, or even a feeling. An additional problem that occurs when retrieving a memory is the subject's choice of words to describe what it is that he observed. The interviewer listening to these words must now interpret what the witness actually saw, and the two meanings may differ greatly.

For example, a witness reports an observation of a suspect, "he rushed across the parking lot." What does this actually mean? The interviewer's definition of *rushed* might be entirely different than the meaning intended by the witness. It is important that the interviewer carefully question the individual to clearly understand what was meant by his word choice.

There are a number of tactics that can be used by the interviewer to assist the witness to expand on the story being told. Already mentioned was silence. In general, people talk when there is silence, thus adding information to what was already said. However, silence by the interrogator during an interrogation is likely to result in the suspect voicing a denial or heading off topic. Another simple tactic to add information is to ask, "What happened then/next?" This encourages the witness to continue his description in the same direction he was telling the story. A simple *um hmm* or *OK* identifies that the interviewer is listening and encourages the witness to continue with his story from that point.

Another technique is to logically explore the memory in order of happening rather than jumping from one part of it to another. Jumping around while attempting to retrieve a memory often causes the witness to omit large amounts of information that otherwise would have been recalled. Additional information also can be recalled when a victim or witness makes repeated attempts to retrieve information on the incident. Much like a jogger warming up, the witness is asked to begin his story at a point before the incident was actually observed. This allows the individual to recreate his mental and physical state at the time of the observation. By using the warm up, the interviewer encourages the witness to reenter his state of being at the time of the observation, thus increasing the likelihood of retrieving the stored memory.

The cognitive interview consists of a number of distinct phases through which the interviewer leads the subject. Each of the following are used to enhance the recollection of the cooperative victim or witness.

1. *Establish rapport.* As in most interviews, the first step is establishing rapport with the individual. One of the primary findings of the researchers was that most interviewers neglect this important component, failing to adequately establish a relationship with the victim or witness prior to questioning, which then hinders the freedom of exchange.

2. *Interview preparation instructions.* The interviewer provides the witness with a set of instructions, which effectively prepares the individual to provide complete answers. The interviewer lets the witness know that it is all right to say that they do not know the answer to a question if they do not recall. The interviewer also lets the witness know that if he does not understand a question, he should ask him to rephrase it or use different words. If appropriate, the interviewer will also discuss with the witness how natural it is to be nervous during an interview. It is during this point as well that the interviewer reminds the witness to be as detailed as possible, providing even minute details when they are recalled.

3. *Reconstruct the circumstances.* The interviewer begins by asking the witness to begin his recollection at some point prior to the incident under investigation. This effectively provides a context for the witness's memory and helps with recall. The interviewer reminds the witness to include as much detail as possible about the people who were present, feelings, or other general observations that may seem irrelevant to them. The interviewer reiterates his previous statement encouraging the witness to be as comprehensive as he can in his recollection.

4. *Change of perspective.* Once the interviewer has obtained as much information as possible from the witness's first recitation, he now asks the witness to change the perspective of the observation. This might include asking what he would have seen if he had observed the incident from another position or asking the witness to begin telling the story from a different point. Another effective technique is asking the witness to tell the story in reverse, which often will result in additional details being remembered. The interviewer may also use memory jogging techniques such as asking if the individual observed reminded him of anyone that he knew. The interviewer might also ask the witness to draw a diagram of the incident to clarify certain aspects of his responses.

5. *Closing the interview.* Once the interviewer has obtained as much relevant information as possible, he should attempt to extend the interview with the witness through general conversation or gathering additional biographical information. By extending the interview the witness often will remember additional details regarding the incident. Prior to leaving, the interviewer should give a statement of expectation to the witness. This statement of expectation tells the witness that he will remember additional details regarding the incident because everyone does. The interviewer then asks the witness to commit to reporting these new details. Obtaining the witness's commitment to call often will result in additional information being reported.

COMMON INTERVIEWER ERRORS

There are a number of common errors made during interviewing, the most common of which is interrupting the victim or witness in the middle of a response. This interruption disrupts the retrieval of the memory and effectively discourages the victim or witness from offering information to the interviewer.

In addition to interrupting victims or witnesses while they are responding, many interviewers use closed-ended questions much too early during the interview. Interrupting the retrieval process with closed-ended questions hampers the recovery of memories much like a speed bump reduces the vehicle speed on a road.

Another common error is the use of rapid-fire questions. Asking questions rapidly does not provide an individual the opportunity to completely answer one question before proceeding to the next. A more appropriate use of rapid-fire questioning is in the latter stages of an interrogation, where the interrogator is attempting to develop an admission, rather than in an interview setting.

Finally, another common problem is the failure of the interviewer to adequately establish rapport with the victim or witness. People are much more likely to cooperate or go out of their way for an individual with whom they feel comfortable, rather than someone who expects or demands they cooperate.

BEHAVIORAL INTERVIEWING

Another form of investigative interview is the behavioral interview. Unlike the fact-gathering or cognitive interview, the behavioral interview is designed specifically to elicit verbal and physical behavior from individuals to eliminate them from suspicion. In this very structured interview the interviewer asks questions and observes the subject's verbal and physical behavior along with the content of the answer to make a judgment about the individual's involvement in the incident under investigation.

In many types of criminal activity, such as arson, theft, burglary, or vandalism, there is rarely a witness and only a minimum of evidence available to the investigator. There was one witness, however — the perpetrator of the crime. This interview relies on the guilty party's fear of detection, which alters the body's autonomic nervous system, contributing to a change in the individual's physical behavior. As the body reacts to the possibility of discovery, the guilty subject's body undergoes a series of physical changes. The heart rate, respiratory pattern, and blood flow in the body change to prepare the individual to either fight or flee the threat. These physiological reactions often can be observed, and may provide indications for the interviewer/interrogator to assist in eliminating individuals or focusing the investigation on them.

In addition to physical behavioral changes, a guilty individual's verbal behavior may be notably differently from a truthful person. The interviewer evaluates the content of the individual's answers along with his verbal and physical behavior to determine whether the individual can be eliminated from suspicion. Each question asked in the behavioral interview has a general principle, allowing the interviewer to determine whether the subject is answering like a truthful person or one who is attempting to deceive.

One question often asked by an interviewer in the behavioral interview is, "How do you feel about the company conducting an investigation into the missing deposit?" The general principle applied to this question is that an innocent person will be accepting of the investigation and expect that it will be carried out fully. A guilty individual is much more likely to deny the need for an investigation or be somewhat put out by the company's decision to investigate. The evaluation of the response to this question and others assists the interviewer in eliminating individuals from suspicion, leaving a fewer number of subjects to investigate.

DIAGRAMS

An interviewer's use of diagrams can help clarify the witness's frame of reference and recollections. If a victim or witness provides a diagram to assist in their recollection of the incident, it should always be dated, signed by the witness, and retained in the investigative case file.

The use of the diagram helps the interviewer visualize what it is that the witness observed. The diagram also locks the witness into his story or alibi, possibly opening new investigative leads relating to the plausibility of the observation. For example, a witness may indicate that he observed an altercation on the street from his bedroom window. After diagramming the position of the window and his position near it, the investigator can now determine whether that line of sight actually exists. If the line of sight for the observation does not exist, the diagram now provides damning evidence of the person's deception.

INTERROGATION

Once the investigation has been completed and a suspect identified, it is time to consider how to confront the individual involved. The purpose of the interrogation is to obtain the truth from the individual with details that independently corroborate the investigative findings.

In many cases it will be the suspect's own words that will provide the final elements of proof to successfully close the investigation. The confession is the crown jewel of any case and links all the investigative findings together in a definitive manner that proves the individual's guilt.

The interrogation process is much too complicated for a single chapter to deal with. However, be aware that obtaining a confession is in fact a learnable process that is customized based on the needs of the suspect. There are a number of ways an interrogator may approach a suspect when attempting to get a confession. Many people learn to interrogate by observing another who then mentors their performance and helps them develop their skills. This works well if one happens to have a mentor who understands the process.

Unfortunately, many excellent interrogators who excel at obtaining admissions are less skilled at communicating what it is that they do and why to the student. Becoming skilled at interrogation requires practice, patience, and an understanding of the process and human behavior.

Preparation

The preparation to conduct an interrogation of a guilty suspect is much like preparing for an interview. The interrogator must clearly understand the case facts and the implications of evidence discovered during the investigation. It is important for the interrogator to be familiar with the investigative findings so he does not have to review information during the interrogation. The interrogator should also anticipate the individual's response to a confrontation by having looked at the suspect's past actions.

Next, the interrogator considers potential problems that might occur during the interrogation. By anticipating problems the interrogator either can avoid them entirely or have a plan in place to address them. Although it is impossible to anticipate each and every problem that may arise prior to the interrogation, the interrogator still should consider the more common pitfalls he may encounter.

- What action should be taken if the suspect decides to leave?
- What action should be taken if the suspect asks for an attorney?
- What action should be taken if the suspect demands to see the evidence?
- What action should be taken if the suspect claims that he is ill?
- What action should be taken if the suspect becomes angry or threatening?

The answers to these and other questions will depend on company policy and the evidence available. However, the interrogator is well advised to consider his responses to these pitfalls in advance of encountering them so he has a ready-made plan.

Another aspect to be considered is the company policy regarding confronting an employee. There may be specific notifications to be made prior to the confrontation or policies, which control the interrogator's actions. The interrogator also should identify the criteria that will be used to determine whether or not an individual will be terminated or prosecuted. Clearly understanding the decision-maker's criteria for action will assist the interrogator in determining what information is relevant to include in the suspect's statement.

DECISION TO CONFESS

The interrogator should also understand why an individual might choose to confess or not confess to a crime he committed. It is counterintuitive that an individual would find a benefit in confession since it may result in their incarceration, termination, and loss of reputation.

As children we are taught that confession is the right thing to do, but then there is a punishment that is associated with the confession. It does not take children long to discover that by lying they may avoid punishment for their indiscretion. As people grow up to become adults, this learned behavior is acted upon and they lie to avoid the consequences of their actions as well.

As a result, the interrogator faces a number of hurdles that must be overcome to convince a suspect that there is a benefit to confession. Most suspects are afraid of one or more of the five most common hurdles:

1. Loss of employment
2. Embarrassment
3. Arrest and prosecution
4. Restitution
5. Retribution from others

In general, the interrogator should anticipate that suspects will be more likely to confess, even in light of the hurdles, when a combination of three factors are present. The most common reason individuals confess is because they believed that their guilt is known and the interrogator can prove it. The second most common reason for confession is a desire by the suspect to put a spin on the story to make his position more understandable. For example, the suspect might offer that he was merely going along with others when in actuality he was the leader of the group. This statement allows him to save face even while confessing to the incident. Finally, some people will confess because they feel guilty about what they have done. These reasons, either individually or in combination, are why an individual normally will confess to an incident.

The interrogator must be careful with his language or he may convey to the suspect that the suspect's guilt is uncertain. For the interrogator to say, "We're pretty sure what happened here" could indicate to the suspect that his guilt is not really known and a lie might extricate him from the situation. It would not be unusual for the suspect, in response to the interrogator's previous statement, to offer a denial of involvement while waiting to see what develops.

The interrogator must take into account these three primary reasons why people confess when constructing his strategy and approach to the interrogation. Simply offering evidence without a face-saving device may make it difficult for a suspect to confess even in the face of overwhelming evidence.

RATIONALIZATION

The backbone of the emotional appeal is the use of rationalization, which offers a face-saving device for the suspect. The interrogator bases his selection of the rationalization on the background of the individual. For example, if the interrogator was aware of financial difficulties in the suspect's background, he might use rationalizations based upon financial pressures.

The previous rationalization could be illustrated by stories that portray people making errors in judgment because of financial difficulties. In essence the rationalization is a face-saving device used by the interrogator to make the individual's actions more understandable. The interrogator might suggest through the use of the story that the individual's theft of money was committed because of a need to take care of his family.

The rationalization allows the individual to save face without removing the elements of the crime. The fact that money was stolen to provide for one's family does not change the elements of the crime of theft. Regardless, the suspect has acknowledged permanently depriving the organization of a valuable asset, which establishes an essential element for the crime of theft.

Even when there is significant evidence proving an individual's involvement in the crime, rationalizations will make it easier for the suspect to confess. In essence he will confirm the evidence while being allowed to offer understandable reasons for having committed the crime.

DENIALS

One of the most common difficulties in any interrogation is a guilty suspect who denies involvement. The interrogator must be prepared to handle two forms of denials that will be offered by the guilty suspect attempting to derail the interrogation.

Emphatic Denial

The most common form of denial is the emphatic denial. The suspect, in response to the interrogator's accusation or later during rationalization, simply says, "I didn't do it." Less skilled interrogators often revert to presenting evidence of involvement to the suspect instead of handling the denial. Or, just as commonly, the conversation will evolve into a did-too, did-not debate between interrogator and suspect.

The optimum way for the interrogator to handle an emphatic denial is to stop it before it is verbalized. The interrogator, observing the physical behavior associated with an emphatic denial, interrupts the suspect and continues with his rationalization. If the suspect is able to verbalize the denial the interrogator must reaccuse him and return to the rationalization.

Emphatic denials also can be used as a measure of progress for the interrogator. The interrogator compares the frequency and intensity of the suspect's denial to the one preceding it, thus determining whether the individual is strengthening or weakening his defense. Normally emphatic denials become less frequent and less intense as the individual moves toward confession.

When emphatic denials do not weaken, the interrogator first should change the rationalization to offer a different face-saving device. If the emphatic denials still do not become less frequent, the interrogator should consider presenting evidence of the individual's guilt or backing out of the interrogation.

Explanatory Denial

Another form of denial is called an explanatory denial. In an explanatory denial the suspect offers a reason or excuse why he could not or would not be involved in the incident. In most cases the explanatory denial will be a truthful statement or one that will be difficult for the interrogator to disprove. The following illustrates a properly handled explanatory denial. The interrogator stops rationalizing and asks for an explanation from the suspect. This will cause the suspect to provide an explanatory denial, which the interrogator acknowledges, changing rationalizations and offering a new face-saving option.

Interrogator:	"... and some people just do things on impulse ..."
Suspect:	"That's impossible."
Interrogator:	"Why is it impossible?"
Suspect:	"I wouldn't want to hurt anyone."
Interrogator:	"Great, that's what I thought all along. That just tells me that it was someone else's idea. You know I remember a time when ..."

The following are some additional examples of explanatory denials:

- I wouldn't do that because I wouldn't want to risk my job.
- I wouldn't do that because I don't need the money.
- I wouldn't do that because my reputation is too important to me.

Each of the preceding statements would be difficult for an interrogator to disprove. Attempting to do so merely offers the suspect an opportunity to move the interrogation away from the incident into a nonthreatening immaterial issue. Instead of attempting to disprove the statements the interrogator accepts them at face value and changes his rationalization to take advantage of the suspect's thought process. For example, if the interrogator was talking about the incident occurring because of a financial need and the suspect said he didn't need the money, the interrogator would agree and change rationalizations.

Interrogator:	"Many people have problems because of financial difficulties."
Suspect:	"But, I don't need the money."
Interrogator:	"Okay then, what that tells me is that this was done on the spur-of-the-moment without thinking. Anyone can make a decision that they later regret. Especially when it wasn't carefully thought out ..."

In the preceding example, the suspect offered an explanatory denial and the interrogator immediately agreed and offered a new rationalization based upon an impulsive behavior. The interrogator also could have blamed peer pressure, opportunity, or used some other rationalization based on the circumstances of the case.

METHODS OF INTERROGATION

There are a number of different ways to conduct an interrogation of a suspect. The interrogator's selection of an interrogation method often is based on the background of the suspect, amount of evidence available, and possible response of the suspect to the interrogation. In instances where a number of people were acting together to commit the crime it may be useful to have multiple interrogators available to confront all of them at one time. It usually is preferable to conduct the interrogation in a surprise fashion, rather than alerting the suspects that they are going to be questioned.

Preparing for the interrogation requires that the interrogator had sufficient rooms, interrogators, witnesses, and resources to handle the number of suspects involved in the incident. In larger cases, such as organized theft rings, this may become as much of an administrative problem as an interrogational issue.

Factual

In cases where extensive factual information and evidence is available to the interrogator he may elect to use a factual approach. However, when considering whether to use a factual attack the interrogator should evaluate the amount of evidence available and whether or not it should be revealed to the suspect. In some instances revealing the evidence may compromise informants or other ongoing investigations.

The most effective use of evidence is to contradict statements or assertions previously made by the suspect. The interrogator should ask the suspect questions to which he will likely lie to conceal his involvement in the incident. Once the suspect has been sufficiently locked into his story or alibi the interrogator can now begin to dismantle it using the evidence discovered during the investigation.

The evidence is presented in a nonemotional fashion by the interrogator. The interrogator offers a piece of evidence that contradicts a previous statement by the suspect and asks for an explanation from the suspect. The interrogator usually starts with seemingly insignificant pieces of evidence that are at odds with the suspect's earlier statements. The suspect at first usually will attempt to explain away the evidence until it becomes evident to him that he has been caught as the contradictions mount.

An interrogator using a factual attack generally will get an admission only to the incident he already knows about and not other areas of involvement. The use of facts establishes to the suspect what his area(s) of exposure are and also tells him what the interrogator likely does not know. This then limits admissions into other areas of wrongdoing that were unknown to the interrogator. A second consideration is that using a factual approach alone, without rationalization, means that the suspect must admit to the crime and to the fact that he is a bad person. Combining rationalization with a factual approach often makes it easier for the suspect to confess since he is able to save face.

Classic Emotional

The classic emotional approach to an interrogation does not require the presentation of evidence. In this approach it generally begins with the use of a direct accusation, which accuses the suspect of involvement in a specific issue.

Interrogator: "Our investigation clearly indicates that you are involved in the theft of the missing cargo from the trailer."

Suspect: "No, I didn't do that"

Interrogator: "No, there is no question that you did, but what we are here to discuss is the reason why it happened."

In response to the direct accusation the suspect almost always will deny using an emphatic denial. The suspect often will continue to deny since he has to protect his initial lie. The interrogator will reaccuse the suspect and then immediately turn to rationalization to offer face-saving reasons why the suspect became involved in the incident. It is not unusual for the suspect to interrupt the interrogator's rationalization to offer another denial. The interrogator must be alert for the behavioral clues associated with a denial so he can interrupt the suspect before he can verbalize one.

If the rationalizations are successful, the suspect's denials will weaken and become less frequent while his physical posture becomes much more open. As the suspect internalizes the rationalizations he begins to think about confessing. Outwardly the suspect's physical behavior appears defeated. The head drops, the shoulders round, and the eyes begin to tear as the suspect goes into submission. By observing the suspect's physical behavior it becomes evident to the interrogator that the suspect is ready to confess.

After carefully observing the suspect's physical behavior and recognizing that it is associated with confession, the interrogator offers an assumptive question. The assumptive question is designed to make it easier for the individual to confess. Instead of asking, "You did this didn't you?" the interrogator asks a choice question based on the rationalization. "Did you plan this out or did you do it on the spur-of-the-moment?" The suspect can make one of three responses to this question. He could select either choice or he could continue to deny. Selection of either of the choices is an admission of guilt to the incident under investigation and is supported by the interrogator, "Great, that's what I thought."

The interrogator then begins to develop the admission, answering the investigative questions who, where, when, why, and how. The suspect is locked into the details of his crime and the admission is fully developed into a confession. Once this has been adequately developed, the interrogator then goes on to obtain a statement from the suspect to preserve the confession for later use.

Wicklander-Zulawski Non-confrontational Method®

The Wicklander-Zulawski Non-confrontational Method® is a modified emotional appeal. The primary strategy in this approach is to avoid forcing the suspect into a position where he has to deny his involvement, which makes it more difficult for him to confess later. Instead, the Wicklander-Zulawski (WZ) method takes advantage of the three primary reasons why a person confesses and structures the interrogator's approach to move the suspect from resistance to acceptance without denial.

The first part of the WZ method uses an introductory statement that helps the interrogator convince the suspect that his guilt is known. The interrogator also has an opportunity at this time to observe behavior and identify other areas of criminal activity that the suspect may be involved in. The introductory statement consists of three parts:

- A description of the security function and its purpose
- A discussion of the different methods that could be used to cause losses or crimes
- How investigations are conducted

When adequately done, the introductory statement is a powerful tool to convince the individual that his guilt is known. It also affords the interrogator an opportunity to behaviorally observe the suspect's responses to a number of different methods of theft or crimes. Many suspects will react behaviorally to methods of theft or crimes that they have committed, allowing the interrogator to gather intelligence relating to the scope of the suspect's criminal activity.

The interrogator then moves through a highly structured planned approach using rationalizations and dealing with internal conflicts in the suspect's mind. This approach concludes with the use of an assumptive question called a soft accusation. Instead of the choice question, which essentially gives an admission to what was known, the soft accusation asks for an admission that may expand the suspect's involvement into other areas of theft or criminal activity. The following is an example of the soft accusation.

Interrogator: "When would you say was the very first time that you took money from the company?"

The suspect may make an admission to this question or pause to consider his response. If the suspect pauses the interrogator will use a follow-up question to achieve the first admission.

Interrogator: "Was it your first week on the job?"
Suspect: "No!"
Interrogator: "Great, I didn't think that was the case."

The suspect now has admitted stealing money, but denied that it was the first week on the job. The interrogator continues to develop the admission with the suspect confirming theft of cash prior to the missing deposit. In this way the interrogator is more likely to get closer to the true scope of the suspect's involvement in theft activity than by focusing on the single missing deposit theft of which he was suspected. In the event that the deposit is the sole theft incident the suspect has been involved in, he will confess to that while strongly denying other activities. The interrogator develops the total admission with the suspect and reduces the confession to some permanent form for later use.

There are a number of additional approaches that an interrogator could use to begin the interrogation. These approaches vary in complexity and difficulty so the new interrogator is encouraged to use those described previously before attempting new strategies. More information and examples on these approaches are detailed in the textbook, *Practical Aspects of Interview and Interrogation.*

Backing Out

There may be instances where the suspect will not confess to the incident under investigation. The interrogator should be prepared to back out of the interrogation without obtaining an admission.

Prior to backing out the interrogator should present the evidence discovered during the investigation. On occasion the individual may be able to explain the evidence or provide proof of their innocence. If the suspect cannot provide an adequate explanation for the evidence the interrogation could continue using one of the emotional appeals. Sometimes presenting evidence at this point will cause the suspect to confess or to lie when confronted with it, which may prove damning at some later point.

If the suspect still refuses to acknowledge his involvement after presenting the evidence, the interrogation shifts to the suspect's knowledge or suspicion of who was involved. From there the interrogator either will discuss the individual's suspicion or talk about why he does not believe why the others were involved.

Another way of backing out of the interrogation is to use the behavioral interview, which allows the suspect to begin to talk. The interrogator asks the questions included in the interview and then slowly draws the encounter to a close.

DOCUMENTING THE CONFESSION OR THE INTERVIEW

At the conclusion of the confession the interrogator should consider obtaining a thoroughly documented statement from the suspect, committing him to the details of his admission. The interrogator should link any evidence by having the suspect identify and incorporate that evidence into his statement. It may also be useful to have the suspect create a diagram to clarify points in the statement. If a diagram is created by the suspect it should be dated, signed, and referenced in the body of the suspect's statement.

If there was not a witness in the room the interrogator now should bring in a witness to listen to the suspect's admission and his commitment to the statement's truthfulness. Once the interrogator has had the suspect repeat his confession in front of the witness both the interrogator and witness should sign and date each page of the document. If necessary, the witness also should complete a statement relating to any relevant conversations or observations made while in the interrogation room with the suspect.

CONCLUSION

The process of interview and interrogation is a complex one, which requires patience and practice. The investigator who masters the skills of interview and interrogation will find that his cases are resolved in a much more professional, timely manner. The statements of victims, witnesses, and suspects lie at the heart of any investigation. Preserving the statement or confession in an accurate manner will confirm circumstances, alibis, and the guilt of those involved.

The following are some suggested readings, which will expand on the ideas presented in this chapter.

SUGGESTED READING

Ekman, Paul. *Telling Lies.* Berkley Books, 1985.

Ekman, Paul. *Emotions Revealed.* Henry Holt & Company, 2003.

Ekman, Paul and Davidson, Richard J. *The Nature of Emotion/Fundamental Questions.* Oxford University Press, Inc. 1994.

Ekman, Paul and Rosenburg, Erika. *What the Face Reveals.* Oxford University Press, 1997.

Gudjonsson, Gisli H. *The Psychology of Interrogations and Confessions, A Handbook.* John Wiley & Sons, Ltd. 2003.

Nissman, David M. and Hagen, Ed. *Law of Confessions.* Clark, Boardman Callaghan, 2004.

Zulawski, David E. and Wicklander, Douglas E. *Practical Aspects of Interview and Interrogation, 2e.* CRC Press, 2002.

Chapter 11

Evidence

Evidence is variously defined as (1) the state of being evident; (2) something that makes another thing evident, such as a sign; and (3) a statement of a witness, an exhibit, and such, bearing on or establishing the point in question in a court of law.

Regrettably, the dictionary definition of evidence in the legal sense unduly limits the scope of the definition by specifying "a court of law" as the only body before which witnesses make statements and exhibits are presented. As a matter of fact, in the private sector, a great deal of evidence is developed, presented, weighed, and decided upon in any number of settings other than a court of law.

Take, for example, internal disciplinary action by a company where an employee was discovered consuming an alcoholic beverage on the job and was under the influence of such beverage. Before the human resources department acts, they require evidence to prove that the employee in fact was consuming and under the influence. Evidence would include the empty or partially empty container of the prohibited beverage, the statement of a witness or witnesses, and anything else that would tend to "bear on or establish the point in question. . . ." For instance, upon taking the bottle away from the employee, the security representative could quickly prepare a handwritten statement concerning the taking of the employee's property for safekeeping and have the employee sign such a statement. The scrawled signature of the intoxicated employee is but another piece of evidence.

The human resources department, after examining and listening to all available evidence, then acts in this particular case, terminating the employee. Later, the company could receive notification from a state or federal agency (or even a summons and complaint from a civil court), alleging that the terminated employee was not fairly treated by virtue of his (or her) sex, age, race, color, or creed, and an administrative hearing may be held to determine if the company's action was justifiable. Without the original evidence used to prove the accusation, it is not far-fetched to envisage the employee being reinstated and "made whole" by receiving all back wages lost due to termination. Evidence is obviously essential not only in the court, but also in business and the industrial community as well.

DEMONSTRATIVE EVIDENCE

There are four kinds of evidence:

1. Judicial notice (that which comes to the knowledge of the court, e.g., the exact time the sun set on a given date).
2. Parole evidence (oral testimony).
3. Documentary evidence (writings).
4. Demonstrative evidence (physical objects).

For the purpose of this work, our primary focus will be on demonstrative evidence and, to a lesser extent, documentary evidence. Most physical evidence is found at the scene of the incident in question, be it a pried-open desk drawer in an executive's office, a stolen shirt discovered in an employee's locker while the employee is being taken into custody for the theft of items on his person, the little nook in the corner of the warehouse where the employee was "sacking out" and imbibing, or the smashed plate glass window of the store through which burglars entered and/or exited during the middle of the night. Whatever the case, the scene is examined carefully for whatever evidence it has to offer. Preserving that scene is critical. No one should be allowed to enter or otherwise disturb that scene until the investigator is satisfied that all the evidence has been identified and collected.

If possible, the scene should be videotaped and photographed before anything is removed. If neither method is possible, a sketch of the scene and its relationship to the rest of the area is recommended. Physical evidence removed from that scene can be so noted on the sketch.

Rules Involving Physical Evidence

There are four basic rules surrounding physical evidence:

1. Get all evidence that can have any bearing on the case.
2. Mark it.
3. Properly wrap, package, or preserve to protect the evidence from contamination or destruction.
4. Establish a chain or continuity between the discovery of the evidence and its subsequent presentation.

Get all evidence that can have any bearing on the case. The emphasis belongs on the word *all*. Put another way, get everything that can have a bearing on the case. If everything really boils down to enormous quantities, such as a freight carload of goods, take a sampling as evidence, treat it as evidence, photograph the rest, and simply recover the balance and return it to its proper place. The strategy of getting everything simply ensures that nothing is overlooked or left behind, because once the investigator leaves the scene, unless specific arrangements have been made to preserve that scene, evidence left will be lost, more often than not, forever. If not literally lost, evidence recovered from an unsecured crime scene during a later search can also be figuratively lost by being excluded from use because the investigator cannot assure the court or hearing officer that the evidence was either there at the time of the first search or remained in an unaltered state until found during the second search.

Remember that, at least in the area of evidence collection, too much is better than too little. From that overabundance one can pick and choose what should be presented in a hearing or in court.

Mark it. The marking of evidence ideally should occur when and where it was discovered, within reason, of course. That is to say, if a crowbar was left on the ground beside the forcibly entered boxcar, the investigator is not obliged to stop in his tracks and mark the crowbar right then and there, but it should be marked prior to its removal back to the office.

Minimally, the marking should be the initials of the investigator and the date. If possible, the case number could be included. This marking must not (1) in any way affect the evidentiary value of the object; or (2) damage or deface or take away from the value of the object.

Avoiding such damage may require some care. In one shoplifting case, an expensive ladies' handbag had been recovered as evidence. It was lined with a light, melon-colored silk fabric. The investigator noted her initials and date with blue ballpoint pen on that lining, rendering the handbag a total loss. Proper identification of the evidence is simply a matter of using some imagination when applying the markings. See Figure 11.1.

If it is not possible to mark on the items, then attach a label and mark on that. If the item is too small to mark on or to attach a label to, put it in a small container, seal the container, and mark on it. Again, if possible, photograph or videotape the small item in order to minimize the need to open the sealed container for a gross visual (as opposed to a microscopic) examination. Marking serves the obvious purpose of making it possible to positively identify the object later, during an administrative or judicial hearing. The investigator may be asked, "Is this the shirt you say you found in Mr. Martin's locker?"

Figure 11.1. Marking physical evidence.

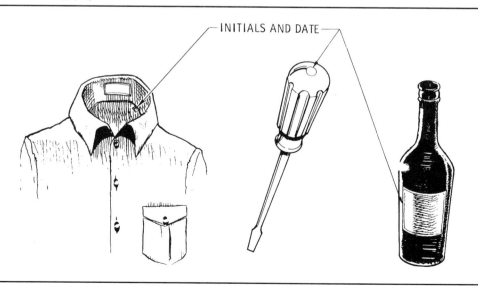

The investigator responds, "Yes, sir."

"Are you positive this is the shirt and not one like it?"

"I'm positive it is the shirt."

"Absolutely positive?"

"Yes, sir."

"How can you be so positive?"

"When I found this shirt in Mr. Martin's locker, I took my pen and placed my initials and the date right here inside the washing instructions tag in the tail of the shirt. Here it is, right here."

Properly wrap, package, or preserve to protect the evidence from contamination. If the evidence is of a fragile nature, such as glass or a plaster of Paris cast, or if the evidence is easily destroyed, such as a plastic or latent fingerprint, great care should be taken to ensure that when the package is reopened the evidence is not destroyed. Common sense gives direction here. If there is a question, seek advice.

Establish a chain of continuity between the discovery of the evidence and its subsequent presentation. Accounting for the uninterrupted control of the evidence is referred to as the "chain of custody" or the "chain of evidence." The so-called "chain" is the inked documentation of each person's possession of that evidence by name, time, and date. The shorter the chain (or the fewer the people who handle it), the better. Ideally, the chain would be only one person, the one who discovered, collected, marked, packaged, carried, and locked it in the vault, and subsequently retrieved it from the vault and carried it to the hearing. The inked documentation (so as to avoid erasures) should be on the outer container or package as well as noted in the investigation file itself.

The evidence storage must be completely secure to prevent the evidence from being altered, damaged, or stolen. Even well-respected law enforcement agencies have found themselves ruing their failure to properly restrict access to evidence storage. The O.J. Simpson vehicle evidence lot fiasco will be long remembered as a classic example of this kind of failure. Ensuring the evidence storage integrity will keep the careful investigator from being forced to explain to the judge and jury why such poorly protected evidence should be relied upon.

Reading Physical Evidence

The condition or state of physical objects can have a great deal to tell us if we come to understand how to read their messages. From the presence or absence of sap (or moisture) at the fracture side of a tree exposed to the sun, natural laws offer valuable information. And the natural laws are not restricted to wilderness areas. They are in play all around us. Take, for example, the dropping of a liquid substance on the floor. The marking of the substance will tell us if it fell at 180 degrees from its source straight down, or if it fell at less or greater than 180 degrees from its source at a slanting angle. If the liquid struck the floor or pavement at 180 degrees, its source was motionless, standing still. If the liquid struck at an angle, its source was moving, and the marking tells us in which direction the source was moving (see Figure 11.2).

Direction of movement on foot is ascertained by one of two types of footprints. A plastic print is an actual depression of the print, such as in mud or snow, which can be preserved by taking a casting, preferably a plaster of Paris casting. A surface print is visible due to a shade or color contrast, such as the print made with a wet, bare foot on a dry surface or the prints left on a dusty surface. The only way to preserve surface prints is to photograph them with oblique lighting to highlight the contrast.

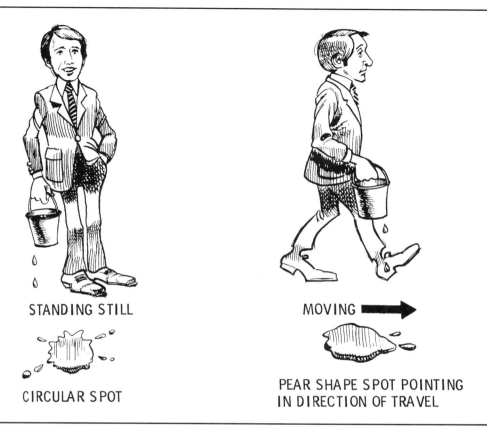

STANDING STILL

CIRCULAR SPOT

MOVING ➡

PEAR SHAPE SPOT POINTING
IN DIRECTION OF TRAVEL

Figure 11.2. Liquid spots.

Two ways to determine the direction of a moving vehicle are shown in Figure 11.3.

Investigators in the private sector frequently are required to investigate incidents on company property, which involve damage to glass. The following points could be helpful:

1. Due to the tensility of glass, high-velocity projectiles (bullets) make a hole generally smaller than the bullet that passed through.
2. Bullets create a cone, without radial and concentric fractures, and that cone is on the opposite side of the glass from the entrance of the bullet (see Figure 11.4).
3. The faster the projectile, the smaller the hole (e.g., a .22 caliber hole will be larger than the hole made by a 30.06 bullet).
4. Larger and slower-moving projectiles knock out portions of glass and leave radial and concentric fractures (see Figure 11.5).

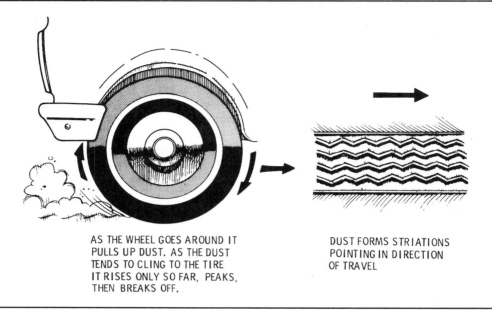

AS THE WHEEL GOES AROUND IT
PULLS UP DUST. AS THE DUST
TENDS TO CLING TO THE TIRE
IT RISES ONLY SO FAR, PEAKS,
THEN BREAKS OFF.

DUST FORMS STRIATIONS
POINTING IN DIRECTION
OF TRAVEL

Figure 11.3.   Vehicle direction.

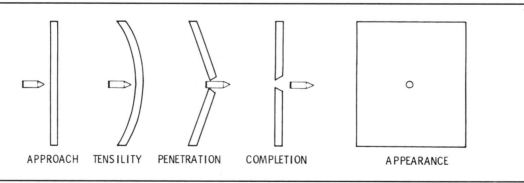

APPROACH   TENSILITY   PENETRATION   COMPLETION   APPEARANCE

Figure 11.4.   Bullet striking plate glass.

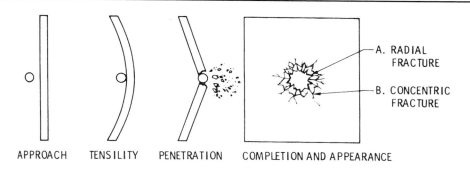

APPROACH   TENSILITY   PENETRATION   COMPLETION AND APPEARANCE

Figure 11.5. Nonbullet striking glass.

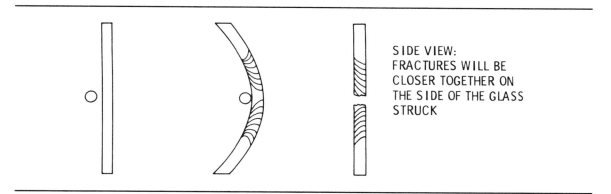

SIDE VIEW:
FRACTURES WILL BE
CLOSER TOGETHER ON
THE SIDE OF THE GLASS
STRUCK

Figure 11.6. Determining which side of glass was struck.

5. Examination of a side view of a broken piece of glass will reveal which side of the glass was struck (see Figure 11.6).

Fingerprints

The evidentiary value of fingerprints has long been established and deserves a word here. There are three types of fingerprint impressions:

1. The visible print.
2. The plastic print (physically imprinted into a material such as putty or paint).
3. The latent print (not clearly visible or discernible until dusted with contrasting powders).

Some investigators in the private sector are very knowledgeable about the science and mechanics of fingerprinting, and can dust, raise, photograph, lift, classify, and make comparisons and identify prints, and they do so in their security roles. This specialized field is, in actuality, in the realm of the public sector. When and if a technician's services are needed, the security department's role should be to safeguard the area and call on the public sector to do the job. If the nature of the investigation does not warrant police involvement but a fingerprint technician's services would be helpful, then hire one on a part-time basis.

What kind of case would *not* warrant police involvement but would warrant a fingerprint technician's services? One example could be the discovery that some unauthorized employee is getting into files that contain sensitive or otherwise confidential information. A very clean obstacle could be placed in a position that blocks access to the files of concern. At the end of the day, or the following morning, that obstacle could be removed carefully and dusted for latent prints. There are any number of such noncriminal problems that must be solved in the work organization, and the evidence of fingerprints can be one of the many strategies used by the security department.

Creativity and Physical Evidence

If there are no tree limbs, saplings, or brush of any kind that can be trampled or broken, signaling that someone has passed through, or no stones on a path that can be disturbed, then create your own signals. Have you ever folded up a very small piece of paper and pinched it into place between the door and jamb, exposing a tiny piece so that, when you returned later, you could tell if someone had opened the door or not? How about running a thin thread a foot high off the floor, tacked down, or in some other way secured in place? Someone passing through or entering would inadvertently break that thread and never know it. The odds are against ever having taken regular baking flour and gently blowing it over a surface with the intention of returning later to inspect that surface with a flashlight. The oblique angle of the light would highlight footprints of whoever walked on that surface. We are too often limited by our own imagination, or the lack of it.

The Case of the Rainy Day Burglar.   An interesting example of observable evidence was a case in which a burglar barely escaped apprehension inside a ten-story department store late one night. The building was surrounded, and for the trapped man to exit the store would have resulted in capture. It became apparent to all that the burglar would wait it out until the store opened its doors to the public at 10:00 A.M.

At about 5:00 A.M., just before the housekeeping crew arrived at the store to start their day's work, it began to rain. All the employees who arrived for work carried umbrellas or wore raingear. Customers started arriving just before 10:00 A.M. They too carried umbrellas and wore raingear. The burglar had been in the building hiding for over 12 hours. He would want to get out as soon as possible. He probably did not know it was raining and would not know it until he left his hiding place. If he did not have rain gear when he entered the store, he would be conspicuous once he mingled with the customers. If he did have raingear, it would be dry.

Every exit was covered by security. Five minutes after the store opened to the public, a man attempted to exit the store wearing a bone-dry coat. It had to be the burglar. It *was* the burglar.

DOCUMENTARY EVIDENCE

In our commercial society, paperwork in all its many shapes and forms lends itself to a variety of manipulations requiring private sector investigative, if not police, involvement. The three most common problem areas in documents are:

1. Anonymous communiqués such as extortions, threats, sexual invitations, sexual harassments, accusations, or notes informing on someone within (or out of) the organization.
2. Counterfeited or altered documents and negotiable instruments such as company bank checks and payroll checks, severance vouchers, raised money orders, gift certificates, and such.
3. Forged signatures of customers, in credit card cases, of company officers in payroll or accounts payable sections, and so on.

The one thing these three areas have in common is the question of *who* is responsible.

Anonymous Communiqués

Anonymous letters or notes are usually computer-printed, typed, or handwritten. "Cut-outs," that is, messages made up of words or letters cut out of magazines and pasted onto a blank sheet of paper, are not common in the private sector. The printed and typed anonymous letters usually are sent to management, and the handwritten notes are more often sent to specific individuals of the company, not necessarily to someone in management. The printed and typed letters tend either to be demanding (i.e., unless the company does so and so, something bad will happen) or they are informative (i.e., "I think you should know . . ."). Handwritten letters tend to be threatening, abusive (usually sexually abusive), or sexually suggestive.

In terms of evidence, the letter and its envelope usually have been handled by at least two or three people before they ever land on the desk of the responsible investigator. If a series of letters arrive from the same source, the handling can be reduced to the investigator. Depending on the nature of the case, he may choose not to open the envelope but rather transport it to the public sector authorities for examination by the crime laboratory and fingerprint technicians. There is a three-phase process in anonymous letter investigations:

1. Examination of the material used.
2. An analysis of the content of the message.
3. Comparison of suspect handwritings or suspect printers and typewriters.

Examining the Material. Careful examination of the envelope flap after you gingerly unseal it and the reverse side of the postage stamp may reveal traces of lipstick. If the letter is sexually abusive to a female, and lipstick is on the envelope, it could be a jealous coworker who is hiding her identity by pretending to be a male author. Other examples of evidence include the postmark (i.e., where it was mailed from), the kind of paper used, and where that same paper can be found. Is it available in the office? Is the paper a quality paper with water-marks (easily seen if the paper is held up to the light)?

Analyzing the Content. What is the author of the letter trying to do? Is the intention clear or disguised? If we understand the intention or objective of the letter, does that narrow down possible authors? Does the language of the letter, in terms of style, choice of words, sentence construction, and so on give any clues? Do the grammar and spelling reflect a poor or good education? Is the author revealing information that only a very few would know? Is the general message realistic (possible) or a fantasy?

Comparing Handwritten, Printed, or Typed Samples. By the time you get to the third phase of the investigation, one or more possible suspects will have been identified. If the letter is handwritten, then handwriting samplers of the suspects will be compared against the letter. A good source of samplers (known writings of a given person) can be the security department's employee bonding file. If more handwriting is necessary, the personnel department's file on the employee or the employee's immediate work area could prove productive. Those files also presumably will contain more recent examples of the employees' writing. If the suspect is not an employee of the same company as the investigator, the security department of that suspect's employer might prove helpful. If the suspect is unemployed, then perhaps one or more educational, financial, or retail sources may have his handwriting on record. If handwriting samplers are needed, they can be found.

Because our handwriting, our penmanship, is learned early and practiced regularly, it develops very specific and identifiable idiosyncrasies by way of habit. Even if we try to hide our writing (usually done by writing with the opposite hand or writing very small), habit creeps in. In a way, handwriting is like fingerprints: No two are identical. The good investigator need not be a questioned document examiner or expert to make comparisons between the sampler and the suspect letter and find identical characteristics on both. That is not to say that analyzing handwriting is simple. It is to say, however, that anonymous letter authors are relatively easy to identify, primarily because there is a good deal of material in the letter to compare. Forgeries are another matter altogether. Typewritten anonymous letters are more difficult in terms of identifying the author. What usually happens, once possible suspects are identified, is that the typewriter on which the letter was typed is located, especially if the machine is on company property. Determining who typed that letter on that machine may not be possible. But the knowledge that a given area of the company is discontented, or that someone in that area is trying to tell management something, can be helpful.

Typewriter comparison, preferably done with a low-power microscope, is more exact than comparing handwriting, because the identifiable characteristics are mechanical in origin. A flaw in the letter "W," as an example, be it caused by accident, during repair, or at the time the particular key was cast in the factory, will consistently be there. And the likelihood of other "Ws" having the same flaw and striking the paper at precisely the same pitch and with the same spacing before and after it, when it strikes, is more than remote.

Computer-generated printed materials provide a different set of problems, which nevertheless can be overcome. Because the ink-jet and laser printing methods do not rely on impact, there are no individual surfaces to be compared as in the flawed "W" just discussed. The questioned document examiner can still do much in advancing the case using other techniques.

As with typewriting, the computer printing comparison will focus on defects in the output. Document examiners frequently will consult the various technical bulletins posted by printer manufacturers on the Internet that detail the precise kinds of defects known to be associated with particular printer models. Being attuned to such identifiable defects allows the document examiner to eliminate many kinds of printers and, based on the equipment inventory within the company, virtually may focus the investigation on one or two offices or individuals.

Other kinds of defects may be more transitory in nature. For example, one print head nozzle of an ink-jet printer may be clogged, leaving telltale artifacts in its output. Gathering and comparing documents from known sources dating from the approximate time frame of the questioned document's origination can also lead the investigation in the proper direction.

Another method sometimes employed in trying to tie a particular document to a small number of suspects is a technique known as orthography, which studies the unique styles with which individuals create documents. As an example, in non-Spanish-speaking regions, the ~ (tilde) is rarely used and most computer users are unable to easily place it into documents. In consequence *señor* most typically is drafted as *senor*. A search of documents that properly use the unusual typographic symbols found in the questioned document may well lead to a specific individual.

In the case of ink-jet documents, although possibly expensive, laboratory analysis of the ink may assist in determining the ink manufacturer and even the printer make.

In some cases, the questioned document examiner, through a thorough knowledge of the development of certain printing and computer technology, will be able to provide significant insight on documents. For instance, let us suppose that a particular contract or letter dating from 1988 is presented as being a genuine claim against corporate assets. Should a document examiner determine that it was printed using a resolution of 600 dots per inch (dpi), she would be able to declare that it could not be genuine by knowing that it was some years later that printer resolution moved from 300 dpi to 600 dpi. Remember, most anonymous communiqués in the private sector are not reported to the authorities. The exception is letters of extortion. The police or FBI will take the letter(s) and envelope(s) as part of the documentary evidence for their case. Security files should contain copies of those letters.

All other anonymous letters should be retained in a specific "anonymous letter" file. If the author is identified and the case is classified under some other category for record-filing purposes, a copy of the original anonymous letter should still be in the anonymous letter file with a reference to the case number. Upon receipt of an anonymous letter, it can be compared to others that have been received over the years. The person who sends an anonymous letter this year may do so again next year.

In one such case, the letter writer, who openly admitted employee status with the company, sent four letters to management over a period of about seven years. These letters were usually complaints about facility conditions or specific supervisory practices; one was information about internal dishonesty. The anonymous employee felt duty-bound to report conditions to management. The interesting thing about that case was the ease with which we could identify the letter as yet another from the same person, even after a lapse of one or two years. The author used the same typewriter, misspelled the same words, used the same format, underlined words, and used the same exclamation mark with the same frequency, and so on. Although we never identified the employee, we came to trust the author and took seriously his complaints or information.

Counterfeited or Altered Documents and Negotiable Instruments

The best evidence in a counterfeiting or altered document case is, again, in the comparison of the good against the bad. The whole array of commercial documents subject to counterfeiting or alteration is beyond the layman's imagination until it is pointed out. Redeemable coupons, scrip notes, refund forms, gift certificates, expense vouchers, payroll checks, accounts payable checks, tickets for passage, and admission tickets are some of the documents or instruments that can be altered or counterfeited.

Although it is not directly related to the discussion of evidence, a word must be said about the necessary strategy in this area, which is threefold: control, comparison, and reconciliation. Control includes quality controls in the printing process; for example, ink colors are stable and consistent so that variations are conspicuous; control by serialization (if appropriate); and control by distribution, that is, meting out given quantities to specific individuals on a need basis with the balance protected by lock and key, use of indicia or signature, and so on. Comparison can be effected by way of samplers appropriately displayed where the media can easily be compared against such samplers. Counterfeiting or alteration also can be detected by reconciliation of the negotiated instruments against the disbursement record; for example, gift certificates numbered 0001 through 0100, all cashed for $100.00, should be reconciled against 0001 through 0100 as issued for $100.00 each.

Forged Signatures

In my wallet are six credit cards, all of which have a place for my signature. I refuse to affix my signature on any one of those cards. Why? If I should lose one of those cards, why should I provide a sample of my signature for the criminal user to copy?

Credit cards probably constitute the bulk of forged signature problems in the private sector. The forged sales check or tab is documentary evidence itself. Further evidence is the handwriting of the forger, in terms of those peculiarities of his handwriting that tend to surface even when writing someone else's name. Another interesting bit of evidence is found in those cases where the forger inadvertently signs his own full name, or own first name, or starts to write his own name and then corrects it to the forged name. If the true party's name is Mrs. Donald Crossen and the forger starts to write a capital "B" instead of "D," habit has forced her to commence writing her own first name, which in this example could be Barbara, Betty, Beverly, or any other such name. That is certainly an important investigative key, but more importantly, it is powerful evidence.

Once the forger is in custody, a handwriting sampler, at least a full sheet, should be taken. Contained therein would be the name forged, as many times as possible. If the forger is willing, a whole vertical column of the forged signature would be desirable. A handwriting expert could testify that the signature on the document was written by the same person who wrote the sampler.

SOME RULES AND DEFINITIONS OF EVIDENCE

Not only must the investigator appreciate and understand the importance of evidence as a tool of the reconstructive process, she must also be sensitive to its ultimate value as proof of culpability. Further, there is invariably some misunderstanding or confusion over evidential terms. Let's consider the following shoplifting scenario as a means of illustrating common terms for better understanding.

A young woman, a college graduate, enters a store, and a store detective observes the following: The woman approaches the handbag department, tears the price tag off the hand strap of a new bag, drops the tag on the floor after wadding it up, then places the items from her old handbag into the store's bag and sets her old bag among the display. She then selects four blouses and enters an enclosed dressing room. She comes out of the dressing room, carrying only three blouses, and hangs those three on the rack. A quick check of the dressing room reveals an empty hanger.

At this point the woman is carrying another store's shopping bag, which appears to contain merchandise. When she entered the dressing room she was carrying only the handbag (plus the four blouses on hangers). She leaves the store without paying for the handbag, and the detective is confident she also stole a blouse. She is approached and detained. She admits the theft of the handbag and one blouse.

The case described involves direct evidence, circumstantial evidence, and physical and material evidence.

Direct evidence also is known as parole evidence, that is, oral testimony. It is always a result of the witness's direct observation or what that witness heard, felt, or smelled. Testimony of the detective's observation of the purse switch is direct evidence. It is a powerful form of evidence because it tends to prove a fact; in this case, the fact that the woman took merchandise without paying for it.

Circumstantial evidence is just as potent as direct evidence *if* the accused fails to provide contrary evidence. In our shoplifting scenario, the theft of the blouse is circumstantial evidence because the detective did not actually see the theft. The circumstances strongly indicate a theft occurred.

Indirect evidence and presumptive evidence are the same as circumstantial. Physical evidence is any object connected with the matter at hand. In our example, physical evidence would include (1) the stolen purse, (2) the abandoned purse, (3) the crumpled price tag that was removed from the stolen purse, (4) the blouse, and (5) the paper bag used to conceal and remove the blouse. Real evidence and demonstrative evidence are the same as physical evidence.

Material evidence is that which tends to prove *part* of the issue. It is material that the culprit assumed unlawful ownership of the purse by transferring her personal effects from the old bag to the new one.

Immaterial evidence is considered to be unimportant and not germane to the issue. The fact that the culprit is a college graduate has nothing to do with the issue of shoplifting. How much money she had in her wallet is also not germane and is immaterial.

Competent evidence is responsible evidence; sufficient to prove a given fact has a bearing on the issue, for example, the removal of the price tag by the woman. Relevant evidence is that which relates directly to the matter, for example, the culprit's admissions of theft, the discovery of the empty hanger, the sudden appearance of another store's bag with contents. Obviously, materiality, competency, and relevancy are very similar.

Best evidence applies only to documentary evidence or writings. Sometimes there is confusion in applying this term; for example, having the actual purse or blouse in the hearing room, instead of a photograph, because the objects are the "best evidence." Best evidence means the actual documents, not facsimiles or copies.

A FINAL WORD ABOUT EVIDENCE

In his text on criminal investigation, James Gilbert makes a point that underscores the thrust of this chapter and is worth repeating here: "Evidence is anything properly admissible in a court, that will aid the function of a criminal proceeding in establishing guilt or innocence. There are many different types of evidence, having different degrees of importance. In general, evidence that is inanimate, or nonhuman, is valued more highly than evidence involving human beings. This is due to the fallibility of the human condition (e.g., loss of memory or purposely altering the truth)."[21]

Bearing this reality in mind, the effective investigator, while seeking out anything and everything that bear upon a case, will place the strongest emphasis and reliance on his own direct observations and on hard physical evidence.

Chapter 12

Written Statements, Admissions, and Confessions

Anyone who conducts investigations as a professional vocation will find himself or herself interviewing hundreds, and probably thousands, of people in the course of a career. In most instances what the person describes simply is noted and reported by the investigator in a memorandum or report. In some cases, however, the investigator will wisely choose to have the individual's information reduced to a written and signed form.

Why is it generally considered a good practice to obtain properly prepared, signed statements from witnesses and suspects? Here are some of the reasons.

1. The witness formally commits to a specific account of the events and observations reported. This raises the comments above the level of mere gossip or chat and properly is accorded more weight and relied upon as more probably truthful than a passing comment. The witness can hardly later claim that the information was passed on in jest or was not intended to be believed.
2. The witness is provided a carefully considered opportunity to measure the words, phrases, and impressions conveyed in her testimony.
3. The witness is able to examine exactly what is to be reported that she stated and endorse that rendition as hers.
4. The witness's memory over time may fade regarding the specific events described in the statement. The statement can be used later as a means of refreshing the witness's memory from her own recollections, and avoids a skewing of her memories as a result of being influenced by reading another person's version of events.
5. Other readers of the statement, such as human resources executives, company attorneys, and investigative managers, can get a true flavor for what the witness had to say without any undue concern for filtering or coloring (albeit generally unintentional) by the investigator.
6. In the minds of third parties, such as arbitrators, judges, unions, and juries, a written statement is virtually incontrovertible proof that the witness or suspect in fact did relate certain information to the investigator.
7. The statement, in certain instances, can be introduced in court as evidence.

WRITTEN STATEMENTS

A properly obtained written statement, and written confessions are a specialized kind of written statement, follows from a properly conducted interview or interrogation. Assuming that the interview has identified all the relevant information available from a particular witness regarding a particular subject, the investigator should commence the preparation of the written statement.

Some witnesses may be somewhat reluctant to provide a signed statement, even after they have fully disclosed the information they know. This attitude can frequently be changed if the investigator offers a plausible reason why the statement is necessary. Seeing the hesitation of the witness to prepare a written statement, the investigator can say, "You know, we've just spent a good amount of time discussing all the things you know and you've given me so much valuable information that I don't want to accidentally misstate what you said to me in my report. Why don't we just take a few more minutes to make sure I get it right?" We have also used a variation of the same theme to get witnesses and suspects to prepare written statements by adding, "You know, I've interviewed so many people in this investigation that their information is sort of running together. Help me be accurate and make sure that I only report exactly what you had to say, no more and no less."

If a written statement is to be fully useful, the investigator should consider including all of the following elements:

1. Identify the author. The information should be explicit enough so that only one person could be the author. Name, date of birth, place of birth, social security number, home address, place of employment, and occupation, as well as even a spouse's name are all factors that can be used to specifically identify a witness or suspect.
2. Date, time, and place. The statement should explicitly identify the date, time, and place where the statement was prepared. This can often be accomplished in the signature area.
3. Voluntarily provided. The statement should explicitly include language that the witness has provided the statement free of compulsion, promise of leniency, or other inducement. It can also document that the person has not been mistreated.
4. Knowing and intelligent. The statement should indicate clearly that the person understood that the statement was being prepared and what was being placed into the statement. The statement also should state that the witness has read all of its contents and made all necessary changes.
5. How statement was derived. The statement should indicate how it arose. A sentence that says the statement was provided to the investigator as a result of the information provided during an interview places the statement into an accurate context for later readers.
6. Close. The statement should contain an affirmation that the contents of the statement are in fact true, correct, and voluntarily provided. It should be signed and dated (including the time) by both the witness and the investigator.

The physical form of the statement can vary greatly; however, some guidelines for both written and word processed statements follow.

1. The statement, if written, should be prepared on lined paper with the text running from the left margin to the right-hand edge of the paper. This prevents any additions to the text at the end of any lines.

2. If the text runs more than one page it should be written so that the text from the last sentence of each page flows onto the first line of the next page. This will assist in reducing claims that pages were somehow added to the middle of the text.

3. Any inaccuracies found by the witness in the text should be lined through and corrected, with the witness initialing each change.

4. The witness should affix his initials before the first word written on each page and after the last word on each page. After the full text of the statement is finalized, in the left-hand margin of each page the witness should affix his signature or initial, the date, and the page number in a format such as "page 1 of 2 pages."

5. If, as often occurs, the statement is actually prepared by the investigator for the witness to sign, care should be taken that the language used mirrors as closely as possible the words used by the witness. The language found in a statement from a very simple laborer with only an eighth grade education will naturally differ from that included in the statement from a college professor. To use professional jargon, words of legal art, or sophisticated terms in such a situation later will be used as an argument that the laborer could not have understood what was being written and signed.

6. Before beginning the preparation of a written statement, ascertain that the witness can read, write, and fully understand English or the language in which the statement will be written. Do more than merely ask the witness if this is true as many illiterate persons in fact are accustomed to concealing this deficiency. Before he signs the statement, have him read it aloud. A surprisingly effective way to prompt this is simply to state that while concentrating on the detailed preparation of the statement you may have missed something and you want to "hear how the whole thing sounds." This is also a good test to ensure that the witness has no trouble seeing what is to be signed. This would later be a problem that must be remedied if the witness wears reading glasses or has any other vision problem.

7. Reiterate during the statement preparation through questions that the witness is not intoxicated, under the influence of drugs, or suffering any mental problem that prevents her from understanding what is being done and what is actually in the statement. Consider including some indicator of this ability in the statement. A simple example, "I am completely sober and have not consumed any drugs or alcohol in the last twenty-four hours."

ALLOWABLE USES OF STATEMENTS

In general, testimony that Marshall told Larry that Milton did something illegal cannot be used in court as a means of proving that the recounted event actually did happen. Generally, the parties before the court have the right to question Marshall directly before the trier of fact (the judge or jury) to determine the accuracy and truthfulness of Marshall's assertions. This is the basic premise of the hearsay rule. In effect, there is no value normally accorded to Larry's testimony that he heard Marshall *say* a certain thing about Milton.

The fact that Marshall even may have put in writing what he told Larry does not change the fact that the hearsay rule will prevent Larry from testifying against Milton by offering Marshall's statements as evidence of Milton's guilt. After all, unless the trier of fact can weigh whether Marshall could be lying, it should not blindly accept the truth of what was said. The right to confront one's accuser accorded to Milton is also enshrined in the constitutional law of the United States as well as the common law of England and the United States. It is difficult to confront a piece of paper.

The hearsay rule would therefore appear to render useless the taking of written or oral statements, at least as far as their utility in court. This would be so but for important exceptions to the hearsay rule that are generally granted by the court to allow the statements to be admitted.

The first exception would come into play if Marshall were to provide testimony to the court that was somehow different from what he earlier had told Larry. The prosecutor could then attempt to prove to the court that what Marshall was now saying differed from the truth. This is known as impeaching the witness's testimony. The prosecutor may enter, through other witnesses, direct and circumstantial evidence that Marshall's new version of events is suspect. One piece of that evidence that could be allowed would be Larry's testimony that Marshall had made a prior inconsistent statement. The written and oral statements given by Marshall to Larry are then allowed as impeachment evidence and Larry may testify about them.

The second exception to the hearsay rule of interest to investigators is where Marshall made admissions against self-interest. In other words, Marshall said that certain things were true that could be harmful to his own interests. In the earlier situation, Marshall's statements, being against Milton's interests, could not be entered as evidence against Milton. However, if they did implicate Marshall himself as being a willing and full participant in the criminal acts with Milton, or in other prohibited conduct by Marshall acting alone, they could be introduced as an exception to the hearsay rule in proceedings against Marshall.

The underlying premise for this exception is that such self-incriminating statements can be relied upon as truthful (under certain conditions) because it is illogical that a person would lie if doing so would bring harm to himself. A third exception to the hearsay rule, one unlikely to be of use with regard to statements collected by private sector investigators, is commonly known as a deathbed confession or dying declaration. Say, for instance, that Larry heard a gunshot and upon rushing to investigate found Marshall dying of a bullet wound. If Marshall were to say that Milton had shot him, his statement would be considered a dying declaration and probably given weight in the subsequent trial against Milton. This exception requires that the person uttering the declaration must believe that he is about to die. It is not important that he actually does die. The exception is premised upon the belief that a person would not wish to die with a lie on his lips and that such statements can therefore be generally believed.

There is no question that an admission of guilt or a full confession, when reduced to writing and signed, is impressive evidence. Even if not always usable in criminal trials, in the other types of decisions made on a daily basis by private parties, such admissions or confessions are given great weight. In a matter of discharge, if a person has made a confession to theft, it is possible for the employer to reasonably rely solely upon that fact as the reason for firing the employee (as long as the confession is otherwise believable). In most cases of both criminal and employment significance, that single piece of evidence is and always will be the deciding factor. Conversely, its absence has undoubtedly served the culprit's best interests in many cases, much to the chagrin of both public and private investigators.

As a matter of fact, the admission (a relatively brief statement admitting culpability with no reference to intent) and the confession (a comprehensive written narrative with details of the offense, including intent and sometimes motive) are so potent, in terms of their damning impact on the accused, that the United States Supreme Court and a host of lesser judicial bodies have come to focus on these

P.J.

My name is Paul Jones, and I live at 475 Seaview Crest Road, Harbor Shoals Beach. My date of birth is March 17, 1978 and I am employed as a warehouseman at Dynamic Frozen Foods, Inc. I am freely giving this statement to Mr. Charles B. Wilson who is an investigator with Dynamic Frozen Foods, Inc. I have been stealing frozen food products from Dynamic for the last nine months.
(in late April, 2004) P.J.
It started out one night when I mistakenly dropped a case box of frozen lobster tails from a pallet in freezer room no. 2. It broke open and some of the boxes were smashed. Earl Marshall and I were working together that night and we decided that we didn't want to get into trouble for breaking it. We split the case up, each of us took three boxes of lobster tails. About two weeks later we were working alone again, that night we each took a forty pound case of frozen filet mignon steaks. We started taking food pretty much every Friday night, every time we would each take a case of meat or seafood. I knew
forty-five P.J.
this was wrong. I think we each have taken about ~~thirty-five~~ cases of food: about half of it was filet mignon steaks and the other half was lobster, crab, or shrimp. I have read and fully understand this one page statement which I wrote, and I marked all needed changes with my initials. I was not forced to give this statement and Mr. Wilson has treated me well. All that I have written in this one page statement is true to the best of my knowledge and belief. P.J.

Page 1 of   Signed, Paul Jones, January 22, 2005, 1:25 p.m.
1 page.   **Witness: Charles B. Wilson, 1-22-05, 1326 hrs.**
P.J.

Figure 12.1. Handwritten confession statement containing corrections and evidence that it was knowingly and voluntarily given.

documents, with particular attention directed toward *how* they were obtained. In detecting what would constitute abuses of one's constitutional rights, the Supreme Court has laid down specific guidelines for officers and investigators in the public sector. Such guidelines — to repeat, for the public sector at this point in time — must be complied with to qualify admissions or confessions as legal and admissible items of evidence in criminal courts of law.

HISTORICAL BACKGROUND

At the beginning of my career in law enforcement, in the early 1950s, trickery, coercion, and even strategies that were psychologically or physiologically abusive were common in obtaining confessions. One technique that struck us as the epitome of deceit was having the investigator pose as a priest; we can recall a discussion in one of our college classes of an actual case of this type. But in those days there were simply no constraints upon law enforcement officers in this area. Deception, and worse, were accepted practices. The same unconstrained "freedoms" were similarly enjoyed in the private sector.

Early Court Decisions

It became evident in mid 1955, with the California Cahan decision, that the pendulum had commenced its swing away from this gathering of evidence through deceit. That landmark case made evidence inadmissible if illegally obtained. In its Cahan decision, the court reacted to what it considered an abuse, the "bugging" of the defendant's bedroom. Charles Cahan was suspected of bookmaking. Thereafter, the public sector of law enforcement became increasingly more limited in its power to search for and seize anything of evidential value. However, those constraints were on the public sector, which "represented the sovereignty of the state," and did not in any way constrain search and seizure in the private sector.

In 1963, the rights of the private sector were challenged but ultimately upheld in yet another California case, *People v. Victoria Randazzo*, 220 Cal. App. 2d. 768, which said that the rule that evidence obtained in violation of constitutional guarantees against unreasonable searches and seizures is inadmissible does *not* apply to evidence obtained by a private person unconnected with government law enforcement agencies. This meant, of course, that investigators in the private sector had a great deal more freedom in gathering evidence than did their cousins in the public sector.

Then, in 1964, in *Escobedo v. Illinois*, the United States Supreme Court took the position that when an investigation changes from a general inquiry into an interrogation, the suspect must be advised of his constitutional right to remain silent and must be given legal counsel if it is requested. The evidence of incriminating statements and confessions was placed under new constraints — but again, not for the private sector!

The 1966 *Miranda v. Arizona* decision went even further than *Escobedo* by requiring the advisement of constitutional rights at the time of arrest, certainly much earlier in the law enforcement process than the formal interrogation. The 1967 Supreme Court decision in regard to *Cault* extended the right to legal counsel to juveniles.

The private sector's immunity from the "Miranda rule" has been tested but the position has remained essentially the same: If the private sector investigator is a private citizen and is not deputized or in any other way affiliated with governmental authorities, he need not advise a subject of his rights.

The Zelinsky Decision

At the time of the Cahan decision in 1955, it was not possible to see clearly the outline of things to come on the horizon. In 1979 there was a California decision that appeared to forecast dramatic impact on the private sector. The case in question is another California Supreme Court decision, *People v. Zelinsky*, 24 Cal. 3d. 357, 1979. Because of the magnitude and potential impact of this case, the facts, as well as some of the court's language, should be of special concern to private security.

The facts of the case were commonplace enough. The defendant, Virginia Zelinsky, was observed by Zody's (a department store) security personnel to place a blouse in her purse, put a pair of sandals on her feet and a hat on her head, and then place her purse inside a straw bag. The defendant then purchased a pair of shoes and left the store without paying for the other items. She was detained and brought back to the security office, where she was subjected to a pat-down search for weapons by Zody's security. After the pat-down, her purse was opened and the blouse retrieved by a security agent. A pill vial, later discovered to contain heroin, was also found. Zelinsky was convicted of possession of heroin and appealed that conviction to the California Supreme Court.

The language of the court in commenting on the case deserves close attention:

> The people contend that the evidence is nevertheless admissible because the search and seizure were made by private persons. They urge that *Burdeau v. McCowell* (1921), 256 U.S. 465, holding that Fourth Amendment prescriptions against unreasonable searches and seizures does not apply to private conduct, is still good law and controlling.
>
> Defendant contends, on the other hand, that only by applying the exclusionary rule 21 to all searches conducted by store detectives and other private security personnel can freedoms embodied in the Fourth Amendment of the federal constitution and article 1, section 13 of the state constitution be protected from the abuses and dangers inherent in the growth of private security activities.
>
> We have recognized that private security personnel, like police, have the authority to detain suspects, conduct investigations, and make arrests. They are not police, however, and we have refused to accord them the special privileges and protections enjoyed by official police officers (see *People v. Corey* (1978), 21 Cal. 3d. 738). We have excluded the fruits of their illegal investigations only when they were acting in concert with the police or when the police were standing silently by (*Stapleton*, supra, 70 Cal. 2d. at p. 103). We are mindful, however, of the increasing reliance placed upon private security personnel by local law enforcement authorities for the prevention of crime and enforcement of the criminal law and the increasing threat to privacy rights posed thereby. Since *Stapleton* was decided, the private security industry has grown tremendously, and, from all indications, the number of private security personnel continues to increase today. A recent report prepared by the Private Security Advisory Council to the United States Department of Justice describes this phenomenon in the following terms: "A vast army of workers are employed in local, state, and federal government to prevent crime and to deal with criminal activity. Generally thought of as the country's major crime prevention force are the more than 40,000 public law enforcement agencies with their 475,000 employees. While they constitute the . . . most visible component of the criminal justice system, another group has been fast rising in both numbers and responsibility in the area of crime prevention. With a rate of increase exceeding even that of the public police, the private security sector has become the largest single group in the country engaged in the prevention of crime." (Private Security Adv. Coun. to U.S. Dept. of Justice, LEAA, Report on the Regulation of Private Security Services, 1976, p. 1.)

The court's conclusion, with but one dissenting vote, was that the evidence (the heroin) was illegally seized and therefore inadmissible. Zelinsky's conviction was reversed. This meant that the exclusionary rule was to apply to private security agent searches.

Ourselves to Blame

How did we in the private sector reach the point where the court system felt an obligation to protect the citizenry from us? Because, intentionally or otherwise, we had abused our prerogatives. As a case in point, also a California case, in *People v. Haydel* the court held that security agents acted improperly in holding an employee and the employee's wife, caught in the act of theft, for a period of five and one-half hours. The couple's small child was with the mother at the time she was taken into custody, so the child was, literally speaking, also in custody. During this period of time, the security investigators obtained four written statements from the employee. One document suggested that the wife and child would be set free in exchange for continued cooperation. Such was not the case.

Although the employee and his wife were caught "red-handed" in the act of theft, and additional stolen goods were recovered from their home, the court reversed their conviction of larceny, using the following interesting language:

> A confession's inadmissibility may stem from civilian as well as police coercion. . . . He signed the second statement after being tricked into the belief that it would free his wife and child from captivity. Section 847 [referring to the California Penal Code Section that spells out the private person's authority to arrest] directs him to take the arrestee to a magistrate or peace officer without unnecessary delay . . . the well-trained and well-financed private security forces of business establishments are heavily involved in law enforcement. . . . The entire process of arrest, detection, incommunicado interrogations, and extraction of signed confessions was the indissoluble product of the arrest under color of state law. The exclusionary rule applies here. . . .

An otherwise excellent piece of investigative work was irrevocably lost in this case because the investigators held their subjects too long and used some deception in gaining the employee's signature to statements. The lesson is clear: Abuses lead to constraints.

TYPES OF CONSTRAINTS

Constraints on Public Sector Investigators

Investigators in private security should be fully cognizant of the constraints, as they pertain to admissions and confessions, under which those in the public sector must operate. They are as follows:

1. Confessions may not be obtained through the use of threats or violence. They must be free and voluntary.
2. Confessions may not be obtained through inducements or promises of leniency.
3. Persons from whom confessions are sought must be informed of their right to remain silent and of the fact that anything they say may be used against them in court.
4. A person suspected of a crime has the right to obtain the services of an attorney, retained or appointed, before making a confession. He must be informed of this right. Interrogation must not be started until the arrival of the attorney if the suspect indicates that he wants legal counsel.
5. A suspect who decides against an attorney may, nonetheless, refuse to answer questions, in which case the interrogation must cease.

6. Police who claim that a suspect has waived any of his rights prior to making a confession must be able to prove that the suspect was fully informed of such rights, that he understood them, and that he or she did knowingly and intelligently waive those rights. The waiver should be written if at all possible. The waiver should spell out the warnings that were given, and should include a statement that the suspect understands and is voluntarily waiving the warnings.

Constraints on Private Sector Investigators

Constraints on representatives of the private sector are currently limited to only two:

1. Confessions (and admissions) may not be obtained through the use of threats or violence. They must be free and voluntary.
2. Confessions may not be obtained through inducements or promises of any kind.

We consider such so-called constraints to be absolutely necessary as well as reasonable, a position most professional investigators in the private sector would agree with.

The problem and danger we see on the scene today are the tendency of some private sector investigators to go beyond these constraints. Specifically, many are now applying the Miranda rule to subjects in their custody. As we stated twenty years ago in our first edition: This must not be done. We should not "Mirandize" anyone unless we are legally obliged to, that is, security personnel who are deputized, commissioned, or have peace officer status. For us to Mirandize now, when it is not legally required, will only set unnecessary, unwanted, and confusing precedents that could accelerate or otherwise cause legal imposition, on those of us in the private sector, of all those constraints now in force in the public sector.

Imagine what problems would surface if we were obliged to advise every person of his constitutional rights! If an employer (and security is the employer's representative) catches an employee with his hand in the company till, in the act of a crime, must the employee be advised of his constitutional rights? Would such constraints preclude the private sector from handling criminal activity as a crime? What of employees caught in borderline criminal behavior, such as padding their expense accounts? Must they also be advised of their rights? Would not the advisement of rights somehow interfere with the normal, necessary, and expected communication between management and employees? If an employee's misconduct is grounds for discharge under company policy, such as the consuming of alcoholic beverages on the job and being under its influence, must that employee be advised of his rights? If an employee wants an attorney, who is to provide one? If an outsider is in the custody of security and that outsider wants an attorney, who provides one? Must security advise people of their rights if criminal prosecution is not considered necessary or desirable?

These and other questions could be paralyzing issues, opening a Pandora's box of problems we do not want or need. The self-imposition of all the public sector's constraints in our private arena is truly foolhardy.

Thankfully, in the years since the Zelinsky decision, the courts have not forced a Miranda requirement on private sector interrogations. Two narrow exceptions have been sometimes recognized: (1) when a specific statute or city ordinance confers police powers on private security officers who detain someone and question them, and (2) when the company investigator, acting in concert with and under the direction of the police, questions a detained individual. These applications of Miranda are less an intrusion of Miranda into the private sector as a recognition that it applies when the private sector investigators intrude themselves into the public sector by becoming agents of the government.

Weingarten Rights

In 1975, the U.S. Supreme Court decided a case that has specific impact only in the area of unionized workplaces. In that case (*NLRB v. Weingarten, Inc.*, 420 US 251), the court imposed upon unionized employers the requirement to allow employees, who have asked for union representation, to have a union representative present at any investigatory interviews that the employee reasonably believes may result in disciplinary action against him.

Although the court did not impose an absolute requirement that the employer make an advisement of rights to the employee similar to the Miranda warnings, in practice some corporations routinely issue such warnings so as to protect against later claims that the employee's Weingarten Rights were violated by the employer. In addition, bargaining contracts between unions and employers may actually require an affirmative warning of Weingarten Rights. Therefore, investigators questioning union members on behalf of their employers should definitely determine the corporate policy in this area prior to starting, especially if there is any reason to think that the particular employee may develop into a suspect during the course of the investigation.

CONFESSIONS AND ADMISSIONS

The Written Confession

Complying with the existing two constraints on private security in the matter of admissions and confessions is simple. Don't threaten, don't use force, don't suggest dire consequences, don't make deals, don't "trade" a concession for a confession. Do solicit absolutely free and voluntary admissions and confessions, and build in the proof of voluntariness in the subject's written admission or confession.

The following contains an example of a typical written confession made to an investigator in the private sector. Note the choice of words that set the tone.

Such a statement should withstand the test of scrutiny in any judicial or administrative hearing. Consider how much this statement tells:

- The author
- The date it was written
- The time it was written
- Who actually composed the words
- How it came about (subject being caught in the act)
- When he first got involved in trouble
- His estimate of the frequency of similar incidents
- His estimate of quantity taken

Statement of Jack J. Doe

I, Jack J. Doe, employee of Ruiter Air Service, make the following statement of my own free will, without duress, threats of any kind, or promise of any reward or immunity, this 19th day of December, 2001.

This evening, at about 9:00 P.M., December 19, 2001, I was in the process of filling my car's gasoline tank from the Ruiter Air Service's pump located in the service yard when I was approached by Mr. Rice of the Security Department. He asked me what I was doing and I told him he caught me taking gas that was not mine to take. At that point, I had taken eleven (11) gallons. We then came to Mr. Rice's office where he asked me about previous incidents in which I took gas from the company. I told him the first time I took gas was in the spring of 2000, during that period when gasoline prices first skyrocketed, I remember that first night I took exactly five (5) gallons because I was low and had a date over in Middleton. I was afraid to alter the pump record because it could easily be discovered. I just cleared the pump reading each time with my key.

I've taken over five (5) gallons a week ever since then. Mr. Rice asked me to compute that loss. I figure at the most, five (5) gallons a week for eighty (80) weeks, which comes to 400 gallons. I understand our cost is presently $1.59 per gallon. My calculation is I've taken $636.00 worth of gasoline from the company and if given the opportunity, I'd like to make restitution.

I know I'm going to lose my job and I deserve to. I truly regret what I have done, but at least I feel better now that it has all come to light and is over. This typed statement was the result of my conversation with Mr. Rice, which took place in his office here at the Ruiter Air Service administrative office. He then typed it up. I've read it and it says what I want to say. Again, this is my statement that I voluntarily offer and Mr. Rice has been very fair with me tonight. (Signed) Jack J. Doe, 10:40 P.M., 12/19/01

Witnessed: Sidney R. Rice, Asst. Security Manager 19 Dec 01

- His calculation of the financial loss to the company
- That the relationship with security was positive
- That the statement was made and signed freely and voluntarily
- That no threats or promises were made

The tone of the statement, which is sincere, is a true reflection of the subject's attitude at the time the statement was made. This usually does not change appreciably. If he later challenges his statement, he will have an uphill struggle because of its tone. It would be hard to perceive a villainous security investigator behind this statement. To add to its voluntary quality, we suggest that a word be omitted in one sentence and that another word be misspelled. Have the subject correct these errors in his own hand and initial the corrections. The sample confession by Jack J. Doe printed earlier is narrative in format. Another acceptable format is the question-and-answer. For example: Mr. Rice: "Think back. Can you recall for me the very first time you took gas?"

Mr. Doe: "Yes, I remember it was on my girlfriend's birthday on April 22 last year. I remember the first time. We had a date in Middleton and I was running late and low on gas. I took exactly five (5) gallons."

We personally favor this format over the narrative. It does, however, require the presence of either a stenographer or tape recorder, with subsequent transcription.

Printed Versus Handwritten Statement

Computer printed statements are preferable if the subject makes corrections and initials them. Why this preference? Printing is easier to read, has a more professional impact, and suggests that time was not a factor (because computer input is quick). It also allows the investigator to assist in composition, which is acceptable as long as it is so noted in the statement.

THE WRITTEN ADMISSION

The written admission may be the only signed, self-incriminating document the investigator can obtain. Whereas the written confession is usually signed at the conclusion of the interrogation, and is frequently reduced to a typewritten document, the admission is taken early in the interrogation, in the handwriting of the subject, and is limited to a simple statement of guilt. Its advantages include these factors:

1. It is secured right after the verbal admission of wrongdoing, which is an emotional peak for the subject. In the eyes of the subject, the simple written sentence or two is no different than the oral admission, so there is less reluctance to sign.
2. If, after some time passes, the subject decides he does not want to sign a confession, the investigator at least has the admission, as opposed to having nothing.
3. Once the admission is secured, its existence tends to mitigate against any later reluctance to sign a full statement, or confession, the logic being, "I've already signed once, so what's the difference?" Typically, an admission comes about in the following manner. The investigator, while on surveillance, observes an employee take a $20 bill from the cash register and put it in his shoe. The employee is taken in custody to the executive offices. Upon being advised that he was observed stealing, he produces the folded bill from his shoe.

Investigator:	(Unfolding the bill) "I appreciate your sensitivity to the problem, Bill, and also appreciate your spirit of cooperation. You said you took it, but you don't know why. That's an important statement. Would you please make that statement here for me? (He hands Bill a tablet of paper and a pen.)
Bill:	"You want me to write that down? Here?"
Investigator:	"Please. Just the way you said it to me."
Bill:	"Why do you want it?"
Investigator:	"I want it as part of my investigative file. I'm not asking you to write down anything that's not true, or anything you didn't say or do, am I?"

Bill: "No, that's what I did and said all right."

Investigator: "Okay. Just put down what you said, but start with the word 'tonight,' because it did happen tonight, right?"

Bill: "Right."

Bill then writes out in longhand or even prints his brief admission, which reads, "Tonight, I took $20 from the register and I don't know why." Bill shows the statement to the investigator.

Investigator: "Good. Now date it. Today's date is June 10, 2001." (Bill dates it.) "Good. Now sign it for me if you will, please."

Bill signs the admission and hands it to the investigator. The investigator signs the document, dates it, and affixes the time of day after the date.

The investigator now has a signed admission of a breach of company rules (improper removal of company funds), the primary concern of the private sector investigator, as well as an admission of theft (a public offense), which may or may not be a matter placed before the judiciary.

VIDEOTAPED CONFESSIONS

Another form of confession documentation is a videotaped session. This is not the norm in most investigations and should be approached very carefully. Even though it does assist in establishing the overall demeanor of the subject at the time of the confession, and in fact may be used to document the fact that the subject was not threatened and understood what was placed into the final statement, it can create certain problems. For instance, the review of a videotape for content is very different than for a printed transcript or written statement, even preparing a statement usually requires the transfer of the audio portion of the videotape onto audio cassettes.

Also, to use videotape on one interrogation and confession may well establish a virtually permanent practice for an organization in all interrogations. Otherwise, one can expect to have to explain why video was not used in another interrogation. The defense may try to imply that the investigator has something to hide about how the interrogations in a nontaped session progressed. One virtue of consistently using videotape is that it acts as an additional deterrent to an investigator carelessly crossing the bounds of professionalism. Knowing that a camera is running actually can act to keep both parties civil and professional, although it can initially inhibit the subject from making admissions.

VALUE OF THE CONFESSION

There is divided opinion over the value of confessions. Charles E. O'Hara, a noted authority and author of the fine text *Fundamentals of Criminal Investigation*, says, "There is a tendency on the part of even professional investigators to exaggerate the value of such a confession and to misinterpret its significance. The written confession does not, for example, prove the matters to which it pertains."[22] He goes on to point out that confession is difficult to get into evidence and that the normal defense is that the confession was obtained by duress, and so on.

That controversy or difference of opinion over the value of confessions rightfully belongs in the public sector. In the private sector, there is no question whatever of the importance of signed statements admitting misconduct or dishonesty. A statement taken from one private person by another private person is an entirely different matter from the situation in which an officer of the law takes a statement from a citizen. In the public sector, such statements serve but one objective: to help sustain a criminal conviction in a court of law. In the private sector, such a statement supports and justifies the action of the company (e.g., discharging employees, terminating contracts, arresting customers) and may or may not be used to help sustain a criminal conviction in a court of law.

How many times has a shoplifter, for example, having been found not guilty in a court of law (where conviction requires evidence beyond a reasonable doubt, the determining factor in criminal law), then turned around and sued the store for false arrest or false imprisonment? In many such cases, the existence of a signed admission of guilt either has discouraged pursuance of the action, or the action has weighed heavily in the preponderance of evidence (the determining factor in civil law) on the side of the defendant (the store).

Written admissions and confessions, then, are an offensive strategy in the public sector where the objective sought is a conviction. In the private sector they are defensive (with offensive capability), and are thus a necessary and valuable strategy.

Chapter 13

The Use of Informants

In a later chapter devoted to the *where* in investigations, our focus is primarily on sources of information in both the public and private sectors. Just about anyone has access to information available in the files of the county recorder, the registrar of voters, municipal court records, bureau of vital statistics, and so on. A variety of data in privately held files are also readily available to any legitimate investigator.

As valuable and indispensable as these general sources of information are to the investigator, private and confidential sources are even more important. Such confidential sources commonly are referred to as *contacts*. Who are they? According to Fuqua and Wilson, "Contacts are people willing to provide information which the investigator would not normally have access to."[23] That distinction alone separates confidential sources from the generally available sources. There are other important differences. Investigative sources, such as those described in Chapter 18 will provide data that could lead to locating a suspect. A private source, or contact, can tell an investigator where the suspect is. The information contained in certain records might well suggest the motive for an act or crime, such as arson, but the right contact can tell the reason with absolute certainty. Records and documents might indicate or even prove that a given incident occurred before or after a specific date; the contact can advise as to the precise time. General sources of information might unfold a pattern upon which an investigator could predict future acts, such as thefts occurring while the supervisor is on a day off, but the informant can provide the specifics of the next planned crime. A contact or informant, furthermore, can advise of individuals who are actively engaged in misconduct or theft when such activity is unknown to management or security.

Suffice it to say that the development and maintenance of good informants have great value for the private investigator as well as the public law enforcement counterpart. O'Hara speaks not only of the pure value but of the productivity of such sources of information: "One informant in the San Francisco area is responsible for an estimated 2000 arrests a year, mostly in narcotic offenses."[24]

PROFESSIONAL CONTACTS

The first category of private sources are professional contacts. They are, for the most part, other investigators or security personnel and security executives. As a rule they provide confidential information only when it is solicited directly.

At first blush it may seem inappropriate to classify other investigators as "private sources," but the validity of this premise becomes clearer when it is held up against the Fuqua-Wilson definition cited earlier. On examination it should be evident that investigator A, working in the public transportation industry, will not automatically obtain the information he desires simply by calling investigator B, who works on the opposite side of the country in the heavy manufacturing industry. There is a very real and legitimate professional restraint that inhibits the passing of information. And investigator B, not knowing investigator A on a personal basis, may very well be hesitant about providing information that the inquirer "would not normally have access to."

On the other hand, there is an equally powerful, unwritten professional code that requires investigator B to assist if possible. How does he resolve this dilemma? More often than not he will refer to a professional publication, such as the membership directory of the American Society for Industrial Security, to verify investigator A's identity and status. If no listing is found, investigator B may refer to the cross-referenced listing of A's employer to determine if any member of that company belongs to or is listed in the directory. If he locates another name, B may call that individual and confirm A's identity. He may even go so far as to advise A's associate of the request for information and inquire if such information is necessary and should be released. Then, and only then, B may provide the information sought. The point is that not many people normally have access to what B has in the way of information; it isn't "readily available."

Where individuals or companies are known to each other, the sharing of information on a private basis is more readily accomplished. An investigator of one company may come into possession of valuable information he will wish to share with another company. For example, during the course of an investigation in company A, information is developed that an employee has a boyfriend who is employed as a receiving clerk in company B. That boyfriend is discovered to be working in collusion with a driver of a trucking firm. The employee of company A is selling to coworkers, at a very low price, merchandise stolen by her boyfriend from company B. An investigator in company B ends up as the recipient of some very valuable and sensitive information from an investigator in company A — a professional source of private information.

INFORMANTS

The second category of private sources are private contacts, more popularly known as informants. It is possible to classify at least eight types of informants:

1. One-time informants
2. Occasional informants
3. Employee informants
4. Anonymous informants
5. Criminal informants

6. Personal informants
7. Mentally disturbed informants
8. Controlled informants

It is by no means a great exaggeration to say that many of the most significant investigations undertaken by a corporate investigator will originate from or be aided by informants. The proper use and management of informants is a crucial skill for the professional investigator to master, but the topic normally is neglected in the formal teaching of the craft. In many respects informants are similar to witnesses, except that generally an informant is unwilling to have it widely known that he is providing information.

By far, the controlled informant represents the greatest potential for producing prodigious amounts of intelligence compared to all other types of informants. We will discuss at length, next, how to properly develop and manage the controlled informant.

The One-Time Informants

The one-time informant usually has very specific information and is anxious to see that information acted upon. The motive behind providing the information commonly is based on moral grounds, that is, what is happening is wrong. These informants give a lot of thought before acting. They are usually nervous about what they are doing, and they seek assurances that their identity will not be disclosed. Some see the act of informing as a civic duty or in keeping with their religious convictions. One-time informers may be employees (who are discussed later as a separate general classification of informants), and if so they tend to view the passing of information as good for the welfare of the company. This is particularly true if the employee has a vested interest in the success of the enterprise. Another variation on motivation for the one-time informant is revenge. The informant may be seeking to get even with someone for a slight or a wrong; evening the score is viewed as "the right thing to do."

In most cases it is difficult to gather additional information from the one-time informant after the initial contact, although not impossible. The difficulty lies usually in the informant's "second thoughts" about involvement. This is not always true. A few such informants are so committed to seeing the matter resolved that they become quite participatory. In one case an informant, a female resident of a nearby community, went through the typical soul-searching. She initially called and stated that one of our employees, whom she identified by name, lived on the same block as her own residence. She stated that the employee in question was using and dealing in marijuana. According to her testimony, the employee was also stealing goods from the company and had a quantity of stolen merchandise in his garage.

What bothered this informant most was the fact that she had two impressionable sons who had always looked up to the employee, who was now bragging about his newly acquired wealth and how easy and profitable it was to steal. Although the informant's fear for her own safety was secondary to her concern for her children, she felt strongly that, if the employee discovered she had informed on him, violence would follow. She was reluctant to stay in touch and provide additional information until she caught her younger son with marijuana. The mother then was fiercely determined that the employee should be brought to justice. Thanks to her, the thief was apprehended and convicted. We never heard from this informant again, although it was later learned that the convicted man moved out of the neighborhood after he got out of jail. The occasion and the circumstances prompted the woman in this case to become a one-time informer.

The Occasional Informer

The occasional informer is an opportunist who will pass along information from time to time, usually if and when it satisfies some need. This is the person who will inform on a supervisor if the supervisor's demise offers an opportunity to advance. Or he may be one who secretly envies the investigator's role in the organization (and in life) and seeks recognition and praise from the investigator or security administrator. Becoming an informant is a way of identifying with the security organization. One clear example of this type of informant was a young college student who had been shunned by a fraternity. He liked to hang around the campus police office and occasionally would provide information about illegal or improper conduct on the part of that fraternity or its members. He acted not so much for revenge as for the acceptance he felt he received from the campus police chief for that intelligence.

Whatever the motivation — which is rarely financial — the occasional informant should be quietly encouraged and praised. He should be made to feel like part of the investigative team. That encouragement alone will go a long way.

The Employee Informant

Although it is true that an employee may be a one-time informant or an occasional informant, employees as a group deserve very special attention and consideration because of their potential as sources of intelligence. This is one category of persons who can effectively be solicited to inform through a structured program.

In any given work force there are employees who either strongly suspect or definitely know of dishonesty in the organization. Some of these employees do not approve of coworkers who steal or condone their dishonest activities. In many cases the frustration experienced by the honest employee who sees others getting away with theft leads to resentment against company management for its failure to stop the thievery. Yet management may be completely ignorant of the existence of any wrongdoing. This type of situation quickly erodes morale. It is not uncommon for the honest but frustrated employee to reason, in effect, "What the hell, if others are doing it and no one cares, I might as well get some for myself." Theft is contagious.

Why do such honest employees not promptly report internal dishonesty, thus avoiding all the frustration, resentment, and possible involvement? There are two principal reasons. In the first place, many employees are unsure of whom to go to with information. Should they report to their immediate supervisor? Perhaps the supervisor is involved in the dishonesty. Should they go over the supervisor's head to someone higher in the company? Going over the boss's head is frowned on in most organizations. Uncertainty holds these potential informants' tongues and adds to their frustration. A second and equally strong deterrent is the fact that the thought of being identified as a company stooge is quite unpalatable to most people. In the vast majority of organizations such a reputation would make working conditions either intolerable or dangerous for the informant. Fear of discovery and its consequences thus leads to silence and continuing frustration.

The problem is that there is no legitimate or structured way for the honest and well-intentioned employee to tell the company what is happening, except by means of an anonymous letter or phone call. Therein lies a golden opportunity for management: Provide a legitimate and structured program for information to be passed up to management.

A number of firms across the country have developed formalized programs aimed at encouraging employees to report dishonesty in a confidential way. Protected anonymity is the key. J. Kirk Barefoot cites one such loss prevention reward program in his book, *Employee Theft Investigation.*[25] A program I designed, which has since been adopted by a number of companies, is called the Silent Witness Incentive Award Program. Its preamble reads, "The Silent Witness Incentive Award Program provides employees of this company with an opportunity to share in substantial awards and at the same time help reduce our losses caused by thieves." For information leading to the detection of a dishonest employee the program paid 10 percent of the value of recovery with a minimum award of $100 and a maximum of $2,500. This program, which is discussed with all new employees, is spelled out in detail in pamphlet form. The pamphlet is distributed to all employees. It reads, in part, as follows:

> When you have any information regarding internal theft, call the Director of Security on his private line (phone number is listed here) and describe to him, or in his absence the Security Manager, what you have observed. Your information will be treated in strict confidence.
>
> If you prefer to remain anonymous, you should outline the complete details of the matter in a letter. Mail the letter through the U.S. postal system to:
>
> Director
> P. O. Box 0000
> Midtown Station
> Middle American City, CA 90009
> "Confidential"
>
> It is not necessary to sign your name; simply write any six-digit number or code in the upper right and lower right corners. Tear off the lower right corner and keep it for identification purposes.
>
> A special bulletin will be published periodically and code numbers eligible for awards will be in such bulletins. If your number appears, you may present the torn off portion of your letter containing the number, either in person or through an intermediary, to the Director of Security (or designate) and receive your award. That presentation may be on neutral grounds, such as in the lobby of a neighborhood bank.

The pamphlet goes on to describe eligibility to participate, which includes all employees except internal auditors, senior management, and security personnel.

How effective was this program? In the first year after it was instituted over 20 employees were apprehended as a direct result of the program. In the second year over 50 employees were caught! These results are startling indeed in view of the fact that, prior to implementation of the award program, not a dozen such cases were referred to security by employees over a comparable period of time.

The Anonymous Informant

Anonymous informants obviously seek to protect their identity. As we have seen with the employee informant discussed previously, the desire for anonymity may come from the fact that the informant is in or closely connected with the firm and does not want to be known as an informant. If the informant is not connected with the firm in any way, he may still wish not to get involved in any way beyond passing along information. What this outside informant is saying, in effect, is, here is some information, do with it what you please. A third type of anonymous informant may or may not be connected with the firm, but what they pass on is not true. It is spiteful, degrading, or disrupting, aimed at causing suspicion, fear, or hostility in the organization. If a formalized informant program is in force, the number of anonymous calls or letters from those in the first group cited here virtually will disappear except for tips received through the structured program.

Outside informants, in fact, may provide good information while insisting on remaining anonymous. However, because of the inherent possibility of false information from members of the third group, anonymous information must rank low in terms of credibility. There is always a greater chance of receiving false or biased information from an anonymous source than from an identifiable informant.

The Criminal Informant

The criminal informant is more commonly identified with the public sector of law enforcement than with private security. Prostitutes, petty thieves, narcotics users, those on parole, and other assorted "street people" frequently pass information to the police. Often they are bartering information for freedom from prosecution, lengthy imprisonment, or a return to prison, although money is the prime motive for some informants. One must wonder how many times hapless and amateurish purchasers of narcotics have been seized by officials because of a tip from the very party who sold the drugs and who then collects a reward.

Although generally considered essential by police and other law enforcement agencies, the criminal informant is not a major source of information to investigators in business and industry. When they do appear on the scene in the private sector, however, as they do from time to time, they are worthy of attention.

In one such case, a caller asked if my employer paid for information. After some discussion of the nature of that information, the caller agreed to a meeting. He then put his cards right on the table. He was a professional forger with a lengthy criminal record including state prison time. He claimed to be currently involved with a forgery ring. He produced nine fraudulent documents for my examination: three bank checks of the company, the type prepared by the accounts payable department to pay company bills. The other documents were three California Department of Motor Vehicles operator licenses and three social security cards. The checks were made payable to three different persons, with addresses included. The same three names were contained on the driver's licenses and Social Security cards. The informant's own photograph was on each license. He had three sets of identification to support the checks, each of which was made out for a sum around $2,500.

According to the informant, the plan was for him to go to three separate banks and establish checking accounts, using the company's checks in each case as the initial deposit. After enough time had elapsed for the checks to have cleared the company's main bank, a member of the gang of conspirators would call each bank branch where an account had been established and determine whether or not the forged check had successfully cleared. He would do this by pretending that he was a service station owner who had a customer wishing to buy an expensive set of tires and wanting to pay by check. Did the customer have enough in his account to cover a $400 check? If the bank said no, the fraud had failed. If the answer was yes, the depositor (who was the informant) would withdraw all the money from the three accounts. The company would remain ignorant of the theft until either an audit or a regularly scheduled bank check reconciliation occurred. The only potential flaw in the plan was the magnetic coding on the checks. The checks were masterfully reproduced, genuine works of art.

The informant sought to sell information on the location where the checks were being printed and the identity of the other members of the ring. He had reservations about his associates and wanted enough money to leave the country and spend an extended vacation in Europe. Our company, it turned out, was not the only intended victim. Other nationally known firms were also in the process of being victimized, and the informant was dealing with them as well as with us. After pocketing the money he was to receive for his information, he would then work with the police until arrests of the conspirators were made, along with the seizure of printing equipment and other materials used in the scheme. His plan was to be en route to Europe while his associates were en route to jail. Bank and company accounting executives, believing that the magnetic coding on the checks could not be duplicated, were confident that the threat described by the informant was not as great as the security department claimed. However, the informant insisted that the coding had been duplicated successfully. The police were involved in the case. The plan unfolded. A number of people were arrested, equipment was seized, blank checks were recovered, and the informant winged his way across the Atlantic.

Oh yes, the checks did clear, in spite of the magnetic coding. Had this informant not approached us, a serious financial loss would have resulted without discovery for a matter of months.

Criminal informant situations, then, do occur in the private sector. They include, but are not limited to, shoplifting arrests where the person taken into custody will offer to deal with the security people, offering to inform on others or revealing such vital information as where stolen merchandise is "fenced." (A fence is a person or organization that knowingly buys stolen property from thieves and sells the goods at a profit.)

The Personal Informant

The personal informant is one who will deal with only one investigator, refusing to provide information to anyone else under any circumstances. Such relationships will often commence with something the investigator says or does. It could be the result of assisting a person whose car won't start, solving someone's problem by composing a letter he is unable to write, exhibiting concern for an individual's family, or even treating the janitor who cleans the investigator's office with respect. The recipient of any one of these actions, knowing what the investigator does for a living, may choose to return the kindness by providing information.

One personal experience offers an illustration, albeit this example is from the public sector, of the sometimes unpredictable motivation of the personal informant. He was my first such informant, a man named Lacey. I received a call one night while doing some paperwork in the Vice Detail headquarters. The caller identified himself as Lacey and asked if I remembered him. I did not. He told me that I had put him in jail for pimping. When he related some of the details surrounding his arrest, I recalled him. He told me that his arrest landed him in jail for six months. He had just been released that day. He wanted to meet me at midnight at an intersection in a rough area of Los Angeles.

"Why do you want to meet me?" I asked.

"I want to talk to ya."

"We can talk on the phone."

"Nope, I want to see ya and talk to ya."

I agreed to the meeting. Several of our brother vice officers deployed in the vicinity at the appointed time, not knowing what to expect. I parked my car near the intersection and approached with some apprehension. Lacey stepped out of a darkened area and said, "Betcha remember me better now, don't ya?"

"Sure, I do," I said, thoughtfully clutching the .38 caliber Chief Special in my jacket pocket.

"Well now, I got two whores lined up for you tonight. Wanna bust two whores?"

"What?"

"Your job is to bust whores, ain't it? And I gotcha two for tonight."

"How come you want to be so good to me, considering what happened the last time we met and you serving six months?"

"Well, it's this way," Lacey answered seriously. "I sat there for six months thinking about me and you, and how you caught me. And I said to myself, of all the times I've been arrested, nobody ever treated me as nice as you did. It made me feel so good that I decided when I got out I was gonna help out the best way I know how. So I lined up two broads for tonight, and I hear there's a guy with a still makin' whiskey over near Compton. I'll line that up for ya in a couple of days or so. I like ya, man, just plain like ya."

Writing this account many years later, I can still see his smile and recall our mutual friendship, and the many cases that one personal informant steered us to. But Lacey would talk to no one else. When we left the vice detail, there was no way we could "transfer" that valuable informant to another officer. He simply disappeared after that, voluntarily we hope.

That was a lesson not to be forgotten.

The Mentally Disturbed Informant

One unique category of informant to be discussed here is, in fact, not a genuine informant at all, at least in our experience. Such people do exist, however, and for the investigator they are a tragic nuisance. They are tragic because they are sick and do not know it; a nuisance because, after your first meeting with them, usually a clandestine one at their request, you cannot easily get rid of them. That usually happens, paradoxically, because the investigator, upon recognizing that the supposed informant is actually a disturbed person, will try to be gentle, understanding, and sympathetic as a strategy to end the meeting. The sick person, for whom rejection is a more typical experience, will latch onto that kindness as a sign of acceptance.

Sooner or later every professional investigator, by virtue of the work itself, will come into contact with the individual who purports to have information but is in fact mentally disturbed. Strangely enough, some of these persons are quite convincing at first. That may be because the investigator wants to believe what he is hearing. But in due course, usually quite quickly, it becomes apparent that the informant has a distorted sense of reality. Their "information" is worthless.

Controlled Informants

Controlled informants, just as all other types of informants, are individuals who possess information regarding a situation of investigative interest and who are willing to provide that information. Typically, however, the controlled informant is a person who has "inside" knowledge or direct involvement in the crimes under investigation and is trusted by those also committing the misconduct. The controlled informant is very similar to an undercover agent, except that she generally does not require the amount of time and effort to become trusted by misbehaving employees that is needed by an undercover agent.

Controlled informant handling is different from typical informant contacts in that it is extremely important that the investigator establish a relationship that goes beyond mere rapport. Why is this so? The informant is typically a member of a group of individuals whose esteem he wants to retain. At the very least, he does not want to garner the hatred of the group members. As Americans, we tend to disdain the "informer," "rat," or "snitch." The fact that the informant chooses to share with the investigator information against colleagues or friends requires him to overcome a natural sense of loyalty to the group. If the investigator does not establish, at least within the mind of the informant, that the investigator–informant relationship is a strong and empathetic one, it will be virtually impossible to keep the informant producing high-quality intelligence. This is best done from the very first stages of informant controlling.

INFORMANT CONTROL STAGES

Working with informants, if done properly, will be managed through several stages, including recruitment, productive handling, and case wrap-up.

Recruitment

Informants come in all shapes, sizes, and types. Some informants appear spontaneously whereas others are recruited especially for an investigation already under way. Many times the employer will receive a call or letter from a coworker, customer, neighbor, ex-spouse, or former friend of the person involved in illicit or illegal activities. Sometimes informants themselves have been caught in misconduct and either selfishly or genuinely want to assist an expanding investigation.

An investigator should attempt to learn why the informant is providing the information. This will assist the investigator in two ways. First, the investigator can gauge credibility of the information based on the motive of the informant. The investigator should see whether the informant is angry with, or a rival of, the suspect and weigh the tip appropriately. Second, understanding the motivation of the informant can give strong clues about how to keep the informant productive in the future.

The following is a list of some of the motivations that prompt controlled informants to assist in investigations:

- Long-term dislike for suspects
- Short-term anger against suspects
- Fear of implication in suspects' activities

- Moral indignation
- Jealousy
- Reducing punishment for his own misdeeds
- Fear of physical harm if misconduct continues
- Legitimate concern for welfare of suspects
- Loyalty to company or community
- Religious beliefs
- Law-enforcement "wannabes"

In one memorable investigation, a company executive was secretly contacted by a new warehouse employee who offered information regarding the large losses of inventory that had plagued the facility. He was a 20-year-old, whom we shall call "Billy," and had recently enlisted in the Army National Guard. When the investigators began to meet with him it was learned that as soon as he began working at the warehouse he saw numerous thefts openly occurring on the midnight shift. He was certain that the conduct, being so blatant and pervasive, would eventually lead to the entire shift being fired. Fearing that being part of a wholesale termination might be a blemish that would prevent him from obtaining the top secret military clearance he had applied for, the young man took steps to secure his future. At the outset he was highly motivated.

Productive Handling

Once the informant has been recruited, and the investigator understands her motives, the investigator must obtain all useful information from the informant. This can sometimes be done in a single meeting; however, in our experience, the wise investigator always leaves the door open for continuing contact with the informant. Often what the investigator believes he understood the informant to say was in fact misunderstood and further clarification is needed. In many cases, once steps are taken to verify the information received from the informant, more questions naturally occur. Frequently, the informant is the logical person who can answer the questions. If the informant is asked, and agrees, to seek out and report information he has effectively become a controlled informant. Controlled informants are frequently prone to fear of discovery. Regular professional contact with the investigator can go a long way toward calming these fears and providing the informant with a sense that her cooperation is appreciated. Also, reinforcing the initial motivation for the informant's involvement can give renewed enthusiasm for continuing the relationship.

The first priority of any informant handling is the security and safety of the informant. The investigator is after all morally responsible for asking the informant to assume certain risks attendant to cooperation. The investigator should train the informant to be careful in keeping the informant–investigator relationship confidential. A careless comment to a spouse, friend, or coworker can easily raise a question or suspicion and jeopardize any ongoing investigation.

The investigator should establish a method of contact with the informant. It is not enough that the informant can reach the investigator — the investigator must be able to initiate the contact when necessary. Few things are as frustrating as wanting to ask an informant for more information and having to wait for the informant to decide she wants to call you. Hours, days, or weeks can pass between receiving informant-initiated contacts and many investigative opportunities will have come and gone.

More importantly, the investigator may learn from other means that the informant's cooperation has been revealed. Reaching the informant in these situations can be critical to the informant's safety and preserving the investigation. A home telephone number, pager, cellular phone, or work telephone number are all acceptable means of contact. The main factor to keep in mind is that the method of contact should in no way identify the fact that the informant is cooperating. A bogus company name, coded pager number, or other false name should be used to protect the informant from having his friends (some of whom may be suspects) overhear a telephone message obviously from a corporate investigator.

Billy's story provides a good example of these principles. Once he was fully debriefed in the first meeting, Billy was told to return to work and keep his eyes and ears open. He was given a pager to carry and an answering service number to call if he wanted to reach the investigators. In the week following the first meeting his story was checked out against company records. The goods that he had mentioned seeing stolen were partially confirmed through inventory records. Supervisors conducted unobtrusive counts of the others and discovered that what Billy had said was true. The investigators recontacted Billy who for a number of weeks continued to provide crucial information that led to the placement of hidden cameras in the areas where the stolen goods were staged before being removed from the complex.

One night the answering service woke one of the investigators at home to say that a male named Billy was calling and claimed that the call was an emergency. Billy told the investigator that he was certain he was "burned" by the other employees, his life was in danger, and he was going to quit in the morning. He was calling from a pay phone after mumbling to his supervisor (who was one of the conspirators) that his girlfriend was sick and he had to take care of her. It was 3:00 A.M. and the investigator merely could have told Billy to go home and call in the morning, but it was clear that the informant was nearing the end of his rope. So, within twenty minutes Billy was seated in the investigator's car sipping coffee in a darkened parking lot. For forty-five minutes they carefully went over the events that had rattled the young man. It became clear that the night-shift supervisor had learned of a routine inventory check by the day-shift supervisor. The night supervisor commented to the night workers that "somebody was checking on them." Absolutely no mention was made by anyone that an informant was operating in their midst. Billy's own paranoia took over and he panicked. The investigator was able to help him calmly work through his fears and pull himself together. Billy was sheepish, but felt enormously relieved. He went back to work the next day, again providing high-quality information for weeks.

Frequent contact between the informant and investigator will serve to keep information flowing. The investigator should carefully observe the informant for any clues that she has possibly had a change of heart about cooperating. Few things can damage an ongoing investigation as thoroughly as an informant who feels misplaced guilt over betraying friends. This often happens if the informant initially came forward after a single event that made her angry with the suspects. As time passes tempers cool and the suspects and the informant will normally become friendly again. The investigator must control the situation and move the investigation along quickly enough that this does not happen before matters are satisfactorily concluded.

This control is best accomplished through building strong rapport with the informant and assuring the informant that his safety and well-being are the investigator's primary concern. Also, taking time to share a cup of coffee or meal with the informant, paid for by the investigator, serves very well to communicate to the informant that the investigator is a friend and does not view the informant as a mere tool. Also, demonstrating prompt response to informant requests for meetings or telephone contact has a similar effect. It is not at all unusual for an informant in an extended investigation to become a little dependent upon the investigator for encouragement and support. Such was the case with Billy. In addition to building rapport, giving the informant small tasks to complete after each contact with the investigator trains them to follow directions and accept small risks to benefit the investigation. At all costs, however, the investigator must train the informant to do nothing suspicious without the direct agreement by the investigator because any overzealous or ill-advised action by the informant can jeopardize the ongoing investigation.

Case Wrap Up

Ultimately, if a case has been successfully investigated and revealed conclusive evidence of wrongdoing, the responsible parties will be apprehended, terminated, and/or sued.

If the informant has been very productive, honest, and cooperative, all these factors should be taken into account by the employer in deciding whether they will reduce the informant's punishment for his own involvement. The investigator should help the corporation fully understand the true extent of the informant's assistance without losing objectivity and becoming an advocate for the informant.

In many cases, in order to protect the informant's cooperative role, the informant is given a sham suspension as an outward punishment. She returns to work later appearing chastised and goes on with her career with the company, with none the wiser. This gesture acknowledging continuing concern for the informant can be very valuable in cementing her loyalty to the company should she later learn of new problems in the workforce. In fact, her reputation as having been caught being a little bad in the past may serve to let other marginal characters in the company be relaxed around her and open up later about their own misconduct. A wise investigator leaves an informant in place predisposed to reactivation when new problems surface.

In the case involving Billy, of the twelve men on the midnight shift, direct evidence was obtained against seven for theft during the covert part of the investigation. During the subsequent interrogations they and four others confessed to additional thefts and on-premises substance abuse.

Billy too was brought in for questioning in his turn. He admitted to a single instance of drinking beer after work on the premises with the rest of the crew, but truthfully denied any thefts, and due to the steering of the interviewers, made no on-the-record statements against others. Due to the involvement of a supervisor in the same drinking, he was given only a one-day suspension.

MAXIMIZING POTENTIAL FOR CONTROLLED INFORMANT RECRUITMENT

Much can be done to encourage honest persons like Billy. As noted earlier, many organizations successfully manage award programs that give incentives to employees who help to protect the company by providing valuable information. This is not at all unlike the Crime Stoppers programs used by public law enforcement to foster tips that solve many violent crimes. A telephone number or post office box address is publicized to the workforce and a guarantee of anonymity is provided. Key to success is acting on bona fide tips and making sure that the workforce learns of it. Also crucial is the publicizing of the fact that awards are being given, although obviously the names of the recipients are withheld.

In the example cited here, there was no established award program. However, the investigators convinced management of the value of Billy's cooperation and a secret cash award was arranged. Billy never anticipated receiving any reward and had easily accepted the loss of a day's pay as a minor cost necessary to ensure his safety. The company chose not to prosecute anyone, and Billy was never needed to testify.

The company decided to reorganize, and ceased midnight shift operations. It realized major savings in labor costs and the inventory losses evaporated. Management was entirely satisfied.

UNEXPECTED DIVIDENDS

It turned out that the story of Billy later developed an interesting footnote. While managing Billy's contacts, the investigators learned that he previously had worked at a company that had been investigated unsuccessfully for similar thefts. Under close questioning he easily provided details of persons, dates, and items he saw stolen while employed there. His prior employer was contacted and the investigators, armed with new intelligence, were able to obtain confessions from a number of employees.

It was clear that but for the rapport and control that the investigators developed with Billy, his first meeting would have been just that, a one-time interview. Skillful controlled informant handling resulted in not one, but two, theft rings being broken up.

TREATMENT OF INFORMANTS

The investigator who speaks scornfully of informants in all probability has no informants or, should one appear, will never be able to keep him. Avoid using such words as "snitch," "fink," "stoolie," or "stool pigeon." Such jargon should be left to the cops-and-robbers of television. It has no place in the professional investigator's glossary of terms. Refer to an informant as a "contact" or a "confidential source."

Irrespective of an informant's motive, always treat him with the same courtesy and respect you would show anyone else. To treat all people with dignity, no matter who they are, has its rewards. That kind of philosophy somehow attracts people with information. To treat people with disdain or disrespect, no matter who they are, also has its consequences, and they do not further the investigative purpose.

THE NEED FOR CORROBORATION

As a general rule information received from an informant is not directly actionable. That is to say, if an informant reports that the head cashier of the firm is embezzling funds and has just purchased a new Cadillac for her boyfriend, the investigator does not set up an interrogation of the suspect. The information received needs corroboration. Does the cashier have a boyfriend? Did she in fact purchase a new Cadillac? How is she embezzling funds? Should the internal auditors do a cash count under the ruse of a routine check? These and many other questions have to be answered before information received from an informant can lead to a confrontation. What information does is provide the direction for further investigation.

This point is well expressed by Gene Blackwell: "Remember that the investigator seeks at all times to upgrade the status of the information he receives by having it verified and corroborated from additional sources whenever possible."[26]

Information from informants that is not verifiable in one way or another has limited value. Where such information can be corroborated, however, it can prove an invaluable aid to investigation. The use of informants, with prudent regard for their limitations and motivations, can be a productive tool for the investigator in the private as well as the public sector. Every investigator who aspires to true professionalism must learn the proper and effective use of this tool.

Chapter 14

Report Writing and Note Taking

It is remarkable how quickly the human mind loses a considerable part of its ability to recall the details of events. This phenomenon applies not only to events merely witnessed but even to those directly experienced. The importance of recording events in writing is clear. If an event is not recorded, it will soon be forgotten entirely or in part, or it will be distorted with the passage of time. Everything else being equal, the difference between a good or competent investigator and one who is considered excellent is reflected in the superior investigator's report-writing skills. Furthermore, there is a direct relationship between the efficiency of a security department or an investigative office and the quality of its records and reports.

Report writing is not a peripheral activity that has little to do with the real business of investigation. On the contrary, the individual who argues that he can investigate a problem and solve it but cannot write reports is comparable to an auto mechanic who says, "I can remove and repair your engine but I can't install it back in your car." If he cannot finish the job, he is not what he claims to be. Report writing is a natural and necessary part of the very job description of an investigator. The investigator who avoids or puts off writing reports, and some do, is in the position of a fireman who avoids fires or puts off arriving at the scene of a fire. Such people are in the wrong business.

DEFINING THE INVESTIGATIVE REPORT

In the absence of a generally accepted formal definition of an investigative report, the following is offered. An investigative report is a clear, comprehensive, written documentation of facts, presented chronologically, which is an objective, first-person recording of the investigator's experiences, conversations, and observations regarding a specific assignment, and from which the events of the investigation can be reconstructed even after a lapse of time. The investigative report reflects, in writing, the investigator's work on a case. As suggested in our definition, it should be able to withstand the test of time. A good report, when read by a stranger five years later, will make as much sense as it did to the author on the day it was written. The ultimate test of a good report is simply this: If the reader of the report has a question, the report is deficient.

NARRATIVE REPORTS

A report is most easily understood when presented in the first person narrative style, and the heart of any investigative report is the narrative body. In many organizations, in fact, the narrative comprises the entire report. An effective narrative report must include the key elements of our definition. Extracting those elements, a good report must be

- A writing
- Told in first person narrative
- Objective
- Factual
- Chronological
- Easily understood
- Comprehensive
- Able to withstand the test of time

A Writing

There is no substitute for the written word when it comes to the investigative report. Despite the availability of computer files, videotape recordings, audio recording capabilities, or any other item of hardware, the report should end up on paper. Even if the investigator dictates his report or inputs the contents to computer records, the net result should be the written word on paper. No other kind of report can be as quickly reviewed, and no other so successfully meets the requirements of being both comprehensive and readily understood. Even with the ease of retrieval that computer files represent, a paper report does not require any equipment whatsoever to access. Copies of it can be easily written on, handed to another person for discussion, and are not subject to the vagaries of hard-drive crashes, power failure, data corruption, or hardware and software incompatibility or obsolescence. The truly "paperless office" is not yet sufficiently reliable, or of universally accepted file and program format, to allow investigators to dispense totally with paper files. Although investigators at different desks may have different software applications programs or hardware, presumably they will always be able to share files the old-fashioned way, opened before them on a real, not electronic, desktop.

Since the final version of the report is in writing, it follows that correct grammar, spelling, and punctuation, as well as legibility will reflect either favorably or unfavorably on the author — the investigator. He does not have to be a consummate stylist, but he does have to be able to organize and present his facts clearly. Lapses in grammar, spelling, and punctuation often have the troublesome result of making things unclear. So, obviously, does an unreadable scrawl.

Told in First Person Narrative

The use of the first person narrative is recommended because, for the average person, a report flows more naturally in this style. If we write as we think and talk, the material tends to become both easier to write and easier to read. The following, for example, is both stilted and unnatural: "The undersigned then asked the victim's supervisor if he recalled the time of the phone call. The supervisor advised undersigned that the call was approximately 3:00 P.M." A more natural first person rendition of this report might read, "I asked the victim's supervisor if he recalled the time of the phone call. He told me it was sometime around 3:00 P.M." The use of such expressions as "this writer," "this investigator," or "the undersigned" is not wrong or bad per se, but it does tend to become awkward and cumbersome.

Again, write as you think, and write for the reader.

Objective

The investigative report is no place for speculation, hypothesis, or opinion (the investigator's judgment or prejudices). If the reader of the report engages in any of these, as a result of the facts presented, that is his prerogative. This is not to say that the investigator should not have opinions or engage in speculation. But any such subjectivity should not be included or reflected in the report itself. If there is any need for subjective expression, it should be made in another or a different report, such as a memorandum to the investigator's supervisor.

Factual

The problem of an investigator reporting nonfactual information in his report, as a rule, does not occur intentionally. The common mistake is for the investigator to assume the facts are there when they are not. For example, "Employee Jones then clocked out at the end of his shift, 4:00 P.M., and went home." Maybe Jones went home. Maybe he went to the Red Rooster Bar & Grill. More factually the investigator's report should have read, "Employee Jones then clocked out at the end of his shift, 4:00 P.M., and left the company property." At a later date that "fact" concerning Jones going home could come back to haunt the investigator.

Consider another example, "Jones left the Red Rooster Bar & Grill at about 9:15 P.M. and drove off in a rented Cadillac; further description and license plate number unknown." The information about the rented car was obtained from a waitress. Factually, the report should have read, "According to the waitress, Jo Dennis, Jones left the Red Rooster Bar & Grill at about 9:15 P.M. and drove off in a Cadillac that Jones claimed he had rented. At this time we have no further description of the car or the license number." The difference between these two statements is obvious. In the first, the investigator includes a conclusion or assumption about the car, based on the waitress's input, but it reads like a fact. The second statement is indeed a report of facts. It is a fact that the waitress gave certain information. There may be some question about her telling the truth, but there is none about what she reported. The reader of the report would unquestionably view the information about the rented car differently, depending upon which report was read.

Chronological

The investigator's report is a record of his own work. The chronology of the report, then, is concerned with the investigative process, not with the crime or incident under investigation. The chronologically structured report is the unfolding, in order of time, of what the investigator did. The following report offers a typical example.

> On Tuesday morning, November 16, I interviewed subject Jones's landlady, Miss Rose Hovely, who told me that Jones rents a small room in the rear portion of the garage for $135.00 weekly. She said that Jones moved in during the 4th of July holiday weekend earlier this year, and every week pays his rent with rolled coins, mostly quarters and dimes. She said she personally didn't like to handle the coins, they were heavy to carry

to the bank. When she asked Jones why all the coins, she said he told her he was a coin collector. "Some coin collector he must be," she said. "Whenever he comes home after too much drink, there's coins lying around the driveway and grass by his door."

I returned to the General Offices and met with the head cashier, Mrs. Rubin Angelo. She produced for my examination the history of daily vending machine receipts for 1999 and 2000 by machine, location of machine in each facility . . .

How the report unfolds will coincide with the investigator's verbal testimony concerning the same events as it might be given in an administrative or judicial inquiry. Observe the chronology unfolding in the following testimony:

Q. Now, after taking the report of an unexplained decrease in vending machine revenue and after conducting a second and more thorough investigation into the newest employee's background, Mr. Smith, then what did you do?

A. I went to Mr. Jones's residence and spoke to his landlady.

Q. Why?

A. I wanted to determine how Mr. Jones paid for his rent. If it was by bank check I was hopeful the landlady could tell me which branch. Once I knew the branch I hoped to learn if he made deposits with coins.

Q. Did you discover his bank and branch?

A. No, I didn't.

Q. What did you discover, if anything?

A. I learned that Mr. Jones has always paid his rent with rolled coins.

Q. After learning that, what did you do?

A. I returned to our general offices and . . .

The chronology of the crime under investigation will be pieced together and presented, either in summary form as an introduction to the report itself or in a summary of a suspect's confession. That chronology, however, is secondary to the sequence of events in the investigation itself.

Easily Understood

The report must be written so that it is easy to understand. Small, familiar words are better than words of many syllables. Short, clear, direct sentences are preferable to long compound or complex sentences. The *Security Investigator's Handbook* recommends sentences of no more than twenty words as a good rule of thumb.[27] If technical terms must be used in the report, define or explain them. The report is not meant to be a literary masterpiece, but rather an accurate and easy-to-understand story of the investigation.

Comprehensive

A report is comprehensive when it has both scope and depth in terms of specific and pertinent facts. That is not to suggest the report should be wordy; on the contrary, it should be as brief as possible. But some space must be devoted to detail when detail is germane. Take, for example, the description of a person who is considered the responsible party in a crime. A comprehensive report would include all of the following in the description:

- Name, including aliases and nicknames
- Address and phone number
- Sex
- Race
- Age
- Height
- Weight
- Hair color and style
- Color of eyes
- Build
- Complexion
- Beard
- Teeth
- Unusual mannerisms or voice accent
- Dress habits
- Birthplace
- Amount of education
- Occupation
- Avocation or hobby
- Relatives and friends

In one investigation, a number of people were meeting during evening hours in the back room of a public restaurant. As part of an investigation underway it was important to identify those in attendance. Because all participants in the gathering had to arrive by vehicle, the logical approach was to identify them through the vehicles, by running the license plate numbers through the department of motor vehicles.

There was an inordinate delay in getting the desired information. Finally, we called for the responsible supervisor. We were advised that the name of one party obtained through the vehicle license records was a mysterious name. The investigators could not account for it, resulting in the delay. We asked to see the report. It read essentially as follows:

Surveillance teams in position on N, S, and E sides of the lot at 1830 hours. Suspect vehicle arrived at 1915 hours, followed by below listed vehicles:

Time	License No.
1915	DDC 768
1918	JPR 098
1922	BVD 432
1925	EXS 101

On the following day the investigators took that list of licenses and followed through on them. Most vehicle license information comes back from motor vehicle departments as follows: License #FFE343, 2000 Ford, Joe and/or Mary Henn, 8424 Camelback, American City, Nebraska. Comparison of vehicle and owner identities indicated that a mistake had been made. It finally *was* determined that two numbers in one of the license plate identifications had been transposed.

The failure of the investigators in the listing of autos during their surveillance was one of comprehensiveness; the report lacked the necessary depth of detail. The human error that always creeps into detail work, in this case the error of transposing numbers on a license, would have been detected immediately if the initial listing of numbers had been done in something like the following fashion.

Table 14.1.   Listing reflecting human error

Time of Arrival	License #	Auto Make Approx.	Yr.	Color	Style
1915	DDC 768	Nissan	97	White	Van
1918	JPR 098	Buick	98	Maroon	Regal
1922	BVD 432	Ford	92	White	Pickup
1925	EXS 101	Jeep	95	Blue	MPVH

Had an investigator then transposed the numbers of the second car's license plate, the vehicle license information on record might have shown "JPR 098" to have been a 1994 Toyota instead of the 1998 Buick that was observed in the field. A comparison of the two reports would immediately have disclosed the error and given direction for further investigation to resolve that error. Such is the value of comprehensive information.

The Test of Time

As our definition of an investigative report suggested, the report should be so written that the events of the investigation can be reconstructed from the report even after a prolonged lapse of time. Consider whether this is true of the following example.

> John McCall from headquarters called Mr. Switzer, senior investigator, on September 19, 1995, and reported his suspicion that a cashier in Unit 33 was slipping twenty dollar bills out of banded bundles. Thus daily bulk counts failed to reflect shortages, but when bundles were broken for use such bundles were short. On Sept. 22, 1995, I observed Catherine Goltz slip a bill from a banded bundle just after opening the safe at 8:00 A.M. She was removed from the cashier's office and taken to the human resources office, where she admitted to me her theft of this day as well as numerous prior thefts, as listed below. . . .

At the time this report was written, it might well have been quite clear in its record of events. At that time there was no question whatsoever about the *who, what, where, when,* and *how* of the matter under investigation. But that report will not necessarily stand the test of time, as a closer examination will show. At the time of the report, we may assume, every security supervisor and investigator knew John McCall; he was an up and coming internal auditor and very pro-security. In fact, John passed on more information to security than the rest of the internal auditors combined. It was also well known that internal auditors worked out of the headquarters operations. And everyone knew that unit 33 was the numerical designation for the facility in Stanton. But in the course of five years a number of things changed. Perhaps McCall left the company for a better position the same year the report was written, and the chief internal auditor was promoted and transferred to another division of the corporation. Three years after the report, the internal audit function was part of an organizational realignment, and was moved out to the data processing facility. At the same time unit number 10, an old and unproductive part of the operation, was closed down. Following that, the numerical designations for other units were abandoned. And finally, as luck would have it, the investigator who wrote the report and his supervisor both moved on to other jobs.

In the short span of five years, this report obviously leaves much to be desired. It would have been improved dramatically if the original writer had simply included John McCall's title and department, and if he had avoided using a code number instead of the proper name of the location cited in the report. Eventually, it is true, the information given in the report can be tracked down, but that is not the point. The content of an investigative report should not require research later. It should not require questions.

Nor are the omissions already cited the only missing pieces in this sample report. Consider that part of the report about observing the theft. How was it observed? The report does not offer a clue. At the time the report was written it may have been common knowledge that cashiering operations had built-in surveillance grills in the ceiling. Investigators would lie concealed above the ceiling and observe the employees handling money. But what if, two years later, a court determines that procedure is an invasion of privacy and, as a result of that decision, surveillance positions overlooking work areas become a thing of the past? We are personally aware of similar surveillance arrangements that were later a source of astonishment to new investigators.

Many things change with time. The investigative report written today should not cause confusion or be incomprehensible a few years later.

STRUCTURED OR FORMALIZED REPORTS

The heart of the investigative report, the narrative body, often constitutes the entire report, as previously stated. Some organizations, however, make use of a more structured form that includes a heading section, the body or narrative, and an ending or conclusion. The latter is simply a statement of the status of the investigation, no more and no less.

The heading portion of a preprinted investigative report form usually calls for answers or information that fits into boxed spaces. Almost anyone can fill these out without difficulty. An exception might be the type of form sometimes used in the private sector that includes the nine parts of a *modus operandi*. Here some confusion can set in about the kind of information required. Table 14.2 suggests the types of answers required to those nine basic questions.

Table 14.2. Nine parts of a *modus operandi*

Question	*Answer*
1. Time of attack	Date and time the offense was committed.
2. Person attacked	Type of person attacked, e.g., female child.
3. Property attacked	Type of location where the offense took place, e.g., single story retail store.
4. How attacked	The way in which the person or property was attacked, e.g., theft of goods.
5. Means of attack	Instrument, tool, device, trick, or method by which the person or property was attacked, e.g., placed goods in lining of jacket designed to accommodate stolen items.
6. Object of attack	Why the crime was committed or attempted, e.g., to sell stolen goods for money to support drug habit.
7. Trademark	Any peculiarity that may serve to distinguish the offense or offender from others, e.g., crawls behind counters in the store to avoid detection.
8. What the suspect said	What and how the suspect spoke to victims or witnesses, not to the authorities, e.g., upon discovery claims he's looking for the men's toilet.
9. Transportation used	Description of vehicle used. If no vehicle seen or heard, so note.

NOTE TAKING

It is difficult to imagine an investigator writing a formal comprehensive report, whether in a structured format or as a complete narrative, without referring to notes taken during the course of the investigation. Good note taking is as important in the investigative process as it is in college courses. It is essential. There are three specific needs for on-the-spot notes by the investigator. These are:

1. *Recording times.* It would require a very superior intelligence to recall accurately all the dates and times that are so important in the investigation.
2. *Recording full name.* Besides full names of witnesses, including their proper spelling, notes should list their title or rank, address, home and business phone numbers. The investigator cannot rely on securing printed business cards from everyone connected with the case.
3. *Recording quotations.* Quotations can be a powerful part of the investigative report. If a person is to be quoted directly in the report, however, those words will lack credibility unless backed up by the investigator's notebook. That is because the report is frequently not written until the case is finalized. Days or even weeks may have elapsed, and it is a difficult challenge to try to explain how you can recall someone's exact words days or weeks later.

The notebook should be small, pocket-sized, and bound so that pages cannot be added or removed. A 3″ by 5″ notebook will fit conveniently into a breast pocket of a man's coat or jacket.

In a formal hearing, attorneys often will attempt to authenticate or discredit the investigator's report and his memory of events by determining the time differential between the date of the incident or conversation and the time when that incident or conversation was written in the formal report. Invariably the investigator called as a witness will be asked something like the following: "Your report (or testimony) is very explicit about what Miss Hovely said about the coins, yet you wrote the report six days after that conversation. Did you make any notes during or immediately after that conversation?" If the investigator says no, his report (or testimony) immediately loses credibility and force. If the investigator says yes and is able to produce those notes when asked to do so, his report (or testimony) becomes credible and impressive.

The fact that, as indicated in this example, the investigator's notebook can be asked for and examined by an adversary attorney or hearing officer is an important consideration. The investigator should not write anything in that book that might mitigate against the case. For example, one investigator who was interviewing neighbors about a suspect employee made a personal note in his notebook that read, "Employee must be gay." Such a comment could raise all kinds of claims of bias and lack of objectivity about the investigation and unnecessarily discredit the real, objective work of the investigator.

LARGE CASE REPORT FORMAT

The report format discussed earlier, centering on a chronological narrative prepared at the close of the investigation, will be sufficient for the majority of investigative reports prepared by private sector investigators. There will be infrequent occasions, however, where individual investigations may take months or years to complete and include hundreds of interviews and many (tens or hundreds of thousands) document pages.

Obviously, preparing a report of this kind of investigation from beginning to end at the conclusion of the investigation would be very hard. Even with superbly written notes, when weeks or months pass before a formal record is completed, there will inevitably be a loss of detail, which good notes will otherwise jog from the investigator's memory if reviewed shortly after the notes are written.

A strict narrative rendition of the large case investigation inevitably will result in a mass of information that any user will find extremely difficult to use efficiently. In these cases an alternative reporting methodology needs to be adopted.

Emphasis

The emphasis of the large report format differs greatly from the routine report format. The large report format concentrates on the events under investigation, not the investigation itself. The large report is not a single running document prepared from notes at the end of the investigation. Though it may be prepared at the close of the investigation, the large report format relies on an intermediate step between note taking and final report preparation, known as memorandum preparation. The large report format is organized by topic, not organized by the investigation chronology. The large report format also is organized with the end-user's needs (when they can be reasonably ascertained) in mind.

Event Concentration versus Investigation Chronology Concentration

Event concentration is adopted in keeping with presenting a clear understanding of the matters under investigation. In some cases the event will be a certain industrial accident, in others the events could be a series of related criminal offenses of various types committed over a multiyear period.

Following the course of events in a large investigation forces the reader to go back and forth in time. For example, suppose Terry is an investigator in the fraud unit of a large corporation and receives an assignment to investigate a single check forgery. During the course of the investigation Terry may uncover and successfully break up a forgery ring in operation.

Inevitably, a report based on the chronology of the investigation will start in the middle of the chain of relevant events. Terry's investigation will initiate when some forgeries have already taken place in the present. He will then likely discover past events of a similar nature, which will lead him to obtain proof of the present conspiracy, and he will attempt to detect, document, and stop future events as they happen. Terry's chronological report will give a clear "blow-by-blow" picture of what he did, but may not be very helpful to present what the criminals did. Therefore, the large investigation report must center on the individual events or offenses of the subject.

Memoranda to File

A large investigation sometimes will go virtually nonstop for weeks or months. It may involve the work of a team of many investigators, each of whom is engaged in numerous concurrent endeavors. The means by which all the efforts and findings of the ongoing investigation are documented is the use of the memorandum to file. The memorandum is in essence a report of each individual interview, significant record examination, important telephone conversation, and interrogation of the investigation. The typical memorandum to file is illustrated in Figure 14.1.

```
Memorandum To File

From:     Henry Goddard

Date:     June 11, 2005

Case:     E-73-05

Subj.:    Attempted Interview of William Taylor
```

```
On June 11, 2005 at 10:15 a.m. I arrived at the home of
William Taylor, located at 543 Second Avenue, Apartment 1,
Zedburgh.  I asked a woman who was locking the front door
whether William Taylor was home.  She said that Taylor was
not home, and had gone to Las Vegas for three days on
business.  I identified myself to her and gave her my
business card.  She gave me, at my request, the telephone
number for Taylor's employer, Express Duplication Services
(555-2277).  She said that her name was Beth Chester and
that she is Taylor's sister.  She further said that she is
in town for the duration of Taylor's trip caring for his two
children as Taylor is a divorced custodial parent whose ex-
wife lives in Philadelphia.  She gave me the number at the
residence (555-1887), and agreed to ask Taylor to call me at
my office the following morning when he makes his next
nightly call to check on the children. I departed at 10:22
a.m.
```

Figure 14.1. A typical memorandum to file.

The memorandum will show the name of the author, date of preparation, the case name or number, and the specific subject covered. It will also contain the detailed narrative of the event, interview, or other investigative activity described and should be written as close in time as circumstances permit to those events.

The various memoranda to file from an investigation will be placed in the overall case files. Generally, there should be a master memorandum file that will contain all the memoranda generated in the investigation in chronological order. Copies of the memorandum can be made and placed in any number of subfiles according to the organization scheme of the specific investigation. In the example of the memorandum to file shown in Figure 14.1, subfiles could be maintained under Goddard, Henry (the author, especially if numerous investigators are contributing to the case); Taylor, William (the individual sought to be interviewed); Chester, Beth (unlikely unless she becomes more important to the investigation later); or even the Taylor residence address or the name of Taylor's employer.

In some investigations, subfiles are established concerning individual criminal offenses, individual suspects, individual methods or schemes discovered, or any other temporary topic that helps the investigators keep the information logically organized and easily retrievable.

The use of computer files is especially helpful in a large case. Having the ability to rapidly search the entire text of hundreds of memoranda contributed by several investigators by a specific name, date, or other term can easily bring together every mention of that one factor and help to organize the chaos associated with large masses of information.

Report Organization

A large report should generally be organized into a number of distinct parts, making it easy to use by the reader of the report. Even though each report and organization producing those reports will have different requirements, the following should be considered for including in large reports.

Case Synopsis. The case synopsis is a very brief statement that introduces the reader to the overall investigation and its primary conclusion. The following is an example:

> Investigation was conducted from June 1, 2000 until December 7, 2000 into a series of suspected embezzlements at the Sharps Hotel. On December 7, 2000 William Taylor provided a confession statement in which he admitted taking cash received from guests from March 17, 1998 until his departure from employment at Sharps Hotel on May 15, 2000, totaling some $543,210.98. Taylor said that he spent the money paying off gambling debts incurred while on frequent gambling trips to Las Vegas. The loss has been confirmed and acknowledged by the fidelity bonding company and the matter is under further investigation by the Zedburgh County District Attorney's Office.

In three sentences a reader comes to understand what happened, where it happened, how it happened, when it happened, who did it, and why. In addition, the reader learns the current status of the matter.

Executive Summary of Findings. The executive summary is very much appreciated by readers of large reports because they are spared being dragged through the entire investigation history to learn the most important information. The executive summary normally will be a numbered listing of the significant findings. For example, the summary for the case alluded to earlier might look like this.

Executive Summary
1. William Taylor was employed as a chief cashier at the Sharps Hotel from October 19, 1990 until May 15, 2000 when he was discharged for excessive absences from work.
2. Taylor admitted that he took virtually all cash generated from room rentals paid fully in cash at the time of checkout. He deleted the record of the room sale from the computer.
3. The scheme was discovered after Taylor was fired when his assistant found original daily room revenue sheets with the cash payments circled and totaled. In following up, the assistant was unable to find a

computer record of the rentals but was able to recover guest registration cards and cash receipts from stored files. She then alerted the general manager and security director.

4. Subsequent recovery of archived computer files and a hand search of the guest registration records was undertaken going back until January 1, 1998. The first identified taking appeared to be $554.00 on March 17, 1998 from the revenue generated from the rentals of rooms 1066, 1754, 1775, and 1812.

5. A total of 335 separate dates were identified in which total diverted cash was estimated as being $543,210.98. The recovery and examination of documents, including canceled guest checks and registration records, lasted from June 1, 2000 until December 3, 2000.

6. Investigation of Taylor's background revealed that he filed for bankruptcy on November 15, 2000 claiming to have assets of $22,345 and debts to various Las Vegas and Reno casinos of $195,500.

7. The Second Fidelity Insurance Company has reviewed the initial findings of the investigation and has agreed to pay the fidelity bond limit of $500,000 less the deductible of $10,000. A copy of this report is to be sent to Second Fidelity.

8. The Zedburgh County District Attorney's Office is conducting a follow-up investigation and is awaiting the receipt of a copy of this report.

Topical Sections. The report is then presented in sections by topic. Some of the sections in a large investigation report such as the Sharps Hotel example could be

1. Evidence of Cash Received
    a. Suspect Guest Registrations
    b. Cash Receipt Slips from Files
    c. Daily Cash Sales Summaries Found in Taylor's Desk
2. Evidence of Computer Deletions
3. Bank Records Reflecting 335 No-Cash Deposits
4. William Taylor Employment Background
    a. Personnel File
    b. Record of Training
    c. Termination File
5. Las Vegas and Reno Casino Records Relating to Taylor
6. Bankruptcy Court Records Relating to Taylor
7. Divorce Court Records Relating to Taylor
8. Schedules Listing All Suspected Losses
9. Statements of William Taylor
10. Timeline of Taylor Misconduct
11. Timeline of Investigative Activity
12. Memoranda to File
13. Listing of Witnesses and Exhibits
14. Exhibits

Each topic area should summarize the information developed and the methodology used to develop the information. All the relevant memoranda to file are included in a section wherein they are chronologically presented. Exhibits would include such items as the actual copies of key documents, photographs, lengthy interview transcripts, and such. The narrative summaries in each topic section of the report should footnote or make other references to the exhibits that support the finding or otherwise illustrate the point being made.

It is very useful to users of such large reports to receive the reports in both written form (frequently requiring several binders and boxes) and digital form (computer diskette or CD).

SUMMARY

Whether in standard chronological or large report form the finished investigative report is a reflection of the skill level of the investigator. Effective report writers will observe and remember these basic principles:

1. Use a personal notebook that will serve as a basis for your report.
2. Write as though you are telling someone what happened.
3. Use small, easy-to-understand words. Avoid technical or professional terms if possible. If that is not possible, define or explain the terms.
4. Be impartial and objective in what you report.
5. Report only what you know to be a fact; do not report assumptions.
6. Normally, write the report as a chronological unfolding of events.
7. Be certain the report is understandable in terms of what actually happened.
8. Be certain that important information is not omitted.
9. Be prepared to support quotes with notes. Quote exactly. If offensive or obscene language is used, quote it, don't soften it.
10. Be sure the report raises no unanswered questions.

IV. APPLYING INVESTIGATIVE STRATEGIES

Chapter 15

Problems Arise: The *What* of Investigation

In a corporate setting, there is little occasion for starting investigations unless it is known that something has happened, or is happening. Few organizations find it worthwhile to open investigations absent some strong allegation or other indication of serious misconduct. There are issues of resource management, disruption of operational activities, and protection of reputations that are important factors to consider before investigations will commence. It is generally unwise to begin an investigation absent adequate predication to believe that a prohibited act has occurred.

Corporations do routinely conduct examinations of departments, offices, sections, and workgroups to determine compliance with established controls, policies, and directives. These are audits, not investigations, and are an integral part of what the accounting profession calls the *control environment*. Audits help to discover some frauds against companies, and if routinely and rigorously conducted, create a general atmosphere that will deter some problems. Investigations occur when such deterrence is believed to have failed.

In the classic litany of investigative questions including *who, when, why, how,* and *what*, it is this last that is normally most conspicuous at the outset of any investigation. A somewhat fuzzy picture of the *what* of an investigation presents itself early on, very frequently upon the discovery of missing money, inventory, or other property. The investigation will normally proceed with the goal of bringing that picture into sharp focus. By answering the other questions posed in our investigative litany we manufacture and polish the lens by which that focus is achieved.

In this and succeeding chapters in this section we examine how the factors of the *who, what, when, where, why,* and *how* of an investigation in the private sector can be applied to the following case study. (Changes to the actual case facts have been made to protect identities and clarify presentation.)

Thefts from Old Midtown Church: Continuing Case Study

Losses Alleged: The What Emerges

One Thursday morning the controller of a large religious organization in the city telephoned me, asking for a meeting. Arriving at the headquarters building, I met with him alone in his office. He said that there might be something amiss with the weekly collections of a particular church. For our purposes, we will call it Old Midtown Church.

One of the volunteers who counted the money every Monday morning had called the controller to mention her suspicions. They were somewhat vague, but seemed to center around three things the counter had noticed. First, the overall amount of collected funds had dropped off over the prior two years at the same time that church attendance seemed at an all time high. Second, the total collections from the various Saturday and Sunday collections seemed to contain much less cash than the counter remembered being the case in earlier years. Finally, the counter had begun to notice that checks had appeared in the collections that were anywhere from one to three weeks old. Based on the counter's many years of volunteering, this all seemed very strange.

The controller explained the procedures for collections handling employed by the church.

1. *During each service, members of the congregation would circulate through the church collecting the donations of the membership. Donations were in bills, coins, and checks. Many of the members used preprinted envelopes and about the same number did not. The money was left on a small stand at the front of the church for the remainder of the service. Between Saturdays and Sundays, there were six different services presided over by any of three possible ministers.*

2. *At the end of the service the presiding minister would take the money, put it into a small canvas sack, and cross the parking lot to the church office building. Once inside, the minister would go to the office of the business manager and open the safe, placing the canvas bag into the safe and closing and locking the door before leaving. Only the ministers and the business manager of the church knew the combination to the safe.*

3. *The combination to the safe had not been changed in over a decade.*

4. *On Monday mornings the church business manager would arrive and unlock the safe at about 7:30 A.M.*

5. *At about 8:00 A.M. the head counter would arrive and proceed to the business manager's office. The head counter would place all the previous weekend's collection bags into a plastic tub and carry them to a small dining room in the church office building.*

6. *The counting team, already assembled in the dining room, would begin to sort the money and count the cash and checks. The preprinted donation envelopes, which bore a registration number identifying the donor's household and a handwritten notation of the amount of the donation, were kept for later use by the church office staff for input of the individual donations into the church computer system.*

7. *The counting team would fill out a weekly donation receipts sheet, roll the coins, and segregate the cash from the checks in order to assist in the preparation of the weekly deposit. The receipts sheet separately listed the total amounts received in cash and check.*

8. *The weekly donation receipts sheet and the money were taken by the head counter back to the business office and placed back into the still open safe. The head counter would lock the safe and depart.*

9. *Sometime later in the day, the business manager would open the safe, prepare a deposit slip based on the donation receipts sheet provided by the counters and take the deposit to the bank.*

I told the controller that this all seemed interesting, but fell short of proving that any actual theft was happening. He said that he had felt the same way when the information was given to him.

The controller told us that he had done an analysis of the donations history for that particular church and compared it to other churches in the area. For one month each year a head count was conducted of all the organization's churches in the city. From this he was able to determine a rough estimate of comparative attendance. Collections were reported monthly by each church. Comparing the two sets of information, he was able to produce some preliminary analysis. He shared the following findings.

1. *Old Midtown Church had enjoyed good growth in attendance during the prior three years. In fact there were two additional services added to the Sunday schedule to accommodate the popularity of the church. Other churches in the area had suffered some loss in attendance.*

2. The other churches' annual collections seemed to fluctuate in accord with the changes in attendance. In other words, when their attendance dipped, donations dipped. When more people came, collections increased.

3. Old Midtown's collections seemed to have dropped about twenty-four months earlier and stayed lowered, rising only slightly when attendance grew. Still, collections were significantly lower than three or four years earlier, even though overall attendance was now higher.

This analysis, showing suppressed collections during a period of rising attendance, seemed to provide additional cause for concern. The controller did not believe that the new members were poorer than the general organization's membership. He believed that the neighboring church's attendance and collections drops were attributable to people joining Old Midtown (and taking their money with them).

The controller felt that the possible dollar loss could amount to about $500 per week. Given that this may have been going on for two years, the potential loss estimate at the initiation of the investigation was substantial (24 months × 4 weeks = 96 weeks; 96 weeks × $500 lost per week = $48,000).

It was agreed that we would begin our investigation at once. Until some initial investigations could be undertaken, we agreed that no one at Old Midtown other than the pastor would be told about the investigation.

Chapter 16

Crime and Solution: The *How* of Investigation

There are two primary questions of *how* in the investigative process: How was the crime or act accomplished and how can the crime be solved or the culprit be caught? Both questions deal with strategy: the strategy of commission on the part of the criminal and the strategy of solution or correction adopted by the investigator.

To some extent, the detection strategy is often dependent on the strategy of commission; that is to say, you cannot catch an embezzler until you know how the embezzler is diverting funds. It does not automatically follow, conversely, that once you know how the crime was committed you will know how to solve it. The crime and its solution remain separate issues, despite the fact that one must follow the other, as the following case illustrates.

The Case of the Telltale Flour. In a processing unit of a warehouse operation, a serious morale problem had developed. An undercover agent was placed in the unit to determine the cause of the problem. The agent soon reported that the male supervisor of the unit was showing favoritism to one female employee to the point where she worked only if she felt like it. It was further rumored that her favored treatment, which was causing resentment among other employees, was the result of her generosity in bestowing sexual favors on the supervisor, an activity that was taking place somewhere on company property during the shift. An investigator's search of remote and likely areas of the property revealed irrefutable evidence of sexual intercourse taking place in a dark and rarely used stairwell behind some barrels stored on the bottom landing. The illicit activity and the "commission strategy" were now apparent. How to catch the supervisor in the act was not so clear. The investigation to this point had revealed what was happening, where it was happening, who was involved, why it was going on, and how it was occurring. One unknown factor remained: When was it happening? Until that answer was found, the case could not be resolved.

A number of solution strategies were possible. Some were tried or considered; most were rejected. The solution strategy required catching the couple in the act. It was not possible or practical to place an investigator on that stairwell landing and wait for the supervisor and the employee to arrive, because they would discover the investigator. It was not feasible to survey the landing with a television camera, nor was it possible to use cameras to cover all the various doors that provided access to that stairwell. A hard-wire microphone (a microphone and recorder-amplifier physically connected with a cord or wire that conducts the sound) failed because the wire picked up the radio signals of a nearby public radio transmitter. A wireless microphone with its own transmitter could not penetrate the concrete and steel stairwell enclosure. And it was not possible to put security personnel in or around the work area because their presence would have been so conspicuous as to deter the very activity we wanted to discover taking place.

Any solution strategy must consider the full range of possibilities open to the investigator, and make use of those adaptable to the particular circumstances. In this case the decision was made to enter the stairwell early in the morning, before employees arrived, and to carefully blow a small quantity of baking flour from the cupped hand to form a fine layer of flour on the floor of the stairwell landing. Then, at timed intervals, the patrolling security officer was to shine the beam of his flashlight at an oblique angle to the floor to determine if footprints were in evidence in the flour. The inspection intervals were supervised by an investigator in order to ensure that the supervisor under investigation was on the job and not near the stairwell, to avoid the risk of having the strategy discovered. Footprints were duly noted, and each day the floor was swept clean and new flour blown onto the floor.

After several days of surveillance it became apparent that the activity took place daily during the morning coffee break for the supervisor's section. Once the time of the event was determined, the couple was soon caught in the act. The supervisor was discharged for misconduct. The young woman resigned. Employees of that section were pleased that management had acted to correct what the employees considered to be an intolerable condition. Morale returned and productivity increased.

The thrust of the *how* aspect of investigation, then, is twofold; it seeks to learn, first, how the crime or activity was carried out and, second, to develop an appropriate strategy of solution or apprehension.

SCIENTIFIC DETECTION METHODS

Observation, hypothesis, and testing are the core of the scientific method. Once again the Book of Daniel, Chapter 14, teaches us that ancient methods were effective. Today's techniques of crime scene examination and the use of detection powders are merely updated applications of common sense.

> Cyrus the Persian was king of the Babylonians who had an idol named Bel. Daily, six barrels of flour, forty sheep, and six measures of wine were left for the idol to enjoy. Each morning the offerings were gone. Daniel, one of the King's favorites, was questioned by Cyrus: "Why do you not worship Bel?" Daniel replied that he only believed in his living God and Bel was merely an idol made by hands. Cyrus pointed out how much Bel consumed each night as proof that he was indeed a living god. Daniel assured him that Bel was merely clay and bronze. Cyrus threatened the priests with death unless they named those who consumed the food and drink, or if they could prove it was Bel, then the King promised to kill Daniel for his blasphemy. Daniel agreed.
>
> The customary offerings were laid out, and the priests bade the king apply a seal to the door to the temple, saying that if the seal was unbroken the following morning and the food

eaten, then Daniel should die. Before the doors were sealed Daniel ordered his servants to bring ashes, which they sprinkled throughout the temple. Only the king observed. In the night, through a secret passage beneath the idol, the priests, their wives, and children entered the temple and ate and drank all that was left for the idol.

In the morning the king went to the temple and ordered the seal broken. From the open doorway it was clear that the offerings were gone. Daniel stayed the king's entry, and pointed to the floor. The king saw the tell-tale footprints. The priests and their families were arrested and showed the king the secret entryway. Cyrus condemned those who would have had an innocent Daniel executed.

Cyrus gave the idol to Daniel who destroyed it and the temple.

HOW WAS IT ACCOMPLISHED? (COMMISSION STRATEGY)

The investigative effort to determine how some act was achieved is either *exploratory* in nature, such as exploration by trial and error, seeking to physically recreate the crime or action, or it is *inspectional* in nature. The latter approach may involve an examination of all steps or processes, looking for loopholes that logically could explain or prove how the deed was accomplished. In general, the investigative effort at this stage is reconstructive. However, where the activity is ongoing, as in the case of the supervisor's misconduct discussed earlier, it may be necessary to use covert or constructive means.

Developing the *How* by Exploratory Means

Identifying the *how* by an exploratory approach means just what the word suggests: systematically searching, probing, looking, tracking down every piece of evidence, and following up every lead to see where it takes you. It means trying to put oneself in the criminal's shoes, even, as the following case of burglary demonstrates, literally following in his footsteps.

The Case of the Locked House. A fellow employee and executive of the company, though not connected with the security organization, was the victim of a residential burglary. Over the weekend his home had been entered and quantities of his personal property were removed.

There was no evidence of forcible entry. The police came to the house, examined the premises, and made their official report. Along with the victim, the police theorized that one of the two doors to the home must have been inadvertently left unlocked.

Two weeks later the executive, who lived alone, returned to his house after spending the night with a friend, only to find that the place had been burglarized again. This time more property had been stolen. Again, there was no evidence of forcible entry.

Since there was no question about a door being left unlocked after the first experience, the official theory this time was that the burglar must have let himself in with a key. Considerable time and effort were expended in tracking former residents of the house, two single girls, and it was discovered that they had lent the key to the house to one or more boyfriends. While this possibility was being investigated, the executive called in a locksmith and had both door locks changed. Shortly thereafter, the house was burglarized once more, this time while the owner was out of town on a business trip.

By now the executive was alarmed. He began to suspect that close friends might be making imprints of his keys in wax, clay, or even on paper and, knowing his schedule, were letting themselves into the house with a newly cut key made from the impression. He was becoming that desperate. The central issue, of course, was more concerned with how entry was being made into the home than who was doing it.

Although the matter was under police jurisdiction, I wanted to help the company executive if I could. The problem was affecting his work. I wanted to see if I could get in by slipping the locks, by climbing a tree and entering through an attic vent, or in any other way gaining entrance, other than by using force or causing visible damage.

I started at the front door, attempting to slip a pliable plastic card between the edge of the door and the strike plate to push or force back the bolt until it was flush with the edge of the door, thus disengaging the lock. I could not slip the lock. The door's hinge pins were on the inside and not exposed. Had they been accessible, I would have looked for evidence of their removal, which would have allowed the door to be opened from its hinged side.

I worked my way counterclockwise around the house, checking doors and windows, looking for any way in. At the rear of the house I noted dirt smudges on the stucco siding below the kitchen window. The only logical explanation for dirt to be ground into the stucco was that someone had his shoe against the side of the house. The kitchen window was of the louvered kind, horizontal slats of glass that fit into metal sleeves. The panes or slats can be rotated outward to a horizontal plane to allow ventilation, or closed to a near-vertical plane. Close examination of the glass louvers revealed fingerprint smudges on every one. I removed the slats from the sleeves of the frames and, by placing my foot on the exterior of the house, at the same height as the dirt smudge I had seen, I was able to hoist myself up and through the window. Satisfied, I left the house the same way I had entered. I replaced each slat and rotated or pressed them down to the original closed or vertical position.

I told my amazed associate, "That is how your burglar friend comes and goes." He said he had wondered why, following one of the burglaries, a house-plant next to the kitchen sink and the louvered window had been tipped over. Now we knew how the crime was being committed. That knowledge offered direction for the next step, which could have been to stake out the home from the inside in order to apprehend the burglar or to correct the weakness in the physical barrier of the home. The executive in this instance chose to have vertical steel bars installed over the window. The pattern of burglaries ceased.

Developing the *How* by Inspectional Means

In attempting to discover how a crime was committed, it is often possible to use inspectional analysis. The investigator must examine internal procedures and practices of the company's operations, examining them for any weakness that the criminal might have taken advantage of. The approach is essentially the same whether one is looking for an accounting loophole exploited by an embezzler or a failure in accountability for goods leaving the company's premises at the shipping dock. The following case shows how a detailed reconstruction of an operating procedure can show where loss is occurring.

The Case of the Missing Checks. The restaurant operation of a major department store came under suspicion when the general manager noted the net result of the newly acquired Rotary luncheon business amounted to a disappointing $300.00, far below the projected $600.00 or $700.00 planned for. He called the treasurer of the Rotary organization and discovered that the treasurer had cancelled checks for over $600.00 that had been properly endorsed and processed by the company. This meant that one of two possibilities was true: Either normal business went down on Tuesdays when the Rotarians had their luncheon meeting at the store's restaurant or someone was stealing. The general manager suspected theft and referred the matter to security for investigation. If someone was stealing, the question was how? Not only was it important to learn how, but also how much and for how long.

The restaurant operation followed a very standard procedure. Each waitress was issued a bound guest checkbook and by policy recorded the date and check numbers contained in that book. For example, on August 16, 1999, Book #3455500–3455549 was issued to Marie Waters. Each guest's order, or party of guests' orders, were written on the guest check along with an itemization of the food and drink served. When the guest finished eating, the check was totaled by the waitress and given to the guest as an invoice. The guest presented the invoice, along with cash or a credit card for payment, to the restaurant cashier. The cashier inserted the guest check into a document certification "throat" of the cash register and then certified or recorded the amount of the sale. This certification process imprinted the amount on the guest check. All checks, along with the inner continuous register tape (called a detail tape), charge sales checks, and any voided transactions constituted the transaction media for that operation. And, like most business records, they were retained.

Each employee authorized to handle sales transactions used a specifically designated ID key that was part of the imprinted certification. Also, each transaction was supposed to be certified on the register at the time it was negotiated; that is, while the customer was standing there.

Theoretically, then, one could go back in time and determine, on any given date, how many transactions occurred, for what amounts, and by whom recorded and to verify each transaction on the detail tape with a certified guest check. If there were five hundred transactions on the tape, there should be five hundred certified guest checks. Not only should there be five hundred guest checks, but the checks should be consecutively accounted for by their serialized numbers.

In this investigation we reconstructed the guest checkbooks for Rotarian luncheon days. That meant that we attempted to reassemble the used books by locating and placing in proper order each certified check from a book to see if any were missing. Figure 16.1 provides a sample of the type of check involved. In this case, as suspected, checks were indeed missing.

On Rotary luncheon days, the restaurant manager served as hostess and cashier. It was the manager who was stealing. And now we knew how she was doing it.

Restaurants with a strong luncheon trade experience a hectic peak at that time. Typically, guests who have finished their lunch line up to pay their tabs and return to work. And, typically, cashiers in this situation tend not to certify each transaction at the time it is processed but rather to make change from an open register drawer and, later in the afternoon when things have quieted down, to go back and certify each guest check for its written face value. Missing guest checks told us that the manager-cashier would set aside several larger checks, total them on a scratch pad, and remove the exact amount of the grand total from the register. The money, along with the uncertified guest checks, went into her purse. The register never reflected a loss or shortage because the sales were never recorded.

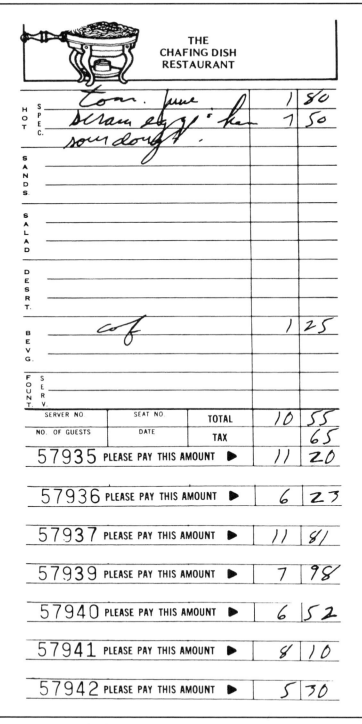

Figure 16.1. Reconstructing guest checks in numerical sequence to reveal missing checks.

With the strategy of the crime understood, it was then possible to develop the solution strategy. Because there was no way to place the cashier's area under surveillance, we chose to have integrity shoppers pose as luncheon guests the next time the Rotary Club met at the restaurant. Of the several guest checks gathered by our shoppers, the manager stole the receipts of one. Acting on that evidence, we were able to secure an admission of theft. We then opened the floodgates and overwhelmed the thief with evidence of losses dating back several years.

Of interest then, and even now, was the woman's admission of how she would tear up the guest checks into little pieces and let them flutter out of the wind-wing of her car on the way home at night — the window of a Lincoln Continental she had purchased with our receipts!

HOW CAN THE CRIME BE SOLVED? (SOLUTION STRATEGY)

In many cases the strategy of commission suggests the strategy of solution, as we said at the beginning of this chapter. The basic strategy, at least, often is indicated. Certainly that was the case with the restaurant manager who was stealing by failing to ring up checks. Why not let her steal one of your own sales as the triggering mechanism for the case? Likewise, if an employee is suspected of stealing money from the cash register at closing time each night, it follows that surveillance should be conducted of that employee at that time and at that location.

This concept of allowing the strategy of the crime's commission to suggest the strategy of solution is exemplified in the following case history.

The Case of the Dusty Shelf. An alert store detective had been inspecting back stock areas when she was puzzled by the odor of what smelled like fresh sawdust. Following her nose, quite literally, she found sawdust on a shelf in a narrow, unlit stockroom. Behind boxed merchandise on that shelf she found the source of the sawdust — a hole drilled through the wall. Leaning on the shelf and looking through the hole, she realized that she was peering into a dressing room used by female customers to try on swimwear.

The first process of elimination in determining the *who* of this case was relatively simple. Customers had no access to that behind-the-scenes part of the store. Without question, the hole had been drilled by an employee — probably a male employee. Because the stockroom housed lingerie items, a male salesperson could never justify his presence in that room. Our "Peeping Tom," then, would have to be in a job classification that would not arouse suspicion if he were seen coming or going or in that room. That narrowed it down to someone in either housekeeping or maintenance.

Carrying this process further, the sawdust chips were relatively large, indicating that the hole was drilled by hand with a brace and bit, the type of tool commonly used by professional carpenters and maintenance people. The most common drill found in the nonprofessional's toolbox is the quarter-inch electric drill. The conclusion was that the guilty employee would probably be found among the maintenance crew.

I asked three key people in that store, the detective, the store manager, and the personnel manager, which maintenance man, in their opinion, might be a voyeur. Each picked the same man, basing that opinion on such common observations as the fact that this individual was always talking to female employees; although he was married, he was rumored to be dating some employees; and, according to the personnel manager, she had caught him looking at her one day "with the strangest expression on his face." Hardly evidence, but the unanimity of opinion suggested that the employee named — call him Robert for purposes of this history — was the most likely suspect.

The location and type of construction of the stockroom made it difficult if not impossible for the room to be placed under surveillance. There was, thus, no way of knowing when Robert would choose to peer through the peephole at unsuspecting customers. Even if he were seen going into that room, there was no guarantee that you could walk in and catch him leaning on the shelf with his eye to the hole. The dressing room might be unoccupied at any given moment, for example, and the suspect might decide not to wait but rather to come back later. How could he be caught in the act, his eye to that hole? The strategy of solution adopted was to attempt to control both the time and the customer, and to signal that information to our suspect in order to induce him to watch when we wanted him to watch.

Putting myself in the suspect's shoes, in a mental exploratory process, I considered who would be the most satisfying to watch undress. The prettiest girl in the store? The girl he apparently liked most? Neither, I thought. The greatest satisfaction would come from observing someone the voyeur disliked most, the secret satisfaction of having seen her exposed and vulnerable. But whom would Robert dislike most in the store? The person who came to mind was the personnel manager. Ironically, personnel people often have a way of irritating other employees.

The personnel manager agreed to assist in the strategy of solution. The manager of the swimwear department was then called to the personnel manager's office and was asked to cooperate in playing out a brief scenario. She agreed, and the two women rehearsed the roles I had sketched out for them. With the little scenario ready to be enacted, I stood on the desk and loosened one neon light tube in the fixture directly in front of the door to the personnel manager's office. The stage was now set. The secretary called the maintenance department. Robert, our suspect, answered the phone. The secretary asked if he could come to the personnel office to replace a burned-out neon tube.

Robert arrived with a stepladder and a box of new neon tubes some fifteen minutes later. While he was standing on the ladder in the process of changing a tube, the swimwear department manager arrived on cue. She paused at the open door of the personnel manager's office and called out, "Marian, that lovely blue swimsuit you ordered last week just came in. Do you have time to come down and slip it on?"

"Oh wonderful!" the personnel manager exclaimed. "I'll be down in about five minutes."

This exchange took place in Robert's hearing. The swimwear manager, in fact, had casually taken hold of the ladder as she spoke to Marian. It was later reported that Robert came down that ladder fast, and in his haste to get out of the office he folded the ladder on one of his legs.

Minutes later the maintenance man was caught in the narrow, unlit stockroom, leaning over the dusty shelf with his eye to the hole that overlooked the dressing room. Subsequently, he admitted not only boring that hole but also several other smaller holes designed for the same purpose. He also admitted the need for professional counseling.

The employee was terminated, the holes were patched, and fortunately it never became public knowledge that a "Peeping Tom" had been watching lady customers undress in that store.

THE *MODUS OPERANDI*

More often than not, if an incident is repeated, how a crime or misconduct occurs is predictable. That is to say, the method of operation or *modus operandi* of the criminal is consistent. This in turn can indicate the solution strategy. If an employee steals funds by fraudulently preparing return or refund documents, you can count on that employee to pursue the same specific avenue of theft because, as he perceives it, it is a winning way. If a holdup artist uses a note to announce his intention to rob, that robber will consistently use a note. If a burglar is a residential daylight burglar, you will not find him operating at night against commercial establishments. Commenting on this predictability, Charles O'Hara writes of the repeating criminal ". . . he judges the value of his methods solely on the basis of successful accomplishments. Having achieved a few minor successes, he is loath to alter his operational procedure, his reluctance stemming from superstition, lack of imagination, and inertia. A summary of the habits, techniques, and peculiarities of behavior is often referred to as the modus operandi or MO, a term which means no more than method of operation."[28]

SELECTING THE SOLUTION STRATEGY

Whereas there is predictability and consistency in how a crime occurs, the MO, there is no such consistency or predictability in how the crime can or will be solved. Earlier in this chapter we said that the strategy of commission *suggests* the strategy of solution. Underscore the word suggests.

There are usually many different ways to solve a crime or apprehend a criminal. Take the case of Robert, the voyeur in the department store. A situation was contrived that, as it unfolded, led to Robert being caught in the act of his offense. But what if the personnel manager had refused to participate in the scenario? What if the swimwear department manager had been unwilling to cooperate or a poor actress? Or what if company policy, or the interpretation of that policy, had prohibited the strategy used? In any of these circumstances, an entirely different solution would have been required.

Consider the alternatives. One solution might have been to install a 35-mm camera loaded with infrared film that would take a series of still photographs once the switch was activated by pressure on the shelf. A variation of that solution would be the installation of a low-light CCTV camera. Another and very different detection strategy would be to dust the back part of the shelf and the wall behind it through which the hole was bored with one of three powders that fluoresce brightly under an ultraviolet lamp. Then, at least two times each day, the suspect could be exposed to such a lamp without his knowledge that he was being tested for the presence of the powder. Those powders can easily be ordered from supply houses selling to the law enforcement trade, and are commonly known as theft detection powders.

Yet another solution would be the installation of a pressure switch that, when the shelf was depressed by someone's weight, would cause a bulb to light in the corridor down the hall from the door to the stockroom. The light would burn only when the weight was on the shelf; it would go out when the pressure on the shelf was removed. The investigator could monitor the light and open the door to the stockroom only when the lighted bulb told him the voyeur was leaning on the shelf to get a better view.

In assessing these and the various other possible strategies that would apply to a given case, the investigator should consider the following factors:

1. If a given solution strategy failed, would it expose the investigative efforts?
2. Which solution strategy would put the suspect at the greatest disadvantage once caught?

3. Which strategy is the simplest in terms of manpower requirements, technology, the need for sophisticated equipment, and so on?
4. Which strategy would take the least time to implement?
5. Which would be the least expensive?

First consideration would be given to the effectiveness of the strategy if it were successful, and to the potential harm if it failed. But the other questions listed take into account the practical realities of most investigations. The best strategy is one that takes the least time, manpower, and expense — and works. The question of *how* in its twin aspects — the strategies of commission and solution — obviously plays an important role in the investigative process. The way an investigator answers this fundamental question will be a direct reflection of his overall performance and investigative skills.

Thefts from Old Midtown Church: Continuing Case Study

Confirming the Loss: The How Answered

The first step, as far as we were concerned, was to confirm that the loss was actually happening and to try to find out how it was being caused. An initial set of tests was devised, which entailed surreptitious observation.

Meeting at the church office late on a Sunday night, the controller and I, along with his and my assistants, conferred with the pastor, Reverend Williams. Reverend Williams deactivated the alarm to the business manager's office. It was monitored by an alarm company's central station. The controller had checked and found that there were no unexplained alarms during the prior three years. The only alarms generally had happened when one or another of the ministers had forgotten to disarm the alarm after a church service.

Reverend Williams admitted us to the church business office where my staff photographed and videotaped the entire office interior. They also inspected the windows and door locks of the office as well as the safe. There were papers piled high on filing cabinets, bookcases, and shelves immediately in front of each window. The inner windowsills were covered in a thick coat of dust. It was evident that they were never opened. In fact, some of them seemed to be painted shut. There was a window air conditioner mounted in a corner window. Its mounts also painted over, the air conditioner clearly showed that it was not being removed to effect entry.

An inspection of the outside of the office showed a low hedge growing against the outer walls. It and the soft earth below the windows indicated no disturbance for quite a while.

Our inspection also checked the rooms adjacent to and above the business office. Each of the walls, floors, and ceilings were completely intact. The door to the office was locked with three separate devices. There was a lock in the doorknob. There was a separate dead bolt with keyways on both sides of the doors that would make leaving through the door impossible once it was locked without exercising force on the frame and door. Also, on the outside of the manager's office was a push-button combination lock.

Reverend Williams told us that a couple of years earlier the business manager had said that she did not like leaving the door unlocked during the day when she was away from her office and did not want to carry her keys each time she left her office. Only she and the ministers had the combination to the push-button lock. If she closed her door while she was in her room during the workday, office staff was forced to knock for admittance.

The safe was approximately thirty inches tall, twenty-four inches wide, and twenty-four inches deep. It was old, but appeared sound. At our initial inspection we found it locked. It was also so heavy that the concerted efforts of two investigators were needed to push it even a few inches. Reverend Williams told us that the business manager was always very strict with the safe. Whenever a new minister came to the church and was given the combination, she admonished him never to write it down. She warned that if she ever learned that a minister had written it down she would have a locksmith change the combination and charge the minister for the expense. As far as Williams knew, all the ministers abided by the rule, and the business manager certainly never needed to write it down herself.

While the investigators were conducting the premises security inspection, the controller's staff was given the six canvas bags from that weekend's services by Reverend Williams. They repaired to the dining room and proceeded to count all the cash, checks, and coins not in envelopes. By the expedient of holding donation envelopes up to a bright desk lamp they were able to easily determine the amounts of checks and single bill donations. Where multiple bills were sealed in an envelope, they tore the envelope open and counted the cash, taking the envelopes with them. They then refilled each canvas bag. They noted down the total amount of each check as well as the total currency collected by denomination. They confirmed that every check received had been dated either that day or the day before.

In this way, after about two hours' work, we were able to know exactly how much money had been left in the safe on Sunday night, as well as how much of it was in checks, and the total number of one, five, ten, and twenty dollar bills donated. A little after midnight we left. I was fairly certain that there was no likelihood that a burglar was breaking into the office. Within forty-eight hours we should be able to tell whether a thief was working on the church staff.

On Tuesday afternoon the controller called me. He told me that the report of the church counters had been received. The differences between their report and the surreptitious count of Sunday night were interesting. Most obvious was the fact that the total documented by the counters was over $1,000 less. At my request Reverend Williams had arrived at the office early and enjoyed several cups of coffee as he socialized with the counters. He helped the head counter carry the cash tub back into the manager's office. He accompanied the head counter back to the business manager's office, personally holding the safe door open as the money was locked away. We were certain that the counters had not taken the money.

I had arranged with the head of security at the bank where the funds were deposited, to have the deposit inspected when it was received. It was found to contain less currency than the controller's staff had counted on Sunday night. The curious thing was that while the total loss was only about $1,200, the difference in cash deposited was almost $1,500. In looking further, there were checks found in the deposit that had not been in the safe on Sunday night. They were all written one to five weeks earlier, and together totaled a little more than $300. Also, some of the checks that had been observed Sunday night were not included in the deposit made Monday afternoon.

Based on the information obtained in this first test, we formed the following hypothesis for how the money was being taken.

1. *Sometime after the last Sunday night collection was placed in the safe by one of the ministers, some person or persons were accessing the funds and taking out cash and checks.*
2. *The thief effected entry into the office and safe by both key and combination. The alarm was not tripped at the time of the entry.*
3. *For some reason, the checks stolen during earlier weeks had been substituted for some of the cash taken during the early morning hours of Monday.*

We began to set about deciding how we could conclusively solve the crime. After weighing the options that seemed obvious by the case facts, we decided to plant a camera hidden in the office of the business manager covering the safe and desk area.

Chapter 17

Identifying Suspects: The *Who* of Investigation

The first of the basic questions in investigations is directed at establishing who is responsible for a given act. It should be understood that there are many other questions of identification that might be asked in any investigation. Who can be trusted to keep the inquiry quiet if confidentiality is needed? Who can provide technical information or assistance? To whom should the investigation be assigned? Who might know who did it and be willing to inform? Considering the type of investigation, who might be the most effective interrogator after the responsible party is caught?

But the most important and popular question asks *who* is the responsible person or culprit? That question is the very stuff of which mystery novels are written, the reason such stories are called "whodunits." After determining what happened, which is usually (though not always) apparent, all minds immediately commence the speculative process designed to discover who could have done it.

THE PROCESS OF ELIMINATION

In the fanciful world of mystery novels, the suspect is usually one of a small cast of clearly defined characters. It had to be the butler, the disinherited nephew, the brother-in-law, the wife in the wheelchair, and so on. Interestingly, in most cases in the private sector dealing with internal problems, there is also a relatively small cast of possible suspects. Take, as a typical example, a series of thefts from a cash register. If a total of seven employees have access to that register, it is from that small cast that we must identify our prime suspect.

As in the murder mystery, the first steps are designed to eliminate who it isn't. The disinherited nephew is the most likely candidate but he could not possibly have killed the old man because he was locked up for drunk driving in the city jail at the very hour the crime occurred. This process of elimination is applied until only a few suspects or preferably one is left.

In our register theft case, we would plot or chart the history of the losses and compare that history to the record of the seven employees' attendance, as illustrated in Table 17.1. This graphic chart tells us that employee Leland can be eliminated because he was off work when a theft occurred on February 23; Beutok because he was out ill when two thefts occurred on February 19 and 20; Daniels

Table 17.1. Cash register timetable

FEBRUARY	Mon	Tue	Wed	Thu	Fri	Sat	Mon	Tue	Wed	Thu	Fri	Sat	Mon	Tue	Wed	Thu	Fri	Sat	Mon	Tue	Wed	Thu	Fri	Sat
	1	2	3	4	5	6	8	9	10	11	12	13	15	16	17	18	19	20	22	23	24	25	26	27
Cash Shortages	$20		$20	$40	$40	$40	$20		$40		$40		$40				$50	$50		$40	$50			
Wagner				X						X						X						X		
Leland		X						X						X						X				
Morton		X						X						X					X					
Beutok				X						X						X	X sick	X sick				X		
Daniels	X						X						X						X					
Sanchez		X						X					X	— V A C A T I O N —					X					
Rundstedder				X	X sick					X					X					X		X		

X = DAY OFF

because he was off duty when three of the thefts occurred, on February 1, 8, and 15; Sanchez, because he was on vacation during one week when three of the losses occurred; and Rundstedder, because he was sick on Friday, February 5, when $40.00 was taken. Only Wagner and Morton remain as suspects and deserve watching. The process of elimination has reduced the number of suspects from seven to two, greatly simplifying the investigation.

The Case of the Anonymous Letter.   In one actual case a college student received an anonymous letter concerning his fiancée. The letter was obscene and luridly graphic in describing the alleged sexual orientation and history of the young woman the student loved and was about to marry. Although he did not believe the charges in the letter, the student was deeply disturbed to know that someone who knew both him and his betrothed would write such a letter. He did not wish to involve the police or postal authorities, but he did ask for my assistance as the chief of campus police.

We listed on a piece of paper everyone who knew the young man and his fiancée. That list constituted our cast of characters; on that list was the suspect, the author of the letter. Since we were in possession of a typewritten letter, the next task was to obtain, secretly, samples of typed material from the typewriters owned or used by all those persons on the list. The sample was to be one full paragraph taken from the offending letter so that a direct comparison could be made. Typewriter after typewriter was eliminated because the samples could not match the original letter. Finally, all the student's friends and work associates had been eliminated, at least in terms of typewriters known to exist. There were only three machines left to be checked — the three in his parents' home. Somewhat reluctantly at this point, the student brought in sample paragraphs from two typewriters, one in his father's study and the other in his brother's room. In each case the type did not match the original.

I asked about the third and last typewriter in his home. Where was the sample from that one?

"Oh, you can forget that one," he said. "It's my Mom's. Besides, it's in her bedroom and she spends a lot of time up there. I don't think I can get to it anyhow."

After some persuasion the student brought in the typed sample from his mother's typewriter. It matched! The student refused to believe it, becoming very upset and defensive of his mother. I did not accuse her but simply told him that, in my judgment, the original offensive letter had been typed on his mother's machine. He wanted proof. Through the low-powered microscope he was able to note the same distinctive type characteristics that I had found.

Several days later the young man's father came to the office, quite angry. He calmed down after making the same microscopic comparison. Shortly after this discovery the student and his father confronted the mother with my findings. She then admitted authoring the letter. She did not want her son to marry for fear of losing him. The drama-packed emotional confrontation and confession brought recognition of the mother's need for medical help.

No chart was feasible in this second case, but the same process of elimination was applied to determine which of the suspects was innocent, until only the guilty one remained.

READING THE PHYSICAL EVIDENCE

In some cases, either through chance or circumstance, the elimination process is not necessary. A proper reading of the physical evidence will point the investigator toward the offender.

The Case of the Missing Eyeglasses.   One night several students scaled a main building on campus and draped over the facade an uncomplimentary message aimed at the school's administration. Lying on the roof after the escapade was a pair of eyeglasses. The cleanliness of the glasses indicated that they had not been exposed to the elements for any length of time but had been left there recently. The obvious conclusion was that they belonged to one of the students who had hung the sign.

The thickness of the lenses made me wonder how their owner ever got down from the roof without them, let alone climbed up to the roof while wearing them. It was reasonable to assume that the owner could not go very long without a new pair of glasses. If the local optometrists could not identify the owner through the lens prescription, they could be alerted to notify me if and when anyone showed up seeking new glasses with the same prescription. Those eyeglasses were like a calling card. Before the day was out, the student's identity was known. A local optometrist recognized the glasses. I called the subject and told him that I had his glasses and he could pick them up at my office. He wanted to know where I found them. When I informed him, there was a long silence on the phone. I asked him about that silence later. He said, "I was just thinking to myself . . . what if I'd done something *really* bad?"

A Case of Red Paint.   The semester was about to end. Summer vacation was a matter of days away. I was called at about seven in the morning at my home by a member of the administration of Scripps College, frantically reporting that a great deal of damage had been done during the night to statuary and Shakespearean reliefs at the college.

At the scene I found that someone with a bucket of red paint had prowled the inner courtyards and passageways, applying the paint to the genital areas and breasts of a large number of wall reliefs and statues. The removal of the paint would be very costly; moreover, it could well cause the loss of some of the details created by the artists.

By carefully examining the paint droppings on the tile and stone flooring, I was able to follow the route the vandals took as they moved from art object to object. Partial sole markings left in some of the paint droppings also established that there had been more than two persons involved.

The last object painted was near the front and side of the building complex, adjacent to a broad expanse of lawn that separated Scripps from the neighboring men's college. By crouching close to the ground it was possible to track the red drippings on blades of grass across the lawn. The trail brought me to the wall of the home occupied by the men's college president. Painted on the wall in letters three feet high was a lurid, two-word obscenity. In terms of how we think in the private sector, the damage done to the statuary was a misdemeanor, but the writing on a president's house changed the case to a felony!

I continued to follow, at times on hands and knees even though dressed in a business suit, the trail of infrequent drops scattered on the leaves of grass. It led back across the lawn to a clump of bushes at the side of Scripps College. There in the bushes was the paint can and brush. The can was not really a paint can but a container used to package candy. The brand was unfamiliar. It was a product manufactured in Phoenix, Arizona. The paintbrush, too, was not really a paintbrush. It was a wadded up portion of *The New York Time*s, of a recent date.

Who composed the cast of characters for this offense? The evidence pointed to immature students of the men's college. Why immature? My experience with the upperclassmen of Claremont Men's College, an outstanding academic institution, convinced me that none of these older students would be involved in such a foolish and destructive episode. Female students at Scripps, on the other hand, would not be likely to deface their own campus. Moreover, they had no quarrel with the president of the men's college.

Given this conclusion and the evidence I had tracked down, my task then was to identify those freshmen and sophomores at Claremont Men's College who (1) came from the greater Phoenix area, and (2) subscribed to *The New York Times*, or any two young men who roomed together at the college and who together would meet my twin criteria. Within an hour those few students whose homes were in the greater Phoenix area were listed. Shortly after that the mailroom provided me with the names of those students who received *The New York Times*.

One freshman met the criteria. His dormitory room was empty when I called there. The door was unlocked and I went in. The chrome handles of the bathroom sink were sticky with red paint. The soap bar and the white interior of the washbowl were pink and also sticky with red paint. The balance of the New York newspaper not used as a paintbrush was still in the room. I left the building and went to the parking lot set aside for that school. The student's automobile, parked in the lot, was examined. Red paint drippings were visible on the ground behind the car, as though a can had been opened there and the paint transferred from one can to another.

The physical evidence gathered within a few hours was enough to lead to the identity of several young men, who were subsequently dismissed from college. The trail of red paint and the evidence were able to point to the culprits, but only when that evidence was read accurately and the judgment was made eliminating older Claremont students and Scripps College students. Finding the physical evidence that is there is only the first part of the investigator's challenge. He must also be able to interpret the significance of what he finds.

THE INVESTIGATIVE INTERVIEW

Often the available physical evidence alone is insufficient to point to the *who* of an incident. In such cases the investigator must track down every possible detail that might be relevant. One of his tools is the careful and thorough questioning of any person or persons affected, whether victim or witness, as the following case illustrates.

A Case of Kidnap and Rape.   Late one spring evening I received a call from a house mother, the resident manager of one of the female dormitories at Pomona College. She reported that she had a serious problem and insisted on my presence. When I arrived, there was a campus police unit as well as a local city police unit parked in front of the dormitory. Both units advised me that a campus unit had been requested and the city unit had acted as a backup. When they reached the scene they were informed by the house mother that a girl had been raped, but the manager then refused them admittance to the dormitory.

Once inside the building I had a brief conversation with the reported victim about what had happened. Although she seemed to be in a state of shock or near-hysteria, she told me that she had gone to the basement of the building, where the coin-operated washer and dryer were located, to do one load of washing. When she pushed through the double swinging doors of the washroom, she was startled to see a young man standing there, brandishing a knife. According to the girl's story, the attacker forced her to crawl out of the basement through an open transom window. He followed her out. After climbing over a wall that surrounded the dormitory area, she was forced into the back seat of a four-door sedan. There she was trussed up, lying on her stomach while wrists and ankles were bound behind her back. With the girl helpless on the floor of the car, the man drove up into the nearby mountains. There he raped her.

After the attack he drove back into town, releasing the girl at the intersection closest to the dormitory. She could not get in because it was past lockout time, the hour when every girl had to be inside. She pounded on the door until the house mother heard her and let her in.

Immediately after this initial interview I had the girl transported to the hospital for (1) a vaginal smear for evidence of semen, (2) a medical douche, and (3) medication to calm her. Before she left I told her that we would meet again in the morning, along with the local police, and talk more in depth. After the girl left I examined the scene of the alleged attack, carefully inspecting the basement area. Lying on the floor just inside the double swinging doors was a box of detergent, some of which had spilled on the floor; two quarters; and a few items of intimate apparel. Nearby was an open transom window; beneath it was a bench. While standing on the bench I was able to peer outside. I could see clear foot impressions in the flower bed. I set a cardboard carton over those prints. (I would take plaster of Paris casts of those footprints the next day.)

At the hospital the following morning, a representative of the police and I sat with the girl to get more details about her experience. The report of the attending doctor had confirmed that there was a seminal deposit. The girl described her attacker. During the course of the questioning a number of details were gone over carefully. She had been wearing a "baby-doll" nightgown when she went to the basement, a sheer, loose, short-sleeve pullover top with matching briefs. She did not attempt to run, even though she was out of the building first through the transom, because she was afraid. She scaled a six-foot wall, although she probably could not do it again. She had no idea what kind of car was involved. She did not fight or resist the man because he threatened her. While up in the mountains, the attacker at first had tied her wrists to separate trees, her arms stretched out in a spread-eagle position. Later he had untied her, and she admitted that, during the drive back into town, he had left her untied and sitting up on the front seat of the car.

It became apparent that the police representative was skeptical of her story. He became aggressive in his questioning. To one question she admitted that she was not a virgin. For my part, I continued the interview with the belief that she was telling the truth — in which case I needed specific details, as suggested by the following exchange.

"Can you recall if the rear-view mirror hung down, came out from the windshield, or came up from the dashboard?"

"I don't remember."

"Was the front seat and seat back cold or warm?" It had been evening, and the answer would indicate a cloth or synthetic seat covering.

"Cold, come to think of it."

"Was the radio turned on in the car?"

"Yes, I remember music, and I remember him saying he wanted to hear a news flash if there was one . . . about us."

Of the many minutiae included in the questioning about the car, the following proved invaluable: "Did you see any words, numbers, or symbols on the dashboard?"

"One time I put my foot up on the dash, and I remember the word 'Eight' was right by my toes."

"Printed or in script?"

"Script. And in chrome. The word went up at an angle like this." The girl motioned with her finger.

"Did he smoke?"

"Yes, cigars."

"Cigars!"

"Yes, . . . in fact, I remember, on the way back, he put the stub of his cigar in the ashtray and it started to smolder. I was choking on the smoke so I reached over to close the ashtray. He yelled at me, 'Don't push in that ashtray. You'll put out the light!' Then I realized there was some kind of light connected with the ashtray, and the light shone down around my legs."

In interviewing a victim or witness, it is important to get every detail possible. In searching questions about the suspect rapist, I asked the girl to recall everything he said to her, sometimes repeating questions in the effort to learn absolutely everything she could remember. As I continued to probe she suddenly said, "Oh! I remember one thing he said that I didn't understand at all. He said, 'The landscaping at Pomona College stinks!' "

When I left the girl at last I had a considerable amount of information about the *who* of this case. I set about locating a man about twenty-five years old, blond, stocky, about 5'8" tall, whose choice of words coupled with his coarse, rough hands suggested that he was a blue-collar worker or laborer. I knew also that he had an opinion, for whatever reason, on landscaping. Additionally, he drove a two-toned, light-over-dark, 4-door sedan that did not have cloth seats and had very dirty, uncarpeted floors.

The search in this case was complicated by the fact that the police were of the opinion that no crime in fact had been committed. They believed that the girl had been out having fun and was caught by the dormitory's lockout policy. To protect herself against any disciplinary action, she contrived the kidnap and rape story.

Believing otherwise, I asked the maintenance people of the college to provide me with a list of every contractor and subcontractor who had worked on or around the institution. At the same time automobile manufacturers were queried in an effort to identify the auto used in the crime. Was there any model auto equipped with a light switch connected to the ashtray and also a chrome script "Eight" that ran at an upward angle on the passenger side of the dashboard? The answer came back; there was one such car, for only two model years, the 1952–1953 Pontiac.

I requested that the police ask the Department of Motor Vehicles for a listing of all 1952 and 1953 Pontiacs registered in Los Angeles and San Bernardino counties. They felt that was asking too much. I then asked if they would assist in obtaining auto registration information for all the license plates on such cars that I could come up with. They agreed, despite their belief that I was on a wild goose chase.

Meanwhile, contractor after contractor hired at one time or another by the college failed to throw any light on the search. About the fifth day of this full-time effort, I called a water sprinkler contractor who had subcontracted an installation at the college the previous year. I made the call just before lunchtime, asking the now routine question, "Did you have a young man working for you while here on the campus, someone in his mid-twenties, about five-eight, with blond hair?"

"Sure did," came the answer. "His name's Bob Greene." (This name is fictitious for the purpose of this work.)

"Where's Bob now?" I asked, attempting to sound calm.

"Gee, I don't know. Haven't seen Bobby in a year, I guess."

"Don't you have his last known home address?"

"No."

"You must have some kind of records for tax withholding purposes, workman's compensation, and the like."

"Oh, I don't keep those kinds of things. My bookkeeper keeps all that."

"What's her name?"

"It's a him."

The contractor gave me the name and phone number of the bookkeeper. I called him immediately, explaining that the contractor had given me his name, and asked if he could provide me with Bob Greene's home address. Within a few minutes I had the suspect's home address, which was in a neighboring city. I went home for lunch but could not eat. I left the table and drove to the address on the note tucked into my shirt pocket. Parked in the driveway of the house, which was in a somewhat run-down residential area, was a dirty, two-toned, light-over-dark, 4-door, 1953 Pontiac sedan. On the back seat of the car lay a rope. The seats were covered in vinyl, the floors uncarpeted and dirty. Cigar butts were in the ashtray.

Later that afternoon, Bob Greene was picked out of a police lineup as the assailant by the victim of his attack. Before the day was out Greene admitted the abduction and rape of the girl. He was convicted for his crimes and served time.

COMBINING TECHNIQUES

Often investigations rely upon a combination of interviews, physical evidence, observation, informants, decisiveness, and luck. Stubborn persistence should not be forgotten.

A Case of Cash and Diamonds.   We had frequently conducted investigations of items stolen from office buildings, identifying various responsible night workers (janitors, guards, clerks, etc.). The particularly vexing thing about one case was that we were the victims.

On a Tuesday morning I heard the president of our firm making a commotion in his office. Going to investigate his outburst, I was informed that the petty cash box in his file cabinet had been pilfered of eighty dollars. I had left it unlocked and was relieved that my offer to make up the loss was declined. We were pretty busy and decided not to do anything at the time other than ensure that in the future the cabinet was properly locked.

On Wednesday I heard my boss exclaiming loudly — much louder than on the prior day. He told me that the cash box again had been accessed and fifty dollars were gone. He admitted that he had left a spare key in an unlocked desk drawer.

Our professional pride wounded, we began to investigate. We lifted a number of latent prints from the cash box and planted a dummy key. We placed a hidden CCTV camera and recorder to cover both the drawer where the key was and the front of the file cabinet opposite the desk. Our camera would catch the face of the thief as he retrieved the key and any subsequent attempt to use it.

I contacted the building manager and found that there had been about a dozen petty thefts in the prior ten days. Change, snacks, and postage stamps had been taken from offices. He gave me a list of victims and permission to contact them. He also gave me copies of the relevant janitor and guard sign-in logs. I learned that there were no signs of forced entry and all victims said that they had left the items unsecured in their offices. All losses appeared to have occurred at night. The last interview was significant. A law office located on our own floor had reported only the loss of postage stamps. When I spoke to the managing partner of the firm, he invited me into his office.

Closing his door, he said he had not reported one item. The firm had accepted a woman's diamond ring as a surety against their services in her planned divorce. It was worth several thousand dollars and was missing. The client had not yet been told of the theft. I said we hoped to have the thefts resolved soon.

Analysis of the guard and janitorial logs was inconclusive, as there were several people who had been present on each night associated with a loss. Our hidden camera would be key.

The next morning we found that the file cabinet had been forced open with a tool. While inspecting the scene we found a small tool box disturbed. It had been opened, but not relatched. Checking its contents, we agreed that only the small hatchet could have made the pry marks found on the cabinet. There were small streaks of paint matching the cabinet on its blade.

We played the videotape. The recording showed the room darkening as the sun went down and remaining that way for several hours. In the mid-evening the black turned to murky gray as the outer office's lights turned on. Later, the scene became fully light as the room was entered by an older woman followed by a man. The woman stepped to the side of the desk and retrieved the trash can, blocking the man's face. When she exited, the man's back was turned to the camera as he dusted the area next to the filing cabinet. He wore a black t-shirt, the back of which had a picture of a white pit bull dog. He left, his face having never been exposed. The lights went out and stayed that way, no one was visible again.

The drawer had definitely been opened, but no one was seen in the office except the janitors. We ran the tape back, looking for any telltale signs of a shielded flashlight or other illumination that could have been used. Although it took hours to accomplish, on the second time through we caught something. Just prior to the entry of the janitors into the room, a small light-colored shape floated across the screen. It was faint, but it was definitely there. It appeared suddenly just in front of the file cabinet and lingered there for a few seconds, it then moved a few feet to the left and sank toward the floor (where the tool box was). A moment later it floated up toward the front of the cabinet, hovering there for about thirty seconds. Then it abruptly disappeared. That was it, nothing else was gained from a full review of the tape. The mysterious shape was tantalizing. We replayed the tape again and thought that the light object floating in the dark was the same shape and size of the white pit bull printed on the back of the male janitor's shirt. We were close, but we still did not definitely have the *who* of the investigation solved. We figured that we probably could begin a sweep among the janitors until we located the fellow whose size and shape fit that of the male janitor in the video. On the other hand, we really didn't have a crime or other misconduct to tie to him.

We reluctantly decided to bait the drawer again with money. This time we left the desk lamp on to light the room. It was not exactly a stage spotlight, but we knew it would be an improvement.

The next day we found over $100 taken. The videotape clearly showed a male (whose face was not well illuminated) go to the file cabinet, pull the drawer open, and reach into it. His hand went from the drawer to his pants pocket. He closed the drawer and left. We felt much better. From the general build, and a wristwatch, we felt certain that it was the "white pit bull" guy. We had but to wait for him to return with the older woman to confirm his identity with the room lights on. Unfortunately, he did not return. Instead, two women arrived. We decided that we would change tactics and grab him in the act. Early in the next janitorial shift we secreted an investigator in the ceiling above the file cabinet with a narrow view of the scene below. Two others of us hid in an electrical room, ready to rush the thief when our partner radioed that a theft was under way. Seven long hours passed, the women janitors came and went, and nothing happened. No male.

Sometimes one must be patient and keep surveillance going for many, many days and nights before something happens. Intuitively we sensed this would be fruitless. Besides, we were getting frustrated. We approached the janitorial supervisor who came to our office. He was clearly thirty pounds lighter and significantly older than the man in the video.

We explained that we were investigating thefts in the building and wanted his help in identifying someone. We showed him the tape of the man in the pit bull shirt. He looked intently at the man and then at us. Do you recognize him or the shirt? Yes. How? I gave him the shirt; he is my son. Where is he now? He's just started a two-week vacation. Can we rely on you to bring him to our office tomorrow? Yes, what is missing? Some money and a ring. The interview ended. Our instincts told us he would return.

The next morning, the two men arrived early. We took them into a conference room. The younger man clearly had not slept, and sported fresh bruises on his face. His father gravely placed several hundred dollars in cash and a diamond ring on the table. We took only what we had lost and began to prepare a receipt. The older man expressed his deep regret and told us his son, who said nothing, was prepared to accept the consequences of his actions. We felt pity for both of them.

We were interrupted by a staff member who said a man who insisted on seeing us immediately was in the lobby. We went to talk to him. It was the partner of our neighboring law firm. He was frantic, saying that he had just received a call from his client who was on her way over with her husband. They had reconciled and she wanted to pick up her ring. We told him to go back to his office.

We returned to the conference room and announced that we were going to let the issue pass as a private matter. Both visitors seemed immensely relieved and immediately left. We took the ring next door and laid it on the desk before the attorney and his client, announcing that we had personally guarded it the entire time it was in our custody. The client beamed and thanked the attorney for having private detectives secure her precious ring.

Unlike public investigators we could, and did, decide our course based on our own priorities. We didn't have a cooperating victim in the single largest theft. We had been made whole on our own thefts, for which there was very marginal evidence, anyway. The son had received swift and certain justice at his father's hands. We went back to producing billable time, and replaced the file cabinet lock, pleased that we hadn't spent a fortnight in the ceiling waiting for the thief to return from his vacation.

SUMMARY

Investigation is a very inexact science, which we must nonetheless approach as a science. An intriguing aspect of the cases cited in this chapter is that these cases were solved more by common sense and persistence than by sophisticated skills. Check every possibility, get others to assist, follow up on the most minor piece of evidence, obtain every possible detail, trust your intuition, and stay with the search tenaciously — these are the laws of our "science."

In seeking to identify the *who* of a case, remember the following:

- Eliminate those who could not have played a part in the incident.
- Collect and analyze all available evidence.
- Look for relationships between evidence and possible suspects.
- When appropriate, obtain the assistance of law enforcement.
- Make full use of available information sources (e.g., automobile manufactures).
- Do not jump to conclusions or prejudge the case.
- Make full use of the investigative interview.
- Persist, persist, persist.

Thefts from Old Midtown Church: Continuing Case Study

Covert Camera: Determining Who Was Stealing

In the following week my investigators entered the business manager's office and placed a small CCTV camera with pinhole lens. It was roughly the size of a pocket box of matches. My investigators glued it to the back side of a silk leaf on an artificial potted plant in the back corner of the office. The pot sat above and behind the safe. Shooting through a 1/16-inch hole in the leaf, the camera provided a view of the door to the office, the back of the manager's desk, and the top of the safe. Anyone entering the safe would be facing the camera both while entering the office and when stopped before the safe. Based on the depth of the dust on the plant and surrounding shelf, we knew that no one bothered with that area of the office. Our "planted" camera seemed safe from discovery.

The video feed from the camera was connected by a short cable to a wireless video transmitter mounted behind the cabinet upon which the pot rested. Its antenna was pointed to beam its signal upstairs. In the room above, a small guest room used by visiting ministers, the receiver was positioned along with a time-lapse video recorder and small monitor. It was agreed that Reverend Williams would admit a team of investigators late Sunday night.

At the appointed hour, the investigators arrived at the church office. They conducted a safe count, similar to that of the previous week. They checked the video feed and found it to be working perfectly. They started a tape in the time-lapse recorder set at a speed that would cover a full twelve hours. They again departed at around midnight.

The next day we got a call from Reverend Bill who said that the volunteer counters' weekly donation receipts sheet had been filed. While the business manager was out of the office he had secured a copy of it. He faxed it to our office and we compared it to the previous night's safe count. Again, the total listed was more than $1,000 less than we had counted. The total amount of cash counted was $1,100 less than Sunday night. The amount of checks were about $100 more than there should have been. A hit clearly had occurred.

Reverend Bill brought the videotape to our office. He was able to certify that he had the only key to the guest room and he had kept the tape on his person from the time he took it out of the recorder until bringing it to our office. Our investigators began a chain of custody document and took control of the tape. It was soon being reviewed in our conference room.

The camera, highly light sensitive, allowed for decent resolution during the hours of darkness from the illumination cast by the parking lot lights outside the office windows. No one entered the office. At a few minutes after 7:00 A.M. the door was opened and the business manager came in to the scene. She put a large handbag under her desk and sat down. She turned on her desk lamp and took out a book from her desk. Reverend Williams told us that the manager read the Bible for thirty minutes each day, and gave strict instructions that she was not to be disturbed before 8:00 A.M. A few minutes passed before the screen suddenly went to "snow." Nothing but static played on the remainder of the tape.

As professionals, we know that technical failures happen sometimes, but this was a bitter blow to those of us present. From viewing the tape, we could not tell how the system had failed. Reverend Williams was able to tell us that he had been in the building that morning and did not believe that any unusual visitors had called and no one had gone into the business manager's office between the time she entered and the time the head counter had arrived. I sent one of the investigators back to the church with the pastor, admonishing him not to return until the system was operating fully. Thirty minutes later the investigator called us to report that the system was working again. He said that when he and Reverend Williams started the system he had noted that the receiver's antenna was pointing straight down. Having been involved in the initial installation, he knew that this was not as it had been left. He asked Reverend Williams whether he had been in the room that morning. The Reverend sheepishly admitted that he had been so anxious about the impending theft that he had come to work early and decided to "check" on the camera and recorder to make sure everything was running. The receiver was pointed down at the floor at what seemed to be an odd angle. The pastor thought it was amiss and realigned it directly at the floor. The transmitter actually was located below and about ten feet to the side of where the receiver was situated. The original antenna angle had been about forty-five degrees from the perpendicular, pointing directly at the transmitter's antenna. Reverend Williams had certainly "fixed" the installation, and of all times, just when a theft might have occurred!

Based on what was seen on the videotape, we were able to determine that no one had entered the office prior to the business manager. Based on what Reverend Williams had said, we knew that she had been alone in the office until the counter arrived at about 8:00 A.M. Reverend William's further observations with the counters determined that they had not taken the money.

We therefore were able to eliminate all parties other than the business manager as suspects in the apparent thefts. We felt certain that a week later we would have our thief "captured in the act" on tape. We felt confident that we had answered the who in our investigation; the manager's name was Helen Moore. Our attention in the intervening week turned to the matters of when, where, and why.

Chapter 18

Finding Information: The *Where* of Investigation

In attempting to determine who was involved in a crime or incident under investigation, the emphasis is on the search for identity. When attention turns to the question of *where* in an investigation, the emphasis is one of discovery. The question of *who* is people-oriented. The question of *where* is location-oriented. As with the first question, there can be a number of location questions that might be relevant to a given case. Where is the offender? Where is the evidence? Where are the fruits of the crime? And where can information be found that assists in the investigative process? Locating individuals, physical evidence, or stolen goods, when they are not discoverable through the routine of physical search, is often a matter of knowing where to look for the right information.

The effective investigator knows where to find the information he needs, just as an effective lawyer knows where to research case law. Sources of information are all around us. Some may be so conspicuous and familiar that their potential is not realized, as the following two investigations illustrate.

The Case of the Missing Mascot. The student body president of Claremont Men's College reported that someone had stolen the school's mascot from an unlocked building over the weekend. The issue was an emotional one. As a rule, students take a dim view of the theft of their mascot. The prize in question was a life-sized stag deer, poised on a platform that could be carried by four to eight men on their shoulders. The size and weight of the mascot made it obvious that several people had to be involved in carrying it off, and that a truck or trailer had to be used to remove it any considerable distance from the college.

Security officers who had patrolled the area over the weekend were asked if a truck or trailer had been seen near the building that housed the stag. One officer had observed a Chevrolet car pulling a yellow, tandem-wheeled trailer in that immediate area. The auto was occupied at the time by what appeared to be college students, and nothing particularly suspicious was observed by the officer.

Even though the possibility of finding any physical evidence was remote, I checked the area carefully. My search came up with a wing nut lying in the gutter of the street alongside the building from which the stag was removed. The wing nut had yellow paint on it. The wing nut appeared to be of the type that is used in pairs to hold the rear gate of a trailer in place.

Turning to the first basic investigative question, I asked myself who could steal a college's mascot. College students from a rival school, of course! What would be the motivation for absconding with their rival's prized possession? Again an obvious answer suggested itself. The thieves probably intended to parade the captured stag, with something less than decorum, at the next football game in which the rival schools met. If that premise was true, the potential for a small riot was clear. The stag had to be recovered before the game in question.

Where Was it?

The telephone directory held the answer. I obtained a phone book for every city in which a rival college was located. I began with the book for the city in which the college that was scheduled to play Claremont the upcoming Saturday. Using the yellow pages of the directory as a guide, I telephoned every trailer rental agency in that city, asking, first, if their trailers were painted yellow and, second, if they had a tandem-wheeled trailer. In my calls to the third city on my list, which was the home of the University of California at Riverside, I received affirmative answers to both of my questions. Riverside was scheduled to play Claremont Men's College in a football game in three weeks. I then asked if the four-wheeled trailer had been rented over the past weekend. It had been. I asked the man on the telephone if he would check the tailgate to determine if the trailer was missing one wing nut. There was a short wait until he returned to the line. He said, "Why yes, it is. How did you know?" There was a puzzled note in his voice. "I have it and I'll bring it over," I said. "I'll be there in an hour and a half."

The rental agency was a Riverside service station. When we returned the wing nut to the tailgate of the tandem-wheeled trailer, we then examined the rental agreement. It contained the name of the renter, his driver's license number, address, and automobile license number.

I took my information to the University Police at Riverside. The renter of the trailer was a registered student. When confronted with the evidence, he admitted his involvement and told us where the stag had been hidden. As we had guessed, the thieves intended to use the mascot to put down their Claremont rivals during the forthcoming game.

The student body president of Claremont Men's College and several other students triumphantly returned the stolen stag to their campus, thanks to one wing nut and a telephone directory.

The Case of the Stolen Calculators. Another case that hinged on locating stolen property involved the theft of ten expensive, small calculators from a Broadway Department Store. One of the company's many stores specifically ordered the calculators from the manufacturer. The shipment arrived in that store accompanied by an invoice. The invoice was approved and forwarded to the accounts payable department of the finance division for payment. The calculators were placed in a locked stockroom behind the camera department. The manager of that department saw the calculators in their original shipping carton on several consecutive days. Then the calculators disappeared.

Security was advised that the calculators were gone. An investigator from the main office was assigned to the case and dispatched to the particular store. A search revealed the original shipping carton in a trash deposit. Several key employees of the store, including members of management, were questioned about the calculators. One member of management seemed unduly nervous. There was, however, no evidence against him or anyone else.

Two weeks passed and the case remained unsolved. Only one possibility suggested itself. The nervous management employee, whom we will call Mr. Dunbarr, was conspicuously upset each time the investigator reappeared at the store. The conclusion was reached that Mr. Dunbarr was the thief, despite the fact that he was known as a very religious man and a leader in the community. If he stole the calculators, what did he do with them? If they could be found, we could possibly connect them with Dunbarr. But without them there was no evidence against him, only suspicion.

In thinking the matter through, it became apparent that the special order for the calculators must have been put through to satisfy a request. An order for ten units would have come from a commercial source rather than a private party. Further, it was concluded that Mr. Dunbarr would be one of the few individuals who could walk out of the store carrying a large box or parcel without arousing suspicion. He must have carried the calculators out and delivered them to the party who had placed the initial order. It seemed probable that that party might be ignorant of any wrongdoing. The calculators might have been paid for in cash or a personal check made out to the executive under suspicion.

If this hypothesis was correct, the next logical assumption was that the purchaser naturally would have acted to protect his legitimate investment by forwarding the product warranty cards identifying each calculator to the manufacturer.

We pulled the serial numbers from the invoice. The next morning a call was placed to the manufacturer, located in another state on the other side of the country. All ten warranty cards had been received. They had been mailed to the manufacturers from a travel agency in a community near the Broadway store.

A team of investigators went to the travel agency. The stolen calculators were observed in use on various desks. The owner was asked to talk in the privacy of his office. There he openly discussed his interest in and eventual purchase of the calculators from the Broadway. He had dealt with one of the store's executives, a gentleman who was a friend and a member of the travel agent's church, Larry Dunbarr.

"How did you pay for the calculators?" he was asked.

"By check. I would never carry that much money around on me."

"To whom was the check made payable?"

"To Larry. He said he'd take care of it back at the store."

"Do you have that cancelled check back from the bank?"

The agent was becoming agitated. "There's obviously something seriously wrong or you wouldn't be asking me these questions."

"That's why we're asking questions. It appears you may be the innocent victim of receiving stolen goods."

"How could they be stolen when I got them from your company?" he protested.

"You may have made payment for the calculators, but that payment was never received by the company. As far as the company is concerned, the calculators are missing from the inventory. Stolen, if you please. And you have them. That doesn't look good, does it?"

"But I paid for them," the agent cried. "One thousand dollars!"

"Mr. Green, you got a real bargain for a thousand dollars, and you know it. The truth of the matter is, either you were in collaboration with Mr. Dunbarr and knew these calculators were 'hot,' or he took advantage of you. We tend to think the latter is true and we expect your cooperation. We want the calculators — we'll give you a receipt for them — and we want your cancelled check."

We received the travel agent's cooperation.

If such simple and readily available sources of information as a telephone directory and the warranty files of a manufacturer can make the difference between success or failure in an investigation, imagine the almost unlimited number of sources that are ignored, unknown, or untapped.

The detailed listing of private and governmental information sources on the following pages is by no means all-inclusive. Nor does the listing here always imply easy access. In some areas the information is extremely difficult to obtain. In others the information is there for the taking. The important point is to appreciate the vastness of the sources of information available to the investigator. How one accesses these sources is essentially a matter of skill, ingenuity, personal contacts, and tenacity.

SOURCES OF INFORMATION IN THE PRIVATE SECTOR

In seeking to discover the *where* of an investigation, the diligent investigator will familiarize himself with the wealth of files and records in nongovernmental sources containing information pertaining to persons, companies, personal property, and real property. Not all personal records are equally accessible, but a great deal of information *is* available, although sometimes only under subpoena after the filing of litigation.

Banks

Savings accounts can provide information regarding the balance in the account, dates of deposits, whether deposits were made in cash or by check, and amounts of deposits. Amounts and dates of withdrawals are also on record. Checking accounts contain the same information regarding deposits plus check activity, including the number of checks written during a given period, to whom, and for what amounts. Banks also keep records of large currency transactions, the date and time of each entry into safety deposit boxes, and other information that can be of use in investigations.

Loan Companies

Loan applications reflect employment data, primary income and other sources of income, property owned and its location, state of indebtedness in terms of amounts and to whom owed, and a variety of personal and family data.

Credit Reporting Agencies

Most trade, professional, and business entities have their own credit reporting agency, such as retail credit agencies. They have information in detail about customers by name, marital status, spouse's name, number of dependents, present and former addresses, how long at an address, credit rating, companies that have dealt with a customer before, and that history. The major business (as opposed to personal) credit reporting agency is Dun and Bradstreet, which maintains historical data on businesses and the principals connected with the business.

Escrow Companies

Escrow company files will contain the details of numerous real property and other financial transactions. Similar to the records held in real estate offices, the escrow company files will show the bank of origin of payments made in real estate transactions, as well as any special instructions regarding the disposition of deposits, payment of expenses, and conveyance of property sent by the principals involved in transactions.

Title Insurance Companies

Title insurance company records identify the owner of a given piece of property, latest address of that owner, date property was purchased or sold, and the amount of that transaction.

Telephone Companies

From just a phone number in the telephone directory one can determine where the phone is located and the identity of the subscriber. Other phone company records contain information on the length of service at that address and where previous service was located, monthly billings, and an itemized record of toll calls. There are also "reverse guides," listing subscribers by address as well as the alphabetical listing. Unpublished telephone numbers are on film. Wireless phone companies also frequently list each number called by the wireless subscriber, along with certain incoming calls.

Other Utility Companies

Applications for cable TV, water, power, and gas service will reveal some personal information on subscribers, as well as where they had previous service, when service commenced, and a history of usage. Most utility companies maintain records by address, so occupants of a given address can be identified (except for rental property where the landlord pays the utility bills).

Van and Storage Companies

Moving and storage records will reveal where an individual came from and when, or where he is going. If goods have been stored, it may be possible in some circumstances to examine the goods in storage.

Insurance Reporting Services

Your firm's counsel or risk management executive can direct you to the agency that maintains files on bad risks and histories of claims filed against carriers.

National Insurance Crime Bureau

The National Insurance Crime Bureau (NICB) is an industry-supported organization that lends insurance and investigative expertise to member companies as well as law enforcement agencies. NICB personnel conduct investigations, intelligence analysis, and training as part of the organization's overall mission to help identify, detect, and prosecute insurance fraud artists. NICB Special Agents also provide expert witness assistance to prosecutors, especially in theft ring cases. The organization also compiles and publishes insurance fraud studies.

Funeral Directors

In addition to financial data on the deceased and facts about the estate and survivors, funeral directors are often privy to a great deal of gossip and other casual information about the survivors as well as the deceased.

Taxicab Companies

Cab companies maintain records of trips, including the time and location at which a taxicab took on a fare, the passenger's destination, and amount of fare. Some packages are also sent by cab. Some individuals will have cabs pick up liquor and deliver it to themselves.

Auto Rental Agencies

The records of car rental agencies will reflect driver's license information, local address of the renter, mileage driven, and the names of others authorized to drive the rented vehicle. The same records will also have a description of the car rented, telephone number where renters can be reached, any credit cards used, information on the method of reservation, as well as the home and business addresses of the renter.

Drugstores

Prescription files of drugstores will reflect, for each prescription, the doctor's name and address, date prescription was written and date filled, type of drug (from which it may be possible to determine the ailment), and patient's name and address. Drugstores also maintain a poison register that records type of poison purchased, the quantity, to whom it was sold, and reason for purchase.

Film Processing Company

A neglected source, film processors may be able to provide photographs of a subject, his family, friends, and surroundings.

Real Estate Offices

The records of realtors will include the asking and selling price of a given property, names of seller and purchaser, amount paid down, name of the mortgage company holding the first trust deed, and a description of the property, often quite detailed. Most realtors belong to local multiple listing services, which can provide information regarding properties offered for sale as well as historical data relating to similar properties in close proximity to a subject property.

Real Property Appraisers

Property appraiser files will list important information about individual properties at particular points in time, including a detailed description (often accompanied by photographs) of a subject property and other properties used as comparison sites. They will often typically note the individual bank or finance company officer who ordered the appraisal.

Hospitals

Hospital records contain patient information, including their treatment and medical histories with that particular facility, as well as insurance data and other personal information.

Newspapers

Newspapers, like any other business, maintain files on the names and addresses of subscribers and advertisers. In addition, the newspaper "morgue" file is a cumulative file on every person whose name has ever appeared in the paper, including a photograph if one was used in a story. Newspapers also maintain a library of every issue in the paper's history.

Schools

School records include the name and address of every student, with date of birth and place of birth. Personal data on each student will include name and address of each parent, the parent's occupation and place of employment, whom to call in the event of an emergency, and the family doctor's name and number.

Colleges and Universities

In addition to personal data similar to that found in schools, college and university records may provide such information as extracurricular or off-campus affiliations and activities, academic objectives, grade-point average, major field of study, financial status of the student, and work history while attending school. Class yearbooks include student photographs. Some *alumni associations* also have up-to-date mailing lists of graduates, with a current history of each.

Housing Projects and Landlords

The administration offices of housing projects maintain files on tenants by name, address, age, number of children, former or forwarding address, place of employment and salary (if salary is a determining factor in residing in the project, which is normally the case), rent payment history, and history of complaints by other tenants, if any. On-site managers and neighbors may have personal information about individuals and their families not normally found in office files. Landlords of privately owned rentals maintain information similar to that kept by housing project offices.

Better Business Bureau and Chamber of Commerce

The Better Business Bureau keeps files on all scam operations and operators in the community. The Bureau can provide information on the business reputation of local or distant businesses or can report that no derogatory information about a business has been recorded. The local Chamber of Commerce can provide a map of the community with an overview of climate, growth, primary industry, population, and other data. The Chamber of Commerce will also have information on local businesses, and will have copies of back issues of the city directory.

DIRECTORIES AND PERIODICALS

The telephone directory cited in a case history earlier in this chapter is only one example of an almost inexhaustible quantity of printed matter available to the investigator as sources of information. As one small example, take three publications in the security industry: *Security Management* magazine, *Security* magazine, and the American Society for Industrial Security's membership listing by member's name and by the member's company's name. These three publications are a mine of information about who we are, where we can be found, what we do, and how we go about doing our work. The same kind of information is available about almost every occupational specialty in this country, from accountants to zoologists.

The following list suggests some of the most common and useful directories. No attempt is made here to list the enormous number of periodicals available covering every field; in this connection the directory of periodicals is a valuable source.

City Directories

Each city publishes a directory containing the name, address, occupation, and sometimes the place of employment of residents of that city. Back issues can provide the same information covering previous periods.

Directory of Physicians

The American Medical Association (AMA) publishes the *Directory of Physicians* in both hard copy and CD-ROM versions. Listings of more than 700,000 physicians are included, which provide names, addresses with zip codes, medical school and graduation year, when first licensed in the listed mailing address state, and any specialties or certifications. Similar information is available at the AMA Web site on its AMA Physician Select page.

Reader's Guide to Periodical Literature

As opposed to data concerning the periodical itself, the *Reader's Guide* lists magazine articles by author, name of magazine, and title of article. The articles are also listed under their general subjects. An electronic version is also available.

U.S. Identification Manual

When the authenticity of a piece of identification is in question, the *U.S. Identification Manual*, a privately published guide, can be consulted. It contains color samples of drivers' licenses, military and government identification cards, and license plates. Similar pictures are provided of bank credit cards, travelers' checks, and commercially issued credit cards. It also contains a list of 24-hour telephone numbers for verification of U.S. government investigative agencies.

Who's Who

The *Who's Who* contains biographical information on prominent persons. Similar biographical compilations are available covering prominent individuals in different fields of endeavor, including authors, scientists, and such.

Baird's Manual of American College Fraternities

Baird's Manual provides a complete listing of fraternities and sororities, both active and inactive. Data for each organization include the history, objectives, numbers and locations of each, and their individual publications, if any. This manual is printed very infrequently (last in 1990) and should be considered only for deep background purposes.

INFORMATION SOURCES IN LOCAL GOVERNMENT

Government agencies at every level often seem to be in the business of collecting and maintaining files and records of every description. Although privacy limitations may restrict access to some personal information, most of the data accumulated in such files are a matter of public record and available to anyone. Municipal and county records useful to the investigator include the following sources.

Tax Collector

Records of the local or county tax collector include the names and addresses of property taxpayers, legal description of property, amount of taxes paid on real and personal property, and the status of taxes — whether delinquent, for example. Tax records also include the names of all former owners of a given piece of property.

Building Department

Building permits record the name and address of applicant, location of construction, amount and cost of construction, and blueprints and diagrams showing details of the building. The files may also name the licensed contractors responsible for the construction.

County Recorder

The County Recorder's office is the repository of such records as all papers pertaining to real estate transactions, mortgages, certificates of marriage, wills, official bonds, transcripts of judgment, births and deaths, and bankruptcy records. The detail included in some of these records is quite extensive. The birth certificate, for example, includes name of infant; sex; date and hour of birth; exact location of birth; if the birth was premature or full term; the parents' names, ages, addresses, and occupations; length of time in the occupation; mother's maiden name; the condition of the infant; and the name of the attending physician.

The death certificate is an even more striking example. It gives the name, address, sex, age, race, birth date, and birthplace of the decedent; place, date, and time of death; how long the decedent had been in the community, the country, the hospital (if death occurred herein); whether the decedent was a veteran and, if so, what war; the social security number; marital status with name and age of spouse; occupation of decedent; parents' names; mother's maiden name; and the name and address of the person who is reporting the death. If death occurred while under a doctor's care, the medical certificate would reflect the doctor's name, how long the decedent was under treatment, the last time seen alive, and the doctor's statement as to the cause of death. If the decedent died while *not* under a doctor's care, a 'coroner's certificate will reflect whether death was accidental, suicide, or homicide; date and location of death; whether death occurred at work or not; and, finally, the disposition of the body, including information concerning burial, cremation, or removal (with place and date), and funeral director's and embalmer's names and license numbers.

This kind of exhaustive detail is common in most governmental records. Marriage license applications and divorce filings similarly offer much information to be searched.

Registrar of Voters

The affidavit of registration reflects the name of the voter, age, address, occupation, political party affiliation, state of birth, where and when naturalized if foreign-born, any physical disability that prevents the registrant from marking his own ballot, and the last previous place of registration.

Welfare Department

Very complete files in the welfare department include information on where and when a person worked, salary, what property the recipient owns, property owned by relatives, state of health, criminal background information, and detailed data concerning immediate members of the family.

County Recorders Civil and Criminal Indexes

The *Civil Index* lists all civil actions, usually alphabetically by plaintiff and defendant, and by date with a reference file number. Criminal actions in the Superior Court are listed alphabetically in the criminal index by defendant with a reference file number to the criminal files (see next).

County Recorders Criminal Files

In addition to reflecting the type of crime, the County Recorders Criminal Files include a transcript of the testimony given in the preliminary hearing, which in turn provides names of all officers and witnesses, and a copy of the probation department's report on the defendant's background.

County Recorders Probate Index

The *Probate Index* lists actions alphabetically by the name of the estate or petitioner for causes of action relating to adoptions, incompetence, insanity, and termination of probate.

In some jurisdictions the information held in county recorder civil, criminal, and probate indices will be found in the courthouse for the trial courts handling each type of matter.

INFORMATION SOURCES IN STATE GOVERNMENT

Various state departments maintain voluminous files on individuals and corporations. Many either are open to inquiries by ordinary citizens or will provide information for a small fee. In addition to the specific officers and departments noted here, most states have a regulatory relationship over vocations such as doctors, dentists, athletes, pharmacists, barbers, optometrists, veterinarians, chiropractors, contractors, embalmers, and nurses. Personal data would be available in these and other vocational files, in some states through a department of professional and vocational standards.

Secretary of State

The Secretary of State has records of all articles of incorporation of businesses, associations, and churches. The same source also has a record of all names that have been legally changed, and maintains records on election returns and candidates for elective state offices.

Controller

The State Controller keeps an account of all warrants drawn on the state treasury, examines and settles accounts of all persons indebted to the state, and inspects the books of persons charged with receiving, safekeeping, or disbursing state funds.

Department of Agriculture

As might be expected, the Department of Agriculture controls weights and measures and performs other tasks related to agricultural activities within the state. It has information on dairies, state-licensed veterinarians, stallion registration, and cattle brand registration, among other agricultural data.

Department of Motor Vehicles

Records of automobile ownership, past and present, are maintained by the state's Department of Motor Vehicles. Files include licensed operators of vehicles with a history of moving violations and accidents. In many states, photographs of licensed drivers are available. In general, files may be accessed in two directions. If the driver's name is known, data can be provided on make and model of vehicles owned and operated, and the license numbers. If a vehicle license number is known, its owner can be identified. In recent years, due to federal pressure, states have begun to restrict the availability of motor vehicle information. It is still available in some states to ordinary citizens for a small fee, usually by mail. Law enforcement agencies have direct and swift access.

Department of Industrial Relations

This department maintains files on industrial accidents and, usually, oversees trade apprenticeship programs. Its files also may include records on unfair labor practice problems based on charges of discrimination.

Department of Natural Resources

The Department of Natural Resources maintains complete files on such matters as mining operations, parks, forestry activities, fish and game licensing and violations, and oil, coal, or gas operations within the state.

Department of Alcoholic Beverage Control

Files kept by the Alcoholic Beverage Control Board include information on licensees reflecting name, addresses (both home and business), marital status, and detailed background history.

OTHER SOURCES

Online Information Sources

Many of the sources of information previously assembled in difficult to access forms are now much more widely available through the use of the Internet.

There are innumerable sites on the Web comprising some 170 terabytes of data (more than seventeen times all the books in the Library of Congress), many of which will provide general background information that can be of use to investigators. Some can provide very specific information about individual persons and companies. Some are available at no charge, some require a paid subscription or have per-search charges.

The constantly evolving nature of the Internet means that any list of sites quickly becomes outdated. However, following are the kinds of sites, with a few examples, that have been useful to investigators.

General Information Sites

Often, the private sector investigator is confronted by an investigation dealing with persons or subject matters about which little is personally known, or archived in firm records. In those instances accessing some of the following often proves very helpful in obtaining general background information.

Search Engines

Search engines are well known to be the basic method of conducting Web-based searches for relevant information. They are generally free to access and are updated continually for new information and sites, although they do not always do as good a job in removing outdated sites.

PUBLISHING/JOURNALISM RESOURCES

By using publishing and journalism resources, it is possible for an investigator to locate persons who are acknowledged experts in virtually any field worthy of note. If, for instance, one wished to obtain information on forensic entomology, one could easily find articles in general or specialized periodicals for background information. The names of more prominent experts undoubtedly would become obvious and direct contact could be initiated if in-depth information is desired.

American Journalism Review

Earlier we noted that newspapers archive vast amounts of information contained in their news morgues. Through the use of the Internet it is possible to pull the cumulative information from thousands of news organizations. One excellent method of researching these sources is an online source known as the *American Journalism Review (AJR)*, which has well-organized links to magazines, newspapers, broadcasters, and even news services. *AJR* claims to link over 18,000 sources. In addition, there are links to reference sites of common use to journalists. As an example of the efficient organization found on this site, newspapers can be found by location (state, nation, continent, etc.), or type (Major metros, Dailies, Non-Dailies, Business, etc.). This site is located at http://ajr.newslink.org/.

PubList.com

In some cases investigators want background on a specific publication itself. One quick way to obtain thumbnail data is at a site that calls itself *The Internet Directory of Publications*. PubList.com lists publications and publishers and claims links to over 40,000 publishers. An individual listing will show the publication title, subtitle, type, frequency, editor name, subject matter, and circulation. The address of the publisher, any parent company, telephone numbers, and Web site home pages are also listed.

Records Held by Government

State, local, and federal government agencies collectively compose a vast repository of information. The degree to which that information is readily available to online researchers is extremely variable, depending upon, among other things, agency budget, governing privacy/public-access statutes, agency staffing and expertise, as well as that agency's commitment to granting wide access to information.

If one desires to be complete while researching government records online, this is an area where there is little choice but to either get advice from professional researchers, obtain a good guidebook, or both. One comprehensive guide is *Public Records Online*, which contains a very readable explanation of how public records are filed across the United States, down to the county level. It also has a state-by-state listing of federal, state, and county public records repositories and the extent to which records are available online. It also includes a directory of over 400 private companies that provide public records research, and a chapter with lists of government Internet sites such as the Library of Congress, the Supreme Court, and the National Technical Information Service.

Databases

In the last decade the number of databases available on subscription or fee-per-use bases has grown significantly. Many of them compile private and public information that can be of significant utility to investigators. Some of them have been in use for two decades, such as *Lexis-Nexis*. Others are newer, but nonetheless have come to prominence, in part by purchasing existing data providers. ChoicePoint's CDB service is one such example. Typically, these private databases can be used to do extensive research on individuals, including residential histories, telephone numbers, business affiliations, publications written for, as well as other useful applications. Some such companies also will coordinate the retrieval of documents from public agencies.

Published Investigations Guides

There are numerous books published that will teach one to conduct research efficiently. Two very dissimilar examples are offered. *The Guide to Background Investigations*, updated every two years since it first appeared in 1987, is a large, detailed guide of over 1,900 pages, which provides exhaustive information on a county-by-county basis of public records throughout the United States and provides information relating to such diverse background topics as military records, state medical examiners, pharmaceutical licensing boards, vital statistics, GED test scores, bankruptcy records, and driving records, among numerous others. It measures almost $11'' \times 8\,^3/_4''$ and is virtually the "bible" for serious background researchers.

On the other end of the spectrum is *The Investigators Little Black Book*, a diminutive volume filled with 2,500 real-world information sources of practical use to investigators on a day-to-day basis. The entries in this directory are extremely brief, some little more than an agency name and telephone number; however, it is what is likely to be very well thumbed by working investigators — a practical listing of useful information. At $8^1/_2'' \times 4''$, this book, together with the encyclopedic *Guide to Background Investigations*, will provide investigators the starting point for almost any research investigation.

With respect to sources of information about individuals at the federal government level, very little can be said of current value to the investigator, simply because very little information is available. This is primarily a result of Right to Privacy legislation.

This is not to say that a one-on-one relationship with a representative of any given federal agency would not be useful and productive. The opposite is true. If, as an example, a post office inspector and an investigator from a major corporation had a case of mutual interest, undoubtedly there would be an exchange of information. The same applies, of course, at the state and local government level as well.

In the same vein, no attempt has been made to list as potential sources of information the many law enforcement agencies at every level of government. Again, the one-to-one personal relationship, based on mutual need and respect, can produce results that otherwise would not be possible. Even in the so-called "information age," trust, confidence, and professional courtesies are the lifeblood of the professional investigator in search of "where" to get the information vital to the case.

Chapter 19

The Time Factor: The *When* of Investigation

The question of *when* in the investigative process is obviously time-oriented. The question seeks to isolate and identify a significant time factor, be it a time before or after a known event, a span of time between known events, or a specific time.

Known time can eliminate possibilities; for example, a bus could not make it from the east side of town to the west side in ten minutes. It can also eliminate suspects; for example, when the fire started, Harry was on his day off. Further, the determination of when an offense occurred or is occurring gives direction to the detection strategy. If money is being pilfered from a given location regularly, for example, it simplifies the investigation to determine that the pilferage must be occurring between 5:00 A.M. and 7:30 A.M.

With regard to criminal offenses, the entire issue of the statute of limitations revolves around the time factor. The perpetrator of the crime must be identified and moved against within one year after the commission of the offense (the general rule for petty or misdemeanor offenses) or within three years (the general rule for major or felony offenses). Consequently, if the discovery of a crime takes place months or years after its commission, the task is to prove that the offense occurred within the period specified under the statute of limitations.

Through this text, in citing examples and case histories, as well as other common observations both actual and hypothetical, many kinds of observations tell us something about time. In many of these examples the times determined are only approximate, but even such approximations can be valuable, as this review suggests.

1. Placing the hand on the hood of a car: Reveals the car has *recently* been driven if the hood is warm.
2. Matching paint on the door of one car and body of adjacent vehicle: Suggests contact was made between parking and discovery of the paint.
3. Coals in center of fire: Suggests *when* the fire was last fed.
4. Post mortem lividity: Reveals time of death.
5. Rigor mortis: Helps determine time of death.

6. Sap in a tree limb fracture: Suggests *when* the branch was broken.
7. Damp side of stone turned to the sun: Shows *when* stone was disturbed.
8. Dry clothing of a suspect when it is   Reveals amount of time suspect has been inside
   raining: the store.
9. Cash register "plot chart":   Establishes which employees could or could not
                                                have committed thefts, based on the time factor.

Just as much energy and imagination may be expended to determine the significant time factors in an investigation as are devoted to determining who did it. And again, as in other aspects of the investigative process, much can be achieved through the application of common sense and the power of observation.

METHODS OF ESTABLISHING TIME

Self-evident Time

Perhaps a classic example of establishing the precise point in time when an incident occurred is the case of the smashed watch on the wrist of the dead driver of a vehicle that careened off a mountain road, an accident unobserved. More often than not there is no way to determine time with such precision, but there are a surprising number of what might be called self-evident time indicators. The simple situation of a teakettle boiling on the fire is one example; it could not have been at the boil for long or the water would have evaporated in steam. Among literally thousands of such examples that could be cited is one involving a typed document dated in the 1960s that had been typed on an IBM Selectric typewriter prior to the production of the Selectric. Or a 1980s document printed on a particular printer before such printers were available. The evidence speaks for itself.

A minor incident offers further illustration. It occurred when, by chance only, I noticed a quantity of rubbish and trash that had been dumped illegally along an isolated dirt road in a remote area reserved for nature studies. The trash appeared to have been recently dumped, as indicated by the fact that the papers were not weathered in any way.

Personal trash is often an interesting source of information in any investigation. In this case I wished only to identify the person who chose to litter this protected natural area. Among the trash was an envelope addressed to a resident of a neighboring community. It was postmarked three days prior to my discovery. Also found among the rubbish was a personal note addressed to the same individual.

In my official capacity I telephoned the party in question, a woman, and instructed her to get back in her car, drive out to the area, and retrieve her trash. At first she feigned ignorance, claiming that she had just walked in the door upon returning from a two-week vacation. She could not possibly have done what I accused her of. It was not difficult to convince her that she should clean up the mess she caused. Had there been no way to pinpoint the time factor in this matter, however, her story would have been more difficult to shake. As it was, the evidence of *when* was impossible for her to overcome.

Significant Time Variations

Relevant considerations of time can frequently be determined by noting a variation in an established process or pattern of activity. Theft of money is a typical problem in the work environment, whether the victim is the company, an employee or guest, a client or customer. Usually the discovery of a loss requires an immediate assessment of when the theft could have occurred. Determining the time factor is usually a key to identifying possible suspects.

A typical example is theft from cash registers that hold money overnight when the premises are closed. In the usual procedure, all the money in the register is removed temporarily at the end of each working day. From that total quantity, a daily "bank" or working fund is subtracted from the total and replaced in the register. The drawer is then closed. The balance of the money removed from the register represents the day's receipts from that register, which are deposited. The following morning a person other than the one who closed the register the previous night opens it and counts the "bank" (which is always the same amount, such as $100.00). If there is a variation from the established amount, that variation must be reported.

Most registers and terminals have the feature of an inner "detail" or "journal" tape that records each transaction as the day progresses; for example, the thirty-third time the register was opened on April 16th was a sale in the amount of $23.46 by employee Smith. Additionally, in a normal operation, some member of management will clear each register, usually with a special key, at the start of the day's business. This clearing allows for the daily audit of sales, and each day starts back at the zero transaction number. Put another way, a series of "No Sales" are rung on each departmental and clerk's key, erasing the previous day's totals. The register then awaits the new day's business. The first time it is activated, it will record that transaction as number one. (Note: Earlier in this work we discussed a different strategy whereby the transaction numbers continue day after day and the sequence is important, which is obviously a different control than discussed here.)

When the employee opens the register/terminal in the morning to verify the bank, that entry constitutes the first transaction. If on that entry the bank is found to contain only $80.00 instead of the established amount of $100.00, there is a $20.00 shortage. In determining who could possibly have stolen this money, the investigation must first determine, if possible, when the theft occurred. Did it happen at night during the closing procedure? At night after the closing procedure? In the morning during the clearing procedure? After the clearing procedure but before the first regular transaction? Or during the first normal transaction?

As a rule, such thefts do not begin and end with one act. They tend to occur with growing frequency until the culprit is caught. Given the circumstances outlined, the investigator would take the detail tapes for days on which no losses occurred and compare them with the tapes for days of loss. If the person who opened or closed the register took the money, the tapes would show no variation. The same would be true if the management or security representative who cleared the registers was the thief. (In fact, these three persons would be unlikely to steal from this particular source.) The tape comparison frequently will reflect an additional entry for those periods when theft occurred. If a night crew remains in the building for housekeeping or maintenance purposes, the culprit's entry will be a "No Sale," and it will follow the last legitimate entry made during the closing procedure. In effect, the tape will show two closings. If, on the other hand, the thief enters the register after it is cleared in the morning or at night, the tape will reflect two number one entries. The legitimate initial entry is actually the second of the day.

In this example, as in many other situations, a variation from the established norm can help to pinpoint the time factor.

Determining Time by Incidental Records

The time an incident occurred can sometimes be determined by an examination of incidental records, as in the following cases.

In one case, while working as a vice investigator, we seized a pornographic film that portrayed felonious conduct, an unnatural sex act. Before the District Attorney would issue a criminal complaint, it was necessary to establish that the unlawful action occurred and was photographed within the past three years. The act in question was being performed on a living room sofa, in front of which was a coffee table. On the table was a newspaper. Enlarging the picture made it possible to read the headline on the newspaper. A check of all the newspapers in the metropolitan area disclosed which paper had carried that headline, and on what date.

In a very similar case, empty beer bottles were in some of the scenes photographed. At that time a popular California beer packaged its product with a large gold-and-red "X" as the dominant part of the logo on the label. The brewery referred to its beer as "age-dated," and indeed each label bore a black printed date in the very center of the X. In this case, the frame of the motion picture including one of the beer bottles was enlarged to a size where the date on the label could be read. As in the case involving the newspaper headline, the photographs could not have been taken at an earlier date. Filming had to have occurred on or after the dates established, making it possible in both cases to establish that the incidents occurred within the period covered by the statute of limitations.

Today, thanks to a major brewery that has adopted a strategy whereby their product reflects a "born on" date, some investigator is going to solve a future case.

Another example of determining time by way of an incidental document was the discovery of a store receipt in the pocket of a dead man. The time of death was unknown. The dated receipt established that he had to have died on or after that date.

As a final illustration, there was an incident in which a customer of a retail store complained about the quality of help she received while shopping for a bedspread. Her note sharply criticized store management for permitting horseplay at the expense of good customer service. The complaint concluded with the statement that the customer had made her purchase in spite of, not because of, the employees in the department. She insisted, moreover, that she would never shop there again.

The customer did not mention the day or hour of her experience. However, her charge account reflected the purchase. The cash register certification on the sales check showed not only the date but also the transaction number. The detail tape on the register certifying the sale showed that more than sixty transactions had occurred that day; the customer's purchase was next to the last one. The documentation revealed that the incident occurred on a Wednesday at the very end of the evening. Armed with that intelligence, store management was able to take corrective action.

There are an almost endless variety of incidental records created in business and personal matters. The investigator should be attuned to the kinds of situations within the investigation's circumstances that could have created records. This is not an exhaustive list of such records, and should only be looked at as a starting point for creative thinking.

Access Control Records.   Automated facility access control systems using key cards, key pads, and biometrics devices will show date, time, door/gate used, and identity of each entry, and sometimes, exits.

Alarm Service Records.   Burglar and fire alarm services will record the location, date, time, and type of alarm. Systems will also record the date and time of alarm activation/deactivation and identifiers of person conducting same.

Appointment Calendars.   Shows date and time of appointments with name(s) of persons met, sometimes with location of meeting.

Automatic Teller Machines Transaction Slips.   Transaction slips will show date, time, transaction type and amount, account number, and location of transaction.

Bank Account Statements.   Will show name of account holder, account number, period covered, dates of deposit, dates particular checks cleared, and amount of those checks.

Building Systems Records

Many building management systems will record the date and time of activation of services in the building or individual areas or suites. Such records may show movement of elevators, turning on and off of lights, air conditioning, and so on. They may also identify persons using same.

Canceled Bank Documents.   Checks, deposit slips, cash-out slips, cash-in slips, and transfer memos will document some or all of the following: date and time of transaction, transacting branch, transacting teller, amount of transaction, form of funds (cash, check, etc.).

Cellular Telephone Records.   Cellular telephone service providers will log the date, time, duration, and number called for each call placed. Even if detailed billings are not ordered by the subscriber, the provider may still have data.

Correspondence.   Most business correspondence will show date of origination as well as other date indicators contained in communication.

Diaries and Journals.   Personal or business journals and diaries, sometimes kept electronically, often will provide accounts of key events written about closely in time to those events.

E-mail.   May show date and time of message being sent, opened, forwarded, or replied to, as well as electronic routing from origin to ultimate recipient.

Facility Entry Logs.   Many buildings and businesses log the name of persons entering as well as the date and time of entry and exit.

Faxes.   On received faxes, the date, time, and originator are listed. On sent fax confirmation reports, the date, time, and receiver are listed along with confirmation of status of a successful or failed transmission.

Guard Tour Confirmation Reports.   Many security forces electronically record the movements of personnel through areas being patrolled. Date, time, and location of guards as they patrol are electronically or mechanically recorded.

Letter/Parcel Markings.   Postal service and package delivery services record varying time information. They can include date and time the item was accepted for delivery, amount paid for delivery, times of arrival at various points along the way to delivery, and the person accepting delivery.

Movie Tickets.   Ticket stubs may show all or some of following: film name, date and time the ticket was purchased, show time, theater name and auditorium number, and the identity of the person selling the ticket. They may also show the date and time of exit.

Parking Facility Tickets.   Generally will show date and time of entry into a parking facility.

Payroll Records.   Time cards, time sheets, and payroll registers will show the date and times of employee presence at, or absence from, work.

Private Telephone System Records.   Some company telephone systems have the capability, although little used or known, to record the date, time, and number called of each outgoing call placed. They can also identify a specific telephone extension placing a call.

Reservation Records.   Whether from an airline, hotel, auto rental agency, restaurant, or entertainment venue, reservation records document that the business expected the person on a specific date and possible time. They are not conclusive that the person was actually present. They will generally also document the date and time the reservation was made, along with the name and phone number of the person making the reservation.

Sales and Delivery Receipts.   These may show date and time of sale, items sold, date and time of delivery, customer name, address and telephone number, amount paid, amount due, due date of subsequent payment, customer account number, names of the sales and delivery person, and the signature of the purchaser and receiver.

Security Surveillance Videotapes.   Shows the activity in a specific location with the date and time recorded.

Telephone Messages.   They frequently show the date and time of call, substance of message left, return telephone number, and identity of the person taking the message.

Telephone Toll Records.   Long distance billing records will show date and time a toll call is placed, the called number, and the duration of the call. Some company systems will provide up-to-the-minute recordation of the same information, allowing retrieval before bills are received.

Traffic Citations.   Citations place a vehicle, and often an individual, in a particular place at a specific date and time. They also provide the name of the issuing officer who can be a witness to other details.

Voice Message Systems.   Answering machines and voice mail systems will record the date and time of a call as well as the specific voice message recorded.

DETERMINING TIME BY EVENTS

Many events play an important role in our lives. These events tend to be time benchmarks. They may be daily events, if the focus is on recent times, or they may be of an annual nature, such as Christmas or one's own birthday. The effective investigator is able to use events to help establish the time factor when it is relevant.

The Case of the Telephone Tap.   In one investigation, a manager was asked when he first noticed his phone acting strangely.

"Oh, maybe three or four months ago," he answered vaguely. "I don't recall exactly."

"Well, this is October. Do you think it was in the middle of summer?"

"Yes, I do know it was in the summer."

"Maybe you can associate that first suspicion with something that happened during the summer. Did you take a vacation this summer, for instance?"

"Right! And it was just after I got back that I noticed something funny. I remember now, we went to Nebraska to visit with my wife's folks, and to spend the Fourth of July in their town. We got back the third Monday in July, and that's when I got the first funny feeling."

The vacation was a significant event that made it possible to establish when something else began to occur.

The Case of the Customized Bed.   In this pornography case, felonious sexual activity recorded on film was performed on what appeared to be a large, customized bed-divan. The scenes were obviously shot in the home in question and on that bed. The people were identified. But there was nothing in any of the footage that offered a clue as to when the filming occurred. If the time of the offense could not be established, there would be no complaint and no prosecution.

Investigators came upon this case unexpectedly and made the arrests without a warrant, based on our observations. While still in the house following the arrests, two investigators drew the owner of the home aside and engaged him in conversation. He was implicated in the crime and was at that time under arrest. The conversation was light, however, and in due course came around to his nice home and its furnishings. Noting the oversized divan, one investigator commented, "Man, that is one beautiful sofa."

"Thanks. It's custom-made. Makes into a bed."

"A bed! You're kidding."

"No, a king-size bed. Here, look at this." He started to remove the cushions to show us how it worked.

"Where could a guy get one like that?"

"Like I already told you, it's custom-made. You gotta have it made up special."

"It must be expensive."

"Yeah."

"Mind if I ask how much?"

"You gotta talk to the guy who makes 'em. The price could be anything; it all depends on the fabric for covering, the size, and the quality of the mattress. If you're serious, I'll give you the manufacturer's name and address. He's in Culver City."

"You know, I'm so impressed with the one you have, I'd like to have one just like it," said the investigator. "Will he remember yours?"

"Absolutely. Mine he'll never forget because it's the biggest one he ever made, and my check was the biggest he'd received, at least up to last year."

At this point of the conversation, the subject produced from his desk drawer his receipt for the bed-divan and handed it to the investigator to record the name and address of the company that had made the unit. The date of purchase was recorded on the receipt. The *when* of this case (which was successfully prosecuted) was established at the moment the receipt was produced.

HOW TO PREESTABLISH TIME

A number of steps can be taken prior to the occurrence of any incident that will help to establish the time factor when something does take place that requires investigation. The following suggestions are basic:

- Add a date and time generator to your CCTV recording surveillances.
- In still photography surveillance, or in CCTV or motion picture surveillance that is triggered by action, have a clock in the field of focus.
- In a basic and rudimentary intrusion detection system, aimed not at apprehension but at determining when the intrusion occurs, have a trip device that stops a clock.
- In any alarm receiving hardware, or in any access control program, add or modify the system so as to receive hard copies showing the times of the breaks or passages.
- Use sealing devices to secure envelopes, packages, entryways, vehicle compartments, or storage areas. Sealing devices include metal "railroad" seals, wire, and plastic seals that look like small padlocks, tape, or even staples. Inspection of the seal when the item is sent and again when it is received should show the seal intact. If it is damaged, you know when the damage occurred (i.e., en route). If seals are placed on stationary locations, they should be inspected on a regular basis. If the seal is found damaged, you know the time frame in which entry occurred. (Note: Sealing wax or specialized item-sealing stickers and tape could and should be used more widely. We have seen many cases, for example, in which money was sent from one floor of a building to another in a plain envelope stapled shut. When the envelope arrived there was less money and two sets of staple holes, the original holes and the new set made when the envelope was restapled. A seal would expose this type of theft — anything that would show damage or destruction if the sealing agent was defeated.)
- Implement count systems. Count the number of items at the end of the day; recount them in the morning. If a dozen steaks have disappeared from the refrigerator, you know when the thefts are occurring.

The Case of the Missing Furs. In one case we secretly implemented this kind of counting system in a warehouse fur storage area, a locked room, as a result of reports of missing furs. The counts revealed a shortage on a Sunday. Only one person was on duty that day: the security officer. A television camera was installed to monitor the interior of the locked fur storage room. The lens was disguised behind an electric appliance wall receptacle, the type you plug your toaster into. The following

Sunday the camera was activated. It was monitored in another building a short distance away. Before much time passed, the security officer was observed entering the storage room, which he had no reason to enter. He removed a very expensive full-length mink coat, boxed it, and left the room. He carried the box from the building and placed it in his car, at which time he was apprehended.

An enterprising security management will find other ways to build the time factor into established operations and procedures. And when incidents take place out of his control, the effective investigator will be alert to physical evidence, variations in patterns of activity, incidental documents or evidence, and significant events that will help to establish or at least to limit the time factor so critical in many investigations.

Thefts from Old Midtown Church: Continuing Case Study

The When Answer Walks in the Door

On the Thursday after our unsuccessful camera surveillance, I received a call from the controller. He said that he had just concluded an extraordinary call, and had the number of someone for me to ring. Although we had beseeched each witness not to discuss the inquiry with anyone, we knew that eventually something would leak. We hoped that it would not happen before the following Monday and also that it would not get back to Helen when it did.

The two days of interviews among the trusted members of the church community had indeed leaked, but with entirely unexpected results. The controller said that he received a call from a woman named Charlene who claimed to have a lot of information to offer regarding Helen Moore and her family, and would be happy to share it with us. I was startled, but asked the controller whether he thought the informant could tell us much we had not already learned. He laughed and said he thought we just might have gotten a big break. Charlene's last name was Moore, and until six months before she had been married to Helen's son, living in a house on a large lot in a city two hundred miles away. I immediately took down the number and arranged to meet Charlene in our office that same afternoon.

The atmosphere was electric as we waited for Charlene to arrive. It is rare that one gets an opportunity to debrief someone who might be an actual insider in an embezzlement scheme. When Charlene arrived she presented herself as a poised and confident woman in her mid-twenties.

Our first priority was the security of the investigation, and I asked Charlene about how she had learned of our inquiry. She said that her mother was a member of the church and the former pastor had called her after his interview with us to ask her if she knew anything likely to be of use. Since Charlene had shared some of her observations with her mother in the half-year since the break-up, her mother naturally told her to call the church.

Charlene told us that she had known Helen's son, Sam, all her life, being raised in the same neighborhood and attending the same church. After high school she went away to college and returned to live at home after the normal four years. She ran into Sam a little while after coming home and they dated for about a year before deciding to marry.

Charlene told us that once Sam announced the engagement, Helen dominated all the wedding planning. Charlene and Sam initially intended a simple wedding, in part because of Charlene's mother's limited means, and in part because of their own tastes. Helen immediately rejected those ideas and would hear nothing of her son "settling" for anything understated. She offered to give ten thousand dollars toward the wedding as long as she was allowed to "make sure everything was just right." She eventually called all the shots. Though Charlene admitted that it was a lovely affair, she felt that she and Sam were essentially mere guests at a "Helen extravaganza."

Sam and Charlene planned a modest honeymoon at a tiny romantic getaway. As her wedding gift to the couple, Helen offered a trip to San Francisco at a first class hotel. Charlene was at first pleased, until she found out that Sam had agreed to let Helen and one of his nieces come along. Charlene was unhappy, but Sam said that after his mother had been so generous, how could they refuse to let her come? Besides, Sam said, if she came along, he was certain that she would pick up all the meals and incidental expenses. Charlene, sorely disappointed, reluctantly agreed because she felt that a full week in San Francisco would be a wonderful experience.

As matters played out, however, San Francisco occupied less than half the honeymoon. The rest of the time was spent on what Sam said was a "surprise" for his niece — four days in Disneyland. When Charlene suggested that Helen and her granddaughter go to southern California without the newlyweds, Helen retorted that of course they would all go because Sam loved Disneyland. Sam gleefully nodded his agreement, and Charlene was trapped.

In the two years of Charlene and Sam's unhappy marriage, Helen continued to try to run their lives. When the job opportunity came up for Sam in a city two hundred miles away, Charlene pushed him to take it. Although it would mean a few months of a commuter marriage until Charlene could finish her graduate degree, she thought that establishing a home far from Helen would be the best thing for their marriage.

Again, things did not go as hoped. During the first few weeks Sam was in the new city, Helen took it upon herself to fly there on weekends to help him find a house. After all, Helen explained, she was a real estate professional and could save "the kids" all kinds of money by making sure they were not "cheated" by unscrupulous sellers.

On one of the few weekends Charlene was able to visit, she and Sam found a perfect little house on their own not far from where Sam worked. They were intending to make an offer just as soon as Helen looked it over and was able to negotiate the price down on their behalf. Charlene went home happy.

In the middle of the week she got a call from Sam. He and Helen had made an offer and it had been accepted. Charlene was overjoyed until she found that it was a different house. Sam told her that when Helen had arrived she had rejected their selection as being too small for a big family and proceeded to search the local area for a more fitting property. They had found a much larger house on a substantial lot. The only drawback was that it was located about an hour away from where Sam worked, but he was assured by his mother that it was sure to appreciate. He said that the commute wouldn't be so bad; after all, that's what his mother had said.

Charlene pointed out that they could not afford the mortgage that would be left after their modest down payment. Sam laughed and said that that was the beauty of the arrangement, his mother had given him $40,000 for the down payment and they could use their money to make a few "minor repairs" the property needed.

This was the gist of the remainder of their marriage. It continued until Sam told her that Helen was thinking of retiring in about a year and he wanted her to move in with them. Charlene gave up thinking that Sam would ever cut the apron strings and instead she filed for a divorce, having never actually been to the new house except as a visitor. On her last visit she saw that one of the bedrooms had already been furnished with some of Helen's things. Sam had said that this was just so Helen would be comfortable whenever she came to visit.

Charlene told us that one day during their engagement she was visiting Sam at Helen's house when Helen came home from work very angry. Charlene said that Helen ranted about how the ministers had always mistreated her and were going to renege on a promise to give her a pension. Charlene said that this was the only time she remembered seeing Helen so enraged. It was shortly thereafter that Helen had offered to pay for the wedding.

Charlene recalled being with Sam when he would visit his mother. Sam and Helen would go into a back room and talk with the door closed for a few minutes. Afterward, Sam and Charlene would leave. Almost always she noticed that Sam would have an envelope. In it was always cash, which Sam told her was a repayment on a loan that he had made to Helen. Charlene was mystified, since as far as she knew, Sam had never had money *of his own, and if anything, actually was borrowing money from Helen. On a few occasions Charlene saw that the money was in Old Midtown Church envelopes. Most times Sam was given five or six hundred dollars, always in ones, fives, and tens.*

Charlene had asked Sam where his mother was getting the money to give to him. He said simply that he never asked her and, besides, Helen deserved any money she got, especially because she had devoted her life to a church.

Charlene's account of the large cash spending by Helen seemed to track with the twenty-four-month time period in which donations had been lagging. We were becoming confident that we knew the time frame of the triggering event. The "when" seemed to have been sketched in when Charlene walked in the door.

Chapter 20

Establishing Motive: The *Why* of Investigation

In dealing with the question of *why* in the investigative process, we find ourselves in the intriguing as well as controversial area of motive. Motive is that logic or reasoning that constitutes the very root cause of a criminal act or misconduct.

Investigators must have better-than-average insight into human behavior and motivation. However, there is a point beyond which the investigator should not attempt to tread. As an example, one easily understood motive is the narcotic addict's need for money to support his habit, resulting in the theft of company funds. That is an apparent or applied motive. Why the person uses narcotics to begin with involves a much deeper examination of motivation, but it is one that belongs more properly in the realm of the psychologist or psychiatrist than the investigator.

Another dimension to the consideration of motive can also be troublesome. That is the ultimate value of motive to the investigation. In *Fundamentals of Law Enforcement*, Brandstatter and Hyman state, "It is almost always necessary to determine the motive for a crime for a successful prosecution. In addition, determining the motive can be an effective first step in discovering the identity of the criminal or the innocence of a suspect."[29]

The assertion that an understanding of the motive behind a crime is "almost always necessary" for successful prosecution may be more true of the public than the private sector. As we saw in an earlier chapter, a successful prosecution is always the ultimate goal in the public sector; it is a secondary consideration in private security.

The emphasis on motive is particularly questionable as it pertains to the crime of theft. We have talked to hundreds of people who have committed theft, including even trusted security personnel, and most of them have been unable to offer a satisfactory explanation of why they did it. Too much weight can be attributed to motive. It is desirable to know why an employee stole property. It can make the whole investigation more comprehensible, perhaps. It could very well be helpful in preventing similar thefts in the future, but it is not essential.

On the other hand, as the authors assert in the same quotation, determining the motive can be an effective first step in discovering the identity of the culprit. Answers to *why* can lead to *who*.

The case of Robert the voyeur in a previous chapter offers a good example. How was Robert identified as the prime suspect in this case? Three knowledgeable people in the store were asked, "Who would do such a thing?" That question led to a probable identification of the suspect. But the same three people could just as easily have been asked, "Why would a person bore a peephole in a ladies' dressing room?"

The answers might boil down to the conclusion that such a person has a perverted or unusual interest in women or has failed to mature sexually in his relationship with females. Who has exhibited or suggested a possibly perverted or unusual interest or sexual immaturity? Robert. What evidence is there? He spends an inordinate amount of time with and attention toward women; he is apparently unfaithful to his wife, suggesting immaturity; and he has been known to stare at women. The answers to *why* someone would do such a thing can lead to the *who*.

Brandstatter and Hyman also state, "Motives are often uncovered by determining who benefited from the crime."[30] That is to say, reversing our previous point, *who* can lead to *why*. Again, however, although there can be both interest and importance to the investigator in knowing the motive, we have some trouble with the degree of importance attached to knowing why when we already know who, particularly in the private sector where there is administrative recourse as well as judicial. It is nice, even helpful, to know why; it is *essential* to know who.

MOTIVATION AND DETECTION STRATEGY

There is a clear and important value to the investigator in the private sector in understanding motive as well as knowing who committed a crime when the motive can be used in the detection or apprehension strategy.

The Case of the Early Morning Striker. A highly unusual case involved an employee who was obviously mentally sick, but successfully evaded detection. The case surfaced with the discovery of a paper plate containing human feces along with a hand-printed note saying, "The pooper strikes!" The plate was discovered in an elevator by employees arriving before the building was open to the public.

The shocking and repugnant discovery caused alarm and concern among the staff and had a negative effect on morale. Over a period of days a succession of plates were found in various locations throughout the building, each accompanied by the same kind of note with the added word, "Again!" Through handwriting comparisons, investigators were confident that they had identified the responsible employee, a janitor. The evidence was not conclusive, however. Surveillances failed to catch the janitor and his activity continued.

Morale among employees deteriorated rapidly. It became apparent that random surveillances in all probability would continue to be unproductive. The problem was the culprit wasn't consistent in where he left the disgusting plate. It was impossible to survey the entire interior of a three-story, 150,000-square-foot building. The problem was finally brought to my attention.

Without a doubt, the suspect had a troubled mind and a perverted sense of humor. That was why he was engaging in his "game." Because his motive was perverted, it appeared that the best way to catch him would be to trigger or trip that perversion at a time and place under our control and surveillance. The next morning investigators entered the building during the early hours prior to the arrival of the janitorial staff. The suspect was known to be assigned to vacuum the third floor. Two undressed mannequins, a male and a female, were set up in a relatively remote location on that floor. The female mannequin was arranged lying face down with the legs spread apart. The male mannequin was placed close to the female, as though looking at her.

Surveillance of that scene commenced. As time passed, the suspect could be heard going about his chores, working his way toward the mannequins. When he came to the prearranged scene and saw the mannequins, he stopped in his tracks and stared. Suddenly he dropped his cleaning equipment and ran off, disappearing from the view of the investigators conducting his surveillance. Some minutes later he reappeared on the scene, carrying a can of spray paint. He began painting the genital area of the female mannequin. At this point he was promptly taken into custody for defacing company property.

The janitor subsequently admitted defecating on the paper plates, writing the notes, and placing his bizarre message at various places around the building. He was a sick man and knew it. His sickness could not handle the mannequin scene. It was in recognizing or speculating *why* someone would do such a demented act that gave rise to the strategy that triggered him to act. He was terminated and taken into police custody for psychiatric examination. Calm was restored to the building.

The Case of the Frustrated Clerk.   Another example of the value to the detection strategy of knowing the motive for a given act was a case in which a customer was the recipient of an obscene letter.

The customer accused a credit employee in one of the company's stores of being the author of the letter. According to the customer, she had had a confrontation with the employee over her monthly statement. The customer admitted giving the employee a "tongue-lashing" during their confrontation. She received the obscene letter in the mail two days later. The customer's manner was aggressive and abrasive.

The employee, a pleasant woman in her fifties, had been with the company over eighteen years and had a good performance record. Management did not and could not believe that she would author a letter filled with such obscenities. Such an action was simply not like her.

Feeling that the problem might be resolved in the store without the security department's involvement or assistance, the store manager sat down with the employee, told her of the customer's accusation, and asked her if she had sent the letter. The employee emphatically denied having written it. Because the case was then at an impasse and the customer was putting pressure on the store, the manager referred the matter to the security department. In addition to its obscene comments, the letter referred to the customer as a "slob of a woman" who came into public places with her hair in curlers and her toes sticking out of house slippers. After an analysis of the letter's contents and a comparison of handwritings, I was convinced that our employee did indeed write the letter in question. But why? What was her motive?

At the beginning of this chapter, motive was defined as the logic or reasoning behind a crime or misconduct. In this case the logic seemed apparent. The employee's letter was no more or less than a venting of eighteen years of accumulated frustration over customer abuses, frustration that had never found an outlet. The employee's anger had finally erupted in a single act of resentment.

Understanding that reasoning behind the letter, I talked to her. The fact that she had already lied to her superior about the letter made a second interrogation very difficult. However, because I understood *why* she had acted, I was able to talk to her about the difficulty of her work, the frustrations, the abusive way customers can treat employees whose only response can be a smile and the avoidance of any visible reaction. This is actually a rather unnatural relationship between human beings. Because I understood the motive, the strategy of my interrogation resulted in her admission of guilt.

MOTIVES FOR THEFT

Psychologists cite three factors that commonly motivate individuals to become dishonest: need or desire, rationalization, and opportunity.[31]

Need or Desire as Motive

Motivations that come under the category of a perceived need or desire may originate in a problem the individual sees as unshareable or unsolvable. The problem may be financial, stemming from gambling indebtedness, a drug dependency, living beyond one's means, or an extraordinary expense for the family such as cancer treatment. It may be a personal problem such as an extramarital affair, an unwanted pregnancy, or alcoholism. And it may even involve antagonism toward the company, expressing a desire for revenge over the failure to receive a promotion or because of resentment against specific supervisors. The need may be more purely psychological, prompted by a problem such as kleptomania. Some thieves steal from a need to appear successful, or even out of worthy motives with no desire for personal gain, such as a need to help others. Others steal to reward themselves with a "gift" or "prize" to compensate for stressful, unpleasant, or unhappy experiences. The "gift" makes them feel good. The desire, finally, may simply be the taking of something wanted but unavailable that they can't afford.

Rationalized Motives

The thief who rationalizes his actions manages to convince himself that stealing is not really wrong. Common rationalizations include the following:

- It's all right to steal because what he takes was going to be thrown away.
- It's all right because he is only borrowing what he takes.
- It's all right because he is underpaid and deserves what he is stealing.
- It's all right because others are doing it successfully and it would be stupid not to engage in the same thing.
- It's all right because the owner (or company) is so big that what is taken will never be missed.
- It's all right because the boss steals, and if he can do it then so can the little guy.

There is, of course, no real limit to the number of excuses that can be found to justify an action, however wrong.

Opportunity as Motive

In our opinion, opportunity does not of and by itself constitute a motive to be dishonest or to steal. Many people have countless opportunities but never steal. Rather, opportunity is a necessary element in theft and must exist in conjunction with one or more of the impulses categorized here under need or desire or rationalization.

Hidden Motives

The real motivation for an incident can be hidden by what appears to be the obvious motive. The terrorist's desire for publicity may mean more than the need to cause damage or reap monetary gain. Even an action that appears to be an open-and-shut case of robbery may result from more obscure and complex motives, as the following case illustrates.

The Case of the Man with the Shirt. A robbery incident took place some years back in a major retail store. An employee walked into the store's public restroom for men and discovered a customer lying unconscious on the floor. The customer had been stabbed in one eye with an ice pick and his wallet had been taken. Witnesses recalled two young men hurriedly leaving the area some minutes before the discovery of the attack.

The customer lost his sight in the wounded eye and subsequently brought suit against the store. The thrust of the civil action was that the company had failed to provide the necessary security or safeguards to protect its customers, and that the customer had the right to assume he could safely use those facilities provided for public use. It was a negligence suit.

The official police report stated that the customer had a need to use the restroom. According to the victim he entered the restroom and observed two Hispanic male youths who approached him. One was holding an ice pick in his hand. They demanded his wallet. He was reluctant to part with it, whereupon the boy with the ice pick jabbed the instrument into his face, penetrating the eye. He fell to the floor unconscious. The wallet was removed from his trouser pocket, and the two youths fled. The wallet was never recovered. The assailants were never identified or apprehended.

Management was concerned that this should happen in the store. Why did it happen to this customer?

An independent investigation conducted by the security department turned up additional information. At about 10:00 A.M., right after the store opened to the public, the customer who was later to be victimized, easily identifiable because he was wearing a neck-brace, approached an employee working on the main floor and asked her for directions to the men's restroom. This was about five hours prior to the robbery. About an hour later the same customer purchased a name brand white dress shirt and, at the conclusion of the sale, asked the salesgirl the location of the men's restroom. At about 1:00 P.M. another salesperson returning from her lunch period happened to observe the customer with the neck-brace standing outside the store next to a doorway. He was carrying a store bag, the size issued with the purchase of a dress shirt. And sometime between 1:30 and 2:00 P.M., the same customer asked an employee working on the third floor for directions to the men's restroom. She directed him back to the main floor. At 3:00 P.M. the man was found unconscious in that restroom.

A background investigation of the customer disclosed that he was the proprietor of a men's haberdashery not many miles from the department store. The type of shirt he purchased in our store was in the inventory of his own store. As we probed deeper, a criminal check confirmed our growing suspicions. The customer had a criminal history of lewd conduct offenses in public restrooms. He had made a small purchase to legitimize his presence in the store for several hours. He may have asked numerous clerks about the location of the restroom in the hope that there was more than just one. Although what happened in the restroom could not be proved, it was apparent that the man had solicited the two youths with a sexual proposal. His own action had undoubtedly prompted them to attack him.

Once the details of our investigation were made known to the plaintiff, the civil action was dropped.

MOTIVE AND RESPONSE

Sometimes the *why* of an incident can help the company or individual targeted to react or respond more effectively. Bomb threats, an all too common hazard faced by companies and institutions today, are a good example. The extent of the response to the threat bears a direct correlation to the perception of the motive for it. A series of malicious attacks against a number of stores in Los Angeles offer another illustration.

The Case of the Broken Windows. The case began with a series of incidents in which my company suffered considerable damage to several large plate glass show windows, each costing hundreds of dollars to replace. In the first store victimized, each window had been shattered by a half-inch hexagon nut, apparently hurled against the glass by a slingshot. A few days later another store of ours had an identical experience. Then, on an almost daily basis, similar incidents continued.

Why were our windows being broken?

The attacks then took a new direction. In our downtown store, someone came into the store with a paper sack containing rats, set the sack down on a counter and abandoned it. Soon the rats were out of the sack and running about the store, sending customers and salespeople shrieking with fright into the streets. Across town, in another store, someone squirted an acid on the sleeves of all the men's suits, causing a total loss of a large quantity of merchandise. Hexagon nuts continued to break windows, and it was discovered that our stores were not the only ones besieged. Other merchants were experiencing similar attacks.

At last, as the pattern of attacks became clearer, the *why* became known. A large newspaper was involved in a labor dispute. Discontented strikers were taking unsanctioned action on their own, attempting to win at the bargaining table by intimidating advertising accounts of the paper. The theory behind the campaign was simple. If those companies that normally advertised in the paper stopped advertising in return for a cessation in harassment, the cash flow of the newspaper would diminish drastically. The paper would be forced to meet the union's demands.

Now we knew our enemy. The attacks made a bizarre kind of sense. The company refused to be intimidated and continued its advertising program, but knowing that various incidents would continue as long as the advertising continued to appear in the newspaper enabled us to take preventive measures as well as to institute detection efforts.

The response to one type of attack offers an example. Various companies in the city, including ours, were victimized by the use of the chemical *butyl marcaptan*, the odorizing agent for natural gas.

The effect of butyl marcaptan is staggering. One small vial, no larger than an iodine bottle, would be opened and set carefully among merchandise. Before long the area around that bottle would take on an odor remarkably similar to vomit. If the bottle was knocked over, which usually occurred, the odor was magnified many times, driving people away. Every fixture and every item of merchandise in the immediate area had to be burned or otherwise destroyed.

Once this threat was known and understood, however, security people were directed to carry or have immediately available a counteragent to the noxious chemical. The counteragent came in spray cans. The sooner it could be applied, the less damage occurred.

The security department's protective objective shifted from an emphasis on theft to patrolling for "customers" who were not really shopping but intent on disruptive actions or malicious damage. The motive for the attacks gave us, the victims, purpose and direction in ways we could act upon. Additionally, establishing a communication network with competitive stores and with a variety of law enforcement agencies helped to stem the frequency of the attacks.

Until we knew the motive behind these acts, we simply reacted to each event. We were not able to respond intelligently and purposefully.

SUMMARY

The process of security investigations essentially involves information collection and, through the application of sound reasoning, analyzing that information to answer questions or solve problems that threaten loss to the company.

Through such basic techniques as undercover investigation, surveillance, background investigation, and the variety of internal strategies that may be used to expose covert crimes, the investigative process develops information. As the investigation focuses on specific acts or individuals, additional procedures are used to build a case, including interviewing suspects and witnesses, the analysis of physical evidence, obtaining statements and confessions, and information gained from clandestine sources such as informants.

All this effort is directed toward answering the fundamental investigative questions, the *who*, *where*, *when*, *how*, and *why* of a crime or incident. The investigator will ferret out and follow up every conceivable piece of information that might be useful in identifying *who* was responsible for an incident. To do that successfully he must know *where* to look — where to find information. He will seek to narrow the scope of his inquiries by limiting and defining the time factor. In solving a crime, his investigative strategy is often dependent on finding out *how* the crime was committed. And quite often, learning who was responsible for a given action requires an understanding of human motivation, determining *why* the crime was committed.

In accomplishing this, the investigator must be imaginative and resourceful. He must be tireless and determined. He must understand people, and he must be able to apply logical reasoning. But he is not a magician or, in truth, a Sherlock Holmes who pulls answers out of a hat. His success, when he enjoys it, is more often the result of applying common sense and uncommon persistence. The work is time-consuming and frequently tedious, but it is also a challenging work of deep personal satisfaction to those rare men and women who bring to it the resources of skill, effort, and character that make the successful investigator.

Thefts from Old Midtown Church: Continuing Case Study

Closing the Circle: The Confrontation of Helen Moore and Afterward

The Confrontation. On the third Friday of the investigation, four days after our failed camera surveillance, we met with the controller, his church superiors, and their outside legal counsel. We presented our findings to date and it was agreed that we would allow one more Monday morning theft (hopefully to be actually videorecorded) and then confront Moore.

On Sunday night another midnight count was conducted of the safe's contents.

The next Monday morning dawned with the optimistic expectation and nervousness that frequently accompanies "game day" at the conclusion of an interesting investigation. At 5:00 A.M. one of our investigators met Reverend Williams at the church office and they secreted themselves in the upstairs observation room. At about 5:30 A.M. I received a call at the office confirming that the camera and recording system were working perfectly. I directed that at 7:00 A.M. the time-lapse video recorder was to be changed from twelve-hour recording speed to six-hour speed, so as to capture more frames per second of crucial activity.

At 7:10 A.M. I received a call from our investigator in the field calmly reporting that Moore had arrived.

Twenty minutes later I received a much more animated telephone report that Moore had gone for the bait early and hard. I was told that immediately upon coming into the office Moore had placed her large handbag under her desk and turned on her desk lamp. Curiously, she then turned off the overhead lights. This would have made it almost impossible to tell from outside that she was in her office.

Moore then swiveled her chair around toward the safe, facing the camera. She bent down, presumably to manipulate the combination dial. A moment later Moore pushed her chair backward in order to pull the safe door open. She reached under her desk and pulled her handbag onto the floor between her and the open safe. She then extracted a plastic bag of the kind commonly used at supermarkets for customer purchases. She snapped the bag before her, filling it with air and opening it wide. Moore then took out a canvas collection bag and reached in, pulling out several handfuls of what appeared to be cash, checks, and envelopes. All went into the plastic bag. She did this again with each of the other collection bags. In a little more than a minute she had filled the plastic bag about half full. She stuffed it back into her handbag and pulled out a dark-colored cloth that was placed on top of the open handbag.

Moore then put the canvas bags back into the safe, closed the safe door, and turned back toward her desk. Incredibly, she then reached into her desk drawer and pulled out a large black book. Placing it on the desk before her she began to apparently read quite intently. Reverend Williams knew that she was reading the Bible given to her by the former pastor.

At about 8:00 A.M. I received a third call from the church. The report from my investigator was brief: (1) the head counter had just been observed being admitted to the office by Moore and taking the collection bags out of the office in a plastic tub and (2) Reverend Williams was getting pretty steamed watching Moore calmly reading the Bible after raiding the safe. No one else had been in the office once Moore had settled into her devotional reading.

At about 10:00 A.M. the report came from the field that the counters had completed their duties and the tub of money was back in the safe. I directed that the next phase of the action commence.

We had learned earlier from the controller and Reverend Williams that Helen had pointed out some area in the payment of money to the headquarters of the organization where she felt that Old Midtown Church was being unfairly treated. We had devised a plan to capitalize on her own interest in this regard.

Reverend Williams, at my suggestion, went to Moore and told her that the organization had hired a fiscal consultant who was conducting an overall review for the controller on the financial management of the churches. She was told that she and the other churches' business managers were each being individually conferred with by the consultant. Williams claimed to have forgotten to tell Moore earlier of the appointment made for her that day with the consultant. She was told that he had just checked his calendar and noticed the appointment that was set for only thirty minutes later.

We had decided earlier that if at all possible Moore would be asked to drive herself to our offices. We wished to later demonstrate that she had not been physically controlled and forced to attend the meeting. Moore, upon being given the address to our office, said that she was too unfamiliar with the area and wondered if Williams would drive her. With extraordinary presence of mind, Williams told Moore that his car was to be used later by someone else, but that he would be happy to ride with her as her guide. She agreed and they left.

A few minutes later my investigator called me to say that prior to leaving Moore had taken her bag from beneath her desk, gone to the safe, took out the money bags, placed them into her handbag, closed the safe, turned off her desk lamp and closed her office behind her.

Moore was introduced to me less than an hour later at our offices. She was not carrying a bag. At the start of the interview she was asked if she wanted anything to drink or to use the restroom. She declined. Knowing how long these kinds of interviews can take, we had made provisions for sandwiches, fruits, and soft drinks to be available at an appropriate lunch hour. Moore and I chatted for a few minutes, during which she described to me her hip problems, and her eye problems, and her general limitations caused by becoming, in her words, "an old lady." She was thus far attempting to give the impression of a mild-mannered senior citizen. I made a point of asking her how she felt at the time. She laughed and said she was fine, but just liked to complain.

In the space of the next forty or so minutes I asked Moore about the general handling of funds at the church and whether she had any good ideas for how other churches could manage their finances. She shared some surprisingly cogent ideas about how to make sure the volunteer counters did not take any money. She also said that it was important that employees do not take money home and that the duties of preparing deposits and taking the deposits to the bank should be segregated. She also complained that for years she had asked for an armored car courier service to take the collections to the bank, but this had been denied by a succession of parsimonious pastors. She said that this had made her increasingly afraid of being robbed over the years as she drove to the bank each Monday afternoon.

While we talked, Moore chattered on about her family and how she had put each of her kids through private schools and college. She said she was planning to retire in a couple of years to live with her son in another city. She told me that he had been recently divorced. She was glad because "that girl" had been putting all kinds of strange notions into her son's head, wanting him to buy a silly "cracker box" of a house.

During the initial interview, Moore claimed that on Monday mornings she would arrive at about 7:30 A.M. and read from her Bible. She said she would unlock the safe a few minutes before 8:00 A.M., when the counters began to arrive. She said that she never entered the safe, instead she only left it unlocked and let the head counter retrieve the collection bags. She said she never touched the collection until the counters had completed their work.

I eventually excused myself and told Moore that I had forgotten some materials needed for the meeting on my desk. I met with Reverend Williams and my investigator who had pulled the videotape and returned to our office. Williams told me that he had passed a nerve-wracking drive with Moore to our office, hoping not to give away the true purpose of the interview or to give in to an urge to verbally tongue lash Moore for the thefts. After parking her car, Moore made a point of placing her purse in the trunk, explaining to the pastor that she was nervous about being mugged.

My investigator passed to me a set of six still video prints of the key few minutes of Moore's activity in front of the safe with her plastic bag. I placed these "aces" in my pocket, retrieved a large file emblazoned with Moore's name, and returned to the room.

During the next two hours I interrogated Moore. She was told in a simple and straightforward manner that it was known that she had been taking money from the church and that we had ample proof. She was then told that we knew that there had been a number of factors leading up to the thefts, and that chief among them was the failure of the church to allow her to use an armored car courier. This additional control, so she was told, would have been sufficient to keep her on the straight and narrow. Instead she had been allowed to take the money out of the office, sometimes not even being able to get to the bank until Tuesday mornings. Thus on numerous occasions she was in the unenviable position of having thousands of dollars of money in her home where she, a struggling single mother devoted to the welfare of her children, was being continually faced with the bills for her children's education. It was little mystery to me, I told her, that she had succumbed to temptation and need in moments of weakness.

Moore immediately latched onto the theme I placed before her. She admitted that she had been taking money, but that it had happened only a few times and not at all for several weeks or months. She cried and said that I was right, and that even at that moment the money to be deposited was sitting in her purse in her car. She volunteered to go and get it to show me how much money she was responsible for.

I agreed, and she left in the company of two investigators whom I told her were being provided to safeguard the money as she walked back from her car. A few minutes later she returned with her bag. She opened it, reached in, and plopped a canvas bag onto the table, saying that this was typical of what she was expected to carry to the bank. On the top of the contents of her bag I could see what appeared to be a black sweater covering what lay below.

I asked Helen if she had any other church property in her possession, either with her or at home. She said absolutely not. I asked her if she would have any objection to my looking through her bag. She visibly gulped and said no. She held it open for me to see, and I asked her what was under the sweater. She silently removed the sweater revealing a white plastic grocery bag. I asked her what the bag contained. She scowled and said simply, "more church money." She gave me the bag that I emptied onto the table. During the next half hour she and I counted the checks and cash she had attempted to steal. It totaled almost sixteen hundred dollars.

Helen agreed to prepare a confession statement in which she admitted that she had been taking church money for more than two years. By the time she completed her estimate of the thefts, we were both astonished by the amount, nearly $100,000. She adamantly denied that any of her family had received any of the money or knew about the thefts. She did confirm that Sam's wedding, the house down payment, and even the honeymoon trip were unwittingly paid for by the members of the church. She also told us about her own car and one she had recently bought for Sam that were "financed" in similar fashion. She admitted that she would come in early on Mondays, rifle the collection bags, and take the stolen checks and cash home. She would sometimes put the stolen checks into later deposits to make up some of the cash she took.

I did not need to use the video still images in my interrogation of Moore.

Helen agreed to allow a search of her car and home by our investigators. In the car were found numerous deposit slips and bank statements of the church. In her home were found dozens of donation checks from the preceding weeks, along with other property of the church. Significantly, it was observed that most of the furnishings of the house were gone. She told our investigators that she had recently had a moving company pick them up and deliver them to Sam's home, where she intended to eventually live. She planned to rent out her town home and live in the city with friends from the church while she finished her final year at Old Midtown. She was to eventually sell her town home and pay off the mortgage on Sam's house.

It was clear that in the next year Moore was planning to salt away the fifty thousand dollars for her retirement annuity. She had spent her career at Old Midtown preparing for her golden years. She had gotten a nice home in the country to live in and paid for the education of her son that enabled him to get a good job with which he could support her. Her social security retirement income, supplemented by monthly annuity payments, and freedom from daily living expenses would have allowed her to continue to indulge in the occasional shopping spree or trip to Disneyland with her children and grandchildren.

Afterward

In the aftermath of the investigation the religious organization directed that our findings be supplied to the police. Helen was discharged and began lengthy settlement negotiations with the church. Eventually her town home was deeded over to the church and sold.

We prepared a lengthy report detailing all our findings and provided each document and image necessary to inform the police of the full extent of the investigation. The police told us that our investigation was sufficiently complete, that they needed to do very little beyond subpoenaing Moore's bank records to show more money going into her accounts than her legitimate income would cover. The police detective assigned to the case, a highly skilled and experienced white-collar crime specialist, worked under a crushing caseload of other unsolved cases, which prevented him from making much headway.

Reverend Williams happily reported that after telling the congregation about the losses, the membership dug deep into their pockets. Weekly donations shot up almost $2,000 and he chuckled as he told me that now maybe a staff pension plan *could* be started. More than two years passed as we went on to other cases.

Finally, less than two months before the three-year statute of limitations lapsed, Helen Moore was indicted by the grand jury on felony theft charges. She had moved by then to another state and eventually was located and extradited. At her arraignment she pled *Not Guilty*. Two months later she entered a change of plea to *Guilty*, asking the court to defer entering the conviction for two years while she was under the supervision of the probation department. At this writing, the court had not ruled on her petition.

The police detective told us that when he interviewed Moore she had recanted her statement to us and claimed that we had merely misunderstood what she had to say, explaining that the money in the white plastic bag had been given to her by the counters who had failed to include it in their work. She stubbornly kept to this line until the detective dealt out the video still images of her filling the bag. Her eyes narrowed and she scowled at the detective before declaring that she wanted to have an attorney present.

Conclusion

This case study illustrates many of the techniques discussed in this book. Analysis of records, surreptitious observation, searches of public records, witness interviews, an informant interview, interview and interrogation of the subject, and searches and recovery of physical evidence all played key roles in the success of the case.

Persistence also was important in this case. Many clients would have lost patience after the first failed video surveillance, regardless of whether they had contributed to that failure. Some would have forced a premature confrontation or merely sternly warned the manager that she was being watched. In this case, however, the client persevered and continued to trust in the investigators.

Postscript

As professional investigators we fully acknowledge the role good fortune played in this and many investigations. What would have happened if the head counter had not come forward? Or if Charlene had not learned of the investigation and been inclined to talk? Or worse, what if Helen had learned of the investigation first and stopped stealing before being caught on video? Luck then is important to the art of investigation, but so is the willingness to capitalize on the openings it presents. On the wall in our investigators' office is found the slogan "Luck = opportunity + preparation. WE MAKE OUR OWN LUCK."

To the readers of this book we simply wish "good luck" in your investigations.

V. TECHNOLOGICAL AND SPECIALIZED INVESTIGATIVE TECHNIQUES

Chapter 21

Imagery

In investigations there are many important uses for imagery. The investigator in the private sector should become at least moderately skilled in three different kinds of imagery: film photography, CCTV video camera recording, and video camcorder recording. Although the various kinds of imagery discussed overlap each other in terms of function and purpose, each format is particularly well suited for different kinds of investigative imagery.

What are the reasons for imagery in investigations? Fundamentally, an image captures a magnitude of information that in many cases would be impossible to reliably reproduce in a strictly verbal or written manner. Simply put, a picture is worth a thousand words. We are able to take in the entirety of a situation with a single good image. With a series of images of the same scene we can be led to important detail and critical evidence.

As important as an image's comprehensiveness are its consistency and objectivity. An image presented to different people at different times does not rely on either the imprecise language a narrator might use, or the unintentional variations of descriptions utilized, or the differences in interpretation that each listener might employ.

In the context of private investigations, some of the typical uses of imagery are:

- Depiction of a general location of a key event or incident
- Depiction of the aftermath of a crime, either in its effect (as in a vandalized storefront) or in the arrangement of articles left behind (such as in a burglary crime scene)
- Depiction of a surreptitious act (such as a cashier placing money into a pocket)
- Depiction of an open but illicit act (such as the delivery of stolen goods by truck to a noncustomer)
- Depiction of the condition of a key piece of evidence (such as impressed writing on a notepad)

Still Photography

The capturing of still images during investigations normally is done through the use of film or digital camera photography.

Film Photography

Film photography has been used for more than a century in the investigation of crime. In a modern context, it remains a versatile and extremely useful tool. Many investigators will continue to use film as the primary method of documenting still images for the following reasons:

1. Film provides the highest degree of resolution readily available to investigators.
2. Film can be forgiving of a novice photographer's mistakes.
3. Film is conveniently packaged and can be processed at virtually innumerable locations.
4. Original film and resulting negatives can be stored and are not alterable in the same way that digital and video media can be.
5. The amounts of money, training, and experience already invested in film photographic equipment are substantial and are not lightly abandoned in favor of other technologies.

Film Photographic Equipment

The standard investigative film camera is the 35-mm single lens reflex (SLR) camera with detachable lenses (see Figure 21.1).

Viewfinder Cameras

Cameras generally are constructed to allow the operator to view the scene to be photographed in one of two ways. Viewfinder cameras, such as those in disposable prepackaged film cameras, have a small window slightly above the actual lens opening. Although this may be fine for general scene and party snapshots, the slight offset between the viewfinder window and the lens can translate to differences literally between what the photographer "saw" and the camera "captured." Most viewfinder cameras come with either fixed lenses or simple zoom lenses of limited magnification.

Viewfinder cameras should be considered suitable for use only by initial persons on a scene who have access to no other equipment and are not able to preserve the scene until other equipment and trained operators arrive. Examples might be security guards who are documenting an auto accident prior to removal of the vehicles, or noninvestigative corporate managers who are first at the location of an incident and must quickly capture the essence of the scene prior to beginning a cleanup or restoring access to an area.

Of course, there have been times when an investigator is at a location where image documentation was not anticipated and other equipment is not readily available. We have on occasion made a quick run to the corner convenience store for a disposable camera in order to document a situation or scene that could not be preserved in any other manner.

The one kind of situation where the disposable viewfinder camera is in fact the camera of choice is in a pretext where one wishes to appear as someone other than an investigator. Disposable cameras are very nonthreatening and virtually no one would suspect that a person using such a camera was a professional investigator. We have used such a camera when posing as tourists or students. When the identity of a specific subject employee is crucial, such as aboard a cruise liner with hundreds of employees, investigators have had the subject pose with them as a picture was taken. No one ever suspected the true intent of the picture taking was to solidly capture the identity of a thief.

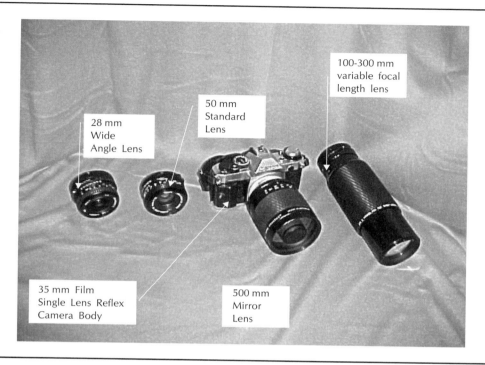

Figure 21.1. Recommended photographic film camera kit for investigations. Lens selection allows for full range of documentation of static scenes or surveillance.

Single Lens Reflex Cameras

The 35-mm SLR camera, through an arrangement of prisms and mirrors, allows the user to view the scene through the actual lens, exactly as it will be positioned and focused on the photographic film.

A selection of detachable lenses will be used to achieve different levels of magnification and field of view. The standard lens provided by manufacturers with SLR cameras is a fixed focal length 50-mm lens, and often is used to depict a "normal" view of a scene. Higher-powered lenses, also known as *telephoto* lenses, are used to provide greater magnification of a scene or object. In most cases, investigators will use telephoto lenses that are not fixed, but are of variable focal length, commonly known as *zoom* lenses. A typical lens selected for surveillance will be a 100–300-mm lens. An important consideration in the selection of lenses is the fact that with increased magnification necessarily comes a narrowing of field of view, a reduction of the width of area that the image will capture. Also, longer lenses can be heavy and must be kept relatively still to obtain unblurred images. Figure 21.2 illustrates the differences in magnification and width of field achievable using a selection of typical lenses utilized in investigations.

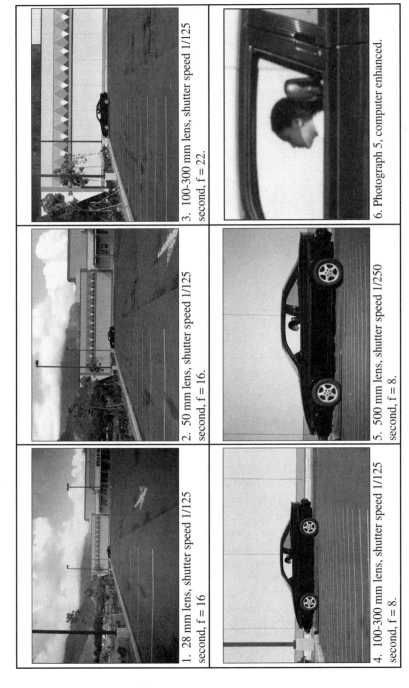

1. 28 mm lens, shutter speed 1/125 second, f = 16

2. 50 mm lens, shutter speed 1/125 second, f = 16.

3. 100-300 mm lens, shutter speed 1/125 second, f = 22.

4. 100-300 mm lens, shutter speed 1/125 second, f = 8.

5. 500 mm lens, shutter speed 1/250 second, f = 8.

6. Photograph 5, computer enhanced.

Figure 21.2. Comparison of film lens capabilities and an example of a computer enhanced photograph.

Many investigators will choose to use automatic cameras that have pc
automatic focus, and automatic exposure capabilities. These can be very hel'
if they can be overridden manually by the operator to compensate for ﬁ
assumptions made by the camera's processor when shooting through glass ᴄ

Instant Cameras

Instant cameras, which produce a photographic print without the necessity of lab processing, aᵢ
sometimes used in investigations. This is because it allows the investigator to see immediately whethe₁
a usable image has been captured. This, however, comes with the limitation that such instant cameras
will not generally allow for ready reproduction of the photographs. Also, compared to other types of
film, instant images tend to be more costly to produce.

Film

Photographic film for investigations in the private sector should be color print film as opposed to black
and white or slide film. Although black and white can be very versatile, the number of processors that
will take black and white film is greatly limited when compared to the ubiquitous one-hour photo
processor. Also, good color pictures provide much more information than black and white images.

Film is graded by its ISO rating, which can range from ISO 50 to ISO 1600; this frequently is
referred to as the film's *speed*. The higher rated films are much more sensitive and require shorter exposure times and less ambient lighting to capture usable images. The 35-mm SLR cameras will be set,
manually or automatically, to match the camera's ASA setting to the ISO of the film.

The lower numbered ISO ratings use fine silver halide grain coatings on the film and provide
extremely fine images that can be enlarged or "blown up" with minimal "graininess." The lower ISO
rated films (below ISO 200) typically would be used for portraiture and images of still objects requiring very fine detail, such as hairline fractures in failed metal fittings from an industrial accident or
other forensic laboratory photography. The lower ISO films being less light sensitive typically are used
in conjunction with flashes or other artificial lighting in controlled situations. Otherwise, the longer
exposure times that lower speed films require make them unsuitable for capturing images of moving
objects or people. Movement across the scene at long exposures will create blurred images.

A good all-around film for investigative photography is ISO 400 film that is usable in many situations, including general scene documentation and daytime surveillance. It can also serve quite well
in documenting fine detail if proper magnification at the time of picture taking is used.

A technique known as *push film processing* can be employed to allow lower ISO rated films to be
used as if they were higher speed film. This requires special photo processing that cannot normally be
handled by the typical one-hour photo processing operation. In near total darkness, infrared film can
also be used; however, the resulting images may provide misleading darkness or lightness information.

Digital Photography

In recent years the use of digital photography has become more commonplace in both the consumer
and professional markets. Digital photography is quickly gaining acceptance as an alternative to film
photography in most investigative applications for some of the following reasons.

1. Digital images can be produced without the use of a processing laboratory.
2. Most digital cameras incorporate small review screens allowing for instant confirmation that a particular image has been captured.
3. Digital cameras allow for instant deletion of images that are either redundant or unusable for other reasons.
4. Digital images are easily incorporated into computer files for easy use in reports and presentations, as well as transmission via e-mail to other users. Once copied to a computer file, the image can easily be marked, enhanced, or cropped for the emphasis the investigator wishes to make in using the image.
5. Digital images can be printed from the user's computer in color or black and white with selectable degrees of quality ranging from 300 dots-per-inch drafts on plain paper to 9600 dots-per-inch prints on glossy paper that are nearly indistinguishable from film photographs.
6. The ability to completely obtain, review, and produce images in-house guarantees full confidentiality of the image content, which cannot always be assured when outsourcing photofinishing using film.
7. Some digital cameras store images on standard computer diskettes that are inexpensive, abundant, and immediately usable in computers without any accessories. Others utilize memory media of various types, typically a *flash card*, and require special cables to transfer images to computers.

Accessories

Investigators should have available to them some or all of the following items when deploying for photographic assignments.

- Spare film, data storage media, and batteries
- Flash attachments
- Lens cleaning kit
- Notebook for recording a photographic log of each image including shutter speed, lens focal length, lens aperture setting, time, date, subject, location, and direction of each shot
- Additional camera support such as tripod, monopod, shoulder or chest support, or window mount
- A full range of lenses, hoods, and filters likely to be useful in the assignment
- Motor drive to automatically advance film and cock shutter

Closed Circuit Television Video Imaging

Closed circuit television (CCTV) cameras and time-lapse video recorders have been used for decades by the security industry to observe and document areas being secured. They are commonly seen by the public in banks, retail stores, and airports. Their use in investigations is especially valuable.

CCTV cameras initially were manufactured using tubes as the video pickup device. Tube cameras are being largely supplanted by the charge coupled device (CCD) camera that has several advantages over tube cameras. General-use CCD cameras tend to be more light sensitive than tube cameras. CCD cameras tend to be smaller and less susceptible to damage or image "burn-in" associated with bright light being shined directly at the camera. CCDs, using light sensitive semiconductors instead of bulky tubes, can be placed into very compact cameras.

Investigators will use two types of CCTV installations: overt and covert. In overt installations the camera and any housing containing it will be readily visible to passersby. This is the typical arrangement in shopping malls, airports, retail stores, banks, and other areas where cameras are being used to prevent the commission of crimes. For the investigator, who will frequently be engaged in reconstructive investigation of past crimes, securing originals or copies of CCTV camera tapes of the areas where crimes may have occurred can be a crucial step in evidence gathering.

Security camera installations typically involve the placement of cameras in high traffic, restricted entry, and high robbery risk areas. In most installations the video signal is sent to the monitoring and recording station by means of wire cable. There are a number of wireless transmission methods that are used when installing a cable would be difficult or cost prohibitive. Radio frequency (RF) and microwave are two wireless video transmission methods. Systems may range from single cameras to those utilizing hundreds of cameras.

Managing multiple cameras normally takes one of two approaches, switching between cameras or simultaneously displaying multiple cameras on a single monitor. Even simultaneous display has more than one method. Some small systems will utilize a *splitter* that divides a monitor screen into small segments (two are typical) that allows for a segment of the video from multiple cameras to be observed. Thus a two-camera splitter will allow half of the image from each camera to be passed on to the monitor or recorder. Obviously, this also results in half of the scene from each camera not being observed.

Newer technology is beginning to come into general use that uses *multiplexers*. Multiplexers typically allow for more camera feeds to be displayed than do splitters. At present, up to sixteen camera views can be displayed with multiplexer technology. The advantage of multiplexers is that the entire image from each camera is passed on for viewing or recording. In those cases where more than four cameras are multiplexed, it is necessary to utilize larger monitors, as the resulting individual image can be quite small on a nine-inch video monitor. In addition, it is possible to display the feed from a single camera on demand on a separate monitor without affecting either the viewing or recording of the feeds from the other cameras. This capability is especially helpful during investigations where the action captured on only one camera may be relevant to the investigation and the other camera views can be distracting to the investigator or image viewers.

Video Recorders

Video recording of CCTV normally is accomplished using VHS tape recorder systems. In an investigative context, especially during constructive investigations of ongoing acts, tape recorders, which slow the recording mechanism down significantly, can allow a standard T-120 videotape to be used to record hundreds of hours of activity. This is achieved by reducing the numbers of frames per minute recorded on the tape. There is some degradation of picture quality and motion can seem jerky at slower speeds. In fact, some extremely slow speeds may not even record a single picture per second, leaving gaps in time during which action taking place is simply not recorded.

In cases where a compromise must be struck between increased time coverage and image frequency, it is recommended that speeds not slower than 24-hour speed be used. This is one-twelfth speed when a two-hour, T-120 tape is used, but can still provide five pictures per second.

An alternative strategy to employ is to have the camera operating constantly but the video recorder set to begin recording only upon an event triggering an alarm. Regular door contact or motion detection alarms can be wired to the recorder and begin the recording. Motion detection features of the video system itself can compare a static image (such as the interior of a storeroom) to the live camera feed. When there is a change in the live camera image in all or part of the image, such as when the door opens or an individual enters the area, the recorder is triggered automatically to record. This can be very helpful in those situations where the access to the video recorder is restricted to infrequent intervals and continuous taping cannot be expected to cover the entire suspect time period.

One possible problem associated with such a triggered recording scheme is the necessity to convince management, unions, or courts that no one else could have entered the area and perpetrated the crime. After all, they need to accept the fact that the alarm sensor was not malfunctioning or somehow defeated. With a time-lapse recording of the entire time of the video surveillance, a straightforward review of the tape will convince anyone that no other persons entered the scene.

A reasonable compromise is to have the recorder set at a slow time-lapse recording speed for the entire time up to the alarm. Once an alarm or motion sensing system is triggered, the recorder automatically switches to normal speed. Some systems allow for the system to revert to slow speed once the motion or other alarm criteria are no longer present. Others switch back from normal to slow speed recording after a predetermined amount of time passes.

In addition to time lapse video tape recording, equipment has been developed for both industrial and consumer Digital Video Recording (DVR). Rather than magnetic tape media, a digital recording is made to a hard-drive similar to that found in computers. At the consumer level, users can record their favorite television shows for later viewing. Utilizing a specialized DVR unit, the user can record, and rapidly search, more than 300 hours of recorded programming.

Industrial DVRs can record up to sixteen camera feeds and provide for weeks of around-the-clock video recording. Some equipment allows for remote viewing of the video via Internet connections. This may, in some situations, allow for a lessened chance of detection as there is no need for tapes to be changed at the site by investigators. If there is a recording made of relevant evidence, imagery normally is transferred to another hard-drive or compact disc for storage and preservation.

Covert Imaging

Private sector investigators routinely will use hidden or covert cameras to determine information important to an investigation. In most cases the answer sought is who is responsible for the undesirable activity. In others it may be when certain activity is occurring or how something is being done. The covert installation of camera equipment is a valuable tool in capturing misconduct as it occurs.

Sometimes covert imaging can be accomplished using overt camera installations. A simple example is a situation where an overt camera is mounted above the rear door to a business through which deliveries pass. Such cameras are used primarily as safety viewers by the persons inside to establish identity before admitting drivers. Often they are not attached to video recording systems. Suppose, however, that night shift workers at a business are suspected of allowing outsiders to enter the premises for unauthorized purposes, such as theft. It is often a simple matter of introducing a recorder somewhere in the system to allow for secret recording of the arrival and departure of those visitors to the company's premises.

More frequently, however, a hidden camera installation will be called for. Although there are film cameras manufactured for certain applications, by far the more likely imaging device will be a CCTV camera. CCTV cameras, given the extremely small sizes afforded by CCD camera technology, can be covertly employed in numerous housings. Cameras routinely are hidden in sprinkler heads, smoke detectors, picture frames, books, power outlets, and other items commonly found in homes and offices. In addition to static installations, CCTV cameras can be placed into very small housings or lens covers to imitate pagers, watches, clothing buttons, and even eyeglasses, allowing use by investigators in an undercover role.

Pinhole lens technology has also allowed for much of this versatility. Holes the size of the letter "o" on this page are more than ample for this kind of installation. We have been able to capture usable images through holes only slightly larger than the period at the end of this sentence. One memorable installation used a literal pinhole through wallpaper in an office. The executive was unable to detect the hole being used even after being told where to look and viewing a live image of himself on the video monitor.

Figures 21.3 and 21.4 show different hidden camera and lens packages available for use. This technology is becoming almost mainstream, with dozens of hidden video camera packages being touted as "nanny-cams." They are used to monitor in-home caregivers for possible child abuse.

Covert Installation Considerations

It is important for the private sector investigator to do preliminary work to first determine whether it is proper to install a covert camera in the area(s) under consideration. The foremost consideration is whether the parties who enter the area under observation enjoy a reasonable expectation of privacy. The act of acquiring evidence of drug use, malingering, or theft in an area where such expectation of privacy exists may create a legal liability for the investigator and the company. Invasion of privacy is a tort that can lead to substantial costs associated with damage awards and legal defense. Such suits can be brought against both corporations as well as individual investigators.

In some jurisdictions it is also a criminal offense to install a video camera in areas where the individual has a clear expectation of privacy. In addition to invasion of privacy claims, there is an additional consideration for investigations that take place in a situation involving a workforce represented by a labor union. In 1997 the National Labor Relations Board ruled that,

> (T)he Union has the statutory right to engage in collective bargaining over the installation and continued use of surveillance cameras, including the circumstances under which the cameras will be activated, the general areas in which they may be placed, and how affected employees will be disciplined if improper conduct is observed.[32]

It appears therefore that it would certainly benefit an investigator to have a covert installation plan reviewed by legal counsel for invasion of privacy, compliance with existing labor agreements, and unfair labor practices *prior* to completing the installation. Company management should definitely also review the installation plan and approve it prior to installation by a corporate security investigator. As has been stated earlier, the company investigator must not create excessive risk of liability while con-

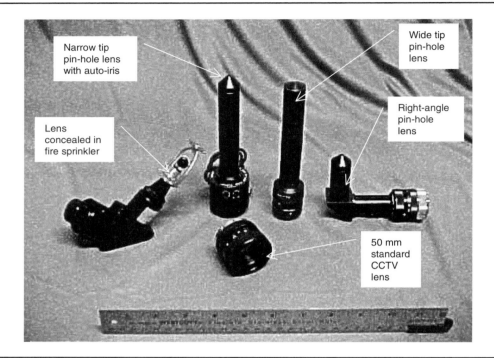

Figure 21.3. CCTV lenses typically used in investigations.

ducting investigations. A clear understanding of the complex issues involving these matters should be obtained *before* placing a hidden camera in the workplace.

Beyond the legal consideration are the practicalities of the installation. The investigator first must answer each of the following questions before a hidden video installation should be undertaken:

1. Is the activity under investigation primarily one that can be visually depicted? In other words, can seeing the activity occur result in usable evidence? Persons breaking into a storage locker probably would be a suitable activity to document by camera, while someone talking on the phone discussing company secrets would probably be unsuitable.
2. Is there a location where the camera may be hidden that will afford a view of the suspected activity?
3. Is there a means of retrieving the stored video images without the subjects or others becoming aware of the surveillance?
4. Is there a ready means of powering the camera and recording equipment?
5. Will the components of the installation (camera, recorder, cables, power supply) remain undetectable during the likely duration of the installation?

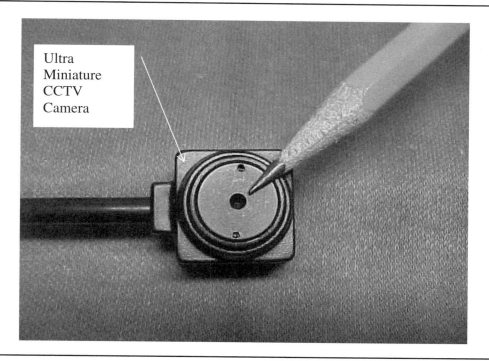

Ultra
Miniature
CCTV
Camera

Figure 21.4. Extremely small pinhole CCTV camera easily concealed for covert applications. Pencil points to actual pinhole lens opening.

6. How often will the tapes be changed and reviewed? Will the review be of all tapes, or only after a specific crime or incident that is known to have occurred?
7. How often will tapes be reviewed to ensure that the equipment is still properly functioning?
8. Are there means and opportunity to place the camera without being detected doing so?

Video Camcorder Imaging

The video camera-recorder combination commonly referred to as a "camcorder" is probably the backbone of the imaging program in any private sector investigations organization. Where still imaging, either film or digital based, can capture single images, a video camera will capture literally thousands in the same time period. For the normal investigator, the camcorder represents the best current technology for easily documenting scenes, actions, and people.

There are several videotape recording formats commonly used by investigators. They are primarily VHS, VHS-C, Super-VHS, Super VHS-C, 8 mm, and Hi-8 mm, all analog formats. The various formats will deliver differing levels of resolution that are expressed in numbers of lines of resolution.

A VHS video camcorder should deliver 240 lines of resolution, 8 mm will deliver 300 lines, Super VHS/Super VHS-C/Hi-8 mm will deliver 400 lines of resolution. For the best identification of suspects, or when the highest degree of detail is necessary, the investigator should use a format with the highest level of resolution that can be afforded.

In contrast to the resolution that can be achieved by affordable field video camcorders likely to be used in private investigations, conventional film photography can provide resolutions of 4,000 to 6,000 lines. This is achieved, however, at a trade-off of convenience of image production (requiring photo-finishing services), numbers of images, and actions that can be captured in nonstaged moving situations, size of telephoto lenses necessary to achieve comparable zoom, and limited low-light capabilities without the use of a flash.

Camcorders also will provide zoom features generally superior to that found in conventional film cameras of comparable size and weight. Zoom functions in camcorders typically will be of two kinds, optical and digital zoom. Optical zooms can range to about 24 times standard focal length, and digital zooms can provide over 300 times standard magnification. The optical zoom is similar to that found in still film photography; the glass lens in the camera will physically move to create a greater focal length, resulting in greater magnification. Once the limits of the optical zoom are reached, electronic effects are manipulated by the camcorder to digitally simulate further magnification. This can result, in extreme digital zooms, in images that are little more than individual points of color and light that cannot be coherently identified.

Field Imagery

The use of film photography or video camcorders in the field by private sector investigators normally will be to document one of two conditions: a static object or set of objects in a scene, or action taking place at a particular date, place, and time by specific individuals. The first type of documentation, used in reconstructive investigations, normally will be completely overt, such as a crime scene documentation assignment or photographing a specific object of physical evidence.

The second method, used for constructive investigations, normally will be applied covertly, such as in a surveillance of employee misconduct or a burglary stakeout. Covert CCTV installations have been discussed earlier, and surveillance applications are discussed in the surveillance chapter.

SCENE DOCUMENTATION

Imagery is used as a regular means of documenting scenes of investigative interest by private sector investigators. In many instances accidents, burglaries, or vandalism are preserved by means of imagery. The purpose of such scene documentation is to allow the visual evidence available at a scene to be reviewed and evaluated at a later time by the investigator or others (such as management, attorneys, union representatives, or courts).

The points listed here are used whether the medium employed is still film, still digital, or videotape.

1. Attempt to document the scene prior to the movement of any items found therein.
2. Document the scene as much as possible from the outside before intruding into the relevant area.

3. Take images of the scene from different perspectives, such as from the four corners of the room.
4. Take images of the scene from the perspectives of the first responder, walking through the scene and stopping at each location where he or she stopped, documenting what was visible from those positions.
5. Take images of the scene from the perspectives of witnesses who are able to identify where they may have been at various times during the incident under investigation.
6. In order to document the specific location of an individual item of interest in a scene, take successive images of the item that "move in" to the object. Do this by means of wide-angle shots taking in the entire area, followed by a medium zoom shot that shows the specific item in relation to other items in the scene, followed by close-up shots of the object.
7. Document the individual items of evidence in the location where first seen upon arrival.
8. If an item has been moved, first document it in its relocated position. After all other images have been taken, position the item where it was first found and take images in that original position.
9. Prior to moving furniture, take images with cameras held above the furniture pointed down at the area behind the furniture to document original positions of items found there.
10. Take measurements of the distances from important objects in the scene in relation to one another; prepare a sketch of the scene using same.
11. Keep a log of still images taken that includes date, time, direction, lens aperture, and shutter speed settings used, as well as a brief description of the picture taken.
12. At the start of each tape or roll of film, make out a small card on gray stock giving particulars that correspond to the log, including roll or tape number, date, and location being documented. Make similar cards and images for each new room or area being documented. This assists later in keeping the photographs or other images properly identified when sorting through large numbers of pictures that may appear to be similar but are of different locations or times.
13. Where possible, take images of individual pieces of evidence with an item of known length also in the image. Typically, a ruler placed next to an item will allow the image to convey the size of the item. For larger items, a stick marked with alternating dark and light bands of known width (six inches, one foot, etc.) allows for a quick reference to the size of the item for later image users. Such size reference objects placed in the image are known as *scales*. Scales are commercially manufactured and available through forensic laboratory supply houses, but in a field situation, anything of known size can be used to prove scale such as a 3″ × 5″ card, a notebook. Even a cigarette or pen can be used.

THE FUTURE OF INVESTIGATIVE PHOTOGRAPHY

In October 1999, the National Institute of Justice's Law Enforcement and Corrections Standards and Testing Program published its *Video Surveillance Equipment Selection and Application Guide* (NIJ Guide 201–99). It provides an excellent overview of the then current technology and its likely future use in investigative imagery. It states in part:

With all the advances in videography today, there will come a day in the not-too-distant future when still photography will no longer be the preferred technique for recording data for most law enforcement and corrections needs. As the resolution and electronic shutter speeds of video equipment continue to improve and the costs of video units are reduced even further, the current advantages of conventional photography will diminish. Also, digital video and multimedia computing could have a significant impact on the future of video surveillance and how the data are gathered and processed.[33]

In many cases, the *who*, *what*, *how*, and *when* of a situation can be visually depicted. Whenever a matter under investigation contains relevant visible details, investigators must be prepared to capture those details by using the correct imagery system.

Chapter 22

Computers in Private Sector Investigations

A CHANGING INVESTIGATOR'S WORLD

In the decades since the first edition of this text was introduced, America and the world have moved from the Industrial Age to the Information Age. In many ways, as a result of being part of that world, crime itself has changed. Our everyday language reflects this evolution.

Consider that only a few years ago having a virus primarily meant we were in for muscle aches and fever, not business interruption; denial of service was a sign in the window stating: "no shirt, no shoes, no service," not a deliberate attack on global electronic commerce; a cracker was a snack food and a hacker was an inept golfer, not cyber criminals capable of threatening a nation's security; and bombs once were logically dropped on an enemy's headquarters as part of traditional warfare whereas today logic bombs are used to reach into a corporate headquarters and bring defeat in info-war.

The crimes that now confront the professional investigator have been clearly added to by the vulnerabilities of computers and our society's dependence upon them. At the same time the computer has given us tools of immense power to investigate "traditional" as well as "computer" crimes.

Computers in private-sector investigations most frequently will fit into one of two categories: as investigative tools or as objects of evidence.

Within these two categories are a number of subcategories, the most obvious of which appear to be the following.

COMPUTERS AS INVESTIGATIVE TOOLS

- The computer is used to collect investigative information; that is, Internet research on arcane subjects or real-time monitoring of system intrusions.
- The computer is used as a processing and analyzing tool; that is, the automated searching of text found in mass records.
- The computer is used in the presentation of investigative information; that is, when graphs, diagrams, or photographs are digitally assembled and displayed. An example is found in Figure 22.1 where the Old Midtown Church Case Study is diagrammed.

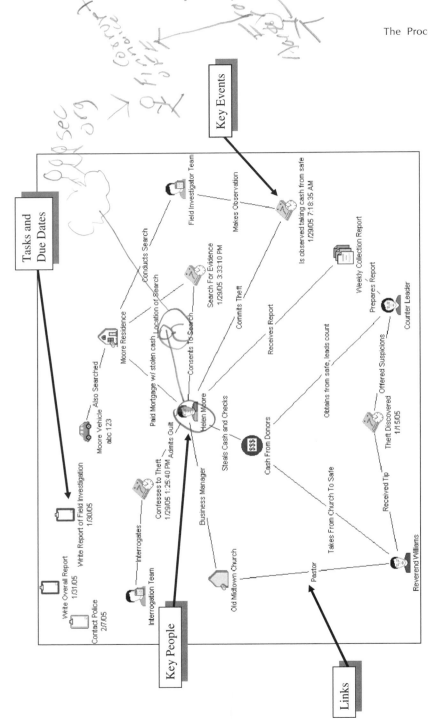

Figure 22.1. Chart from CaseRunner, an investigation management program. This software allows for quick visualization of the case information and tracking of tasks to be completed.

- The computer is used as an investigative management tool; that is, when the work flow or document management of a large case is automated.

COMPUTERS AS OBJECTS OF EVIDENCE

- The computer as an instrument of crime; that is, the computer is actually necessary to the commission of a crime.
- The computer as the site of an intrusion or direct attack; that is, it's a crime scene, much like an R & D lab that has been burglarized.
- The computer as a repository of evidence of computer crimes and noncomputer crimes; that is, a computer can contain files relating to crimes, such as the accounting records kept by an embezzler working in the accounts payable office.
- The computer itself as the fruit of a crime; that is, when the entire computer or its components are stolen, such as in the case of a laptop computer theft.

Certainly, in any investigation it would be possible, even probable, for the same computer to fit into multiple roles within the two respective categories. For example, in a large fraud investigation, a single computer could be used by an investigator to

- Lay out the case management plan
- Sort information from several thousand canceled checks
- Create and archive interview transcripts and reports
- Diagram links between individuals or to create time lines of relevant events
- Process digital images of documents, people, and locations
- Prepare a final report

The computer as an investigative tool will be used exactly this way, to varying degrees, in most private sector investigations. Similarly, an intruder could sit at a single computer and

- Load certain hacker software tools to enable the alteration of data or the compromising of passwords
- Log onto an attached network to steal valuable proprietary information while leaving behind altered data
- Plant a virus likely to cause a loss of system functionality or the destruction of data

As such, the computer at the same time would be the site of an intrusion, the means by which a theft was conducted, and the repository of evidence of the crime. In each role the computer probably would hold valuable evidence. Although such multiplicity of roles is common during investigations, the investigator must never allow a single computer to be used across the two broad categories. In other words, we do not allow the individual computer containing original evidence to be used as a tool in the investigation. The hazards to an investigation are legion and lethal.

Suppose for a moment that we were to sit at the same computer used by our intruder in the earlier example and begin to operate it as an investigative tool rather than treating it as an item of evidence.

In all likelihood we would alter the data on the hard drive, rendering it useless as court-admissible evidence, while exposing our entire case file to corruption, destruction, and even remote penetration by the hacker. If this is not bad enough, we could definitely gore our professional reputations by giving electronic copies of our final report to other legal and investigative professionals on media that had been infected by the viruses left for us by our culprit.

The only time it makes sense to violate this evidence versus tool separation would be when a computer or network is subject to an ongoing series of intrusions and continued access is allowed for the purpose of gathering information on the identity and methods of the intruder(s) in real-time. This should be done only with the help of highly skilled computer experts experienced in collecting and analyzing computer evidence for criminal court proceedings.

COMPUTERS AS TOOLS

Just as the prevalence of the personal computers in society has led to the everyday use by students, government workers, and business employees of word processing, spreadsheet, and database programs, so have computers entered into daily use by professional investigators. In seemingly growing numbers, special-purpose software programs are being developed and sold to assist investigators in their work.

Even the use of general-purpose programs can net very powerful gains in the ways investigators are able to handle individual cases.

(Note: References to any programs, products, or companies are provided for informational purposes and for conceptual insight only and are not intended to be endorsements. Indeed, it's most probable that with the passage of time, this text will outlive some of the very programs and products referenced here. Readers must conduct their own evaluations prior to using programs, products, or companies.)

Spreadsheet Programs

A spreadsheet program, such as *Excel* or *Quatro Pro*, allows for the arrangement of information (most commonly numerical data) into rows and columns that can be rapidly sorted, compiled, and totaled. This can be very useful to an investigator whenever numerous similar events need to be listed or compared.

As an example, the effective use of a spreadsheet program allowed for us to prove an important element in an investigation of embezzlement by the treasurer of a small county. We already had identified more than three hundred separate instances where cash had been diverted from the county coffers. There were about twenty employees who enjoyed access to the funds during the three years the crime had continued. To have manually conducted a loss/presence correlation analysis of the type shown in Figure 17.1 would have been extremely painstaking and difficult to update as new information became available.

Instead, the use of a spreadsheet allowed for the creation of a list, or schedule, which clearly demonstrated that the only person present for each identified diversion had been the county treasurer. Printing the schedule and presenting it to the jury provided a very simple summary of the information that could be easily thumbed as they deliberated. The county treasurer eventually was convicted and sentenced to ten years in prison for the theft of more than $1.3 million in taxpayer funds.

Another common use of spreadsheets in our white-collar crime practice is the well-planned use of subsidiary and summary schedules during the confrontation of embezzlers. Because embezzlers rarely keep track of the amount and date of each theft, the investigator must assemble the information to assist the culprit's recall and to support later legal action.

In one case, we were informed that a restaurant manager was suspected of stealing from payments made on guest checks. It was estimated to us that the individual losses ranged from five to twenty dollars. Though not exactly the Great Train Robbery, a thorough investigation to identify the full extent of the loss was required. Digging into tens of thousands of guest checks and cash register journal tapes, the review team identified 1,058 separate thefts.

The individual guest tabs were gathered and put into chronological order in three-ring binders. The corresponding journal tapes were segregated into matching manila envelopes. After the thief was confronted and generally admitted his role in the thefts, it would be crucial to establish the total dollar amount of the losses. This is typically the case when a corporate victim will be seeking compensation under an employee fidelity bond or from other recovery sources. Whoever is going to pay will have to be satisfied with the basis for the final amount. Additionally, the amount stolen customarily will be used by prosecutors when the level of the charges to be brought is being decided.

Instead of creating a single schedule of more than 1,000 lines, we chose to break it into separate schedules, each containing the details of only one month. During the interrogation we positioned the stack of binders and journal tapes out of the suspect's sight. At the appropriate time we placed on the table a single schedule sheet and only the original documents necessary to prove that schedule's accuracy to the suspect. The schedule had been preset with spaces for the subject to initial on each line to acknowledge the accuracy of the loss amount. He was asked to compare our data against each guest tab and journal entry. He accepted almost all the items, challenging only a small number, normally with a convincing argument. At the bottom of the page he and I totaled the acknowledged theft amounts. He then signed and dated each of the pages, which were whisked immediately out of sight and replaced with the following month's sheet.

In fairly short order we had secured the suspect's signature on all the subsidiary schedules. He was never scared off by seeing the size of the entire verification undertaking. When we presented him with a summary schedule on which the total from each month had been entered, he was fully convinced of the accuracy of our work. He signed a written acknowledgment after verifying the grand total. Through the use of a spreadsheet program we were able to figuratively feed him the whole elephant, "one bite at a time."

Another use of spreadsheet programs is their capability to graphically represent trends or proportions. Bar graphs, line charts, and pie charts are all effective means of illustrating changes in key factors, such as falling net profits from a company suffering embezzlements, or comparing total hourly sales by respective cashier.

Database Programs

A relational database program can be used to integrate information from large masses of data. One such program is *Access*. Databases allow for the gathering of specific similar items to be displayed in customized reports based upon carefully defined criteria. For instance, we recently had reason to review more than 15,000 individual donations made to over one hundred political candidates. The information had been compiled in *Access*, a database program, by a government office and was made available to our personnel.

Using the customized reporting features of the program we were able to research in a number of ways. For instance, it is sometimes the practice by companies wishing to evade the donation limits in political campaigns to have a selected number of employees make individual donations that are later reimbursed by the company. Depending on the total number of employees involved, quite a lot of corporate money in excess of spending limits can be funneled to favored politicians without the company appearing at all in published donation reports. One feature of such donation "bundling" is the fact that it is typical for the donations to be delivered at one time, so that the politician can be sufficiently impressed by the efforts of the persons delivering the checks en masse. Knowing that campaign finance laws require reporting of the date, amount, donor name, and donor address associated with each political contribution above a certain amount, we used the database program to determine the identities of politicians to whom certain key corporate officers had made donations.

We then ran reports of all donations made to those politicians that were received on the same day as the corporate officers' moneys. After doing this on only a couple of politicians we were able to identify the members of the "bundle" whose donations kept appearing together in identical amounts on the same dates. The pattern we were able to discern identified a number of men and women, as well as their spouses and children, who seemed to have remarkably similar political interests. We did further research on those persons and found that all of them worked for, or had spouses who worked for, architectural, engineering, and construction firms doing business with a single large business entity.

Through interviews we were able to determine that executives from that business had contacted each of the companies to seek funds to be paid to particular political campaigns. Although we were not able to show that the large business actually funded the donations of their vendors, a number of vendors indicated that to preserve their large contracts with the business, they were willing to pay their hard-earned money to the "right" politicians.

Without the ability to rapidly pull names out of the mass of information using a few key criteria, we certainly would have missed the names of numerous donors who were part of the "bundle," and amounts of money each paid. Another powerful use of database programs is the indexing of many thousands, sometimes even millions, of documents, events, and testimony. As long as correct key words are selected for indexing from all letters, checks, testimony, or contracts in a large case, it may be possible to pull needles out of haystacks.

As an example, suppose an investigator obtains documents including letters, canceled checks, sales invoices, and contracts. If the investigator were to have all relevant information for each type of record properly input into the database, he would be able to capitalize on investigative leads as they occurred. For instance, if he came across the name of an individual or company in an interview, he could query the database for all records in which that individual or company's name appeared. He might well be referred to a letter, interview report, or sales invoice where that name was significant and connections to third parties referenced in those records would emerge. He could then better determine how to proceed in the investigation.

In massive cases, databases help the investigator navigate confidently through trackless oceans of information.

Presentation Programs

At many points during an investigation it is necessary to provide briefings or reports to management, government agencies, clients, or others. Typically, this is done in order to provide enough information to allow for decision-making, obtain or maintain cooperation or continued authority to investigate, or to explain the findings of a completed investigation. This can take the form of a simple verbal explanation over the telephone or can actually be part of sworn testimony delivered to executive committees, regulators, legislators, grand juries, judges, or arbitrators.

Generally, such briefings or testimony have as a primary objective the summarizing of large amounts of information. Diagrams, graphs, and photographs are all helpful in this regard. Putting together a number of electronic slides or overhead transparencies can easily be accomplished using presentation software such as *PowerPoint*. Printing the slides onto paper for handouts and notes is valuable for the persons being briefed. Figure 22.2 depicts a typical timeline easily and quickly prepared in *PowerPoint*.

Specialized Software

In addition to the programs generally found in any comprehensive suite of business software, there are a number of specialized programs currently available that can be considered for use by investigators.

Analytical Software

The field of criminal investigation has been enhanced by the use of analytical techniques traditionally utilized in scientific research and military intelligence analysis. One organization that pioneered this kind of application is Anacapa Sciences, Inc. of Santa Barbara, California. Anacapa Sciences developed the basic framework for connecting individuals, organizations, and events through a process known as *link analysis*. The use of link analysis techniques allows investigators to advance investigations beyond what is plainly discernible, by facilitating the development of *inferences*. Anacapa Sciences has trained investigators around the world in its analytical techniques. Those techniques are relied upon by criminal intelligence analysts.

In its Analytical Investigative Methods course material, Anacapa Sciences provides some basic information of use to those unfamiliar with its concepts: Information is material of every description, including that derived from observations, surveillance, reports, rumors, and other sources. The information itself may be true or false, accurate or inaccurate, confirmed or unconfirmed, relevant or irrelevant. Thus, the analytical process requires that information be evaluated, organized, stored, and retrieved. Although not part of analyses, these functions are necessary to support the process.

An inference is the principal product of the analytical process. It is an explanation of what the collected information means. The objective of analysis is to develop the most precise and valid inferences possible from whatever information is available. In addition, analysis serves to identify needed data and, consequently, helps to focus and provide leads for further information collection.[34] As can be seen from these statements, the products of investigative analysis explain what a mass of information means and help point out likely avenues of investigation.

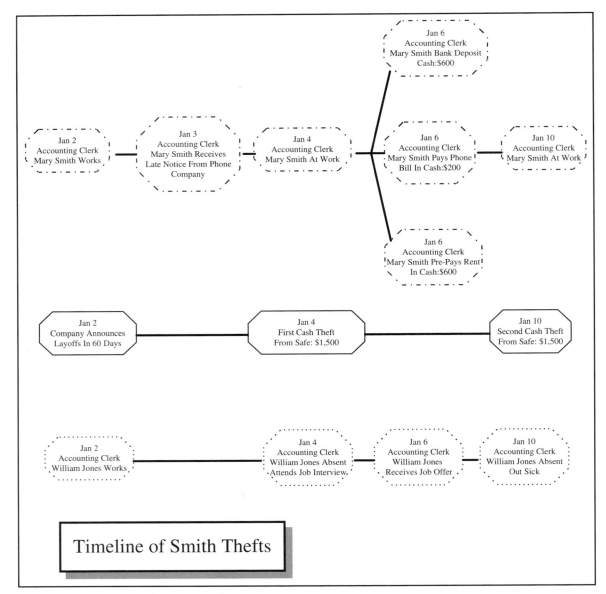

Figure 22.2.   Event timeline prepared using *PowerPoint*.

The diagrams found in Figure 22.3, which are produced using Anacapa Sciences analytical software, provide both explanation and leads development in a hypothetical case of extortion. By looking at the diagrams the following pictures appear:

1. After each of two refusals to accept proposals received from TWU, XYZCO had a number of its locations damaged by arson, bombing, or vandalism.
2. Another firm, ABC, Inc., and an individual named Maas are both linked to TWU through money passed through an intermediary named Lissom.
3. Telephone traffic connects a woman named Grady with TWU through someone named Philpott.

How can this analysis be used in this particular investigation? Several things can be planned by investigators after becoming aware of these links. As a result of identifying the money flow through Lissom, it would be important to research ABC, Inc. and Maas to determine any interest they may have in the XYZCO/TWU negotiations. The telephone traffic analysis would indicate a need to determine the backgrounds of persons associated with the telephone numbers identified. Are any of the subscribers criminals with arson or bombing backgrounds? Is Grady somehow related to ABC, Inc., Maas, or even XYZCO? Further, if Lissom is a conduit between ABC, Inc. and TWU, then targeting Lissom as a person to "turn" for information against both entities becomes an obvious investigative avenue.

In addition to links between persons and businesses, these diagrams assist in the determining of follow-up investigations relating to the key event chronology. For instance, what can be learned about the whereabouts, movements, meetings, and telephone calls made by the linked individuals immediately before, during, and after each of the negotiation meetings and subsequent attacks? By following these leads it may be possible to obtain new evidence to tie individuals to the illegal acts.

Another investigative software package is that offered by i2 Inc., a company founded in England as a result of the development of specialized software solutions for the British Metropolitan Police, otherwise known as Scotland Yard. i2 Inc. markets a very sophisticated analytical tool known as *Analyst's Notebook*, which is used by government criminal intelligence analysts and law enforcement personnel throughout Europe, the United States, Canada, Latin America, and Asia. Even though it is an expensive software program, *Analyst's Notebook*, with over 1,500 worldwide users, is believed by some to be the gold standard for this type of software. i2 Inc. says that its product can analyze information from hundreds of thousands and even millions of records or reports. At that volume of information it is simply not humanly possible to manually process and identify critical links between individuals, or connections between events, unless such a sophisticated tool is employed.

The result of any completed investigation should be an inference presented to management, police, or sometimes even the public. That inference can be one that implicates or exonerates. The use of specialized analytical software can be vital to completing and presenting investigative analysis, especially when there is a mass of information to be processed.

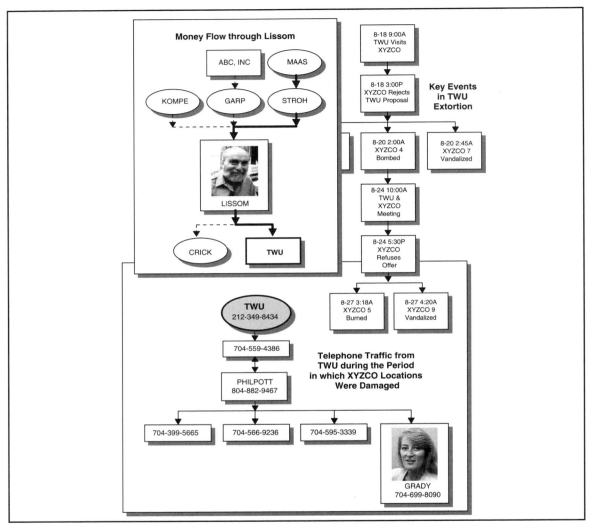

Figure 22.3. Three diagrams useful in sorting out who may be involved in an extortion plot against XYZCO. Provided courtesy of Anacapa Sciences, Inc. Santa Barbara, CA.

Diagramming Programs

It is sometimes necessary for a private sector investigator to prepare diagrams of accident and incident scenes. The precise rendering of objects, buildings, and persons at a scene can be best preserved through a well-documented sketch. Investigators have been sketching crime scenes for years, but now specialized software is available to allow for rapid and standardized scene sketches. One such product is *Crime-Zone* developed by the CAD Zone, Inc. and was specially configured for the needs of working investigators. In wide use by local, county, state, and federal agencies, *CrimeZone* is updated continually as user feedback is received. An example of a *CrimeZone* diagram is shown in Figure 9.1. Other products are also available that allow for similar employment of computer-aided diagramming technology first made popular by the architectural and engineering professions.

A hastily scribbled sketch done at a crime scene may suffice for compiling initial information, but the process of converting it to a usable diagram that will be exhibited in court is made immensely easier by automating the task. In addition to dispensing with the hours spent with pens, rulers, and templates, the investigator can much more easily send copies of diagrams to other investigators, managers, or lawyers via electronic mail. Updating diagrams is also very simple when using a digital rendering.

Investigations Management Programs

There are a number of computer programs available that help investigators to manage information and tasks in investigations. i2, Inc. also produces a program called *CaseRunner*, which combines a link diagramming program, report generator, and investigation task manager to allow the working investigator to stay on top of ongoing investigations. Although the link diagramming program is not the same level of analytical tool as that found in *Analyst's Notebook*, it appears sufficient for those investigations of low to moderate complexity that will normally make up the bulk of an investigator's caseload. It is not designed as a tool for the management of multiple investigators; rather, it is intended for ease of use by individual investigators.

A recent search of the Web found several investigative case management programs being offered for sale. These are cited with information gleaned solely from the posted information for each product:

1. *ICMS (Investigations Case Management System)* by Loss Control Solutions, Inc. This program was developed using *Access* for a large financial institution and appears to include the ability to track the workload of several investigators from its "Investigation Managers Workbench," and seems to provide an overall set of database tools to manage individual investigations, loss trends as well as summaries by individual investigator, loss categories, and time. The product description indicates an orientation toward private sector corporate operations.
2. *CaseInfo* by CI Technologies. This software appears to be largely directed at law enforcement investigation management and allows for task planning, report generation, and automated linking of persons, vehicles, telephone numbers, and businesses. It is advertised to be especially well suited for major case support, allowing the integration of information from multiple investigators and originally was written to support a student murders task force in Florida in 1990.

3. *e@gle.i Investigation Management* by Oakton Computing. This program, jointly developed with the New South Wales Police Service of Australia, is definitely a law enforcement oriented program. The program apparently focuses on tasking workflow, information sharing, and managerial review.

Other Programs

Investigators, typically being highly resourceful, find and adopt all kinds of software not necessarily created for the investigative professional. Programs come from the full range of the complexity spectrum. Two such programs are mentioned here in passing. A very inexpensive program available for download from the Web is a product known as *Cyber-Detective* by InnoSoft Solutions, which includes some simple task management, information source listings, and general tools and tips not often assembled into a single resource for nonprofessionals.

The other is a litigation management software package known as *Summation Blaze* from Summation Legal Technologies, Inc., marketed to the legal profession. It has been used in some of the largest lawsuits in legal history to integrate the endless documents, transcripts, and working notes involved in megalitigation. It often is used with mountains of scanned documents, depositions, and hearing transcripts. Using it, federal litigators were apparently able to instantly produce e-mail evidence in the courtroom to refute testimony offered by Microsoft's highest profile witness in its antitrust case.

COMPUTERS AS OBJECTS OF EVIDENCE

As discussed earlier, the computer can be both the means of committing crimes as well as the "location" where crimes occurred (such as in a computer intrusion or denial of service attack). Accordingly, computers have become a new type of crime scene that requires as much care to process for evidence as the location of any high-profile homicide or bombing scene. In some ways, even more care must be taken than in traditional crime scenes because of the extremely fragile and ephemeral nature of digital evidence.

Additionally, computers are often the high-tech equivalent of a filing cabinet used by criminals to store information that to an investigator can turn into proof of numerous misdeeds including the distribution of child pornography, embezzlement, narcotics trafficking, money laundering, identity theft, sexual harassment, or the theft of trade secrets, to name a few. Such evidence can even be used to prove the selling of a nation's secrets by its own senior counter-intelligence operatives, as was the case of the Central Intelligence Agency's Aldridge Ames.

Specialized Techniques

The techniques for obtaining digital evidence commonly are not fully appreciated by either investigative or computer professionals. On the one hand, an investigator may believe that once a computer file has been deleted it is beyond retrieval. On the other hand, a computer analyst may pay little heed to the manner in which he resurrects that same file and in doing so can utterly destroy its usefulness as a piece of evidence in courts or quasi-judicial proceedings. As a result of the problems caused by this lack of understanding, very painstaking methods have been developed by the law enforcement community. Specialized forensic analysis software has been written to allow for both the culling of information from suspect computers and surviving legal challenges to the information's reliability and authenticity.

Seizing Computer Evidence

Unfortunately, securing computer evidence is not quite as simple as photographing, bagging, and tagging a screwdriver found at the scene of an office burglary. A high-tech intrusion rarely leaves evidence that is easily apparent or durable.

As early as the mid-1980s the federal government was creating methods by which its agents were able to seize, examine, and present computer evidence in court. Michael R. Anderson was one of the early pioneers with the U.S. Department of the Treasury, Federal Law Enforcement Training Center (FLETC) in Glynco, Georgia. Anderson and others developed the first computer evidence courses before 1990 that have been taught to federal, state, and local law enforcement specialists.

Now the head of New Technologies, Inc., a private firm that through its software and training makes current state-of-the-art methods available to both public and private sector specialists, Anderson has provided easily accessible guidance through articles posted on his firm's Web site. Though such articles, and other information available electronically or from other traditional sources, cannot substitute for a fully featured training course, they can still be instructive to an investigator in the cautions they describe.

Corporate Considerations

For the private/corporate investigator, certain suggestions are provided by Anderson to be considered when initially responding to a possible computer incident:

1. Don't turn on or operate the subject computer. The computer should first be backed up using bit stream backup software. When the computer is run, the potential exists for information in the Windows swap file to be overwritten. Internet activity and fragments of Windows work sessions exist in the Windows swap file. This can prove to be valuable from an evidence standpoint. In the case of a DOS-based system, the running of the computer can destroy "deleted" files. For that matter, the same is true of a Windows system. To save grief, don't run the computer.
2. Don't solicit the assistance of the resident "computer expert." The processing of computer evidence is tricky, to say the least. Without proper training even a world-class computer scientist can do the wrong things. Like any other science, computer science has its areas of specialty. We typically get calls "after the fact" and are advised that a computer-knowledgeable Internal Auditor or Systems Administrator has attempted to process a computer for evidence. In some cases, valuable evidence is lost or the evidence is so tainted that it loses its evidentiary value. For these reasons, seek the assistance of a computer specialist that has been trained in computer evidence processing procedures. Do this before you turn on the computer!
3. Don't evaluate employee e-mail unless corporate policy allows it. New electronic privacy laws protect the privacy of electronic communications. If your corporate policy specifically states that all computers and data stored on them belong to the corporation, then you are probably on safe ground. However, be sure that you have such a policy and that the employee(s)

involved have read the policy. Furthermore, it is always a good idea to check with corporate counsel. Don't be in a hurry. Do things by the book! To do otherwise could subject you and your corporation to a lawsuit.[35]

Seizing Computer Evidence

In 1995, a Deputy District Attorney for Santa Clara County, California, named Kenneth S. Rosenblatt published a book titled *High-Technology Crime, Investigating Cases Involving Computers*. Mr. Rosenblatt's expertise was derived from his service as his office's High-Technology Crime Unit supervisor that covered the Silicon Valley. In conducting our research for this chapter, Mr. Rosenblatt's book was found to be constantly referred to by experts consulted and books read. It can probably be considered the bible for investigators seeking to become familiar with the law and methods that should be applied in seizing and initially examining computer evidence. His book provides a step-by-step guide for obtaining search warrants, executing searches, and examining computers. As such, it is primarily oriented to the needs of law enforcement investigators, but should still be read by corporate and private investigators who are serious about conducting investigations relating to high-technology crime.

Rosenblatt lists the priority items to accomplish at the time of executing a warrant:

1. Isolate the computers.
2. Isolate power and phone connections.
3. Confirm that the computers are not erasing data.
4. Check for physical traps.[36]

It is clear that the first steps taken by investigators must be to ensure that the evidence existing at the moment they commence their search is not destroyed or damaged during the hunt as a result of protective measures taken by suspects either in advance of the search or during the search.

Another valuable source of information regarding various laws and methods relating to the seizure of computer evidence is the *Federal Guidelines for Searching and Seizing Computers*, from the U.S. Department of Justice. At the time of this writing it was posted on the Internet at http://www.usdoj.gov/criminal/cybercrime/s&smanual2002.htm. Both Rosenblatt's book and the *Federal Guidelines* make clear that great pains must be taken in preparing for and executing the seizure of computer evidence. Figure 22.4 illustrates the procedural steps taught at FLETC for such searches and seizures.

Examining Computer Evidence

Anderson also lists on the NTI Web pages a number of mistakes and tips to consider when processing computer evidence, especially that found in DOS/WINDOWS-based computer systems. This information is cited to provide background information for investigators so that they can understand what a computer forensics expert should or should not be doing — it is not a substitute for engaging the services of such an expert in the case where computerized evidence must be examined.

Mistake #1: Run the Computer.   The first rule is *NEVER* to run any programs on the computer in question without taking precautions (e.g., write protection or by making a backup copy). Also, you

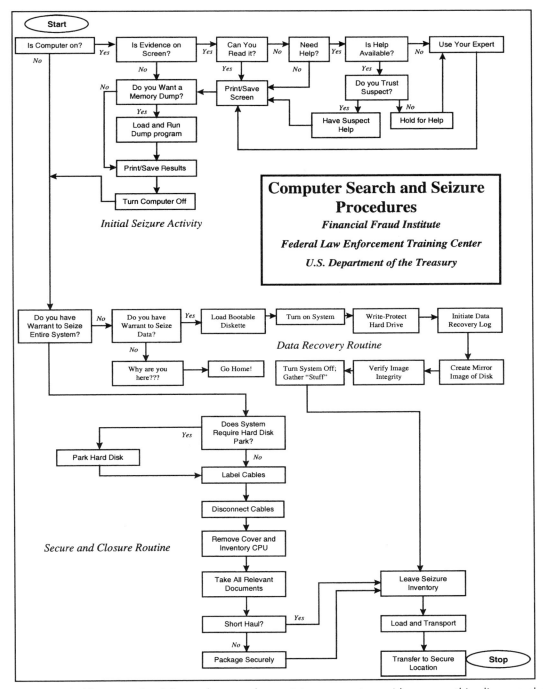

Figure 22.4. Nothing may be left to chance when seizing computer evidence, as this diagram shows. Provided courtesy of Mr. Carlton Fitzpatrick, Financial Fraud Institute, FLETC.

should not boot or run the computer using the operating system on the computer in question. It is relatively easy for criminals to rig their computers to destroy hard disk drive content or specific files by planting decoy programs or through the modification of the operating system. By way of example, the simple DIR instruction that is used to display the directory of a disk can easily be rigged to reformat the hard disk drive. After the data and destructive program have been destroyed, who is to say that the computer was rigged or that you were negligent in processing the computer evidence? This is one of the first points we illustrate when training law enforcement or corporate computer investigators.

Mistake #2: Get Help from the Computer Owner.   It is potentially a serious mistake to allow the owner of the computer to help you operate the computer in question. I like to equate this to asking some thug to help you unload the 9 mm you just found under his car seat. Don't do it. I recall one case a few years ago ... The defendant was asked to answer questions about the computer evidence and was allowed access to the seized computer in the process. He later bragged to his buddies that he had encrypted relevant files "right under the noses of the cops" without their knowledge. The good news is that the computer specialists had made a bit stream backup of the computer before giving the defendant access to it. As a result, his destructive act became another nail in the coffin at trial.

Mistake #3: Don't Check for Computer Viruses.   You can imagine how credible your testimony might be as the expert witness for the government if you were the one that infected the computer evidence with a computer virus. It might get even worse if you carry that a step farther and infect several of the computers in the police department in the process. *ALWAYS* use fresh diskettes and check all diskettes and hard disk drives with good quality virus scanning software before you fall into this trap.

Mistake #4: Don't Take Any Precautions in the Transport of Computer Evidence.   Computer evidence is very fragile. Heat and magnetic fields can destroy or alter it in a very short period of time. The heat of summer in a car trunk or the magnetic field created by an operating police radio in the trunk of a squad car can ruin computer evidence. If a good defense attorney can show that you were negligent in storing or transporting the computer equipment, your case may be in jeopardy and you may spend some time in civil court defending your agency against a lawsuit. Use good judgment and this issue won't be a problem.

Mistake #5: Run Windows to View Graphic Files and to Examine Files.   The Windows swap file can be a valuable source of data fragments, passwords, and network logons. The running of Windows by the computer specialist can destroy evidence that exists in the swap file. Furthermore, running NetScape or other Internet browsers can destroy or modify evidence stored in the form of bookmarks, graphic files, and/or cache files. Many times Windows is needed to review specific graphic files and other file types. However, the running of Windows should not take place until a bit stream backup has been made and the Windows swap file has been processed and analyzed for potential evidence in the form of data fragments.

Tip #1: Bit Stream Backups.   Normally computer evidence is preserved by making an exact copy of the original evidence before any analysis is performed. It is not enough to just make copies of computer files using a conventional backup program. Valuable evidence may exist in the form of erased files and the data associated with these files can be preserved only through a bit stream backup. Specialized software is available to law enforcement agencies that perform this task (e.g., SafeBack).

Regarding floppy diskettes, the DOS DISKCOPY program will suffice. A bit stream backup of the evidence provides a level of insurance should things go bump in the night. It is always a good idea to make a bit stream backup before processing computer evidence.

Tip #2: Temporary Files. Word processing programs and database programs create temporary files as a by-product of the normal operation of the software. Most computer users are unaware of the creation of these files because they usually are erased by the program at the end of the work session. However, the data contained within these erased files can prove to be most valuable from an evidence standpoint. This is particularly true when the source file has been encrypted or the word processing document was printed but never saved to disk. Like magic, these files can be recovered.

Tip #3: Windows Swap File. The popularity of Microsoft Windows has brought with it some added benefits for computer investigators in their quest for new sources of computer evidence. The Windows swap file acts as a huge data buffer and many times fragments of data or even an entire word processing document may end up in this file. As a result, careful analysis of the swap file can result in the discovery of valuable evidence when Windows is involved. New Technologies, Inc. has developed software that automates the analysis of the Windows swap file. With this software a 40-meg swap file can be processed and evaluated in just a few hours. Using traditional methods and tools, such analysis used to take several days.

Tip #4: Document Comparisons. Many times duplicate word processing files may be found on computer hard disk drives and/or floppy diskettes. Sometimes subtle changes or differences between versions of the same document have evidentiary value. These differences can easily be identified through the use of the redline and compare features of most modern word processing programs. The use of this trick alone can save countless hours of time that could be wasted making manual comparisons from one document to another. Because the resulting file is modified by the word processor, be sure to work from copies when using this tip. Automated forensic tools created by New Technologies, Inc. can also be used to help expedite the process. Such tools are particularly helpful when multiple computers are involved.[37]

Steps advocated by FLETC for computer evidence analysis are illustrated in Figure 22.5, and reflect many of the steps mentioned by Anderson. Unless the investigator or computer analyst examining the computer is trained and experienced to do each of the steps listed, it is strongly recommended that such a person be located by the investigator in charge of the case and enlisted to assist. If investigators are fortunate enough to be provided with legitimate access to the computer files and programs used by the target of an investigation, they potentially stand just outside the digital equivalent of Ali Baba's Cave. The trove of evidence that may lie within reach should not sway us to unwise and hasty action. After consulting with legal and computer forensics experts, and not before, the investigator can confidently say "Open Sesame!" and commence the electronic search.

A FINAL NOTE

As the profession of investigations continues to track criminals through both real and cyber crime scenes, there is little doubt that each new method of digital attack and obscuring of evidence will need to be countered and overcome. However, certain constants will remain for the determined

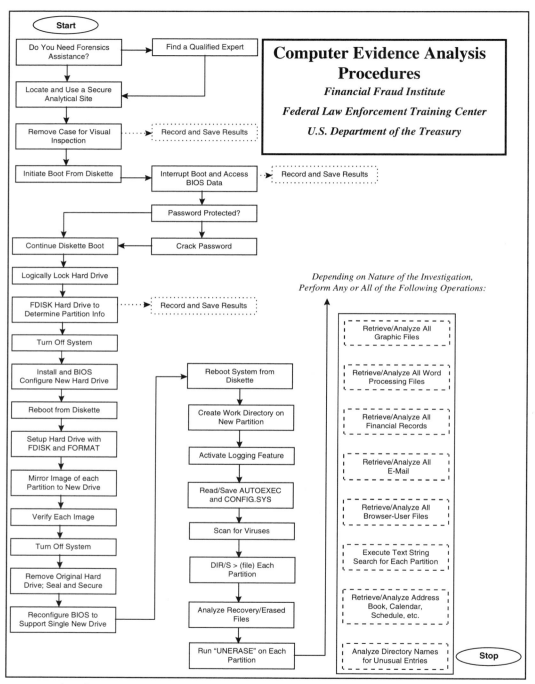

Figure 22.5. Flowchart of procedures illustrates the complicated nature of forensic computer examination. Provided courtesy of Mr. Carlton Fitzpatrick, FLETC.

investigator. While we proceed with the seizure and examination of ephemeral digitized evidence, we should keep in mind what the authors of the *Federal Guidelines for Searching and Seizing Computers* wrote:

> It is important to remember throughout the process that as dazzling and confounding as these new age searches and seizures may be, they are in many essential ways just like all other searches. The cause must be just as probable; the description of items, just as particular. The standard investigative techniques that work in other cases (like finding witnesses and informants) are just as valuable in computer cases. The evidence that seals a case may not be on the hardware or software, but in an old-fashioned form: phone bills, notes in the margins of manuals, or letters in a drawer.[38]

Chapter 23

Targeted Violence Investigations

Examples of Workplace Murderers

Current Employee

Honolulu, November 2, 1999 — Byran Uyesugi, a photocopy repairer convinced that his coworkers are conspiring against him, brings a high-capacity semiautomatic pistol to work and kills seven coworkers. He is later found in his van at a park and surrenders after a stand-off with police.

Fired Employee

Chicago, February 5, 2001 — William Baker, convicted of stealing from his employer a number of years earlier, returns to the factory where he worked and shoots eight employees, killing four. He commits suicide. He was about to begin serving his prison sentence on the theft case.

Domestic Violence Spillover

Jackson, January 11, 2005 — David Lynn Jordan allegedly arrives at the government garage where his wife worked, killing her. According to witnesses, he then shoots two bystanders outside the building. He is arrested by police while leaving the area.

Former Employee Robbery Murder

Queens, May 25, 2000 — Former employee John Taylor and accomplice Craig Godineaux, in an early morning robbery, herd seven employees into the basement of a neighborhood restaurant. They cover the victim's heads with plastic bags, bind them with duct tape, and shoot them until they expend all their ammunition. They are caught within two days by police.

Disgruntled Customer

Atlanta, July 29, 1999 — Failing as a stock day trader, Mark Barton kills his wife and two children, leaving suicide notes at his home before visiting the stock office where he traded. Once there he opened fire, eventually killing nine victims in two office buildings, before fleeing. As police close in on him five hours later at a gas station he kills himself. He blamed the stock office workers for his financial failure. Barton was also the chief suspect in the 1993 murders of his first wife and mother-in-law at a campground.

Traditionally, investigators have had the task of gathering evidence relating to a known crime that has already occurred, or one that is believed to be already occurring. In those cases either normal reconstructive or constructive methods will be applied. The *who, what, where, when, why,* and *how* aspects of the process of investigation will guide the investigator to collect and present evidence that can be used to justify appropriate action. As we have previously discussed, in the public sector the goal is normally the bringing of criminal charges, whereas in the private sector, the goals of loss prevention, economic recovery, and employment termination are typical.

There is, however, one kind of investigative problem that differs significantly from these norms. This type of investigation centers on the problem of targeted violence and has received increasing attention in the past twenty years. The relevant questions are not merely "what happened?" or "what is happening?" Rather, they are "what is likely to happen in the future?" and "what can be done to prevent it?"

The approach that has developed since the early 1990s is known as Threat Assessment and Management, or TAM. Although it was first applied in the areas of workplace violence, dignitary protection, and domestic violence policing, TAM has acquired significance on a broader scale. Since September 11, 2001, its general principles have been adopted in the areas of homeland defense and counter-terrorism.

For our purposes, however, we will concentrate on workplace violence prevention because this is an area of frequent occurrence in which private sector investigators can make important contributions. Therefore, knowledge of workplace violence is essential.

TYPES OF WORKPLACE VIOLENCE

There are generally considered to be four categories of workplace violence.[39] They are:

Type I: Violent acts by criminals with no other connection to the workplace. Entry is solely for the purpose of committing a crime such as robbery.

Type II: Violence by customers, patients, students, clients, inmates, or others receiving goods or services from the organization.

Type III: Violence by present or former employees against supervisors, employees, or managers.

Type IV: Violence by persons who have a personal relationship with an employee, but who do not themselves work in the organization.

The first two types of violence will tend to be addressed through normal crime prevention strategies and typically are investigated in a post-incident or reactive context. These violent incidents tend not to involve perpetrators who are targeting specific individuals for violence. Examples are the convenience store or gas station stick-up robbery or the outburst of anger that a drunken patron may direct at a bartender. This type of outburst is known as *affective violence* and is typically an emotional reaction to a stressor in the immediate situation.

In the last two categories, there is much more likely to be a specific individual who is being selected for violent victimization by the perpetrator. This is known as "targeted violence," and is the kind of violence that frequently exhibits a number of warning signs. If those warning signs are properly detected and assessed, they can give the organization the opportunity to steer the situation away from a violent outcome.

This kind of violence will tend to be what is known as *predatory violence*, which is violence that is planned, purposeful, and emotionless. The perpetrator will engage in behavior that is akin to hunting the intended victim(s) and may provide clues to intentions, methods, and targets prior to an actual attack. It is in these situations that TAM is intended to be used.

SIGNIFICANCE OF WORKPLACE VIOLENCE

Homicides represent a minority of deaths at work according to the Federal Bureau of Labor Statistics (BLS). In 2003 there were a total of 5,559 workers who died as a result of injuries sustained while working. Of that number, only 11%, died as a result of homicide.[40] This amounted to some 632 workers who were murdered while working.[41]

Statistically, during an average week in 2002, 348 American workers were assaulted while working and 12 were murdered. This does not take into account the number of employees whose lives were affected by assaults, threats, stalking, bullying, intimidation, or vandalism that did not result in death or injury.

The economic costs are also significant. One team of researchers estimated the societal costs at approximately 6.5 billion dollars between 1992 and 2001 as a result of worker fatalities due to homicide.[42]

It is clear therefore that workplace violence exacts a high cost from American workers and industry. The personal suffering by individual victims, their families, and surviving coworkers lasts far beyond the actual events. In addition, the costs to organizations in days lost from work, damage to corporate image, and loss of worker confidence in their safety at work cannot be ignored.

A COMMON MISTAKE

When information is received indicating that employees are troubled by the statements and actions of a coworker, customer, or someone otherwise associated with the workforce, any number of thoughts may be triggered in managers. Some examples are

- That's just how Joe is, a little bit cranky, but that's it.
- Everyone is simply overreacting to a minor situation.
- Until something actually bad happens, there isn't anything we can do.
- If I just leave the situation alone it will blow over.
- Disputes among employees are their business, let them settle it themselves.
- Even if he did say something scary, I'm sure he didn't mean it.
- Nothing really bad would ever happen here, that kind of thing happens only in other places.

These statements all represent a common mistake made by organizations: denial. Managers often deny that there is a situation that could result in violence. They may deny that they or the organization have any responsibility to prevent a situation between employees from escalating to violence. They may also deny that there is anything effective that can be done to proactively manage the situation away from becoming lethal.

Denial in these cases is a failure to appreciate the reality of the situation, often to the detriment of everyone involved.

THREATS

The topic of threats is an area in targeted violence prevention that carries great potential for misunderstanding that leads to ineffective action or overreaction. In many organizations there exist workplace violence policies that prohibit employees from making verbal threats against others. The statement, "I'm going to kill you," will generally be understood as a threat and action will be taken. What about the statement "If you fire me, I'm going to kill you?" Some might consider this a threat, while others, noting the conditional nature of the statement (the "if you fire me"), might not. Consider too the statement, "Unless something around here changes, people are going to get hurt." Is that a threat, or not?

The ambiguity involved in these situations requires that we establish definitions. The term "threat" tends to be used in two ways.

- Threats Made: The purest form of threat is an unconditional statement of intent to do harm. It is characterized as a communication.
- Threats Posed: A person, situation, or act that is regarded as a menace. It is characterized as a danger.

Another definition we will use here is *instigator*, a person who either has made a threat or poses a threat to the targeted victim(s).

Threats Made

When a disturbing communication is made by an instigator, many organizations, including law enforcement, will measure it against either an internal policy or a penal code definition. Unless the unequivocal intention to commit bodily harm is present within the statement, many managers, investigators, and police officers will simply shrug their shoulders and say that since no direct threat was made, no rule or law was broken, and therefore nothing can be done.

In other instances, when the unequivocal statement of intent to do harm is made, many organizations, driven by so-called "zero tolerance" workplace violence policies, will automatically take punitive action, sometimes including termination of employment or criminal prosecution.

There has been some significant research completed regarding threats to do harm that indicates the need to take a more thoughtful approach to threats made. For many years a myth was believed that the persons most likely to carry out attacks are those who make direct threats. In the 1990s the U.S. Secret Service, the National Institute of Justice, and the Federal Bureau of Prisons studied the behavior of 83 persons who carried out actual attacks, or came close to attacks, on prominent public figures. As a result of that research it was concluded that "persons who pose an actual threat often do not make threats, especially direct threats."[43] It was further concluded that, "although some threateners may pose a real threat, usually they do not."[44]

This is not to say that simply because a direct threat has been made that one can afford to discount it as an indicator that violence may occur. In the areas of school violence, domestic violence, and workplace violence, it is not uncommon for direct threats to precede violence. Threat management experts Frederick S. Calhoun and Stephen W. Weston provide a means of sorting the confusion regarding threats. In their book, *Contemporary Threat Management*, they introduce the concept of what they term the *Intimacy Effect*.[45]

Essentially, it is believed that greater intimacy between the instigator and the target will make direct threats more reliable as preincident behavior. For example, an ex-husband who tells his former wife that he will kill her is doing so in the context of ultimately having been intimate with her. The Intimacy Effect would dictate that such threats should be weighted very heavily in a threat assessment investigation. An individual citizen, who writes a threatening letter to the president of the United States, having zero intimacy with his target, would be considered a low risk for actually carrying out an attack.

Threats Posed

While there are many who make direct threats who never attempt an attack, the lack of any threats made cannot lead the investigator to necessarily conclude that there is no threat posed. The central concept of a Threat Assessment investigation is to attempt to determine whether, at the present time, it appears that the instigator poses a threat to the target.

Persons known to possess all of the following should be considered threats posed to the target(s).

- A grievance
- Violent ideation
- Capability to mount an attack
- Preattack planning and preparation
- Movement toward target proximity

Lacking one or more of these factors probably lessens the threat posed, although movement toward target proximity would not necessarily be relevant if a mail bomb or other similar device delivered by a third party is likely.

Red Flags

It should be clearly understood that there are no reliable profiles that can be of meaningful use to TAM practitioners. No set of attributes will be present in all of those who perpetrate lethal targeted violence. Likewise, the absence of those attributes should not be taken as a signal that the instigator does not pose a danger to a particular target. For these reasons "profiling" is not a responsible approach to take when considering potential targeted violence.

Some factors have been identified in cases involving targeted violence that do bear attention. Organizations should train supervisors and employees to be aware of these red flag items.

If they are present, the red flags should not be used to conclude that any danger is actually posed. In fact, in the majority of instances individuals who exhibit one or more of these items never will carry out, or even desire to carry out, targeted violence.

The presence of the red flags should signal to the organization that some level of assessment should be performed to determine whether further concern is justified. Only after an adequate TAM process is completed, is it wise to specify appropriate action by the organization. In many cases, TAM investigation will determine that the person of concern lacks the grievance, violent ideation, inclination, means or preparation necessary to carry out an attack.

Employees should be encouraged to report the red flags, or any other reasons that cause them concern, to the TAM team with the understanding that no negative action will be taken against the person of concern solely on the basis of their report. To do otherwise may make employees hesitant to share information at an early stage when there still exists ample opportunity to address the situation while it is of manageable size.

Red Flags
1. Bringing weapons to work.
2. Alcohol use on the job.
3. Illicit drug abuse.
4. Recently acquiring weapons, especially in conjunction with dispute events.
5. Fascination with weapons.
6. Hypersensitivity to normal criticism.
7. Harboring grudges in conjunction with imagined or actual grievances.
8. Preoccupation with themes of violence.
9. Outbursts of anger.
10. Interest in highly publicized incidents of violence.
11. Loss of significant relationships including marriage or other intimate relationship.
12. Legal or financial problems.
13. Ominous, specific threats.
14. Suicidal/homicidal thoughts or speech.
15. Stalking or placing employees under observation.
16. Indicating a belief that others mean him harm.
17. Being frequently sad, angry, or depressed.
18. Extreme disorganization.
19. Marked changes in behavior or deteriorating hygiene.
20. Actual or expected job loss or job-related discipline.
21. Those surrounding instigators fear violence.

No list of red flags or warning signs can be exhaustive, and the fact that something of concern to employees does not appear on this list should not prevent the TAM team from considering it when deciding to proceed with a formal assessment.

TAM Teams

TAM is a complex undertaking that has the twin objectives of determining whether the current situation apparently is moving toward a violent act and specifying a set of measures the organization can undertake to steer the situation away from violence. Unless the investigator is very experienced in the specific demands of TAM, and has a high degree of authority in the organization to commit resources and vary from standard practices, policies, and procedures, the investigator working alone cannot hope to match the abilities of a properly configured team.

The practice of creating specially-trained teams has arisen in order to provide the talents of a multidisciplinary group to both sort out the complexities and handle the numerous tasks associated with quality assessment and planning in the high-stakes endeavor of targeted violence prevention.

These teams are known by a variety of names. They may be called Threat Management Teams, Incident Management Teams, Threat Assessment Teams, Crisis Management Teams, or go by any number of "committee" names. In any case, the teams often will include TAM-trained representatives from the following parts of the organization:

- Human Resources or Personnel department
- Legal department
- Security department
- Facility Management or Building Management

In addition, someone in the management chain above the affected employees often will be included so that the team has sufficient information regarding the day-to-day operations of the relevant department.

Certain outside consultants often will be contacted to assist the team in its assessment and planning duties. Some such consultants may include:

- Outside legal counsel
- Psychiatrists or psychologists experienced in violence risk assessments
- Investigators who specialize in TAM work
- Employee Assistance Program counselors
- Background Research firms

It is highly recommended that the organization adopt a formal workplace violence policy and procedural guideline that applies in these matters. This policy should be communicated to all organization employees and be fairly and uniformly enforced. One trend in such policies is the adoption of so-called "zero-tolerance" clauses, by which any employee found to have violated the policy automatically is terminated. Great caution should be employed before adopting this approach as the company has reduced its flexibility in dealing with individual situations. The mere foreknowledge that firing is the inevitable consequence of committing a relatively minor violation may prove to be a precipitator that convinces an instigator that he will have nothing further to lose if he proceeds to a more serious lethal violation.

It is suggested that the organization's policy statement should make clear to all employees that the governing priority of the organization is the safety of employees, visitors, and others while on company premises or business. Given the multidisciplinary nature of the TAM team, if the company policy does not enshrine safety as the prime priority, it is very likely that the team may bog down when it comes to specifying a violence prevention plan in individual instances. This is because human resources, legal, employee assistance, and security professionals invariably will have differing views of what should govern the actions of the organization.

Finally, the TAM team should be headed by a manager with the authority to fully commit the organization's resources to the effort and expense necessary to take meaningful protective measures immediately upon determining that they are essential. This TAM team leader should make the final decision on the organization's response if the team cannot reach consensus. If either the authority to proceed or sufficient decisiveness are lacking in this key person on the team, undue delay, inaction, and very possibly physical harm may ensue.

TAM Principles

To the uninitiated, the too frequent incidence of news reports relating the latest story of workplace carnage gives rise to a sense of disgust and horror that leads one to reject the possibility that any normal thinking person could be responsible for these senseless attacks. The public naturally concludes that the person somehow must have "snapped" and impulsively murdered multiple victims. Although this is the lay person's view, the serious private sector investigator must be aware that another, more professional view, must be adopted.

The process of Threat Assessment investigations relies on a number of major principles that are opposite to the commonly held view of violence.

1. **Targeted violence results from a process of thinking and behavior that can be understood and often detected in advance.** In order to carry out an act of targeted violence, the perpetrator must pass through a series of steps along the way. He must develop a sense of grievance or injustice that motivates him. He must hit upon violence as the only or best option available to him to redress his grievance. He must select the individual or organization to target. He must choose the method of attack as well as the date and time for an attack. In order to do so he may conduct research on the target, including stalking the targeted individual or placing the target site under surveillance. He may need to acquire the means to approach the target, breach any security measures in place protecting the target, and carry out the intended attack to the desired conclusion. The instigator's dispute with the target and subsequent planned violence may take center stage in his life and rise to the level of an overriding obsession that the instigator readily and compulsively talks about to those around him.

2. **Targeted violence takes place in the interplay between the instigator, past stressful events, the target, and the current situation.** It is considered useful to determine how the instigator has reacted to prior instances of unbearable stress. If in earlier situations involving significant losses (home, family, job, position, etc.) the instigator attempted acts of violence (including directed at himself), this information may be crucial to an understanding of how he may perceive his present situation. Likewise, other information regarding the instigator's background may be critical to the assessment process. Where he lives; his vehicles; his access to or familiarity with weapons; his educational, medical, and employment histories are all among the

information about the instigator that the TAM team may require. Information regarding the target will also be critical. The TAM team should seek answers to the following questions. Is the target known to the instigator? Can the target easily be approached at work, home, or other obvious locations? Does the target take the threat posed seriously? Can the target's normal locations be "hardened" (receive additional security measures)? Will the target accept and follow security advice? Finally, the current situation, both in terms of any event likely to trigger untoward acts and the overall atmosphere, environment, and influences acting on the instigator must be examined. Whether the instigator is surrounded by a culture, family, group of associates, or counselors that encourage or discourage violence as a means of addressing problems is also important to determine.

3. **Addressing targeted violence requires determining the "attack-related" actions of the instigator.** As noted earlier, the instigator normally will travel a path leading to an eventual attack. At each stage of this journey, he may communicate information or be observed in behavior that signals his thinking, planning, and preparation. Searching for information regarding these factors is key to the proper assessment of a situation, to determining whether the instigator poses a present danger to the target(s). If for instance, the instigator is known to dislike a coworker with whom she has exchanged angry words, is this sufficient reason to consider her to pose a threat to the target? An assessment investigation that determines that the instigator has acquired a firearm and was seen sitting outside the targeted employee's home in her car would clearly support an assessment that the situation should be of serious concern.

The TAM team must consider all sources of information and resources for taking useful action to prevent violence. Figure 23.1 lists resources that should be considered by the TAM team in its work.

TAM Investigation Methods

The conduct of TAM assessment investigations relies upon the same skills, techniques, and aptitudes of any other kind of investigation. These investigations are best initially considered to be constructive in nature. Low-profile or even covert methods of investigation should be employed to prevent the investigation itself from becoming a factor that triggers the instigator to initiate a hasty attack.

The following should all be considered in TAM assessment investigations by the TAM team:

- Reviewing all in-house file information on the instigator. This should include employment application; background reference checks that were completed at the time of hire; all evaluations by supervisors, coworkers, or subordinates; records of counseling or discipline; any complaints, grievances, or even lawsuits against the employer, coworkers and others; attendance and leave records; training records; and any prior safety or misconduct investigations involving the instigator.
- Examining the context in which the instigator first became of interest to the TAM team. Care should be taken to understand the reasons for the initial report concerning the instigator and determining the credibility of the complainant. The first notice to the TAM team that the instigator concerns a coworker, supervisor, or other company-related person, may contain

Figure 23.1. The TAM Process requires continual gathering of and re-evaluation information to promote safety.

information that will help the TAM team understand the nature of the dispute or injustice that may be at the heart of any motivation to commit violence.

- Researching in the public record any history of court actions (civil or criminal) involving the instigator. If the instigator is involved in a years'-long dispute with a potential target individual or organization, the record may be rich in information that describes the degree of anger that the instigator may harbor against the target(s). Similarly, if the instigator has elevated the grievance to a "cause" or "crusade" against perceived perpetrators of great injustice, the TAM team should carefully consider how committed the instigator may be to punishing the target, regardless of the cost, to himself or others.
- Interviewing persons with historical or current information on the instigator's thinking, capabilities, motives, and plans. Care should be taken that anyone interviewed by the TAM team can be relied upon to not disclose to the instigator that the assessment investigation is being conducted. In some cases, these persons may be part of the instigator's inner circle of friends, family, and associates. They may be concerned by the actions of the instigator and be willing

to become continuing informants, especially if they are convinced that the instigator intends to carry out a lethal attack. The TAM team should determine whether those close to the instigator discount any potential for violence or actually fear the instigator themselves. Either outlook could result in persons interviewed by the TAM team revealing the existence of the TAM investigation to the instigator, something that could inflame the situation.

- Examining the instigator's workspace. In the case of instigators who are employed by the TAM team's organization, and if consistent with established company policy, examining the instigator's immediate work areas may be of immense value to the assessment. If the examination can include a review of the company computer files accessed by the instigator, it may be possible to uncover information relating to the underlying grievance held by the instigator, preattack planning and actions, ritual settlement of his affairs and disposing of his property, and the identity of individual targets not previously known. Also if permitted, the TAM team should try to view the instigator's e-mail traffic on the employer-owned computer system.

- Making direct contact with the instigator. At some point, the TAM team may decide that the benefits of speaking directly with the instigator outweigh any risks associated with initiating such contact. In some cases, contact with the instigator may allow him to vent his frustrations and reduce his sense that only violence can give voice to his grievance. In other cases, the instigator may provide a clear view of her intentions to actually cause violence and accept the attendant consequences. Sometimes the instigator may reveal the amount of research, surveillance, and other attack preparation he has completed. We know of at least one instance in which an instigator described in detail to the investigator exactly who was on his hit list and the gruesome axe-murders he yearned to make. The instigator may prove to the TAM team that he lacks the organization, means, or capability to launch an attack during direct contact. One way to reduce the backlash that direct contact may precipitate may be for the TAM team to utilize covert or undercover contacts with the instigator. A well trained investigator who sits at a bar next to the instigator may get an earful that indicates a deep hatred for the target that is successfully masked at work.

The focus of the TAM investigation always should be upon seeking answers to the question of whether the instigator is progressing toward violence, and if so, how far advanced that progress may be. The answers to those questions are the heart of the actual Threat Assessment.

TAM Countermeasure Planning

If the assessment investigation substantiates a concern that a legitimate threat is posed by the instigator, certain countermeasures or other actions must be planned.

The key question for the TAM team process is simply, "What can we do to promote safety for the target and others during this situation?"

The TAM team cannot plan only short-term immediate safety steps. Although some factors, such as improving access control to the workplace, may be of immediate priority, the team should understand that the instigator may be a lasting problem for the target and the entire workplace. Certain long-term, and expensive, measures may be necessary. For instance, a short-term solution may be to have an armed security officer screen visitors through the main entrance to an office. A long-term solution may be the installation of a hardened entry doorway with electronically controlled access hardware allowing individualized entry devices for all employees. Even after the period of immediate threat has passed, these security enhancements can continue to provide benefit by making workers feel safer in the workplace.

The TAM team must look at all major components of the problem in addressing possible solutions. The TAM team should ask itself, "what can be done to affect the situation in which the instigator operates to reduce the likelihood of an attack?" Likewise, the question, "what can be done to alter the expected event to reduce the likelihood of violence?" also should be answered. Finally, the team should address the question, "what can be done with the target (person or site) to reduce the likelihood of an attack?"

The TAM team should not be afraid to be creative in its approaches to the problem. Although it must be cautious, it often can determine solutions that fit the complexities of the situation well if it is willing to think "outside the box."

Examples of this kind of thinking might include the following. If the instigator is prone to outbursts of anger, should the organization consider convincing the instigator to complete anger management training while receiving psychological counseling or psychiatric treatment? If the instigator is willing but not able to afford the training and other services, should the organization pay for them? Further, if the instigator is going to be fired, and it is known that he is concerned for the long-term treatment of his child's chronic disease, should the TAM team recommend a separation package that includes continuation of medical plan benefits for a certain period paid for by the organization? Also, if the target's current workplace is well known to the instigator, should the organization consider a transfer for the target to another branch or even another city?

In addition, the TAM team should realize that most organizations cannot afford to "go to war" with the instigator. If an organization is pushed, it may fire the instigator or threaten a lawsuit. If an instigator is pushed, he may commit mass murder. He possesses offensive options that organizations simply cannot use.

Provocative, punitive, prosecution-based solutions, will rarely net the enhancement in safety that the organization requires. It is often difficult for organizations to put aside an adversarial posture when dealing with instigators. Such actions tend to increase the intensity of the conflict with the instigator, not reduce it.

The TAM team should seek disengagement from the instigator, not further entanglement in lawsuits or criminal actions. Although doing otherwise may satisfy an organization's desire to somehow obtain "justice," such pursuits rarely will provide a lessening of the safety problem. The instigator may not initially commit a serious criminal act that will lead to long-term incarceration. Making misdemeanor prosecution a centerpiece of countermeasure planning may only increase the likely danger. Courts will only be able to impose moderate sanctions at an early stage, which are unlikely to reduce the threat posed in a meaningful way. A series of arrests for minor offenses, or being dragged through prolonged litigation initiated by the organization, may simply add to the instigator's reasons for viewing himself as the victim of injustice. He may then feel warranted in escalating his responses to this perceived provocation.

Having the instigator escalate to a stage where serious criminal justice sanctions can be employed is precisely what the TAM team should be working to avoid.

The Restraining Order

Many employers, police officers, investigators, and human resources managers believe that the best response to a threat situation is for targeted persons to obtain a Restraining Order (sometimes known as a Protection Order). This is a civil court order requiring the instigator to stay away from the targeted persons and premises and not harass or harm them. The police can arrest the instigator if he approaches or contacts the targets.

Though such an order sometimes can be useful, many people place too much confidence in its true protective power. The following are cautions to consider regarding such Restraining or Protective Orders:

1. The act of being served a court order, typically by police officers, can convince the instigator that the target is escalating the conflict and is not interested in any peaceful settlement to the dispute. Some instigators justify moving to violence in their own minds because they believe the targets have decided to "go to war."
2. The Temporary Restraining Order will be followed by a court hearing at which the instigator and the targets are brought together in a courtroom. In some cases this is exactly what the instigator wants (physical closeness to and interaction with the target) and it results in increased engagement between the parties, rather than the preferred *disengagement*.
3. The court hearing allows the instigator to know the exact time and place where the target will be. If the instigator is bent upon violence, especially after losing the hearing, he is afforded a perfect attack opportunity as the target leaves the secured area of the court complex. Parking lots, and even the courthouse steps, have been the scenes of fatal attacks.
4. In most jurisdictions, the court action must be initiated by individuals, as opposed to organizations, thereby requiring a degree of personalization between the individuals and the instigator. This may focus the instigator's anger at individual targeted persons, rather than a faceless corporation. This is seldom good for the individuals.
5. In most jurisdictions, the arrest of a person violating the Restraining Order will result in a low bail and a sense of humiliation and anger in the instigator toward the targets. Penalties tend to be very minimal fines or brief incarcerations. As such, an arrest has the potential of creating an angrier instigator who may have little regard for the Restraining Order.

Fundamentally, one must consider the wisdom of relying on a person whom we fear is willing to commit murder to conform to rational behavior simply because a court has ordered him to do so. Should we really expect that a person capable of homicide will be deterred because he may commit a misdemeanor contempt of court?

Too often, especially in domestic violence incidents, the victims are shot to death after obtaining the Restraining or Protection Order. Simply put, papers do not stop bullets. TAM investigators and targeted individuals should not think otherwise.

TAM Reports

The TAM team should attempt to express, preferably in writing, its combined opinion on the state of the situation as it relates to whether the instigator appears to intend violence, is capable of carrying out that violence, and has engaged in preattack behaviors. The assessment should detail the methods used in obtaining the information and reaching the opinion, including any input received from outside consultants, researchers, and investigators. The assessment also should provide details of the information that persuades the TAM team that the situation is moving toward or away from violence.

The TAM report also must lay out the recommended steps the organization should take to prevent a violent outcome.

It is important to note that the TAM report, and the assessment upon which it is based, are both valid only as long as the underlying situation remains unchanged. As such, it is a "snapshot" in time, which documents conditions as they were at a particular moment. Threat situations are extremely dynamic, constantly changing as new events occur. Therefore new assessments and management plans may need to also be evaluated in light of these new events or when previously unknown information comes to light. Figure 23.1 also contains a flowchart describing the TAM process and the requirement to sometimes reinvestigate, reassess, and replan, as matters progress.

For example, if the instigator brandishes a firearm on day one, threatening to shoot his estranged wife, the assessment may be that the situation is one of high risk. If the instigator is taken into police custody on the morning of day two, the assessment may be downgraded only to shoot up again in a few hours when the instigator is released on bail. In a similar vein, if the target leaves town for a week to vacation at a location unknown to the instigator, the assessment of danger will probably lower, but it may rise upon the target's return home.

Any TAM report must inform the reader that the assessment is subject to immediate change upon new developments or information.

Law Enforcement Assistance

If there is a truly imminent danger of serious physical attack, or if the instigator is present and is persistently unwilling to leave or desist from unlawful behavior, *the police should be called immediately for an emergency response.*

In less imminent circumstances, a TAM team may decide at some point to obtain help from the local police. If prepared to approach the police properly, the TAM team can maximize the assistance it can expect. Otherwise, such contact can be an exercise in frustration at best and make the situation much more dangerous at best.

It is clear that the police in almost any jurisdiction are inundated with more cases than they can fully attend to. As such, the police concentrate on matters that are judged to be especially serious, such as drug trafficking, organized crime, gangs, and homicides. In most cases, police patrol officers are responding to reports of completed crimes, documenting the available information. Where there is easily obtainable evidence and identified suspects, they will effect an arrest. In cases where a serious crime has not yet been committed, or the evidence is less than perfectly clear, it is rare for the police to go beyond the filing of an initial report. In the more serious crimes, investigations are referred to police detectives to pursue the case. This is not poor police practice, simply a logical allocation of police resources.

Very few police officers or detectives have been trained to see threat situations as matters to be approached with careful assessment and management. Police emphasis traditionally has been upon enforcement after crimes occur.

TAM teams wanting to obtain law enforcement assistance must therefore make full use of the assessment aspects of TAM in order to inform and educate the police on both the gravity of the threat situation and the ways law enforcement can best help.

The following are considerations to review prior to making law enforcement contact:

1. The TAM team should conduct a full investigation and assessment before calling the police.
2. The TAM team should be willing and able to lay out each and every factor leading to a conclusion that the situation appears to be potentially violent.
3. If the TAM team believes that the instigator represents a serious lethal threat, and can point to specific statements and actions by the instigator that would convince anyone to be very concerned, the team should seek police assistance in managing the situation.
4. The TAM team should not ever overstate the credibility or reliability of information that form the basis of its assessment. The TAM team should carefully review all evidence it is considering, and remove all supposition or unsupported conclusions from its assessment. The police will not appreciate later learning that they have been "oversold" on the seriousness of the situation.
5. The TAM team should attempt to contact the police at the highest possible level, preferably through the chief, sheriff, district commander, or precinct commander. Senior police officials, provided with the specifics of a grave situation likely to represent a lethal threat to multiple targets, are much less likely to shrug off the report than the patrol officers. They are also able to command sufficient resources in terms of detectives, officers, and others to effectively help.
6. The TAM team should understand that contacting the police can lead to unintended consequences if the police choose to take aggressive action toward the instigator, such as a confrontation in which he is "warned" by the police on his doorstep. The TAM team should be able to address with the police what the assessment investigation may indicate will happen if such a provocative act occurs.

Law enforcement assistance can be crucial to a good outcome in many threat situations; however, as with Restraining Orders, TAM teams must properly plan how to approach and use police assistance. To do otherwise is unwise and may worsen the situation.

A THREAT IN THE WAREHOUSE

The regional human resources manager of a multinational corporation phoned on Monday afternoon saying that a warehouseman fearfully reported to her a threat by a delivery driver to shoot a supervisor who rescheduled the driver to start his day two hours later than before. They worked at a small branch operation three hundred miles away.

The HR manager was authorized by the corporation to engage our TAM services. A temporary TAM team was formed that included two individuals from out of state: a corporate security manager and a psychologist retained for TAM services by the corporation's national headquarters. The regional HR manager, our office, and a local psychologist who specialized in TAM rounded out the team.

While the corporate officials traveled across the country, we secretly interviewed two workers who provided information about the instigator, Tom:

1. Tom had been fired elsewhere, boasting he had entered the office of a supervisor who had "messed with him," pointed a gun at his head, threatening to kill him if not left alone. A friend hid the gun before police were called. There being no witnesses, Tom was never arrested.

2. Tom reportedly fired a rifle at drunken troublemakers menacing his family at a picnic. Police were not called.

3. Tom became violent when drunk, often brawling with little provocation.

4. Tom's wife, a heart patient, cared for her aged father at their home and also babysat for their two granddaughters. Tom's employment provided the sole family income and health insurance. He was the only one who could pick up another grandchild after school because his old schedule ended so early.

5. Tom said that if fired for refusing the new schedule he would punch the supervisor, leave, return armed, and shoot everyone at the warehouse. He claimed his family would be better off if he went to jail.

6. Both informants, who knew Tom well, were convinced he would carry out the threat.

The team, including the corporate officials, met on Tuesday evening. The HR manager confirmed from company records that Tom's health insurance covered his wife, and that it was widely known that she could not work due to illness. Several members of Tom's family had died at young ages, and he was afraid to die and leave his family destitute. Early contact with low-ranking police officials netted a directive to call "if something bad really happens."

It was decided to directly contact the Chief of Police that night. The corporate security manager placed the call, informing him that there was a grave situation that had called him and the corporate psychologist to town, but that he was hesitant to discuss it on the phone. The chief agreed to meet the following afternoon.

Early the next morning we flew to the small town and secretly met with the local branch manager at a local hotel. He was shocked by the information we had received, but believed Tom was capable of carrying out the threat. Later that day we briefed the police chief and his senior commanders. They pledged their cooperation, and one commander was assigned as our liaison. The police believed Tom could have access to guns.

It was decided that Tom needed to be removed quickly from the workplace and armed security officers placed at the warehouse as soon as he knew he was being suspended. We wanted to get possession of his guns, and allow the two psychologists to interview him at length. Obviously, the physical security of the psychologists during any meeting was paramount. Our office was in charge of the law enforcement and security coordination.

Flying home that night we discussed how to ensure Tom was not armed during the intervention meeting. Passing through the airport security checkpoints gave us an idea. On Wednesday morning we had the HR manager telephone Tom at work and tell him that he was to fly to the regional headquarters to participate in an employee focus group over the next two days. He would stay at a hotel paid for by the company. He agreed.

On Thursday, the HR Manager picked up Tom at the airport, who carried a small bag that he had carried aboard the plane. We were certain that he was not armed.

Meanwhile, we arranged for a provider of armed security guards to have two officers posted at the warehouse each day from 5:30 A.M. until 7:30 P.M., covering all hours that staff was at the site.

The psychologists and corporate security manager waited at the interview site, which included a conference room outfitted with covert audio and video monitored by two armed security officers in a room down the hall. Our investigators coordinated all the diverse parts of the plan.

Upon Tom's arrival, the HR manager introduced him to the security manager and the psychologists. During the course of the next four hours the psychologists spoke with Tom, assessing his attitudes, willingness to follow direction, and introducing him to the idea of his suspension. He was persuaded to allow the police to search his residence and vehicle for weapons. Our office coordinated with the liaison police commander who dispatched a team of detectives to Tom's house. They met with his wife and after conducting the search took away a number of weapons. Tom agreed to meet with a psychiatrist in his town who had previously been contacted by the TAM team psychologists. When he flew home Friday he was calm, had explained the situation to his wife, and understood that the company was going to continue its inquiry into his actions and complaints. He accepted the fact of his suspension (with pay and benefits).

The armed security presence remained in place for a few more days, until it became clear that Tom was continuing his sessions with the psychiatrist. He underwent alcohol treatment and anger management training. The local TAM team psychologist kept in phone contact with him on a regular basis, monitoring his progress and attitudes toward the company. He also conferred with the treating psychiatrist to confirm Tom's compliance with his treatment plan. A few weeks later Tom agreed to separate from the company and accepted a settlement package that provided a small amount of severance pay, extended family health coverage, and the services of a job-hunting firm. At last report Tom had embarked on a new career, with different attitudes about work and coworkers.

This case study illustrates perfectly how a well-ordered response to a frightening initial informant report, using a multidisciplinary team and the Threat Assessment and Management process, can move a potentially violent situation to a safe outcome. The investigative professional can fulfill a crucial role in that team, but only if he understands the proper methods and goals of TAM.

THE LONG VIEW

TAM investigations are becoming increasingly important for investigators in the private sector to master. The opportunities for coworker dispute, employee terminations, or even domestic violence to create real danger for the workplace through targeted violence are incalculable. The stakes can be extremely high, and the complexity of each situation must be considered carefully. Those men and women who undertake to assist in TAM investigations will be called upon to use all the qualities of the investigative professional we described in Chapter 3.

As the specialized approaches used in these investigations have become more widely adopted, the private investigative practitioner is provided with the chance to delay, redirect, or disrupt situations that might otherwise escalate to lethal violence.

Even though the threat may be forestalled today, the instigator may someday return. As such, these cases rarely are considered fully closed. They may become dormant for a while, but as long as the instigator can focus on the target, and is at liberty to mount an attack, the situation will probably bear long-term monitoring.

It should also be understood that in this type of investigation, successes seldom result in public recognition, however, the failures do.

With these things in mind, we believe that investigators must adopt a long view. They must approach the task with all their skill, care, and professionalism, ever mindful of the profound responsibility with which they have been entrusted. Few investigations allow the investigator to work on cases of greater significance, especially to the many employees and their families that are under real threat.

To contribute to the safe resolution of threat situations is both a burden and a privilege that is increasingly within the domain of the private sector investigative professional.

A Worst Case Not Avoided: Domestic Murder, School Murder, Workplace Murder, Mass Murder, Suicide

In May 1927, Andrew Kehoe perpetrated the worst case of school violence in U.S. history. Along the way he also murdered his wife and targeted his boss, and killed himself in the final fatal blast. His discontent was rooted in financial problems that he blamed on high taxes, which he associated with the building of a new school. Kehoe blamed School Superintendent Emory Huyck for leading the campaign to build the school. He had opposed the construction for a long time, and in fact was elected for School Board Treasurer in order to prevent the authorization.

Kehoe's wife suffered from chronic medical problems, which accelerated the financial problems of the family. Eventually, the Kehoe farm was foreclosed upon, and Kehoe faced financial ruin.

Kehoe was hired by the new school as a handyman. In a well-planned scheme, Kehoe traveled throughout the Lansing, Michigan area making small purchases of dynamite and practiced detonating explosives with timer devices. During much of the spring he was engaged in placing a thousand pounds of explosives throughout the school, under floors, in walls, above rafters.

Over two days in May 1927 Kehoe completed his plan. He murdered his wife at the family farm, rigged the farm with explosives, destroyed all fruit-bearing trees, and prevented his livestock from escaping their pens. He also fashioned his pickup truck into a vehicle-borne bomb, using explosives and all the scrap metal he could find for shrapnel.

On the morning of May 18, 1927 the charges at the farm and the school detonated within minutes of one another.

Kehoe sought Superintendent Huyck among the rescuers lifting rubble from the ruins. Kehoe got out of his truck and fired a rifle into a dynamite charge in the back of the truck. The explosion killed Kehoe, Huyck, two other men, and a child who had escaped from the school after the first blast.

As horrific as the outcome actually was, it was planned to be much worse. While the rescuers were frantically working to clear the rubble, they were forced to withdraw from the site by the State Police. An additional 500 pounds of explosives had been found that failed to initially detonate, possibly due to an electrical problem.

Thirty-eight children and six adults were murdered by Kehoe. Though not generally remembered, the 1927 Bath Michigan School Disaster was this nation's worst episode of school violence, and until the 1995 federal building bombing in Oklahoma City, was the worst case of domestic terrorism in U.S. history.

Although this incident occurred seven decades ago, is there a factor one can point to today that would preclude a similar attack from occurring? Practitioners hope that TAM is such a factor.

Sources

CHAPTER 1

1. Henry Goddard, *Memoirs of a Bow Street Runner*. London: Museum Press Limited, 1956, p. 100.
2. *Ibid.*, pp. 100–101.

CHAPTER 3

3. *The American Heritage Dictionary of the English Language*. New York: Houghton Mifflin Company, 1969, p. 978.
4. Donald O. Schultz, *Criminal Investigation Techniques*. Gulf Publishing Co., p. 6.
5. Charles E. O'Hara, *Fundamentals of Criminal Investigation*. Springfield, IL: Charles C Thomas Publishers, 1976, p. 22.
6. *Municipal Police Administration, 4e*. International City Managers Association, 1954, p. 306.
7. *Ibid.*, p. 317.

CHAPTER 4

8. Charles A. Sennewald, *Effective Security Management, 4e*. Boston: Butterworth-Heinemann, 2004, p. 56.
9. Schultz, *op. cit.*, p. 4.
10. *Ibid.*
11. Sennewald, *op. cit.*, p. 4.
12. *Ibid.*, p. 179.
13. Charles A. Sennewald, "Give Your People the Opportunity to Fail," *Security Management* (May, 1979), p. 20.

CHAPTER 7

14. *Garzilli v. Howard Johnson's Motor Lodges, Inc.*, 419 F. Supp. 1210 (U.S. D. Ct. E. D. N. Y., 1976).
15. (Explanatory note.)

CHAPTER 8

16. Saul D. Astor, *Loss Prevention: Control and Concepts*. Los Angeles: Security World Publishing Co., Inc., 1978, p. 89.
17. Roger Griffin, *Failure to Record*. Los Angeles: Commercial Service Systems, p. 1.
18. *Ibid.*, p. 2.

CHAPTER 9

19. James Gilbert, *Criminal Investigation*. Columbus, Ohio: Merrill Publishing Co., 1980, p. 96.

CHAPTER 11

21. *Ibid.*, p. 50.

CHAPTER 12

22. O'Hara, *op. cit.*, p. 137.

CHAPTER 13

23. Paul Fuqua and Jerry V. Wilson, *Security Investigator's Handbook*. Gulf Publishing Co., p. 16.
24. O'Hara, *op. cit.*, p. 159.
25. J. Kirk Barefoot, *Employee Theft Investigation*. Los Angeles: Security World Publishing Co., Inc., 1979, p. 53.
26. Gene Blackwell, *The Private Investigator*. Los Angeles: Security World Publishing Co., Inc., 1979, p. 23.

CHAPTER 14

27. 27. Fuqua and Wilson, *op. cit.*, p. 81.

CHAPTER 16

28. O'Hara, *op. cit.*, p. 666.

CHAPTER 20

29. A. F. Brandstatter and Allen A. Hyman, *Fundamentals of Law Enforcement*. Glencoe Press, 1971, p. 367.

30. *Ibid.*
31. Richard J. Healy and Timothy J. Walsh, *Protection of Assets Manual, Vol. I.* The Merritt Company, 1978, pp. 11–15.

CHAPTER 21

32. Colgate-Palmolive Co., 323 NLRB No. 82 (1997).
33. National Institute of Justice, *Video Surveillance and Equipment Selection and Application Guide,* 1999.

CHAPTER 22

34. Anacapa Sciences, Inc., *Analytical Investigation Methods.* Santa Barbara, CA: Anacapa Sciences, Inc., 1999.
35. Michael R. Anderson, *Computer Incident Response Guidelines.* http://www.secure-data.com/guidelns.html.
36. Kenneth S. Rosenblatt, *High Technology Crime, Investigating Cases Involving Computers.* San Jose, CA: KSK Publications, 1995.
37. Michael R. Anderson, *Electronic Fingerprints, Computer Evidence Comes of Age.* http://www.forensics-intl.com/art2.html.
38. United States Department of Justice, *Federal Guidelines for Searching and Seizing Computers —Introduction.*

CHAPTER 23

39. U.S. Department of Justice, Federal Bureau of Investigation, *Workplace Violence Issues in Response,* p. 13.
40. Bureau of Labor Statistics, http://www.bls.gov/news.release/cfoi.to3.htm, 6/27/05.
41. Bureau of Labor Statistics, http://data.bls.gov/cgi/surveymost, 6/27/05.
42. National Institute of Occupational Safety & Health, http://www2.cdc.gov/nioshtic-2/. . . ,6/27/05.
43. U.S. Department of Justice, Office of Justice Programs, *Protective Intelligence & Threat Assessment Investigations,* p. 14, 1998.
44. *Ibid.*
45. Frederick S. Calhoun and Stephen W. Weston, *Contemporary Threat Management.* San Diego, CA: Specialized Training Services, 2003, p. 48.

Index

A

Access control records, 243
Access program, 283
Accidents, 96
Accounting, 83
Acting skills, as quality of investigator, 23–24
Active listening, 97
ADA (Americans with Disabilities Act), 78
Addresses, fictitious, 85
Admissions and confessions, 162–164
  overview, 162
  types of constraints, 160–162
    overview, 160
    on private sector investigators, 161–162
    on public sector investigators, 160–161
    Weingarten Rights, 162
  value of confession, 165–166
  videotaped confessions, 165
  written admission, 164–165
  written confession, 162–164
Affective violence, 300
Agency qualifications, 42
Agent characteristics, 42
Agent control guidelines, 43
AJR (American Journalism Review), 237
Alarm service records, 243
Alumni associations, 231
AMA (American Medical Association), 232
American Journalism Review, 237
American Journalism Review (AJR), 237
American Medical Association (AMA), 232
American Society for Industrial Security, 12, 13, 168, 232
Americans with Disabilities Act (ADA), 78
Anacapa Sciences, Inc., 285

Anacapa Sciences analytical software, 287
Analyst's Notebook, 287
Analytical Investigative Methods, 285
Analytical software, as investigative tools, 285–288
Analytical techniques, 86
Anderson, Michael R., 291
Annual inventory, 81
Anonymous communiqués, 147–149
  analyzing content, 148
  comparing handwritten, printed, or typed samples,
    148–149
  examining material, 147
  overview, 147
Anonymous informants, 171–172
Appearance of interviewer, 121
Appellate reversals, 48
Application For Employment, 74
Application package, and background investigations,
    68–73
  master indice file, 70–71
  neighborhood check, 72–73
  overview, 68–70
  past employment verification, 71–72
Appointment calendars, 243
Association of Certified Fraud Examiners, 13
Assumptive question, 135
Astor, Saul, 80
Attack-related actions, 307
Audio/visual recording, 120
Automatic cameras, 269
Automatic teller machines transaction slips, 243
Autonomic nervous system, 129
Auto rental agencies, as information source, 230
Auto surveillance, 60–61

B

Background investigations, 67–78
  application package, 68–73
    master indice file, 70–71
    neighborhood check, 72–73
    overview, 68–70
    past employment verification, 71–72
  overview, 67–68
  post-hire screening, 73–78
    comparing bond to application, 76–77
    drug testing, 78
    employment verification and reference letters,
      77–78
    examination of bond, 75–76
    ongoing investigations, 78
    other suitability measures, 78
    overview, 73–75
  workplace violence, 68
Backing out, as method of interrogation, 136–137
Backups, bit stream, 294–295
Baird's Manual of American College Fraternities, 233
Bank account statements, 243
Bank check reconciliation, 84
Banks, as information source, 228
Barefoot, J. Kirk, 171
Behavioral clues, 115
Behavioral interview, 136
Behavior during interview and interrogation,
  115–117
Best evidence, 151
Better Business Bureau and Chamber of Commerce,
  232
Birth certificate, 234
Bit stream backups, 294–295
Blackwell, Gene, 180
Blanket information authorization, 69
BLS (Federal Bureau of Labor Statistics), 301
Bonding form, 75–76
Bow Street Runners, 6
Brandstatter, 251–252
British Metropolitan Police, 287
Broken Windows, case of, 256–257
Bugging, 158
Building department, as information source, 233
Building permits, 233
Building systems records, 243–244
Bulk counting, 84
Bullet striking plate glass, 144
Bundle counting, 84
Bundling, 284
Burdeau v. McCowell, 159
Burning, 60
Business journals, 243
Buyers, 86

C

Cab companies, 229–230
Cahan, Charles, 158
Calendars, appointment, 243
Calhoun, Frederick S., 303
California Cahan decision, 158
California Department of Motor Vehicles, 172
California Supreme Court, 159
Camcorders, 275–276
Cameras, 87
  35-mm single lens reflex (SLR) camera, 266
  automatic, 269
  automatic cameras, 269
  camera photography, 265
  charge coupled device (CCD) camera, 270
  Closed circuit television (CCTV) cameras, 53, 54–55,
    273
  disposable viewfinder camera, 266
  instant, 269
  managing multiple, 271
  photographic film camera kit, 267
  single lens reflex, 267–269
  single lens reflex (SLR) camera, 266
  viewfinder, 266–267
Canceled bank documents, 243
Career paths, 13–14
CaseInfo software, 289
CaseRunner program, 280, 289
Case synopsis, 191
Case wrap up, 178
Cash and Diamonds, case of, 220–222
Cash counts, 84
Cash registers, 82, 89, 214
CCD (charge coupled device) camera, 270
CCTV (closed circuit television video imaging), 53,
  54–55, 270–271, 273, 274
Cellular telephone records, 243
Central Intelligence Agency's Aldridge Ames, 290
Central repository, 70
Certified Fraud Examiner (CFE), 13
Certified protection professional (CPP), 13
Certified Security Consultant (CSC), 13
CFE (Certified Fraud Examiner), 13
Chain of custody, 142
Chain of evidence, 142
Charge coupled device (CCD) camera, 270
Checkpointing, 62
Chester, Beth, 191
Chronological case assignment order, 33
Chronological narrative report, 183–184
Chronology of crime, 184
CID (Scotland Yard Criminal Investigation Department)
  Inspectors, 6
Circumstantial evidence, 151

City directories, 232
Civil Index, 234
Civil liability, 11
Classic emotional interrogation, 134–135
Classroom training, 31
Closed circuit television video imaging (CCTV), 53, 54–55, 270–271, 273, 274
Closed-ended questions, 115, 123–124
Cognitive interviews, 127–128
Colleges, as information source, 231
Collegial atmosphere, 32
Commercial firms, 12–13
Commission strategy, 203–207
    developing "how" of by exploratory means, 203–204
    developing "how" of inspectional means, 204–207
    overview, 203
Communication, 4–5, 21
Competent evidence, 151
Comprehensive narrative report, 184–186
Computer-generated printed materials, 148–149
Computers, 279–297
    changing investigator's world, 279
    as evidence, 294
    as investigative tools, 279–290
        analytical software, 285–288
        database programs, 283–284
        diagramming programs, 289
        investigations management programs, 289–290
        other programs, 290
        overview, 282
        presentation programs, 285
        specialized software, 285
        spreadsheet programs, 282–283
    mistake in getting help from owners, 294
    mistake in running, 292–294
    as objects of evidence, 281–282, 290–295
        corporate considerations, 291–292
        examining computer evidence, 292–295
        overview, 290
        seizing computer evidence, 291, 292
        specialized techniques, 290–291
    overview, 279
    viruses, 294
Confessions. *See* Admissions and confessions
Confidential information, 168
Consistency in reasoning, 24
Constraints, types of, 160–162
Constructive investigations, 3–4, 276
Contacts, 167
Contamination, evidence, 141–142
Contemporary Threat Management book, 303
Control by distribution, 150
Control by serialization, 150

Control environment, 197
Controlled informants, 169, 175, 176, 178–179
Controller
    as information source, 235
    manager as, 32–37
        equipment, 36–37
        expenses, 36
        organization and span of control, 32–33
        overview, 32
        records, 33–36
Control records, 243
Control stages, informant, 175–178
    case wrap up, 178
    overview, 175
    productive handling, 176–178
    recruitment, 175–176
Corporate investigator, 111
Correspondence, 243
Counseling process, 30
County Recorder, 233–234
Cover story, 24
Covert crimes, 79–80
Covert imaging, 272–273
Covert installation considerations, 273–275
Covert versus overt surveillance methods, 53–55
    overview, 53–54
    surveillance by human eye, 54
    surveillance log, 55
    visual surveillance devices, 54–55
CPP (certified protection professional), 13
Creative imagination, as quality of investigator, 25–26
Creative puzzle, 25
Credit cards, 150
Credit reporting agencies, 228
CrimeZone, The , 106, 289
Criminal informants, 172–173
Criminal Investigation, 96
Crisis Management Teams, 305
CSC (Certified Security Consultant), 13
Cumulative file, 231
Curiosity, 18
Custody, chain of, 142
Customized Bed, case of, 245
Cyber-Detective software, 290

D
Databases, 238, 283–284
Death certificate, 234
Deception, 51–52
Degrees in security management, 11
Delivery receipts, 244
Demeanor, during interview and interrogation, 114, 121

Denials, during interrogation, 132–134
  emphatic, 132–133
  explanatory, 133–134
  overview, 132
Department of Agriculture, 235
Department of Alcoholic Beverage Control, 236
Department of Industrial Relations, 236
Department of Motor Vehicles, 235
Department of Natural Resources, 236
Detachable lenses, 267
Detail tape, 241
Detection methods, scientific, 202–203
Detection strategies, 91–92
Diagramming programs, 289
Diagrams, using during interview, 129–130
Diaries, 243
Digital Video Recording (DVR), 272
Direct accusation, 134–135
Direct evidence, 151
Directories, 232
Directory of Physicians, 232
Disciplinary interviewing, 101–102
Display screen, 83
Disposable viewfinder camera, 266
Distractions during interviews, 120
Distribution, control by, 150
Documentary evidence, 151
Document comparisons, 295
Documents, counterfeited or altered, 149–150
Doe, Jack J., 163–164
Domestic violence spillover, murderers, 299
DOS DISKCOPY program, 295
DOS/WINDOWS-based computer systems, 292
Double-cross, 51–52
Drugstores, as information source, 230
Drug testing, 78
Dun and Bradstreet, 228
Dusty Shelf, case of, 207–208
DVR (Digital Video Recording), 272

E
E@gle.i Investigation Management, 290
EAS (electronic article surveillance), 91–92
Education, 11–12
Education Waiver, 69
Effective Security Management, 36
Electronic article surveillance (EAS), 91–92
E-mail, 243
Emergency response, 312
Emotional reactions, 98
Emphatic denials, 132–133
Employees
  interviewing, 100–101
  as type of informant, 170–171

Employee Theft Investigation, 171
Employment verification, 77–78
Energy, as quality of investigator, 23
Entrapment, 50–51
Errors, during interview, 128–129
Escobedo v. Illinois, 158
Escrow companies, 229
Evaluator, manager as, 38
Event concentration, 189
Evidence, 139–152
  chain of, 142
  circumstantial, 151
  demonstrative, 140–146
    creativity and physical evidence, 146
    fingerprints, 145–146
    overview, 140
    reading physical evidence, 142–145
    rules involving physical evidence, 140–142
  documentary, 147–150
    anonymous communiqués, 147–149
    counterfeited or altered documents and negotiable
      instruments, 149–150
    forged signatures, 150
    overview, 147
  marking of, 141–142
  overview, 139
  rules and definitions of, 150–151
Exaggeration, 118
Excel program, 282
Executive summary of findings, 191–192
Exit interviews, 84–85
Expansion questions, 123
Explanatory denials, 133–134

F
Facility entry logs, 243
FACTA (Fair and Accurate Credit Transactions Act of
    2003), 43
Fact gathering, during interviews, 126
Factual interrogations, 134
Factual narrative report, 183
Fair and Accurate Credit Transactions Act of 2003
    (FACTA), 43
Fair Credit Reporting Act (FCRA), 43, 44
Fair Credit Reporting Act Waiver, 69
Faxes, 243
FBI (Federal Bureau of Investigation), 12
FCRA (Fair Credit Reporting Act), 43, 44
Federal Bureau of Investigation (FBI), 12
Federal Bureau of Labor Statistics (BLS), 301
Federal Bureau of Prisons, 302–303
Federal Fair Credit Reporting Act, 70
Federal Guidelines for Searching and Seizing Computers,
    292, 297

Federal Law Enforcement Training Center (FLETC), 291
Female investigators, 100, 104
Field imagery, 276
File memoranda, 189–191
Files
    examining, 294
    fictitious, 85
Film, 269
Film processing company, as information source, 230
Financial analysis, and deployment of undercover agents, 89
Fingerprints, 145–146
Fired employee, murderers, 299
Firms, commercial, 12–13
First person narrative report, 182–183
Fitzpatrick, Carlton, 296
Fixed surveillance, 55–56
FLETC (Federal Law Enforcement Training Center), 291
Foot surveillance, 60
Forged signatures, 150
Forgers, 9
Formalized classroom experience, 31
Former Employee Robbery Murder, 299
Fundamentals of Criminal Investigation, 165
Fundamentals of Law Enforcement, 251
Funding, 10
Funeral directors, as information source, 230

G
Generalists, 10
General-purpose programs, 282
"Ghost" employees, 85–86
Gifts, reward, 254
Gilbert, James, 96, 151–152
"Give Your People the Opportunity to Fail" article, 37
Goddard, Henry, 6–7, 191
Governmental immunity, 11
Government records, as information source, 237
Graphic files, viewing, 294
Graphology, 21
Green book, 17
Griffin, Roger, 83
Grilling, 96
Guard tour confirmation reports, 244
Guidelines, agent control, 43
Guide to Background Investigations, The, 238
Gut feeling, 23

H
Handwritten confession, 157
Handwritten reports, 47
Handwritten samples, comparing, 148
Hearsay rule, 156
Hidden video installation, 273, 274–275

Higher-powered lenses, 267
High-Technology Crime, Investigating Cases Involving Computers book, 292
Horizontal analysis, 89
Hospitals, as information source, 231
Hourly fees, 43
Housing projects, as information source, 231
"How" of investigation, 201–211
    case of telltale flour, 201–202
    commission strategy, 203–207
        developing "how" by exploratory means, 203–204
        developing "how" by inspectional means, 204–207
        overview, 203
    overview, 201
    scientific detection methods, 202–203
    solution strategy, 207–211
        case of dusty shelf, 207–208
        modus operandi, 208–209
        overview, 207
        selecting solution strategy, 209–211
Human behavior, understanding of, 20
Human eye surveillance, 54
Human resources executive, 46
Hyman, Allen A., 251–252

I
ICMS (Investigations Case Management System), 289
Imagery, 265–278
    accessories, 270
    closed circuit television video, 270–271
    covert imaging, 272–273
    covert installation considerations, 273–275
    digital photography, 269–270
    field imagery, 276
    film, 269
    film photographic equipment, 266
    film photography, 266
    future of investigative photography, 277–278
    instant cameras, 269
    overview, 265
    scene documentation, 276–277
    single lens reflex cameras, 267–269
    still photography, 265
    video camcorder imaging, 275–276
    video recorders, 271–272
    viewfinder cameras, 266–267
Immaterial evidence, 151
Improvisation, 59
Impulsive behavior, 133
Incidental records, 242–244
Incident Management Teams, 305
Indirect evidence, 151
Inferences, 285

Informants, 14, 167–180
    anonymous, 171–172
    controlled, 169, 175, 176
    control stages, 175–178
        case wrap up, 178
        overview, 175
        productive handling, 176–178
        recruitment, 175–176
    criminal, 172–173
    employee, 170–171
    maximizing potential for controlled informant
        recruitment, 178–179
    mentally disturbed, 174
    need for corroboration, 179–180
    occasional, 170
    one-time, 169–170
    outside, 172
    overview, 167–169
    personal, 173–174
    professional contacts, 168
    treatment of, 179
    unexpected dividends, 179
Information, sources of
    in comparison of public and private sectors, 10
    general information sites, 236
    in local government, 233–235
    online information sources, 236
    in private sector, 228–232
    publishing/journalism resources, 237–238
    search engines, 236
    in state government, 235–236
Information age, 238
Information authorization, blanket, 69
Information System Audit and Control Association
        (ISACA), 12
Information Systems Security Association (ISSA), 12
Ink-jet documents, 149
Installation considerations, covert, 273–275
Instigators, 302, 307
Insurance and risk management, 43
Insurance reporting services, 229
Integrity testing, 82–83
Intelligence, as quality of investigator, 25
Intelligence surveillance, 87
Internal misconduct cases, 48
International Association of Professional Security
        Consultants, 13
Internet Directory of Publications, The, 237
Interrogation, 95–96, 102–104, 113–138
    beginning of, 108–110
    behavior, 115–117
    decision to confess, 131–132
    demeanor, 114
    denials, 132–134
        emphatic, 132–133

    explanatory, 133–134
    overview, 132
documenting confession or interview, 137–138
do's and don'ts of, 110–111
interviewer appearance and demeanor, 121
learning, 111–112
lies, types of, 117–118
methods of, 134–137
    backing out, 136–137
    classic emotional, 134–135
    factual, 134
    overview, 134
    Wicklander-Zulawski Non-Confrontational
        Method®, 135–136
overview, 113–115, 130
preparing for, 104–112, 119–120, 130–131
rapport, 114–115
rationalization, 132
room setting, 120–121
setting of, 105–108
Interrupting victims, 128
Interviewing, 96–102, 113–138
    behavior, 115–117
    behavioral interviews, 129
    checking perceptions, 102
    cognitive interviews, 127–128
    common errors, 128–129
    conducting interviews, 122–126
    demeanor, 114
    disciplinary, 101–102
    distractions during, 120
    documenting confession or interview, 137–138
    employees, 100–101
    evaluating techniques of, 127
    fact gathering, 126
    interview dynamics, 97–98
    interviewer, 96–97
    interviewer appearance and demeanor, 121
    investigative, 102
    lies, types of, 117–118
    lifestyle interviews, 126
    nonemployees, 101
    overview, 96, 113–115
    preparation, 119–120, 128
    purpose of, 96, 122–123
    rapport, 114–115
    room setting, 120–121
    selling of interviews, 124–125
    statement analysis, 125–126
    types of questions, 123–124
    understanding and establishing case facts, 122
    using diagrams during, 129–130
    victims, 98–100
Intimacy Effect concept, 303
Introductory statement, 136

Intuition, as quality of investigator, 23
Investigation chronology concentration, 189
Investigations
    and post-hire screening, 78
    two categories of, 3–4
Investigations Case Management System (ICMS), 289
Investigations management programs, 289–290
Investigative assignment ledger, 33
Investigative counselor, manager as, 29–30
Investigative function, 29–38
Investigative process, 3–8
    communication, 4–5
    creative process in, 8
    investigation, two categories of, 3–4
    observation, 5–8
    overview, 3, 4
Investigative report, 181
Investigator, qualities of, 17–28
    acting skills, 23–24
    communication skills, effective, 21
    creative imagination, 25–26
    dedication to work, 22
    energy, 23
    good character, 26
    good judgment, 24
    healthy skepticism, 22
    intelligence, 25
    interacting with people, 20
    intuition, 23
    logic, 24–25
    overview, 17–18
    patience, 19
    powers of observation, 18–19
    receptivity, 21
    resourcefulness, 19
    self-initiative, 22
    self-quiz, 26–28
    sense of professionalism, 26
    sense of well-being, 21–22
    stamina, 23
    true success, 28
    understanding human behavior, 20
    understanding legal implications, 20
Investigator Childs, 34
Investigator–informant relationship, 175
Investigator Moss, 35
Investigators Little Black Book, The, 238
ISACA (Information System Audit and Control Association), 12
ISSA (Information Systems Security Association), 12

J
Job placement, 44–47
Job security, 10
Johnson, Samuel, 17

Journals, 243
Journal tape, 241

K
Kehoe, Andrew, 316
Kitchen Cleanup Time, 50–51

L
Landlords, as information source, 231
Language of interrogator, 131
Large report format, 189
Latent print, 145
Law enforcement, 64
Law enforcement contact, 313
Leading questions, 124
Ledger computer file, 36
Legal implications, 20
Lenses, 267, 274
Letter content, analyzing, 148
Letter file, anonymous, 149
Letter investigations, anonymous, 147
Letter/parcel markings, 244
Lexis-Nexis, 238
Lies, types of, 117–118
Lifestyle interviews, 126
Link analysis, 285
Liquid spots, 143
Listening, active, 97
Litigation history, 78
Loan companies, as information source, 228
Location descriptions, 64
Logic, as quality of investigator, 24–25
Low-keyed confrontation, 76–77

M
Mail drops, 86
Male interrogators, 104
Manager
    as controller, 32–37
        equipment, 36–37
        expenses, 36
        organization and span of control, 32–33
        overview, 32
        records, 33–36
    as evaluator, 38
    as investigative counselor, 29–30
    as motivator, 37–38
    as trainer, 30–32
        direct involvement, 31
        on-the-job training with others, 31–32
        outside classes, 32
        overview, 30
Marking of evidence, 141–142
Marriage contract, 68
Marriage license, 234

Master indice file, 70–71
Master record, 33
Material evidence, 151
McCall, John, 186–187
Memory of witness, 127
Mentally disturbed informants, 174
Mental recall, 25
Method of operation, 208–209
Minimization, 118
Miranda requirements, 20
Miranda rule, 158, 161
Miranda v. Arizona, 158
Mirroring, 114–115
Modus operandi (M.O.), 25, 187, 208–209
Morgue file, 231
Motion detection, 272
Motivator, manager as, 37–38
Motives
    and detection strategy, 252–254
    and response, 256–260
    for theft, 254–256
Movie tickets, 244
Moving surveillances, 59–65
    auto surveillance, 60–61
    checkpointing, 62
    foot surveillance, 60
    hardware used in moving surveillances, 61
    overview, 59–62
    presurveillance planning, 62–65
    public conveyance surveillance, 60
Multiplexers, 271
Municipal Police Administration, 17, 26

N
National Institute of Justice, 302–303
National Institute of Justice's Law Enforcement and
    Corrections Standards and Testing Program, 277
National Insurance Crime Bureau (NICB), 229–230
National Labor Relations Board, 273
Negotiable instruments, counterfeited or altered, 149–150
Neighborhood check, and application package, 72–73
Nervous system, autonomic, 129
Newspapers, as information source, 231
New Technologies, Inc., 291
New York Times, The, 216–217
NICB (National Insurance Crime Bureau), 229–230
Nonbullet striking glass, 145
Nonemployees, interviewing, 101
Notebooks, 188
Note-taking, 188

O
Objective narrative report, 183
Objectivity in evaluation, 38

Observation, and investigative process, 5–8
Occasional informants, 170
Odometer checks, 89–90
O'Hara, Charles, 17, 165
Old Midtown Church, thefts from, 197–199, 210–211,
    223–224, 247–249
Omission, 117
One-time informants, 169–170
Online information sources, 236
On-the-job training, 30
Open-ended questions, 123
Oral examination, 102
Oral presentations, 21
Organizationally unacceptable activity, 4
Outside informants, 172
Overlapping missions, 15–16
Overt surveillance methods. *See* Covert versus overt
    surveillance methods

P
Paper and pencil tests, 78
Paperless office, 182
Parking facility tickets, 244
Parole evidence, 151
Past employment verification, 71–72
Patience, as quality of investigator, 19
Payroll records, 244
Payroll register, searching, 86
People interaction, 20
People v. Haydel, 160
People v. Victoria Randazzo, 158
People v. Zelinsky, 159
Perceptions, checking of, in interviewing, 102
Periodicals, 232–233
Perseverance, 17
Personal achievement, 14–15
Personal informants, 173–174
Persona non grata, 70
Perspective, change of, 128
Persuasive demeanor, 121
Photography
    digital, 269–270
    film, 266
    filming equipment, 266
    future of investigative photography, 277–278
    still, 265
Physical evidence
    and creativity, 146
    reading, 142–145, 215–217
    rules involving, 140–142
Physical inspections, 87–88
Physical inventories, 81
Pinhole lens technology, 273
Plastic print, 145

Police assistance, 312
Police Science and Administration degree, 11
Polygraph, 78
Post-hire screening, and background investigations, 73–78
   comparing bond to application, 76–77
   drug testing, 78
   employment verification and reference letters, 77–78
   examination of bond, 75–76
   ongoing investigations, 78
   other suitability measures, 78
   overview, 73–75
PowerPoint software, 285, 286
Practical Aspects of Interview and Interrogation, 136
Predatory violence, 301
Pre-hire investigations, 67, 68, 70, 71–72, 73, 75
Presentation programs, as investigative tools, 285
Presumptive evidence, 151
Presurveillance planning, 62–65
Primary record, 33
Printed samples, comparing, 148
Private/corporate investigator, 291
Private sector investigators, 161–162
Private sources, 168
Private telephone system records, 244
Probationary periods, 68
Process of elimination, in identifying suspects, 213–215
Professional contacts, 168
Professionalism, 12–13, 26
Professional specialty societies, 13
Profiling, 303
Property for surveillance, 57
Protection Order, 311
Psychology, practical, 19
Public and private sectors, comparison of, 9–16
   assistance, 14
   career paths, 13–14
   civil liability, 11
   image, 11
   job security, 10
   overlapping missions, 15–16
   overview, 9–10
   personal achievement, 14–15
   professionalism, 12–13
   scope of work, 10
   sources of authority, 10
   sources of funding, 10
   sources of information, 10
   technical resources, 12
   training and education, 11–12
Public conveyance surveillance, 60
Public Records Online, 237
Public sector investigators, 160–161
Published investigations guides, 238
PubList.com, 237

Purchasing agent, dishonest, 86
Push film processing technique, 269
Pygmalion Effect, 105

Q
Qualifications, agency, 42
Quatro Pro program, 282
Questions, during interviews, 123–124
   closed-ended, 123–124
   expansion, 123
   final, 124
   leading, 124
   open-ended, 123
   overview, 123–124

R
Rainy Day Burglar case, 146
Randall, Joseph, 6–7
Rapid-fire questions, 129
Rapport, 97, 114–115, 127
Rationalization, 132, 135
Reader's Guide to periodical literature, 232
Real estate offices, as information source, 230
Real property appraisers, as information source, 231
Receipts, delivery, 244
Receptivity, as quality of investigator, 21
Reconciling information, 51
Reconstructive investigations, 3–4
Recruiting/qualifying process, 42
Reference letters, 77–78
Refund letter circularization program, 81–82
Register transaction numbers, 82
Registrar of voters, as information source, 234
Report writing, 181–193
   defining investigative report, 181
   handwritten, 47
   large case report format, 188–193
      emphasis, 189
      event concentration vs. investigation chronology
         concentration, 189
      memoranda to file, 189–191
      organization, 191–193
   narrative reports, 182–187
      chronological, 183–184
      comprehensive, 184–186
      easily understood, 184
      factual, 183
      objective, 183
      overview, 182
      test of time, 186–187
      told in first person narrative, 182–183
      writing of, 182
   overview, 181
   structured or formalized reports, 187

Reservation records, 244
Resourcefulness, as quality of investigator, 19
Resource verification, 86–87
Responsible evidence, 151
Reverse guides, 229
Reward gifts, 254
Robert, case of, 209, 252
Room setting, for interview and interrogation, 120–121
Rosenblatt, Kenneth S., 292

S
Safety, 64
Sales and delivery receipts, 244
Scales, 277
Scene documentation, 276–277
Schedule sheet, 283
Schools, as information source, 231
Schultz, Donald, 17, 32–33
Scientific technology, 5
Scotland Yard Criminal Investigation Department (CID)
    Inspectors, 6
Screening applicants, 67
Search engines, 236
Secretary of State, 235
Secret Service, 302–303
Security and Loss Prevention, 11
Security camera installations, 271
Security department investigators, 48
Security Investigator's Handbook, 184
Security magazine, 232
Security management, degrees in, 11
Security Management magazine, 37, 232
Security surveillance videotapes, 244
Self-confidence, 21, 22
Self-fulfilling prophecy, 105
Self-incriminating statements, 156
Self-initiative, as quality of investigator, 22
Self-starters, 22
Self-study interrogation workbook, 31
Semiannual inventory, 81
Seminars about investigation, 12
Sense of well-being, as quality of investigator, 21–22
Serialization, control by, 150
Shoplifting surveillance, 90–92
Shopping, 82
Short-term surveillance, 56–59
Signed statements, 154
Silence, 123
Silent witness, 14
Silent Witness Incentive Award Program, 171
Single lens reflex (SLR) camera, 266
Skepticism, as quality of investigator, 22
SLR (single lens reflex) camera, 266
Soft accusation, 136

Software, 285–288
Solution strategy, 207–211
    case of dusty shelf, 207–208
    modus operandi, 208–209
    overview, 207
    selecting of, 209–211
Specially-trained teams, 305
Speed of film, 269
Splitter, 271
Spreadsheet programs, 282–283
Spy operations, 41
Stamina, as quality of investigator, 23
State Controller, 235
Stationary surveillance, 55–59
    fixed surveillance, 55–56
    hardware used in, 59
    overview, 55
    presurveillance planning, 62–65
    short-term surveillance, 56–59
    very temporary surveillance, 59
Stolen Calculators, case of, 226–228
Storage companies, as information source, 229
Stories, first telling of, 125
Stressful interrogations, 109
Structured classroom experience, 31
Suggestion box and award systems, 88–89
Summation Blaze software, 290
Supreme Court guidelines, 158
Surveillance, 53–65
    covert vs. overt, 53–55
        overview, 53–54
        surveillance by human eye, 54
        surveillance log, 55
        visual surveillance devices, 54–55
    moving, 59–65
        auto surveillance, 60–61
        checkpointing, 62
        foot surveillance, 60
        hardware used in moving surveillances, 61
        overview, 59–60
        presurveillance planning, 62–65
        public conveyance surveillance, 60
    overview, 53
    stationary, 55–59
        fixed surveillance, 55–56
        hardware used in, 59
        overview, 55
        short-term surveillance, 56–59
        very temporary surveillance, 59

T
Tail-wise, 62
Tape, 241–242
Targeted violence investigations, 299–316

long view, 315–316
overview, 299–300
threats, 302–313
    made, 302–303
    overview, 302
    posed, 303
    red flags, 303–304
    restraining order, 311
    Threat Assessment and Management (TAM)
        countermeasure planning, 309–311
    Threat Assessment and Management (TAM)
        investigation methods, 307–309
    Threat Assessment and Management (TAM)
        principles, 306–307
    Threat Assessment and Management (TAM)
        reports, 311–313
    Threat Assessment and Management (TAM) teams,
        305–306
    threat in warehouse, 313–315
    workplace violence, 300–301
Tax collectors, 233
Taxicab companies, as information source, 230
Taylor, William, 191
Teams, 304–305
Technical resources, 12
Telephone companies, as information source, 229
Telephone interview, 120
Telephone messages, 244
Telephone Tap, case of, 245
Telephone toll records, 244
Telephonic report, 47–48
Telephoto lenses, 267
Telltale Flour, case of, 201–202
Temporary files, 295
Test analysis, 21
"Test of time" narrative report, 186–187
35-mm single lens reflex (SLR) camera, 266
Threats, 302–313
    overview, 302
    posed, 303
    red flags, 303–304
    restraining order, 311
    Threat Assessment and Management (TAM)
        countermeasure planning, 309–311
    Threat Assessment and Management (TAM)
        investigation methods, 307–309
    Threat Assessment and Management (TAM)
        principles, 306–307
    Threat Assessment and Management (TAM) reports,
        311–313
    Threat Assessment and Management (TAM) teams,
        305–306
Time
    determining by events, 245–246

how to preestablish, 246–249
significant variations in, 241–242
Time-lapse recording, 272
Titanium example, 25
Title insurance companies, as information source, 229
Tool-and-storage room, 108
Topical sections, 192–193
Traffic citations, 244
Trainer, manager as, 30–32
    direct involvement, 31
    on-the-job training with others, 31–32
    outside classes, 32
    overview, 30
Training, 11–12
Traits of dishonesty, 21
Trash, personal, 240
Typed samples, comparing, 148

U
Ultra-sophisticated surveillance platform, 57
Undercover agents
    arranging for, 42–44
    deployment of, 80–90
        bank check reconciliation, 84
        cash counts, 84
        checking for "ghost" employees, 85–86
        checking register transaction numbers, 82
        daily audit of cash registers, 82
        exit interviews, 84–85
        financial analysis, 89
        integrity testing, 82–83
        intelligence surveillance, 87
        odometer checks, 89–90
        overview, 80
        physical inspections, 87–88
        physical inventories, 81
        refund letter circularization program, 81–82
        suggestion box and award systems, 88–89
        verification of vendor or resource, 86–87
Undercover Investigation Engagement Agreement, 44–45
Undercover investigations, 41–52
    absence of professionalism, 52
    overview, 41–42
    problem areas, 50–52
        deception or "double-cross," 51–52
        entrapment, 50–51
        overview, 50
    techniques and methods, 42–50
        arranging for undercover agents, 42–44
        concluding case, 48–50
        overview, 42
        penetrating for job placement, 44–47
        reporting, 47–48
Unemployment Verification Form, 69

Universities, as information source, 231
Unobtrusive surveillance positions, 55
Unsuccessful interrogation, 104
U.S. Identification Manual, 233
U.S. Secret Service, 302–303
Utility companies, as information source, 229

V
Van companies, as information source, 229
Vaughn, Koral, 26
Vehicle direction, 144
Vendor verification, 86–87
Ventilation, 108
Vertical analysis, 89
Very temporary surveillance, 59
VHS tape recorder systems, 271
Victims, interviewing, 98–100
Video camcorder imaging, 275–276
Video recorders, 271–272
Video Surveillance Equipment Selection and Application Guide, 277
Video-workbook program, 31
Voice message systems, 244

W
Warehouse Dock, The, 50
Weingarten Rights, 162
Welfare department, as information source, 234
Weston, Stephen W., 303
"What" of investigation, 197–199
"When" of investigation, 239–249
    determining time by events, 245–246
        case of customized bed, 245–246
        case of telephone tap, 245
        overview, 245
    how to preestablish time, 246–249
    methods of establishing time, 240–244
        building systems records, 243–244
        determining time by incidental records, 242–244
        overview, 240
        self-evident time, 240
        significant time variations, 241–242
    overview, 239–240
"Where" of investigation, 225–238
    case of missing mascot, 225–226
    case of stolen calculators, 226–228
    directories, 232

general information sites, 236
information sources in local government, 233–235
information sources in state government, 235–236
online information sources, 236
overview, 225
periodicals, 232–233
publishing/journalism resources, 237–238
search engines, 236
sources of information in private sector, 228–232
"Who" of investigation, 213–224
    combining techniques, 220–224
    investigative interview, 217–220
    overview, 213
    process of elimination, 213–215
    reading physical evidence, 215–217
Who's Who, 233
"Why" of investigation, 251–261
    motivation and detection strategy, 252–253
    motive and response, 256–257
    motives for theft, 253–256
    overview, 251–252
Wicklander and Zulawski's interviewing and interrogation seminars, 12
Wicklander-Zulawski Non-Confrontational Method®, 135–136
Windows swap file, 295
Woman's intuition, 23
Word processed statements, 154–155
Work, scope of, 10
Workplace violence
    and background investigations, 68
    significance of, 301
    types of, 300–301
Writing of narrative reports, 182
Written policy, 46–47
Written statements
    allowable uses of, 155–158
    historical background, 158–160
    overview, 154–155

X
XYZCO/TWU negotiations, 287, 288

Z
Zelinsky decision, 159
Zero-tolerance, 302, 305
Zoom lenses, 267